SEXUAL RELATION
IN CHRISTIAN THOUGHT

SEXUAL RELATION
IN CHRISTIAN THOUGHT

DERRICK SHERWIN BAILEY

HARPER & BROTHERS PUBLISHERS

NEW YORK

This book is published in Great Britain under the title of
The Man-Woman Relation in Christian Thought

Library of Congress catalog card number: 59-10326

CONTENTS

INTRODUCTION   vi

I   PRIMITIVE CHRISTIANITY AND ITS BACKGROUND   I

II   THE NEW TESTAMENT   8

III   THE PATRISTIC AGE   19

IV   THE MEDIAEVAL WESTERN CHURCH   103

V   THE REFORMATION AND SEVENTEENTH-CENTURY
     ANGLICANISM   167

VI   THE TRADITION TODAY   232

VII   TOWARDS A THEOLOGY OF SEX   260

     INDEX   304

INTRODUCTION

DURING the past eight years it has been my business to lecture to students and the clergy upon the theology and ecclesiastical history of sexual relation, and the lack of comprehensive and well-documented books on the subject has always proved a serious hindrance to teaching and study. Marriage, of course, has been amply treated by such authorities as Watkins, Lacey, Joyce, and Dr E. O. James; and Dr W. G. Cole has recently broken new ground with a selective enquiry into Christian ideas of venereal sexuality[1]—though this did not reach me, unfortunately, till my own work was almost finished. But there are other aspects of the relation between man and woman than the matrimonial and the venereal, and the student must equally concern himself with matters less often handled by the theologian, such as the ontological and metaphysical factors in human sexuality, the status and social rôle of woman, and the causes and effects of sexual attitudes and stereotypes—to mention but a few. He must also pay particular regard to the traditions by which the sexual ideas of one generation or age are transmitted to the next, thus perpetuating not only truth and insight, but also error and prejudice.

Few things have influenced the pattern of western culture more than the sexual tradition of the Christian Church, yet no attempt has hitherto been made (so far as I know) to give a full and sufficiently detailed account of its development as reflected in theological literature, canon law, liturgy, and ecclesiastical debate. In this book, therefore, I have tried to trace the history of this tradition in its main features from the second century down to the seventeenth, dealing in Chapter III with the early Church, in Chapter IV with mediaeval Christendom, and in Chapter V with the Reformation, and with the Anglican Church in the Tudor, Jacobean, and Caroline periods. This progressive restriction in scope has been dictated partly by practical considerations, and partly by the fact that I have had specially in view the

---

[1] See W. G. Cole, *Sex in Christianity and Psychoanalysis*, London, 1956.

interests of Anglican readers and the needs of students in the universities and theological colleges. Chapters I and II have deliberately been kept as short as possible, since they are intended simply to provide an introduction to the more detailed survey which follows, and outline the background to primitive Christianity and the thought of the New Testament.

In Chapter VI the tradition is evaluated, and its validity and its relevance for the twentieth century are considered; and some of the tasks and problems confronting the contemporary Church in the realm of sexual relation are also indicated. This chapter was written before the meeting of the 1958 Lambeth Conference; hence the concluding paragraphs make no mention of the report of Committee V on 'The Family in Contemporary Society', with its notable departures from tradition which meet some of the criticisms that I have ventured to make, and encourage the hope that more serious theological attention will now be given to the personal and relational aspects of sexuality. In this connexion Chapter VII is specially relevant, for it explores an essential but neglected department of the doctrine of Man, and seeks to define the theological and metaphysical significance of sex. It is less a conclusion, however, than a bridge leading to further and more specific studies in sexual relation which I hope to publish in due course as a supplement to the present volume.

Chapter VII contains, among other things, a discussion of the meaning of sex. The reader may find it helpful to glance first at this;[1] it explains the precise sense attaching to the terms 'sex', 'sexual', and 'venereal' in the following pages, and will obviate misunderstanding. I should also add that for the sake of clarity, 'Man' (capital M) is used for the generic sense—that is, Mankind or humanity, while 'man' (small m) is specific, and denotes the human male.

To assist the student, the footnotes provide ample references to the primary sources, and also bibliographical details of secondary sources; but I have not supplied a bibliography because one is already available which lists, with annotations, more than 200 books and articles on the theology and history of

---

[1] See below, pp. 259 ff.

sexual relation,[1] and I suggest that this be kept at hand as a guide.

The extent of my general indebtedness to other scholars in this field will be apparent, and need not be recited at length. But I would like to make special acknowledgement of the help which I have received from those to whom I have lectured. By question, discussion, and criticism they have contributed unwittingly to my own thought, and therefore to the writing of this book; I hope they will find in its pages a pleasant reminder of our studies together, and an incentive to the pursuit of a fascinating and important subject which is still unduly neglected.

Birmingham,   SHERWIN BAILEY
January 1st, 1959

---

[1] D. S. Bailey, *Sexual Relationship: A Guide to Published Literature,* London The Church Information Board), 2nd ed., 1957 (1s. 4d.).

I

PRIMITIVE CHRISTIANITY AND ITS BACKGROUND

In the attitude of the ancient world to sexual relationship at the time of the appearance of Christianity there can be discerned three features in particular which affected, either positively or negatively, the character and development of the Church's thought and outlook.

Among the Jews, marriage had always been held in relatively high esteem—not primarily (it must be admitted) for its relational value, but because it was the means of propagating the Holy People, of maintaining the institution of the family as the basis of society, and of assuring a shadowy semblance of immortality to a man in the offspring which he had begotten. Consequently the duty of early marriage was represented in rabbinical literature as incumbent upon every Hebrew male;[1] for a man to remain single was a reprehensible evasion of responsibility, and displeasing to God. Likewise, barrenness in a woman was a reproach hardly to be endured; it reflected a certain discredit upon her father,[2] and if it persisted for ten years, gave her husband ground for divorce.[3]

With but slight modification the Old Testament conception of marriage still held in first-century Judaism.[4] Its positive worth lay in the inculcation of a genuine love for home and children, and a

---

[1] Bab. Talmud, *Kiddushin* 29b; cf. *Yebamoth* 63b.
[2] Cf. Ecclus. xlii. 10.
[3] Bab. Talmud, *Yebamoth* 64a, etc.
[4] See D. R. Mace, *Hebrew Marriage* (London, 1953), and G. F. Moore, *Judaism* (Cambridge, 1927), ii, pp. 119 ff.

high ideal of family life. It led also to a rigorous condemnation of irregularity in sexual behaviour—though in earlier times this was penalized only when it infringed a husband's property-right in his wife or, by contaminating a virgin, reduced her chances of matrimony and obliged her father to be content with a smaller bride-price. The Jewish attitude tended to induce a healthy, affirmative view of coitus which to some extent corrected an ingrained disposition to associate venereal acts and impulses with sin and evil.[1] On the other hand, however, it did not affect the acceptance and perpetuation of a double standard of morality which was heavily weighted, as was usual in antiquity, on the side of the male; nor did it conflict, at any rate in theory, with the allowance of polygyny and a unilateral right of divorce—although first-century Judaism was generally monogamous in its ideals and practice.

The dominance of the procreative motif in Hebrew sexual thought was doubtless partly responsible for the fact that the common Jewish view of woman seems to have risen but little above the low estimation typical of most oriental peoples. Her domestic and maternal virtues were esteemed, however;[2] she was honoured as a parent, and on the whole was treated with kindness and affection. Yet in conformity with the theory of sexual relation universally current in ancient times, she was regarded as subordinate and naturally inferior to man, and laboured under various religious and social disabilities; moreover, in certain post-exilic and rabbinical writings there is more than a trace of misogynic pessimism.[3] Nevertheless, since the home remained virtually the centre of community life, the lot of the Jewish woman was not without either its compensations or its opportunities for influence;

---

[1] On the sexual element in Hebrew speculation upon the Fall and the origin of evil, see N. P. Williams, *The Ideas of the Fall and of Original Sin* (London, 1927), pp. 34, 45, 58, 66. 77, and 86.

[2] Cf. the famous eulogy of the good housekeeper in Prov. xxxi. 10 ff.

[3] Cf. Eccles. vii. 26–28; E. Bevan, *Jerusalem under the High-Priests* (London, 1940), pp. 62–63 on the views of ben Sirach (see especially Ecclus. xxv. 13, 16 f., 24; xlii. 13); *Aboth* i. 5 (R. Jose ben Johanan); Bab. Talmud, *Erubin* 53b, *Yebamoth* 63a (R. Hiyya).

under her husband's roof she was respected, and her seclusion was never so restricted or servile as that of the Greek wife in the gynæceum. Despite their manifest limitations and imperfections, the Jewish sexual ethic and conception of marriage were never surpassed in antiquity by those of any other culture, and were maintained with an unequalled consistency.

In its theoretical view of woman and of marriage the Gentile world of the first century did not differ greatly from Judaism, though in practice it was content with a much lower standard, and at best rarely succeeded in realizing even its own ideals. As with the Jews, so with both Greeks and Romans, the declared purpose of marriage was procreation; its object was the production of legitimate offspring (that is, children of citizen caste) in order that the service of the state and the worship of the gods might be maintained. To this end the laws enforced a formal monogamy, while custom sanctioned a double standard of morality which encouraged male promiscuity and condoned prostitution.

Roman tradition preserved a conception of wedlock more elevated than that commonly entertained by the Greeks, especially in the 'sacramental' form of union contracted by *confarreatio*,[1] and in the earlier days of the Republic the *materfamilias* usually enjoyed an exceptional dignity, freedom, and equality with her husband. Nevertheless, her essential subservience and dependent status was reflected and defined in the legal doctrine of *patria potestas*, according to which she remained under the *manus* or authority of her father (or another male relative) until at marriage she passed beneath that of her husband. While emancipation, however, ameliorated the lot of the Greek woman and tended to transform for the better the character of Greek marriage, in Rome it had an opposite effect. There, women in ever-increasing numbers acquired virtual independence by resorting to the privilege of *trinoctii absentia*[2] sanctioned in the laws of the Twelve

---

[1] For an account of this and the other forms of Roman marriage (*coemptio* and *usus*), see A. T. Macmillan, *What is Christian Marriage?* (London, 1944), pp. 27–28, and E. O. James, *Marriage and Society* (London, 1952), pp. 84–89.

[2] That is, absence from the matrimonial home for three nights in the year.

Tables, thus evading the restrictions of *manus*; but this only served to hasten a general moral decline which was marked by the growing prevalence of divorce and by the disintegration of family life.

In two respects the sexual ethic and practice of the Hellenistic world contrasted strongly with that of Judaism. The Greeks had always displayed a certain insensibility to the notion of moral 'purity' in sexual matters, and their hedonism and sensuality, though generally moderated by the ideal of *sophrosunē*, was liable at any time to degenerate into barely disguised licentiousness. The social attitude thus engendered was favourable to venereal indulgence; both hetairism and the lower forms of prostitution flourished, and the *paiderastia* in which male homosexual relationships were idealized, and to some extent institutionalized, led to a widespread toleration of unnatural practices, and especially of *paidophthoria* or the corruption of youths. Gradually infiltrating into Roman society, the baser elements of Greek sexual life undermined the severe puritanism of the early tradition, and produced a parody of the spontaneous naturalism of Hellenic sensuality in the coarse, brutal, and calculated vice for which the imperial city has ever since remained notorious. While stricter morals continued to prevail in many of the provinces where the former ideals of marriage and family life were preserved, the cities and ports of the Mediterranean seaboard rivalled or instructed the capital in licentiousness.

Against this laxity in moral standards and depravity in sexual behaviour the philosophies of the age proclaimed an ascetical ideal which, though contemplative and mystical rather than disciplinary, had always inclined towards mortification of the flesh. Though chiefly the product of a pessimism which abandoned the realm of the material and phenomenal as the irreclaimable domain of evil, this asceticism, in its sexual aspect, was partly due also to the low contemporary view of woman and marriage—a view endorsed by several of the Greek sages themselves. From the time of Diogenes, the Cynics had extolled their master's surly repudiation of worldly possessions and comforts—an attitude which was inevitably interpreted as implying renunciation of wedlock and the family. Stoicism, too, in its search for self-sufficiency and independence of earthly things, tended to reject matrimonial and domestic ties, while Neo-Pythagoreanism inclined towards a dualism which regarded coitus as a defilement and inculcated continence. Nor were these notions of sexual 'purity' characteristic only of Hellenistic asceticism, though they emanated from a Greek philosophical tradition at least as old as Orphism. They were echoed even from within the confines of Judaism in the teaching and practices of the *Therapeutæ* and the Essenes; and a definite ascetical and dualistic strain can also be detected in the thought of Philo.

Upon the sexual thought and life of the primitive Church each of these attitudes left its mark. The Jewish respect for marriage and the family was continued in the ideal of the Christian home as in some sense a 'religious institution'—a microcosmic *ekklēsia*,[1] in which natural relationships were elevated and strengthened by the sharing of a common faith, and charity was practised through the mutual submission "in the fear of Christ" which was enjoined upon all followers of the Lord.[2] In the spirit of the old Israel, the new upheld the divine ordinance and the moral value of wedlock; but avoidance of fornication now tended to supplement, if not to supplant, the procreative motif, and the virgin state was accorded a supremacy which the orthodox Jew would have repudiated as an impious frustration of the purposes of God. On the other hand, by abolishing polygyny and divorce, by laying the obligation of chastity equally upon men and women, and by attributing to matrimony a new and loftier sacramental character, Christianity transformed the Hebrew conception of the union of husband and wife.

Yet in its popularized form the ascetical ideal of the philosophies made a stronger, though more subtle appeal to the primitive

---

[1] This may well be implied in Rom. xvi. 5, 1 Cor. xvi. 19, Col. iv. 15, and Philem. 2 which are commonly interpreted as referring to Christian assemblies for worship.

[2] Eph. v. 21.

Church than did the domestic ideal of Judaism. There was, perhaps, little or no deliberate borrowing from Hellenistic teaching and usage,[1] but the evidence points to some measure of unconscious assimilation. There is no doubt that the rigorist strain, both in the noblest contemporary speculative thought and in the more popular mystery cults, created an atmosphere congenial to the development within Christianity of an asceticism which was markedly sexual in its emphases. This, however, was not the only contributory factor; the Christian attitude to sex and marriage was also partly the result of a revulsion from the immorality of the times and the laxity of pagan religious ideas and practice, both of which continued to call forth the denunciations of the Church.

Over and above these specific influences, there were others of a more general nature which helped to determine the Church's view. Despite their early reputation that they had "turned the world upside down",[2] the first Christians (and their successors) remained citizens of the *civitas terrena*, and showed themselves in many ways to be typical children of their time. Not least was this so in regard to woman, marriage, and sexual relation. Concerning these, they shared with their contemporaries certain assumptions and attitudes which were almost universally current in antiquity, and which they appear to have accepted more or less without question. Furthermore, with all other subjects of imperial Rome save a very few, they submitted to a common civil law by which the status of woman was defined and the formation of marriage regulated; and in all material respects they conformed to the established conventions which governed the social intercourse of the sexes—indeed, in this as in other matters,[3] Christianity displayed from the first a marked inclination towards conservatism. Thus, both directly and indirectly, environment played an

---

[1] See the discussion in K. E. Kirk, *The Vision of God* (London, 1937), pp. 86–87 and 480–487—the latter containing a brief account of pagan asceticism.

[2] Acts xvii. 6.

[3] Cf. St Paul's attitude to the veiling of women in 1 Cor. xi. 1 ff.; also the injunctions in 1 Peter ii. 11–17 and iii. 16 concerning circumspection in behaviour.

important part in moulding the sexual thought of the primitive Church. Yet this was not the only influential factor; the Christian sexual tradition did not originate merely in a synthesis of elements derived from Judaism on the one hand, and from Hellenistic asceticism on the other.

II

✳ THE NEW TESTAMENT

IT is in the Bible, and particularly in the New Testament, that we find the source of those concepts and principles which, from the outset, imparted a distinctive character to the Christian view of sex and marriage—counteracting, modifying, and accentuating various features in the heritage from the past, and in the influence of contemporary culture. Yet the teaching of Jesus cannot itself be described as original in the sense that he proclaimed a new code of sexual conduct or a new ideal of sexual relationship—in fact, he implicitly disowned any such intention. When, against Jewish custom and the Mosaic law, he forbade the disruption of the one-flesh union, he simply claimed to be affirming and restoring a principle which had existed "from the beginning of the creation" in the design of God.[1] The novelty of his teaching consisted rather in its complete contrast to the prevailing spirit and practice of the time—although even in the matter of sexual morals it is important not to over-sharpen that contrast. Despite the exegetical quibbles of Shammai and Hillel, the rabbinical marriage ideal was one of permanent monogamy; while among the philosophers Dion Chrysostom, Musonius Rufus, and Plutarch inculcated a high standard of morality and an elevated conception of the wedded state. Even the notable saying in the Sermon on the Mount: "Every one that looketh on a woman to lust after her hath committed adultery with her already in his heart",[2] has its parallels in the precepts of the rabbis,[3] and recalls

---

[1] Mk. x. 6; cf. Matt. xix. 4.
[2] Matt. v. 28.
[3] See G. F. Moore, op. cit., ii, p. 268 for instances.

similar utterance of the Stoic Epictetus concerning the man who exclaims on beholding a woman: "Lucky is her husband."[1]

While Jesus, in setting before men and women the primordial conception of marriage, condemned not only polygyny and divorce but also every breach of fidelity, St Paul developed[2] to a new height of spiritual significance the nuptial symbolism already familiar to his readers, either through the writings of the Old Testament prophets,[3] or through the notion of the *hieros gamos* in ethnic religion.[4] Christ's loving self-sacrifice for his bride the Church gave an altogether deeper import to the idea of Yahweh as the patient, constant, forgiving husband of Israel—an idea which was itself but a purified version, invested with an ethical content, of the ancient theme of the union between the cult diety and his land or people. From the Christ-Church relationship, moreover, St Paul drew a picture of marriage in the order of redemption, accepting the established matrimonial pattern of the first century with its subordination of the wife to the husband, yet transforming it from within by an infusion of the spirit of its supernatural exemplar. Like our Lord's teaching, St Paul's exposition of this "great mystery" leans upon the biblical principle of union in one-flesh which is derived from the second creation narrative in Genesis.[5]

If there is any element of real novelty in the specific teaching of the New Testament on sexual relation, it is perhaps to be found chiefly in St Paul's profound and realistic treatment of coitus and its significance in the first epistle to the Corinthians.[6] Here his

---

[1] Cf. R. Bainton, 'Christianity and Sex', in *Pastoral Psychology* (U.S.A.), vol. 3, no. 26, Sept. 1952, p. 12 and references.

[2] Eph. v. 22 ff.

[3] Cf. C. Chavasse, *The Bride of Christ* (London, 1939), pp. 19–48.

[4] Cf. L. R. Farnell, *The Cults of the Greek States* (Oxford, 1896 f.), iii, p. 176, v, pp. 217–218; S. Angus, *The Mystery Religions and Christianity* (London, 1928), pp. 62, 90, 112 ff.; S. H. Hooke (ed.), *Myth and Ritual* (Oxford, 1933), pp. 9–10, 34 f., 56, 139; S. H. Hooke (ed.), *The Labyrinth* (London, 1935), pp. 28, 143 f. 230; J. G. Frazer, *The Magic Art and the Evolution of Kings* (London, 1936), ii, pp. 129 ff.; J. G. Frazer, *Adonis, Attis, Osiris* (London, 1936), pp. 27 ff.

[5] Gen. ii. 24; cf. Mk. x. 8, Matt. xix. 5–6, 1 Cor. vi. 16, Eph. v. 31.

[6] 1 Cor. vi. 12–20.

thought apparently owes nothing to any antecedent notions, and displays a psychological insight into human sexuality which is altogether exceptional by first-century standards. The Apostle denies that coitus is, as the Corinthians would have it, merely a detached and (as it were) peripheral venereal function involving no more than an appropriate exercise of the genital organs. On the contrary, he insists that it is an act which, by reason of its very nature, engages and expresses the whole personality in such a way as to constitute an unique mode of self-disclosure and self-commitment.[1] It is curious that this remarkable and pregnant concept should have had a negligible influence upon Christian thought—probably because it invests coitus with a significance which proved unacceptable in the face of rapidly developing ascetical tendencies in the Church.

Such tendencies are already evident in the rigorist temper displayed by certain of the New Testament writings. From the teaching of Jesus on marriage, however, asceticism is almost wholly absent. It is very doubtful whether the saying concerning those who "made themselves eunuchs for the kingdom of heaven's sake"[2] amounts to more than a recognition that as in the past, so now, the service of God may demand a self-imposed continence. Again, the conditions of Christian discipleship laid down in the third Gospel probably reflect its author's 'Ebionism'[3] when they add a man's wife to the list of persons and possessions which he must "hate",[4]— this being St Luke's substitution for the milder "leave" in the Matthæan[5] and Markan[6] parallels. Nevertheless, these passages left their mark upon the sexual thought and practice of the Church, as did also our Lord's choice of the single life as a necessary condition for the fulfilment of his messianic vocation.

---

[1] See further on this passage D. S. Bailey, *The Mystery of Love and Marriage* (London, 1952), pp. 50–54.

[2] Matt. xix. 12.

[3] See K. E. Kirk, op. cit., pp. 73–74.

[4] Lk. xiv. 26; cf. xviii. 29.

[5] Matt. x. 37; cf. xix. 29.

[6] Mk. x. 29.

In the Pauline epistles the ascetical strain is more prominent, especially in 1 Corinthians, where it is accentuated by the eschatological tension under which the letter was composed. St Paul's attitude, however, is peculiarly complex, and has been consistently misunderstood by his critics; he cannot be dismissed as one of " the world's most influential, and therefore perhaps most dangerous, sex reactionaries"—to quote the words of a popular modern writer.[1] He certainly does not conceal his own preference for the single state—indeed, he commends it both "by reason of the present distress", since "the time is shortened", and because it hinders less the service of the Lord.[2] Marriage, on the other hand, he represents as something of a concession to human frailty —a means whereby those not endowed with the gift of continence can avoid the sin of fornication.[3]

Yet this personal bias does not prevent him from recognizing that God calls some to wedlock and some to celibacy,[4] and his precepts addressed to husband and wife regarding their coital relationship are the reverse of what later rigorism would have enjoined. Ascetical practices within marriage are disapproved rather than commended, save when devotion may be thought to require a brief period of abstinence; the married are forbidden to defraud one another of the coitus which is their due, and are reminded that they have conceded each to the other the power over their own bodies[5]—a remarkable attitude, quite out of keeping with the spirit of the first century.

Although these injunctions to the Church of Corinth un-compromisingly set singleness above marriage, the wedded state itself is exalted in the epistle to the Ephesians which, if it does not (at least, in its present form) come directly from St Paul's pen, may fairly be assumed to reflect his more mature thought. Admittedly, this epistle does not expressly reverse or qualify the

---

[1] E. Chesser, *Sexual Behaviour, Normal and Abnormal* (London, n.d.), p. 22.
[2] 1 Cor. vii. 7, 26, 29, 32–34.
[3] 1 Cor. vii. 9.
[4] 1 Cor. vii. 7, 17 ff.
[5] 1 Cor. vii. 3–6.

opinions stated in the earlier letter to the Corinthians; nevertheless, it elevates wedlock in treating of the "great mystery" by
which Christ's union with the Church is signified, and makes no
mention of its negative utility in providing a means for the relief
of incontinence.[1] The Apostle, though he does not conceal his
preferences and prejudices, is certainly no extremist like the
author of the Apocalypse, who saw the great procession of the
redeemed as a company of virgins "which were not defiled with
women"—a phrase which it is difficult to dismiss as merely
hyperbolical.[2] His own temperamental predilection so harmonized
with the mood engendered by expectation of an imminent
parousia that he inevitably stressed the advantages of celibacy—yet
not in such a way as to exclude matrimony, concerning which
there is no doubt that he would have endorsed the command of
the anonymous writer to the Hebrews: "Let marriage be had in
honour among all."[3]

In presenting and estimating St Paul's view of marriage and of
physical sexuality, his theological exponents and his secularist
detractors alike have generally failed to make sufficient allowance,
either for the provenance or for the contemporary setting and
reference of his thought. By some his ideas have been termed
contradictory or paradoxical—and so, no doubt, they appear
when compared with the sexual concepts and standards of the
Hebraic and the Hellenistic traditions, to both of which he was in
some measure indebted. Yet considered in itself, and in relation
to its context and purpose, his teaching has a remarkable consistency and coherence. If he could not affirm the naturalism
typical of his Jewish heritage, neither could he accept for the

---

[1] Eph. v. 22 ff.

[2] Rev. xiv. 4. This verse has always proved something of an exegetical
problem. It has been explained as an interpolation by a "shallow-brained fanatic
and celibate"—R. H. Charles (Int. Crit. Comm., i. p. lv), and as a reference to
those who have abstained from cultic prostitution, or who have not apostasized—
P. Carrington, *The Meaning of the Revelation* (London, 1931), p. 237, where
"virgins" is interpreted simply as a "violent symbol for purity"; but there is no
reason to suppose that the expression does not in fact represent the writer's own
views—see M. Kiddle, *The Revelation of St John* (London, 1940), p. 268.

[3] Heb. xiii. 4.

Church the pessimistic dualism of Hellenistic philosophy. Therefore he chose a middle way, commending celibacy without
condemning marriage, and approving continence in those who
possessed the gift while recalling husbands and wives to the
obligations of their state, and bluntly telling the 'highly-sexed':
"It is better to marry than to burn [with unsatisfied venereal
desires]".[1] To us, this may suggest a low and utilitarian notion of
wedlock, but to most of the Apostle's contemporaries it would
have seemed reasonable enough, and to some unnecessarily
liberal. His realistic attitude to coitus is proof that he was no
preacher of a doctrinaire asceticism; nevertheless, the general
tenor of his thought clearly betrays the influence of the *zeitgeist*—
no man of his time and apocalyptic outlook would have regarded
matrimony as anything but an encumbrance and a distraction to
be avoided by the prudent, and in the circumstances his counsels
show no less tolerance and broad-mindedness than wisdom.

Neither in St Paul's writings nor in the New Testament as a
whole is there to be found any comprehensive or systematic
treatment of sexual matters. Even the seventh chapter of
I Corinthians, so often misunderstood as a definitive statement
of the Apostle's position and teaching, is simply a collection of
answers to questions submitted by the Church at Corinth,
designed to give the enquirers guidance upon specific points.
Nowhere does St Paul go beyond the scope of these questions and
the problems to which they point, but replies briefly, distinguishing where necessary between the commands of the Lord and his
own opinions.[2] It is with a sense of great pastoral urgency that
he advises these unstable Greek converts in the most immoral city
of antiquity about their personal problems of relationship and
behaviour. The End was approaching, and the souls of men and
women were at stake; in such a time of crisis, carefully reasoned
dissertations were out of place. Hence it is futile to seek in this
chapter for any exposition of a complete Pauline theology of sex
and marriage, or to attempt to extort from its miscellaneous,

[1] I Cor. vii. 9.
[2] I Cor. vii. 10, 12, 25; cf. 6, 17, 40.

particular directions and precepts any general system of doctrine applicable to sexual relation. Appreciation of the epistle's occasional character and limited scope might have restrained Christian thinkers from their ready endorsement of its apocalyptic rigorism, and prevented the mischievous distortions of the Apostle's teaching which have been exploited to discredit the Church.

No impartial assessment, however, can ignore in St Paul's attitude to sexual matters an ascetical bias which, though it stops short of dualism, accords but a grudging recognition to marriage, and exalts virginity as a religious ideal. In this comparative evaluation of the two states to the detriment of wedlock lay the germ of a new double ethical standard which was soon to exert upon Christian conceptions of spirituality an influence no less damaging than profound. The eschatological context of the Apostle's words was forgotten, and matrimony was set forth as a way of life, permitted indeed by God and possessing a certain positive value, but intrinsically and in all circumstances less perfect than singleness—a way in which care for "the things of the world" and for what will please husband and wife takes precedence of care for "the things of the Lord".[1] Partly upon this groundless antithesis rested such later ecclesiastical developments as clerical celibacy and monasticism, which tended to encourage the notion of a spiritual élite composed of those who, by renouncing all that was regarded as earthly and carnal, had embraced the 'higher life'.

In this idea of marriage as an accommodation to human weakness and a hindrance to the fullest service of God there is but little appreciation of its dignity and high calling; nor do the writers of the New Testament show much sense of the joys and privileges of family life, or of that love for children which our Lord himself displayed.[2] Indeed, the curt precepts of the 'household codes' in the Colossian,[3] Ephesian,[4] and first Petrine[5] epistles suggest a

---

[1] Cf. I Cor. vii. 32–34.
[2] Mk. x. 13 ff.
[3] Col. iii. 18 ff.
[4] Eph. vi. 1 ff.
[5] I Pet. ii. 13–iii. 7.

Christian domestic ideal approaching in its austerity that of the Romans in the ancient days of the Republic. A nobler and less severe conception appears, it is true, in the injunction to husbands that they should "love" (that is, exercise a self-sacrificing benevolence towards) their wives "as Christ also loved the Church", and "as their own bodies"—being one-flesh with them.[1] Elsewhere, however, the argument is altogether on a lower plane. Husbands are told not to be bitter against their wives,[2] while the latter, for their part, must reverence and be submissive to their spouses after the example of Sarah, who called Abraham "lord".[3] Children are exhorted to obedience, and fathers are bidden to eschew provocation lest it should lead to discouragement.[4] There is hardly any hint here of the distinctive tenderness and warmth of affection which normally mark the marital and parental relation-ships—and which, it must be allowed, were certainly not wanting from the highest pagan view of marriage and the family.[5]

Yet an account of the New Testament attitude to children and the home which halts at this point would fail to do justice to the unique element in the Christian conception of personal and sexual relation. This is perhaps best illustrated in the apostolic teaching concerning woman and her status, where the traditional and the evangelic views are exhibited in clear and unresolved contrast. It is evident that the writers of the New Testament accepted without question the androcentric assumptions underlying the law and the social attitudes of Judaism and of the Græco-Roman civilization; and St Paul even gave these assumptions a semblance of theological sanction by fitting the sexual relation into a universal hierarchical scale, according to which God, Christ, male, and female were set in a descending order of subordination.[6] Woman, so the Scriptures declared, was created for the benefit

---

[1] Eph. v. 25, 28–31.
[2] Col. iii. 19.
[3] 1 Pet. iii. 6.
[4] Col. iii. 20–21; cf. Eph. vi. 1–4.
[5] See further on this K. E. Kirk, op. cit. 76–77.
[6] 1 Cor. xi. 3.

of man,[1] and must submit to him as her divinely-appointed "head";[2] she was forbidden to teach in the church[3] and was enjoined to keep silence,[4] cultivating a meek and tranquil spirit,[5] and learning "in quietness with all subjection";[6] she was reminded, moreover, that Eve and not Adam was first beguiled into transgression[7]—a stigma which long clung to her sex, branding every member of it as a "weaker vessel", irresponsible, and a potential temptress.

On the other hand, the New Testament asserts no less forcibly the spiritual equality of male and female; husband and wife, together and without any discrimination, are "joint-heirs of the grace of life",[8] and in Christ the distinction of sex and its consequences become relatively unimportant.[9] The Gospels, the Acts of the Apostles, and the greeting lists in the Pauline epistles show that this was no empty theory. Women occupied an important place in Jesus' ministry, and in his dealings with them he refused to be bound by the shackles of petty convention;[10] they doubtless shared in the initial outpouring of the Holy Spirit at Pentecost,[11] they were among the first and most faithful converts to the new religion,[12] they displayed charismatic gifts,[13] they devoted themselves to works of charity,[14] they dispensed hospitality,[15] they laboured in the task of evangelism,[16] and they even imparted instruction in the faith.[17]

The revolutionary ethic of Christianity and the personal and

---

[1] I Cor. xi. 9.
[2] I Cor. xi. 3, xiv. 34; Eph. v. 23, 33b; Col. iii. 18; I Pet. iii. 1.
[3] I Tim. ii. 12.   [4] I Cor. xiv. 34.
[5] I Pet. iii. 4.   [6] I Tim. ii. 11–12.
[7] I Tim. ii. 14: but "she shall be saved through her childbearing", ii. 15.
[8] I Pet. iii. 7.
[9] Gal. iii. 28.
[10] Cf. Jn. iv. 27.
[11] So Acts i. 14 suggests; cf. ii. 18—the fulfilment of Joel ii. 28.
[12] Cf. Acts xvi. 14–15; xvii. 4, 12, 34.
[13] Acts xxi. 9.
[14] Acts ix. 36 ff.
[15] Acts xii. 12; xvi. 15, 40; Rom. xvi. 2.
[16] Cf. Rom. xvi. 1, 6, 12; Phil. iv. 2.
[17] Acts xviii. 26.

communal experience of a new life in Christ undoubtedly transformed sexual relationships no less than others, and there is much
to suggest that the position of woman in the primitive Church,
when judged by contemporary standards and notions, was at
first exceptional in many respects. There is also evidence, however, in the first Corinthian epistle and elsewhere, that this newly-
found liberty in the gospel could prove a source of embarrassment
—that it was open to abuse by the faithful and to misconstruction
by unbelievers. Thus the problems which confronted individuals
and local Churches alike served only to heighten an inevitable
tension between what may be called the progressive and the
reactionary elements in the early Christian attitude to woman
and to sexual relation; and something of the resultant perplexity
may perhaps be detected in the curiously abrupt ending to the
fifth chapter of Ephesians, as if the writer had suddenly realized
that his argument was leading him on to difficult or dangerous
ground. Eventually, as we have seen, this tension was eased, but
hardly resolved, as first eschatological and then moral and
expediential considerations brought the thought of the Church
upon sexual matters more and more into harmony with the
conservative and ascetical tendencies of the age.

Although the traditional view of woman and her status, as
expressed in the qualified subordinationism of Pauline and
Petrine teaching, ultimately became one of the dominant and
determining features in Christian sexual thought, it never
obliterated (however much it obscured) the evangelic truth that
in the sight of God male and female are equal. This, together with
an insistence upon the infinite value of every soul for which
Christ died, the supreme obligation of love and forgiveness, and
the application of the rule of chastity impartially to both sexes,
gave a new meaning and potential, not only to marriage but to
every relationship between man and woman. The originality of
the Christian contribution to an understanding of sexual relation
lay, therefore, not in any novel code of morals or conduct, but in
a higher conception of Man than that taught by other contemporary religions and philosophies—and above all, in the offer of a

new life in Christ which had the power to redeem and transform both persons and institutions. Unfortunately the Church has proved slow, not to say somewhat reluctant, to face the radical implications of the New Testament ethic in the sexual realm. Consequently the influence of that ethic is to be seen less obviously in theology and ecclesiastical practice than in the social and cultural changes which are partly attributable to its diffusion in the west—changes such as the emergence of 'romantic' love,[1] for example, and the emancipation of woman.

---

[1] I use the term 'romantic' love, not in its debased modern meaning, but in the sense in which it was employed by Charles Williams—see *He Came Down From Heaven* (London, 1938), pp. 83–113; *The Descent of the Dove* (London, 1939), pp. 132 ff.; *The Figure of Beatrice* (London, 1943).

III

THE PATRISTIC AGE

It is evident from the literature of the first five or six centuries of the Christian era that the interest of the early Church in sexual and matrimonial questions was generally occasional, limited, and practical rather than theoretical or speculative. In an age much given to controversy, it is particularly significant that no dispute arose of such magnitude as to demand a thorough and systematic treatment of the theological principles governing marriage and sexual relationship. Reaction against the prevailing ascetical mood of the time provoked a few light skirmishes, in several of which the redoubtable Jerome was involved; but a short treatise or two at most usually sufficed to refute, silence, and disgrace any who had the temerity to challenge current assumptions or prejudices. Apart from such brief contentions, however, and an unflagging zeal in exalting and commending the virgin state, the patristic concern with sexual matters was relatively slight and narrow. In particular, the Fathers confined their attention almost exclusively to the unions of the baptized, and did not touch more than casually and incidentally upon marriage in the natural order;[1] while even when dealing with Christian wedlock, they made no attempt to work out any satisfactory doctrine of the one-flesh relationship.

The rigorist tendency already noted in the New Testament came to its full development during the patristic age in an asceticism which sought, like its Hellenistic counterparts, to attain perfection through renunciation of the world and subjugation of the body. To this end every means was employed—fasting,

---

[1] For one such passage, see John Chrysostom, *in epist. ad Rom.*, hom. xiii. 4.

solitude, prayer, mortification (not to mention a deliberate neglect of elementary hygiene); but always the decisive test, the critical discipline, was that of sexual continence.[1] This cult of virginity followed inevitably from the ethical dualism implicit in St Paul's comparison of the married with the single state to the advantage of the latter, and found its rationale in the distinction between counsels and precepts. From all Christians a minimal level of spiritual achievement was required; but before some who were called to a 'higher' life than that of the faithful in general a special standard was set, the chief feature of which, in practice if not in principle, was abstention from coitus and even from all forms of association with members of the other sex.

It is hardly surprising, therefore, that much of the small volume of patristic literature dealing with sexual topics is devoted to a vindication of celibacy against marriage,[2] and of widowhood against digamy or remarriage after the death of a first partner.[3] But to maintain and justify this doctrine demanded considerable theological and dialectical adroitness, for since marriage had been instituted and blessed by God and sanctified by Christ, it could not be treated as something impure or evil; yet Christian sentiment would not tolerate any view of wedlock which tended in the least degree to derogate from the presumed superiority of virginity. The ascetical enthusiasm of the Fathers, however, proved equal to this task—though the earliest works which deal

---

[1] See H. Lietzmann (tr. B. L. Woolf), *The Era of the Church Fathers* (London 1951), p. 130. Hermas, *vis.* iii. 8 treats continence as the first fruit of faith, and both Athanasius (*orat. de incarn. verb.* li) and Ambrose (*de virginibus*, i. 12) regard it as a new and distinctively Christian virtue. The *Didache*, in a somewhat obscure passage discussed by K. E. Kirk, op. cit., p. 186 and n. 4, appears to describe celibacy as the "cosmic mystery of the Church".

[2] See e.g., Hermas, *mand.* iv. 4; Tertullian, *ad ux.* i. 3; Methodius, *conviv.* vii; Gregory Nazianzen, *orat.* xxxvii. 10; John Chrysostom, *in epist. I ad Tim.* xii, 2; Ambrose, *de vid.* lxxii; *epist.* lxiii; Augustine, *de bono conj.* viii, ix, xxiii, xxiv; *de virg.* xix; Jerome, *epist.* xlviii; lxvi. 2; *adv. Helvid.* xx ff.; *adv. Jov.*; Athanasius, *epist.* xlviii; John Damascene, *de fid. orth.* iv, 24; etc.

[3] See, e.g., Hermas, *mand.* iv. 4; Tertullian, *ad. ux.*; *de exhort. cast.*; *de monog.*; *de pudic.* i; *Constit. Apost.* iii. 1, 2; Cyril of Jerusalem, *cat.* iv. 26; Minucius Felix, *Oct.* xxxi; John Chrysostom, *in epist. I ad Tim.* vii. 4; *in epist. ad Tit.* ii. 1; Ambrose, *de vid.* lxviii; Augustine, *de bono vid.* vi; *de bono conj.* xxi.

with the subject, Tertullian's three dissertations,[1] *Ad Uxorem*, *De Exhortatione Castitatis*, and *De Monogamia*, are quite uncompromising in their rigorism. All, in substance, are vigorous dissuasives against resuming the carnal ties from which the fortunate decease of a husband or wife has given release; and with each successive treatise the argument grows more opinionated and intransigent until in the last, composed during the author's Montanist period, rejection of digamy is almost asserted as the distinguishing mark of the true Church.

With the single exception of Jerome, however, the rest of the Fathers avoided such extravagances, and were content to extol virginity in more measured and temperate language, pointing out the incommodities and disadvantages of married life and leaving the faithful to draw their own conclusions. Indeed, Tertullian the Montanist himself spoke also for catholics and voiced the settled and moderate opinion of the early Church when he declared, against Marcion, that Christians prefer celibacy to marriage as superseding, not a bad thing by a good, but only a good by a better. "We do not reject marriage", he wrote, "but simply refrain from it. Nor do we prescribe [single] sanctity as the rule, but only recommend it . . . at the same time earnestly vindicating marriage, whenever hostile attacks are made against it as a polluted thing, to the disparagement of the Creator."[2]

Other Fathers delivered themselves to the same effect, maintaining with Gregory of Nazianzus that matrimony is not dishonoured by the veneration accorded to celibacy.[3] An early follower of Basil taught that the obligations of the Christian life applied no less to the married than to monks,[4] and Basil's brother Gregory of Nyssa expressly asserted of marriage that "while the pursuit of heavenly things should be every man's first care, yet if

---

[1] For an excellent translation of these works, with valuable introductions and notes, see W. P. le Saint, *Tertullian: Treatises on Marriage and Remarriage* (Ancient Christian Writers, vol. 13, London, 1951).

[2] *Adv. Marc.* i. 29.

[3] Greg. Nazianzen., *de bapt.* xviii.

[4] *De renunt. saec.*; see W. K. L. Clarke, *The Ascetic Works of Saint Basil* (London, 1925), p. 61.

he can use the advantage of wedlock with sobriety and moderation, he need not despise this form of self-dedication".[1] So also
John Chrysostom held that the wedded state is not *per se* an
obstacle to salvation or to the performance of religious duties,
for with zeal and fervour every married person can observe the
law of Christ and accomplish the prescribed acts of piety.[2] Yet
he could not regard it as the perfect state,[3] for it hinders the freest
possible service of God—a view with which Ambrose concurred,[4]
though he nevertheless condemned any depreciation of matrimony on the pretext of exalting virginity.[5] Augustine likewise
would not have wedlock despised;[6] celibacy, he claimed, is
elevated simply by being set above a condition which is good in
itself[7]—a condition endowed, moreover, with the triple blessing
of children, mutual fidelity, and sacramental meaning.[8] Even
Methodius, who in imitation of Plato composed a somewhat
jejune *Symposium* praising virginity as the goal and crown of
human evolution,[9] allowed that those who had lived chastely
with their wives and had refrained from excessive embraces would
not be denied entrance to the marriage feast of the Lamb.[10]

By means of the convenient distinction between the good and
the better, the Fathers contrived to uphold the superiority of the

---

[1] *De virg.* viii.

[2] Cf. *in epist. ad Rom.* xxx. 3; *in epist. ad Eph.* xx. 9; *in epist. ad Phil.* xii. 3; *in epist. II ad Thess.* vi. 4; *in epist. II ad Tim.* x. 5; *in epist. ad Tit.* ii; *in epist. ad Hebr.* vii. 4; *in cap V Gen.* xxi. 4; *in illud: vidi Dominum,* iv. 2 and vi. 1; *in Matt.* vii. 7 and xliii. 5; *adv. opp. vit. mon.* iii. 13. With the exception of Augustine, John Chrysostom shows a deeper appreciation of the moral value of marriage than do the rest of the Fathers, especially those of the East.

[3] *De virg.* xi; cf. ix and x.

[4] Cf. *de vid.* xiii; *de virginitate,* vi.

[5] Cf. *de virginibus,* i. 34; *de virginitate,* vi; *de vid.* xxiii and lxxii; also *epist.* xlii. 3; lxiii. 40—there are different ways to the same goal, marriage, widowhood, and virginity (cf. *de virginitate,* xxxiv, *de vid.* xxiv and lxxxiii).

[6] Cf. *c. Jul.* v. 66; also *de nupt. et concup.* ii. 32; *de sancta virg.* xviii.

[7] Cf. *de sancta virg.* xxi.

[8] Cf. *de bono conj.; de Gen. ad lit.* ix, 7; *de pecc. orig.* ii, 34; also ii. 39 and 42; *c. Jul.* iii.

[9] *Conviv.* i. 2–4; cf. i. 1.

[10] *Conviv.* ix. 4.

virgin state and the higher merit of continence without yielding to the thorough-going dualism which denounced marriage as evil. But further than this they were reluctant to go. They continued to regard matrimony as a concession to the inordinate desires of fallen humanity and as a refuge for those weaker souls who could not bear the discipline of celibacy.[1] Although they taught that it had been instituted by the Creator for the generation of children, there was a tendency to argue on eschatological grounds that it was no longer necessary solely for the increase of the race,[2] but that it now served also to provide sinful Man with a remedy against concupiscence—indeed, John Chrysostom seems to have thought that this had become its principal purpose.[3] While none denied that marriage, relatively speaking, was a good thing, it was nevertheless tolerated rather than commended, and was depicted in exaggeratedly sombre colours by those more extreme writers who did not scruple to dissuade in the strongest terms where the very Scriptures[4] forbade them to condemn.

These authors rarely fail to remind their readers of the trials of pregnancy, the pains of childbirth, the anxieties of parenthood, and the distractions occasioned by wives, children, and family life.[5] Gregory of Nyssa dismisses marriage as a "sad tragedy";[6] Jerome, in his inimitable and scurrilous fashion, expatiates upon its manifold inconveniences and tribulations,[7] and praises it solely because it produces virgins;[8] Ambrose considers it a "galling

---

[1] Cf. Jerome, *epist.* lxix. 3; *adv. Jov.* i. 13; Ambrose, *de vid.* lxviii; John Damascene, *de fid. orth.* iv. 24; Severus of Antioch, *epist.* § x. 2.

[2] Cf. Eusebius, *Demonstr.* i. 9; Augustine, *de bono conj.* xiii. It is curious how the eschatological motive continued down to the beginning of the fifth century to exert its influence—reinforced, no doubt, first by the persecutions, and then by the threats from the north to the political security of the western Empire.

[3] *De virg.* xix.   [4] Cf. 1 Tim. iv. 3; Heb. xiii. 4.

[5] Cf. Basil, *epist.* ii. 2; Gregory of Nyssa, *de virg.* iii; Ambrose, *de virginibus*, i. 25–26; Gregory I, *moral.* XXVI. xxvi. [44]; and numerous other references. See also n. 7 below.

[6] *De virg.* iii.

[7] See, among other references, *epist.* xxii. 2; xlviii. 18; liv. 4; *adv. Helvid.* xxii; *adv. Jov.* i. 28, 41.

[8] *Epist.* xxii. 20; "I praise marriage and wedlock, but only because they beget celibates; I gather roses from thorns, gold from the earth, pearls from shells."

burden",[1] and bids his brethren reflect upon the oppressive bondage and servitude into which wedded love too often degenerates.[2] Tertullian, it is true, has a famous encomium upon Christian marriage,[3] but it breathes the rarefied air of the cloister and consists of little more than an allusion to the nuptial ceremonies and a catalogue of the religious exercises in which husband and wife engage; nothing is said which could not apply to a couple living in a syneisaktical[4] relationship. On the whole, patristic literature adopts a pessimistic view of matrimony even while it vindicates its goodness, and the Fathers argue from the parable[5] with monotonous frequency that the wedded state produces a mere thirty-fold as compared with the sixty-fold of widowhood or the hundred-fold of virginity.[6]

Nor do they show much appreciation of the family—even though some were married men. The early Church certainly denounced such common pagan practices as abortion,[7] infanticide,[8] and the exposure of unwanted infants,[9] and benevolent Christians were ready to care for any who had been abandoned or orphaned.[10] Yet Tertullian does not hesitate to write of the "most bitter pleasure of children",[11] whom he describes as

---

[1] *De vid.* lxxxi; cf. *de virginibus,* i. 6.

[2] *De vid.* lxxxviii; cf. lxix.

[3] *Ad ux.* ii. 8.

[4] On syneisaktism or 'spiritual marriage' as an ascetical exercise, see below, pp. 33–35.

[5] Matt. xiii. 1 ff.

[6] Cf. Athanasius, *epist.* xlviii; Jerome, *epist.* xxii. 15; xlviii. 3; cxxiii. 1, 9; *adv. Jov.* i. 3; Augustine, *de sancta virg.* xlv; [? *de bono conj.* xiii]; Ambrose, *de virginibus,* i. 60; etc. For other analogies comparing marriage with virginity, see K. E. Kirk, op. cit., p. 241 and n. 2.

[7] See Tertullian, *apol.* ix; Minucius Felix, *Oct.* xxx; Basil *epist.* clxxxviii. 2 and 8; Jerome, *epist.* xxii. 13; John Chrysostom, *in epist. ad Rom.* xxiv. 4; Augustine, *de nupt. et concup.* i. 15; *Conc. Ancyr.* (314), xxi; *Conc. Ilerden.* (524), ii; *Conc. in Trullo* (692), xci; etc. For further material, see *Dict. Chr. Antiq.* i p. 9.

[8] Lactantius, *instit.* v. 9; vi. 20; *Conc. Illib.* (305–306), lxiii, lxviii; *Conc. Ancyr.* (314), xxi; *Conc. Ilerden.* (524), ii.

[9] Justin, *I Apol.* xxvii, xxix; Minucius Felix, *Oct.* xxxi; Lactantius, *instit.* v. 9; and other material in *Dict. Chr. Antiq.,* i, pp. 653–654.

[10] Cf. Augustine, *epist.* xcviii. 6; *Dict. Chr. Antiq.,* i, pp. 684–685.

[11] *Ad ux.* i. 5.

encumbrances avoided even by the heathen,[1] and Ambrose stresses the "troubles of nursing, training, and marrying" which beset the path of parenthood.[2] Injunctions to fathers recommend severity; they are to teach their children the word and the fear of the Lord, and subdue them "with cutting stripes" lest they fall into fornication—for the avoidance of which early marriage is advocated.[3] Little indeed is said of the happiness of life in the true Christian home—of the joys of parental self-sacrifice rewarded in the success and gratitude of the children, and of the salutary discipline and the simple yet satisfying pleasures of the domestic common life.[4] For all these things, good in themselves and good in their moral and spiritual no less than in their social and civic effects, the patristic writers in general display a singular and almost unnatural apathy, remote alike from the best contemporary pagan opinion and from the Jewish tradition in which Christianity was deeply rooted and had been partly nurtured.

Nor do we find only this mere indifference; not a few distressing anecdotes and exhortations to celibacy or monachism reveal a definite and active antagonism to home and family, and show with what ruthless fanaticism some advocated or pursued the ascetical ideal.[5] No bond of affection or blood was so strong, no claim of filial or parental obligation so sacred as to avail against the inflexible determination of such enthusiasts to spurn all worldly possessions and relationships, and the Lucan injunction to "hate" father and mother, spouse and child, was sometimes applied almost literally with a heartless contempt for decency and human feeling. Happily these excesses of rigorism were relatively uncommon, though they do not seem to have been markedly discordant with the sentiment of the age; indeed, the fact that they were tolerated at all, and that they passed without

---

[1] Ibid; cf. *de exhort. cast.* xii.   [2] *De virginibus*, i. 25–26.   [3] *Const. Apost.* iv. 9.
[4] Very rarely there is a hint of a different attitude, as in Minucius Felix, *Oct.* ii; and see below on Clement of Alexandria.
[5] Cf. Jerome, *epist.* xiv. 2, 3; xxxix. 4; cviii. 6; John Cassian, *de instit. cœnob.* iv. 27; v. 32; *coll.* xxiv. 9, 13; Ambrose, *expos. evang. Luc.* vii. 146; *epist.* lxvi. 7; *de virginibus*, i. 63; Paulinus of Nola, *epist.* xiv; xxv. 7; Augustine, *epist.* cxxvii; cclxii.

ecclesiastical censure, is in itself a significant comment upon the early Church's ethical and theological view of the family.

It is clear, however, that at least the more extreme ascetical doctrine of the Fathers was not wholly congenial to every thinker of their time. Clement of Alexandria in particular wrote more sympathetically of the happiness and the unaffected piety of the Christian home.[1] While allowing that celibacy is intrinsically the way of higher merit, he nevertheless recommended marriage as that best suited to the majority of men,[2] and went so far as to maintain that it offers better opportunities than virginity for the attainment of excellence, involving as it does greater temptations and cares, and therefore more occasions for the exercise of self-discipline.[3] He suggested, moreover, that avoidance of wedlock might in some cases proceed rather from cowardice than from a love of continence,[4] and also expressed his dissent from the Pauline opinion that a man cannot both care for the things of the Lord and please his wife.[5]

In an even more liberal vein the "fifth-century Sidney Smith", Synesius of Cyrene, insisted as a condition of his elevation to the episcopate that he should continue to live with his wife in normal marriage. Separation he rejected as an impiety, and clandestine intercourse as unlawful and more befitting an adulterer; and he expressed the hope that he might be granted a large and virtuous family.[6] Even the hermit Macarius of Alexandria was led as the

---

[1] Cf. R. B. Tollinton, *Clement of Alexandria* (London, 1914), i. pp. 283 ff., with references to *Pæd.* ii. 1, 7, 9, and iii. 11. [2] *Strom.* ii. 23; iv. 23.

[3] *Strom.* vii. 12; but Gregory Nazianzen, on the other hand, regarded virginity as "higher and more divine, though more difficult and dangerous" than marriage, which was "safer", *orat.* viii. 8.

[4] *Strom.* ii. 23. [5] *Strom.* iii. 12.

[6] *Epist.* cv (A. Fitzgerald, *The Letters of Synesius of Cyrene* [Oxford, 1926], p. 199). No more children were born to Synesius and his wife after his consecration as bishop of Ptolemais, and it has been suggested that despite his protestation he conformed to the convention of the time and did not retain his wife (see T. R. Halcomb in *Dict. Chr. Biog.*, iv, pp. 775–776); but the evidence is inconclusive—and the protestation remains. Does Synesius's refusal to associate himself with his wife "surreptitiously, like an adulterer" imply that some of the clergy were accustomed thus to circumvent the restriction of marital intercourse demanded by public opinion before it was imposed by ecclesiastical rule?

result of a vision to acknowledge that "virginity matters nothing, nor marriage; there is no difference between the monastic life and the secular. It is the motive alone which God observes; and he gives the spirit of life to all alike".[1]

The most vigorous opposition to the cult of virginity, however, came at the close of the fourth century from three western writers. The cause, like many another, could perhaps have been more fortunate in its advocates; nevertheless, their criticism might have been less barren of effect, and their characters would have escaped calumniation, had they not had the ill-luck to arouse the spleen of Jerome. Their works have now perished, and their arguments survive only as he presents (or misrepresents) them for the purpose of refutation, but the general drift of their contentions is clear.

Helvidius, it seems, had composed a treatise in which he called the Scriptures to witness against the growing opinion that the mother of the Lord remained perpetually virgin, and asserted that her own example demonstrated the equal value of marriage and celibacy.[2] Jovinian, in an attack upon the exaggerations in which the ascetical spirit found expression, had maintained *inter alia* that in the sight of God there is no essential distinction between virgins, wives, and widows, and that the single state has no greater merit than the married.[3] Vigilantius, denouncing such abuses as excessive veneration of relics, scandalous behaviour at vigils, formalism in almsgiving, and the pretensions of monks and nuns, had declared that a wedded clergy is advantageous to the Church, and that the choice of a solitary life was often actuated by a desire to evade responsibility.[4]

---

[1] See K. E. Kirk, op. cit., p. 235 and references.

[2] Cf. Jerome, *adv. Helvid.*; Gennadius, *de vir. illustr.* xxxiii; *Dict. Chr. Biog.*, ii, p. 892.

[3] Cf. Jerome, *adv. Jov.*—especially book i; *epist.* xlviii, xlix, l; Gennadius, *de vir. illustr.* lxxvi mentions Jovinian in a notice of an opponent, and retails one of Jerome's calumnies from *adv. Vigil.* i; Augustine, *de hær.* lxxxii; *Dict. Chr. Biog.* iii, pp. 465–466.

[4] Cf. Jerome, *adv. Vigil.*; Gennadius, *de vir. illustr.* xxxvi; *Dict. Chr. Biog.*, iv, pp. 1141–1143.

With each of these Jerome dealt in characteristic fashion. To Helvidius, admittedly, he was no more than mildly rude; but he made up for this lapse into relative civility by the vituperative polemic which he directed against the other malignants. Disdaining to reason with them and ignoring their exposure of abuses, he merely silenced them with a spate of intemperate invective and puerile argument, interspersed with vulgar sarcasms and slanderous personalities. His attack upon Jovinian even drew remonstrances from his own supporters, who attempted to suppress what he had written, and these he sought to appease by restating his case in slightly more moderate terms;[1] but when he was himself assailed in turn by a certain monk whom he calls a "lounger" and a "noisy newsmonger", he simply answered with base insinuations against his adversary, and made the facetious concession: "I do not condemn wedlock. Indeed (and this I say to make my meaning quite clear to him) I should like everyone to take a wife who cannot manage to sleep alone because he gets frightened at night."[2] Jovinian had already been condemned by synods at Rome under Pope Siricius[3] and at Milan under Ambrose,[4] and Jerome's tirade sufficed to arrest the further spread of his teaching; nevertheless, the orthodox were not entirely happy about their champion's methods, and some ten years later Augustine composed the treatise *De Bono Conjugali* to prove that the defence of virginity did not require any denunciation of marriage.[5]

It was hardly to be expected that Siricius would prove tender to an opponent of asceticism, for in the first authentic decretal,[6] issued five years before action was taken against Jovinian, he had

---

[1] See *epist.* xlviii and xlix.

[2] *Epist.* l. 5. Reference is made to this incident in *epist.* l. 1–2, and in Rufinus, *apol.* ii. 9.

[3] Siricius, *epist.* ii (*ad divers. episc.*): an English translation appears in *The Letters of S. Ambrose* (Oxford, 1881—Library of the Fathers), pp. 280–282.

[4] Ambrose, *epist.* xlii. See also *epist.* lxiii, 7 ff., against two Jovinianists, Sarmatio and Barbatianus.

[5] Augustine, *retract.* ii. 22.

[6] Siricius, *epist.* i *ad Himer.*

attempted by invoking the apostolic authority of the Roman see to prohibit all married presbyters and deacons from coitus with their wives.[1] Although the New Testament does not exclude, and indeed might be interpreted as expecting a married clergy,[2] a rule of celibacy was sooner or later inevitable, given the attitude which at this time prevailed in the Church. It seems that custom had established from a very early date the practice which later became the basis of eastern canon law in this respect—namely, that while a married man might proceed to ordination, an ordained man might not marry;[3] but positive regulations do not begin to appear until the fourth century,[4] and at first any suggestion that matrimonial cohabitation unfits a person for priestly ministrations is strongly resisted.[5]

Eastern usage eventually diverged from that of the West. Swayed by the pleading of the monk and confessor Paphnutius, a bishop from the upper Thebaid, the Council of Nicæa rejected an absolute rule of clerical celibacy,[6] and some two centuries and a half later the Trullan Council established as the law of the Church a modified version of the ancient custom already mentioned. Only lectors and cantors were permitted to marry·after ordination, but a lawfully married man might become subdeacon, deacon, or priest;[7] and to secure uniformity an earlier concession[8] was implicitly withdrawn which had sanctioned the marriage of deacons who, prior to ordination, gave notice of their intention to enter matrimony. Furthermore, the wife of a man advanced to the episcopate was required to separate from him and to retire into a monastery.[9]

---

[1] This rule, however, did not apply to subdeacons and acolytes, who were to be "content with one wife".

[2] 1 Tim. iii. 2, 4, 12; Tit. i. 6.

[3] Behind this practice, of course, lay the principle stated in 1 Cor. vii. 17–24.

[4] *Conc. Ancyr.* (314), x and *Conc. Neocæsaren.* (ante 325), i both presuppose some such rule; cf. later, *Const. Apost.* vi, 17.

[5] Cf. *Conc. Gangren.* (? 343), iv excommunicating any one who objects to a married priest celebrating the Eucharist.

[6] See Sozomen, *Hist. Eccl.* i. 23; Socrates, *Hist. Eccl.* i. 11.

[7] *Conc. in Trullo* (692), vi.

[8] *Conc. Ancyr.* (314), x.   [9] *Conc. in Trullo* (692), xlviii.

In the West an attempt was made at the beginning of the fourth century to impose a rule of abstinence from coitus upon all bishops, presbyters, deacons, and others employed in the service of the altar,[1] and a hundred years later a succession of synods and decretals had more or less established the principle.[2] To secure its observance in practice, however, seems to have proved harder, and the repeated efforts made by councils to enforce clerical celibacy suggests that the ministry as a whole did not view this discipline with excessive enthusiasm.[3] Leo I ventured to soften its rigour a little by permitting the married clergy to retain their wives on the condition that they should "have them as though they had them not";[4] but he also extended the rule so that it applied to subdeacons as well as to those in the higher grades of the ministry.[5] The demand for a celibate clergy continued to create for ecclesiastical authority problems of discipline which even the energetic measures instituted by Gregory VII failed to solve, and a perusal of mediæval conciliar and synodal legislation reveals in many a significant canon the weakness or the insubordination of those upon whom the yoke of continence was thrust.[6]

Both in the East, and in the West prior to the general requirement of clerical celibacy, certain restrictions operated in regard to the ordination of married men, the chief of which related to digamy. Following the injunctions in the Pastoral Epistles,[7] clerics

---

[1] *Conc. Illib.* (305–306), xxxiii.

[2] Cf. *Conc. Rom.* (386), ix (the enactment runs: "Finally, we advise [*suademus*] that priests and levites should not live with their wives"; but since this synod met under Siricius, it is likely that *suademus* here carries a sense stronger than that of mere persuasion); *Conc. Carthag.* (390), ii; *Conc. I. Toletan.* (400), i; *Conc. Carthag.* (401), iv; *Conc. Taurin.* (401), viii; *Conc. Rom.* (402), iii; also Siricius, *epist.* i *ad Himer.*; Innocent I, *epist. ad Victr.*, and *epist. ad Exsuper.*, both in 402.

[3] Cf. *Conc. Araus.* (441), xxii, xxiii, xxiv; *Conc. I Turon.* (461), i and ii; *Conc. VIII Toletan.* (653), vi; *Conc. IX Toletan.* (659), x; *Conc. XVI Toletan.* (731), iii and iv.

[4] *Epist.* xiv. 5; clxvii. 2.

[5] Ibid; but see also Gregory I, *epist.* i. 44, iv. 5, 36.

[6] See below, pp. 148 ff; also J. Wordsworth, 'Christian Asceticism and the Celibacy of the Clergy' in *The Ministry of Grace* (London, 1901).

[7] 1 Tim. iii. 2, 4, 12; Tit. i. 6.

were forbidden to effect second marriages,[1] and none were
admitted to the ministry who were either themselves digamists,[2]
or had married widows.[3] Moreover, by a curious extension of
the original principle, not only had deaconesses to be monogamous,[4] but also widows of the clergy, whom several later
western canons during this period prohibit from remarriage.[5] In
theory the rule excluding digamists applied to all grades of the
ministry, but for a time some relaxation was permitted in the
case of the inferior clergy,[6] and there is evidence[7] that in France,
at any rate, clerical digamy was sufficiently common to compel
the authorities to tolerate it—or at least to deal with it leniently.

At first the attitude to lay digamy was less strict; it was regarded
as lawful and sinless although, in the words of Hermas, the man
who refrains from entering again upon matrimony "invests himself with more exceeding honour and with great glory before the
Lord".[8] Then, as the spirit of asceticism grew within the Church,

---

[1] See Tertullian, *de exhort. cast.* vii; Hippolytus, *philosoph.* ix. 12; *Constit.
Apost.* vi. 17; *Conc. I Toletan.* (400), iv; *Conc. Rom.* (465), ii; Gelasius I, *epist.*
ix. 3, 22; *Conc. in Trullo* (692), iii; John Chrysostom, *in epist. I ad Tim.* x. 1; *in
epist. ad Tit.* ii. 1; Severus of Antioch, *epist.* § 1, nos. 46, 49, 50, 51, 63; and also the
additional references in the notes following.

[2] Cf. *Constit. Apost.* ii. 2; vi. 17; Leo. I, *epist.* iv. 3; *Conc. Valent.* (374), i; *Conc.
Andegav.* (453), xi; *stat. eccl. antiq.* (c. 525), lxix; etc.

[3] Cf. Basil, *epist.* clxxxviii. 12; Leo I, *epist.* iv. 3; vi. 3; *Conc. I Toletan.* (400),
iii; *Conc. Andegav.* (453), xi; *stat. eccl. antiq.* (c. 525), lxix. No doubt this rule was
influenced by Jewish precedent, cf. Lev. xxi. 13, 14. Other regulations forbid
those already ordained to marry widows: see Innocent I, *epist.* ii. 4 (*ad Victr.*);
Conc. I. Turon. (461), iv; *Conc. Rom.* (465), ii; etc.

[4] See *Constit. Apost.* vi. 17; *Conc. II Aurelian.* (533), xvii; *Justinian, nov.* vi. 6;
and cf. 1 Tim. v. 9.

[5] *Conc. I Aurelian.* (511), xiii; *Conc. Epaunen.* (517), xxxii; *Conc. Autiss.* (578),
xxii; *Conc. II Matiscon.* (585), xvi.

[6] *Conc. Araus.* (441), xxv; *Conc. II Arelat.* (452), xlv; Justinian, *nov.* vi. 5; xxii.
42; cxxiii. 14.

[7] *Conc. Agath.* (506), i; cf. *Conc. Epaunen.* (517), ii; *Conc. IV Arelat.* (524), iii;
Conc. IV Aurelian. (541), x; etc.

[8] *Mand.* iv. 4.

second marriage fell increasingly into disfavour;[1] some were inclined to treat it merely as a regrettable concession to incontinence, but others of a more extreme disposition stigmatized it as an indulgence amounting almost to adultery,[2] and condemned a third union as "fornication" or "transgression", and a fourth as unclean or "swinish".[3]

Eventually, however, saner and more moderate views prevailed. Augustine, who did not conceal his regret that the Count Boniface had so soon abandoned his profession of widower,[4] nevertheless recalled the tolerant judgement of Hermas in his recognition that "second marriages are not condemned, but are set in lower honour", and castigated Tertullian for his attack upon them.[5] The East, less tender in this respect than the West, yielded a little to ascetical sentiment; a mild penitential discipline was imposed upon digamists,[6] the crowning was omitted from the wedding ceremony, and presbyters were expected to signify ecclesiastical disapproval of such unions by refraining from attendance at the nuptial festivities.[7] But the West, too, penalized digamy after what was deemed to be a religious profession, such as that of penitent[8] or widow;[9] and in Spain two curious regulations

---

[1] In addition to the references given above (p. 20 n. 3), the following reflect the general attitude of the Church to lay digamy: Epiphanius, *hær.* lix. 6; John Chrysostom, *in illud: Vidua eligatur.* v, vi; *de non iterando conj.*; *in Act. Apost.* xlix. 4; *in epist. I ad Thess.* vi. 2; Gregory Nazianzen., *orat.* xxxvii. 8; Jerome, *epist.* xlviii. 8; lxxix; cxxiii; *adv. Jov.* i. 15, 16; Ambrose, *de offic.* ii. 27; *de vid.* xii, lxxxix; *Hexæm.* v. 62, 63; Ambrosiaster, *comm. in* 1 *Cor. vii.* 40; Augustine, *epist.* ccxx. 3–4.

[2] Tertullian, *de exhort. cast.* ix; Athenagoras, *legat.* xxxiii.

[3] *Constit. Apost.* iii. 2; Gregory Nazianzen., *orat.* xxxvii. 8; cf. *The Gospel of Bartholomew*, v. 7 (M. R. James, *The Apocryphal New Testament* [Oxford, 1924], p. 181). Cf. Basil, *epist.* cxcix. 50: trigamy is a defilement, but "better than unrestrained fornication" (cf. *epist.* clxxxviii, 4, where it is penalized as limited fornication).

[4] *Epist.* ccxx. 2–3.   [5] *De bono vid.* iv [6].

[6] Cf. *Conc. Neocæsaren.* (c. 315), iii, vii; *Conc. Laodic.* (mid-4th cent.), i; Basil, *epist.* clxxxviii. 4.   [7] *Conc. Neocæsaren.* (ante 325), vii.

[8] Cf. *Conc. II Arelat.* (452), xxi—the reference here to *pœnitentia* may relate either to penitence strictly so called, or to a vow of asceticism, which would naturally involve continence.

[9] Cf. *stat. eccl. antiq.* (c. 525), civ; *Conc. V Paris.* (613), xv [xiii].

forbade the remarriage of a widowed queen.[1] On the other hand, digamy was less rigidly interpreted in the East, where account was taken only of marriages effected after baptism,[2] whereas the West disregarded this distinction.[3] While the canon law prohibition of digamous clerical unions influenced the provisions of the civil law, which enforced the ecclesiastical sanctions,[4] the secular regulation of second marriage among the laity was but little concerned with the imposition of penalties upon digamists, and looked principally to securing the rights of the issue of the first marriage.[5]

The most remarkable manifestation of sexual asceticism in the early Church was undoubtedly the phenomenon known as syneisaktism, or spiritual marriage—that is, the cohabitation of the sexes under conditions of strict continence, a couple sharing the same house, often the same room, and sometimes the same bed,[6] yet conducting themselves as brother and sister.[7] St Paul's allusion in the first Corinthian epistle to the relationship between a man and his "virgin"[8] and other references by Hermas[9] confirm the great antiquity of the practice, which seems to have been adopted by Christianity at second-hand from pagan religion.[10] To the patristic age it was known in several forms, each representing an adaptation of the idea to different social circumstances or personal needs.[11] Certain of the solitary ascetics of the desert were

---

[1] *Conc. XIII Toletan.* (683), v; *Conc. Cæsar-Augustan.* (691), v.

[2] Theodore of Mopsuestia, *Comm. in epist. ad Tim. I*, ad loc. cit.

[3] Ambrose, *de offic. cler.* i. 50; Augustine, *de bono conj.* xviii; Innocent I, *epist.* ii (*ad Victr.*), 6; xxiii; Leo I, *epist.* iv. 3; vi. 3. But Jerome argues against the prevailing view, and contends that marriages prior to baptism should be ignored, *epist.* lxix. 2–3; *adv. Jov.* i. 15.

[4] Justinian, *nov.* vi. 1, 5; xxii. 42; cxxiii. 1, 12; cxxxvii. 2.

[5] *Corp. Jur. Civ.*, Cod. V. ix *de secund. nupt.*

[6] Cf. Jerome, *epist.* xxii. 14; Cyprian, *epist.* lxi, 3.

[7] The women so cohabiting were known as *agapetæ, mulieres subintroductæ*, or *suneisaktoi*—whence the term syneisaktism.

[8] 1 Cor. vii. 36–38.   [9] *Sim.* ix. 11; x. 3.

[10] See A. Œpke, art. *gunē*, in G. Kittel (ed.), *Theologisches Wörterbuch z.N.T.*, i, p. 779.

[11] See H. Achelis, '*Agapetæ*', in Hastings' *Encyclopædia of Religion and Ethics*, i. pp. 177b–178a, 178b.

accompanied each by a female hermit who acted more or less as a maidservant to the holy man; in the ancient Irish Church monks and nuns lived together in monastic establishments; and in the towns and cities women shared the dwellings of priests, and even of bishops, as housekeepers or spiritual companions.

At first there was nothing specially clerical about syneisaktism, but with the growing tendency towards a celibate ministry and the popular expectation that the higher clergy, at least, should exhibit in their lives a more than ordinary asceticism, spiritual marriages became increasingly common. It was not long before such unions began to lose the ideal character with which extra-ordinary personal discipline or indulgent sentimentality had invested them, with the result that "out of the ascetic and the bride of the soul there arose imperceptibly the housekeeper, who was suspected to be also the mistress".[1] Finally, by a reversal of the original arrangement, a new form of syneisaktism emerged when wealthy young women or widows, having refused marriage and thus acquired the outward reputation of virginity or vidual continence, sought out clerics or monks to share their homes. In these equivocal relationships the hostess played the dominant rôle and the man was the *suneisaktos*, occupying a somewhat precarious position which "may have varied between house steward, domestic chaplain, and spiritual lover",[2] and sometimes degenerated all too easily into that of the harassed and obsequious *cavaliere servente* described by John Chrysostom,[3] Jerome,[4] and Gregory of Nazianzus.[5]

There is no reason to suspect the integrity of the early experiments in syneisaktism, though they may often have been ill-advised and, as St Paul's counsel suggests, may occasionally have

---

[1] Ibid, i. p. 178a.

[2] Ibid.

[3] See his homily: *contra eas quæ viros subintroductos habent.*

[4] See *epist.* cxvii; in *adv. Vigil.* iii Jerome reveals that this denunciation also provoked a rejoinder from his opponents, who apparently alleged that his picture of the abuse was merely a fabrication. There is no ground, however, for doubting its genuineness.

[5] See *carm. moral.* i.

led to situations of intolerable strain. While spiritual marriage was at first viewed by some with approval,[1] especially if the *suneisaktos* was a widow, it is clear that with the passage of time it speedily lost its original character and eventually became an open scandal which demanded severe disciplinary action by the Church. From the beginning of the fourth century onward, councils enacted against the custom and the demoralization to which it tended, and insisted that no women should reside in the houses of clerics but those whose natural relationship with their protectors would disarm suspicion.[2] Bishops likewise inveighed against the *suneisaktoi*, and took action against those of the clergy who refused to part with their virgins.[3] Finally, since none of these measures availed to eradicate the practice, the aid of the civil power was invoked and a law was passed in the year 420 under Honorius and Theodosius II[4] forbidding all "so-called sisterly cohabitation" and permitting no females to live with clerics of any grade, except mothers, sisters, daughters, and other near relatives. Even this regulation, however, failed in its purpose, as did a later edict of Justinian to the same effect;[5] and the problem of syneisaktism only disappeared when the transparent pretence of asceticism was at last abandoned, and clerical concubinage arose in its place to engage the attention of ecclesiastical disciplinarians and moralists in the West.

---

[1] Tertullian, *de exhort. cast.* xii; *de monog.* xvi; etc. In the first passage, Tertullian even recommends a plurality of such 'wives'.

[2] See *Conc. Illib.* (305–306), vii; *Conc. Ancyr.* (314), xix; *Conc. Nic.* (325), iii; *Conc. Carthag.* (348), iii, iv; *Conc. Hippon.* (393), II. xvi; *Conc. II Arelat.* (452), iii; *Conc. Ilerden.* (524), xv; *Conc. II Toletan.* (527), iii; *Conc. Bracaren.* (563), xv; *Conc. Hispalen.* (590), iii; *Conc. IV Toletan.* (633), xlii; and cf. *stat. eccl. antiq.* (c. 525), xlvi.

[3] Cf. Cyprian, *epist.* lxi; Gregory of Nyssa, *de virg.* xxiii; Basil, *epist.* lv; John Chrysostom, *in evang. Matt.* xvii. 2; *in epist. I ad Cor.* xliv. 3–5; the homily *contra eos qui virg. subintr. hab.* Eusebius, *hist. eccl.* vii. 30 records that one of the charges against Paul of Samosata was that he permitted, and himself associated with *subintroductæ*. Tertullian, whose favourable attitude to 'spiritual wives' has already been noticed, appears to attack syneisaktism as practised by catholics, in *de jejun.* xvii. Syneisaktism is also condemned in Ps-Clement, *de virg., epist. I*, x.

[4] *Cod. Theod.* XVI. ii. 44 = *Cod. Justin.* I. iii. 19.

[5] *Nov.* cxxiii. 29 (541).

Despite its enthusiasm for virginity, the early Church was always careful to maintain the doctrine that marriage is an inferior good, and on that account not to be despised; hence it lent no countenance to those rigorists who so exalted continence as to teach that matrimony is to be shunned as something impure or evil. Few of those who permitted or propagated this view took their stand upon it; rather, it followed as an inevitable consequence of their basic religious tenets. In some cases, reprobation of marriage was but one of many forms in which expression was given to the principle of *egkrateia* or self-control; in others, it was the result of eschatological or perfectionist ideas. Encratism, which had close affinities with Essenism and Ebionism, had already begun to manifest itself in New Testament times; it seems to have been a feature of the Colossian heterodoxy,[1] and Timothy was warned against false teachers who forbade marriage and commanded abstinence from certain foods.[2] Later, the apocryphal Acts (especially those of Paul and Thekla, Peter, Andrew, and above all John and Judas Thomas) and the pseudo-Clementine *Homily*,[3] with its reference to the *Gospel according to the Egyptians*,[4] exhibited encratite tendencies in an extreme form; and it has been alleged that the writings of Hermas are similarly tainted—but without good reason, for the suspected passages[5] contain simply counsels and not precepts of continence. Encratism never became the distinctive or exclusive teaching of one particular sect, but was rather an influence affecting all ascetical movements on the fringe of Christianity.

Gnosticism, with its dualistic premise that matter is inherently evil, gave Encratism something of a dogmatic foundation; it also provided a theoretical justification of sexual asceticism on the ground that marriage and coitus only serve to entrap more souls in the prison-house of the body. Continence, therefore, was

---

[1] Col. ii. 21.
[2] 1 Tim. iv. 3.
[3] The so-called second epistle of Clement; see p. 39.
[4] Ps-Clement, *hom.* xii. 2.
[5] E.g., *vis.* ii. 2; *mand.* iv. 1, 4.

encouraged both as a device to frustrate the purpose of the Demiurge and as a mortification by means of which the zealous Gnostic might bring the flesh into subjection to the spirit. Thus Apelles,[1] Marcion,[2] Tatian,[3] Saturninus,[4] and the Priscillianists[5] (among others) condemned wedlock and procreation as the works of Satan. Julius Cassianus taught likewise, arguing that coitus is a sowing in the flesh from which man reaps corruption;[6] and the Severians, seeing that so many ills proceed from the inordinate indulgence of human appetites, proclaimed that woman, and man from the navel downward, were created by the evil Demiurge— who also made the vine.[7]

Basilides, on the other hand, only recommended and did not insist upon abstinence; he allowed marriage for the purpose of banishing sexual distractions which hindered prayer, and his followers were alleged to have maintained that even the gratification of carnal desires in fornication would procure the same result.[8] There was, indeed, an antinomian as well as an ascetical tendency in all Gnosticism—due partly to contempt of the body; partly to the conviction that to the enlightened soul all actions, whether termed good or bad, are really indifferent; and partly to an extension of the theory of creation by the Demiurge which attributed to him the origin, not only of things material, but also of the moral law. Thus venereal licentiousness became in effect a demonstration, either of the superiority of the spiritual over the

---

[1] See Tertullian, *de præscr. hær.* xxxiii.

[2] Tertullian, *adv. Marc.* i. 29; iv. 11, 34; *de præscr. hær.* xxxiii; Clement of Alexandria, *Strom.* iii. 3, 13, 15, 17; Hippolytus, *philosoph.* vii. 17 (on the Empedoclean influences upon Marcion); viii. 15.

[3] Clement of Alexandria, *Strom.* iii. 6, 8, 9, 10; Irenæus. *adv. hær.* I. xxviii. 1; Hippolytus, *philosoph.* viii. 9; x. 14; Eusebius, *hist. eccl.* iv. 29; Augustine, *de hær.* xxv.

[4] Hippolytus, *philosoph.* vii. 16; Theodoret, *hær. fab. compend.* i. 3.

[5] *Conc. Toletan.* (447), xvi, which anathematized those (i.e., the Priscillianists) who taught that marriages are *execrabilia*.

[6] Jerome, *in epist. ad Galat.* iii. 6; see also Clement of Alexandria, *Strom.* iii. 13.

[7] Eusebius, *hist. eccl.* iv. 29; Epiphanius, *hær.* xlv; Theodoret, *hær. fab. compend.* i. 21; Augustine, *de hær.* xxiv.

[8] Clement of Alexandria, *strom.* iii. 1; see also Irenæus, *adv. hær.* I. xxiv. 5; Epiphanius, *hær.* xxiv. 3; Jerome, *adv. Jov.* ii. 37.

physical, or of the freedom of the gnostic from the bondage of ordinances which had emanated from the Evil One.[1]

Some, however, who pressed the ascetical principle beyond the limit which orthodoxy would tolerate were in theory neither Encratites nor Gnostics. It is doubtful, for instance, whether even Hieracas of Leontopolis should be numbered among the 'self-controlled', though he certainly taught that Christ had come to preach absolute continence, and that since his advent no married person could inherit the kingdom of heaven.[2] Nor does the vacillating Eustathius of Sebaste appear to have been more than an over-enthusiastic ascetic, though he and his followers incurred the censure of the Council of Gangra for their slighting of matrimony[3] and their intolerance of those who accepted the ministrations of wedded clerics.[4] Again, the rigorism of the Montanists was not due to any metaphysical doctrine which involved reprobation of carnal things, but arose simply from a mistaken striving after perfection, which was intensified by ecstatic experience and by expectation of the approaching End. In their view, as it is represented by Tertullian in various works belonging to his third and heterodox period, matrimony was merely a tolerable way of escape from the temptations of the flesh, while digamy (as we have seen) was condemned out of hand. The Novatians, too, denounced the practice of second marriage as no less reprehensible than the pardoning of the lapsed, and in their zeal to achieve a 'pure' Church, refused to maintain communion with digamists.[5]

The accounts of the heresiologists constitute the principal source

---

[1] For references to antinomian sects, see Tertullian, *de anima*, xxxv (Carpocratians); Clement of Alexandria, *strom.* iii. 1 (Basilides); 4 (Nicolaitans, Prodicians, etc.); 5, 18; *Constit. Apost.* vi. 8 (Nicolaitans), 10; Irenæus, *hær.* I. vi. 2–4; xxv. 3 (Carpocratians); xxvi. 3 (Nicolaitans); xxviii. 2 (Basilidians and Carpocratians); xxxi (Cainites); II. xxxii. 1; Hippolytus, *philosoph.*, vi. 14 (Simonians); Augustine, *de hær.* i (Simonians); v (Nicolaitans); vii (Carpocratians).

[2] See Epiphanius, *hær.* lxvii.

[3] *Conc. Gangren.* (mid-4th cent.), i, ix, x, xiv.

[4] *Conc. Gangren.* iv.

[5] See Epiphanius, *hær.* lix. 3; Socrates, *hist. eccl.* v. 22; *Conc. Nic.* (325), viii.

of information regarding the specifically sexual ideas of the gnostic and encratite sects, but a more vivid impression of their general attitude is conveyed by the apocryphal literature of the early Christian era, most of which (though anonymous) clearly emanated from circles of proved or suspected heterodoxy. To Christ himself the spurious gospels attribute only one relevant utterance of real antiquity—the cryptic saying that the kingdom of heaven will come "when ye have trampled on the garment of shame, and when the two become one and the male with the female is neither male nor female".[1] To this may be added two others, from documents of a later date: "A single marriage belongeth to sobriety... he that sinneth after the third marriage [wife] is unworthy of God",[2] and "The disciples of John marry and are given in marriage; but my disciples neither marry nor are given in marriage, but are as the angels of God in heaven."[3] The first and third of these logia certainly represent Jesus as an advocate of extreme sexual asceticism, but it was rather the apostles than the Master himself whom the sectaries claimed as exponents of their tenets.

The various apocryphal *Acts* or romances purporting to recount the evangelistic adventures of some of the Twelve abound in passages and incidents which display a temper of uncompromising rigorism towards every aspect of sexual relation. John, Paul, Thomas and Andrew in particular are shown proclaiming, not the gospel of the New Testament but a gospel of asceticism in which sexual continence figures prominently, and making it their chief business as emissaries of Christ to turn people against marriage, to separate brides from bridegrooms on the wedding night, to persuade spouses to cease cohabitation save as brother and sister, and to stir up dissention in households by inducing

---

[1] From the *Gospel according to the Egyptians*, quoted in Pseudo-Clement, *hom.* xii. 2, and by Clement of Alexandria, *strom.* iii. 13—see M. R. James, *The Apocryphal New Testament* (Oxford, 1924), cited in the notes following as J, p. 11.

[2] *The Gospel of Bartholomew* (? 5th cent.), v. 8 (see J, p. 181).

[3] From the *Book of John the Evangelist* (? 6th or 7th cent.), see J, p. 191.

women converts to shun the connubial bed.[1] Wedlock, they declare, is "a foul and polluted way of life",[2] and entrance into eternal life is impossible for those who continue therein.[3] Coitus is "an experiment of the serpent . . . the impediment which separates from the Lord, the beginning of disobedience, the end of life, and death";[4] it is a "deed of shame and confusion"[5] to be abhorred by the enlightened. Even children cannot mitigate the evil of matrimony, but rather increase it; they encourage in their parents a covetous and unscrupulous disposition and, if not sickly, deformed, or lunatic, inevitably grow up to be dissolute, idle, or criminal.[6]

The sexual outlook of Encratism is Epitomized in a set of extraordinary beatitudes which are put into the mouth of St Paul as he discourses in the house of Onesiphorus upon "the word of God concerning abstinence [or continence] and the resurrection". Four of the blessings pronounced are upon those "who keep the flesh chaste, for they shall become the temple of God"; upon the continent, "for unto them shall God speak"; upon those who "possess their wives as though they had them not, for they shall inherit God"; and upon "the bodies of the virgins, for they shall be well-pleasing unto God and shall not lose the reward of their continence. . . ."[7] Such was the view of marriage and of the family inculcated by the writings which have aptly been described as the "Sunday afternoon literature of the ancient Church",[8] and whose influence upon popular Christian sentiment,

---

[1] See, in addition to the passages cited below: *Acts of John* (ante 150), xxix (J, pp. 233–234); xvii—Latin version (J. p. 261); *Acts of Paul* (c. 160), ii. 5–6, 7–20 (J, pp. 273–276); *Acts of Peter* (ante 200), xxxiv (J, pp. 232–233); *Acts of Andrew* (c. 260), xxxv (J, p. 349); *Acts of Thomas* (c. 200 ?), xlii (J, pp. 385–386); *Acts of Philip* (5th cent.), iv, v (J, pp. 442–443); *Acts of Peter and Andrew*, viii, ix, xiii (J, pp. 458–459); *Apocalypse of Paul*, xxii (J, p. 537); 1 (J, p. 553); etc.

[2] *Acts of Andrew*, Vatican MS fragment, v (J, p. 352); cf. *Acts of Thomas*, xii (J, p. 369); lxxxviii (J, p. 404).

[3] *Acts of Paul*, xii (J, p. 275); cf. *Acts of Thomas*, li (J, p. 389); ci (J, p. 408).

[4] *Acts of John*, fragment (J, p. 266).

[5] *Acts of Thomas*, xiv (J, p. 370).

[6] *Acts of Thomas*, xii (J, p. 369).

[7] *Acts of Paul*, ii. 5 (J, p. 253).

[8] C. H. Turner, *The Study of the New Testament* (London, 1920), p. 12.

though impossible to measure, ought not to be underestimated merely on account of their provenance. They may well help to explain the apparent enthusiasm with which sexual asceticism, particularly in the form of clerical or monachal celibacy, was regarded even by those ordinary Christians of this time who were themselves disinclined to practice what they applauded, and sometimes demanded, in others.

To a few, however, the spirit exemplified in these romances made an irresistible appeal. One young woman, Demetrias, gained the warm approval of Augustine[1] and Jerome[2] for her decision to embrace virginity when the preparations for her marriage were already far advanced, while Ammon,[3] who founded the celebrated colony of Nitrian monks and hermits, and Pelagius, bishop of Laodicea,[4] both profitably employed their wedding nights in persuading their brides to share with them a life of continence. After five years of matrimony, on the other hand, the wife of a pious young Egyptian named Theonas was less disposed to be compliant; she resisted his entreaties that together they should vow themselves to celibacy, whereupon he deserted her for the seclusion of a monastery over which he was eventually called to rule as abbot.[5] Augustine in particular lost no opportunity of commending abstinence from coitus to the married,[6] and it is evident that certain of the more devout ventured upon this

---

[1] *Epist.* clxxxviii. 1.

[2] *Epist.* cxxx. 5.

[3] Socrates, *hist. eccl.* iv. 23; Sozomen, *hist. eccl.* i. 14.

[4] Theodoret, *hist eccl.* iv. 12.

[5] John Cassian, *coll.* xxi. 8–9. Cassian himself is obviously uneasy about the deplorable behaviour of Theonas, as his subsequent disclaimer shows (xxi. 10). He is at great pains to assure his readers that for his part he regards marriage as honourable, that he has not invented this incident in order to encourage divorce, and that the fact that he has recorded it must not be interpreted as an indication of his personal views.

[6] See, e.g., *epist.* ccxx. 12; *de bono conj.* iii (the sooner husband and wife abstain by mutual consent, the better); *de serm. Dom. in mont.* i. 14 [39]; *de consensu evang.* ii. 1 [2]; *c. Faust. Manich.* xxiii. 8; *de nupt. et concup.* i. 12 [11]; and cf. pseudo-Cyprian, *de discipl. et bono pudic.* iv.

ascetical experiment[1]—though doubtless there were some, like Jerome's correspondent Rusticus and his wife Artemia,[2] who proved unequal to its demands.

Although the Church condemned the dualists for their absolute rejection of matrimony, Christian thought upon sexual topics did not at all points conflict with that of Gnosticism and Encratism. There is a similarity of language, and still more, of sentiment between patristic literature and the theosophies and apocryphal romances which makes it impossible to doubt that many of the Fathers were substantially at one with the extreme rigorists in their general *emotional* attitude to marriage and coitus. But they could not harmonize their dualistic inclinations so easily or conveniently with dogma as could the Gnostics, who ascribed wedlock and procreation to the malign invention of the Demiurge. They were compelled by the Church's tenacious and reverential belief in the beneficent Creator-God of the Old Testament to affirm the essential goodness of all his works; yet cultural and temperamental factors inhibited them from treating matrimony and sexuality in the positive spirit of Jewish naturalism. From the impending dilemma, however, the Pauline double ethical standard offered a way of escape; by ranking the single above the wedded state it permitted the Fathers to acknowledge the divine institution and the practical utility of marriage while at the same time subordinating it as a lesser good to virginity and widowhood. Thus predilection was reconciled with theological exigency by a formula which conceded nothing to the heretics, though it could not always disguise the real sympathies of the orthodox.

In support of this solution Christian writers not only invoked the Apostle's authority, but argued also that the advent of Christ had modified God's original intention in creating male and female.

---

[1] Cf. Augustine, *serm.* li. 13 ("We know many of our brethren bringing forth fruit through grace, who for the name of Christ practise an entire restraint by mutual consent"); Jerome, *adv. Helvid.* xxiii; *adv. Jov.* i. 33; John Cassian, *coll.* xiv. 7.

[2] *Epist.* cxxii.

Under the old covenant, they contended, marriage and coitus were necessary—and, indeed, were commanded—in order to ensure the increase of the Lord's people, and the establishment and continuance of a line from which the Messiah might arise. Hence the levirate, the desire of the Patriarchs for a numerous progeny, and the concession of polygyny which somewhat embarrassed the Fathers and provided ready ammunition for anti-Christian polemists. With the arrival of a new dispensation, however, carnal propagation ceased to be obligatory and salvation became dependent, not upon generation but upon regeneration; now the children of God were to be born, "not of blood, nor of the will of the flesh, nor of the will of man", but "of water and the Spirit", through the supernatural agency of faith.[1] Consequently marriage was no longer enjoined as of old, but merely permitted; the preservation of the race could be left to the pagans, but before Christians was set the more excellent way of virginity—it was a time, not to embrace but to refrain from embracing.[2] Indeed, if all would abstain, the City of God would be filled the more speedily, and the end of the world hastened.[3]

Nevertheless, it was recognized that not all the faithful were endowed with the gift of continence requisite for the pursuit of this higher ideal, or disposed thus to accelerate the consummation of the ages. For them, therefore, God's ordinance now served as a means of relieving concupiscence. It remained for Augustine to present the lesser vocation of marriage as one endowed with its own blessings, of which the chief was a sacramental character peculiar to Christian unions,[4] investing them with the symbolism of the Incarnation and of Christ and the Church, and establishing between husband and wife a bond of solemn obligation.[5]

In the patristic treatment of sexual and matrimonial topics one feature particularly compels attention—namely, a curious and

---

[1] Jn. i. 12–13; iii. 5; 1 Pet. i. 23.
[2] Augustine, *de nupt. et concup.* i. 14–15 [13]; cf. *de bono conj.* xiii.
[3] Augustine, *de bono conj.* x.
[4] *De bono conj.* xxiv.
[5] Cf. *de nupt. et concup.* i. 11 [10], 19 [17], 23 [21]; *de bono conj.* xxiv.

sometimes almost morbid preoccupation with physical sexuality, and specially with coitus, towards which most of the Fathers displayed what can only be described as an attitude of settled emotional antipathy. This preoccupation, which in the case of one or two was nothing less than obsessive, caused them to handle most sexual questions primarily if not exclusively in venereal terms. Tertullian, for instance, declares that between marriage and fornication there is merely a legal and not an intrinsic difference, since to each the same act of shame appertains.[1] Likewise Martin of Tours implies that both are essentially similar when he permits himself to draw a deplorable comparison between the ungrazed field of virginity, that of marriage cropped by cattle, and that of fornication uprooted by swine.[2] That wedlock distracts from the service of the Lord was not, in the patristic view, its only defect; it had also this against it, that it suggests either inability to refrain from—or worse, inclination to—an act which some Fathers regarded as voluptuous carnal indulgence, and which few seem to have been able to contemplate without at least a certain distaste or suspicion.

The literature of the period affords abundant and significant evidence of this attitude. Because of the blessing pronounced upon Man: "Be fruitful and multiply",[3] the Fathers could not but deem coitus legitimate when performed by husband and wife with the express object of generation; indeed, this was widely held to be its sole purpose and justification.[4] Consequently some disapproved

---

[1] *De exhort. cast.* ix.

[2] See Sulpitius Severus, *dial.* ii. 10.

[3] Gen. i. 28; cf. ix. 1, 7.

[4] Justin, *I Apol.* xxix; Arnobius, *adv. gent.* iii. 8; vii. 35; Clement of Alexandria, *strom.* ii. 18, 23; vi. 12; Athenagoras, *apol.* xxxiii; Gregory of Nyssa, *de virg-*xiii; Jerome, *adv. Jov.* i. 20 (he further observes that because God made the genitals, this does not require their constant use, ibid, i. 36); Augustine, *c. Faust. Manich.* xxii. 61; xxix. 4, 6. Likewise cf. John Chrysostom on the venereal desire: it is not in itself sinful (*in epist. ad Rom.* xiii. 1), but was not given for adultery, fornication, and lasciviousness (*in epist. ad Galat.* v. 3); cf. *in epist. II ad Cor.* xxiii. 6; also Pseudo-Clement, *Recog.* vi. 12.

of the congress of the married during menstruation,[1] pregnancy,[2] and the period of breast feeding,[3] though Dionysius of Alexandria would permit it at the couple's discretion after the menopause.[4] While there was no denial that procreation is good in itself, there was nevertheless a general disposition to deplore the means appointed by the Creator to that end. Coitus was regarded on the whole as an unfortunate necessity to which the Christian should descend with regret;[5] the devout man, says Gregory of Nyssa, will not be concerned over-much about such "trifling debts of nature".[6]

In a more extreme vein, Tertullian assures his wife that none of the improper and voluptuous acts of their wedded life will be resumed in heaven, for God has not prepared for his own things so frivolous and impure.[7] Similar sentiments often recur in patristic literature. Arnobius writes of the filthiness of coitus (*fœditas cœundi*), its degrading pleasures, and the base nature of the sexual impulse,[8] and regards the genital organs as an unsightly disfigurement.[9] To others the act of venereal intercourse is unseemly[10] and unclean,[11] investing matrimony with shame.[12] Not a

---

[1] Clement of Alexandria, *pæd.* ii. 10; *Const. Apost.* vi. 28; Pseudo-Clement,. *hom.* xxx (it is better that coitus should not occur at such times); *Recog.* vi. 10, 11. The author of the *Didascalia*, however, condemns women who refuse coitus during menstruation, as well as those who think that during this period they have not the Holy Spirit, and do not then pray or communicate; see R. H. Connolly, *Didascalia Apostolorum* (Oxford, 1929), pp. 242–245.

[2] Clement of Alexandria, *pæd.* ii. 10; Athenagoras, *apol.* xxxiii; *Const. Apost.* vi. 28; Augustine, *de bono conj.* vi.

[3] Cf. Gregory I, *epist.* xi, 64, *respons. ad dec. interrog.*

[4] *Epist. ad Basilid.* iii.

[5] Augustine, *serm.* li. 25.

[6] *De virg.* viii.

[7] *Ad. ux.* i.

[8] *Adv. gent.* iv. 19; iv. 21; iii. 9.

[9] Ibid, iii. 10; cf. John Chrysostom, *in epist. I ad Cor.* xxxi. 2: these organs are esteemed the least honourable; but Augustine holds them not to be disgraceful in themselves, but only in their intemperate and licentious use, *c. Faust. Manich.* xxix. 4.

[10] Methodius, *conviv.* v. 4 (*atopēma*); cf. the implications of *conviv.* ii. 7 and v. 8.

[11] Jerome, *adv. Jov.* i. 20 (*immundus*).

[12] Tertullian, *de virg. vel.* x (*contumelia*).

few allusions to Christ's birth of a virgin imply that the carnal relationship of the sexes is staining and destructive of purity.[1] Jerome declares: "If we abstain from coitus we honour our wives; if we do not abstain—well, what is the opposite of honour but insult?";[2] if, as the Apostle says, "it is good for a man not to touch a woman", then it must obviously be bad for him to do so![3] Such weak sophistries provide their own comment upon the views of those who employed them.

Although the *Apostolic Tradition* plainly asserts: "He who has used marriage is not defiled; for those who are washed have no need to wash again, for they are pure",[4] St Paul's authority[5] was frequently invoked to demonstrate that coitus causes spiritual insensibility[6] and hinders devotion,[7] thus preventing that unceasing prayer[8] which the Apostle had enjoined.[9] It followed, therefore, that marriage (with its carnal intercourse) and the priesthood were necessarily incompatible[10]—a point which Ambrose stresses without any mincing of words: "The ministerial office must be kept pure and unspotted, and must not be defiled by coitus"; the married priest is "foul in heart and body".[11] John Chrysostom, however, often more inclined to moderation in sexual questions than his western contemporaries, ventures the hesitant concession that it is possible to live with a wife and yet

---

[1] Cf. Athanasius, *de incarn. verb. Dei*, viii. 5; Hilary, *de Trin.* iii, 19; and many similar references.

[2] *Adv. Jov.* i. 7.   [3] *Epist.* xlviii. 14.

[4] Hippolytus, *Apost. Trad.* II. xxxvi. 10. Similar statements are found in other Church Orders, etc.—e.g., the *Didascalia* (R. H. Connolly, op. cit., p. 255); the *Sahidic Heptateuch* (Sahid. 62 only—see G. Horner, *The Statutes of the Apostles or Canones Ecclesiastici*, London, 1904, pp. 329–330); also the *Canons of Hippolytus*, § 242: "Let those who are married pray whenever they arise from their wives; for wedlock does not stain."

[5] See 1 Cor. vii. 5.

[6] Tertullian, *de exhort. cast.* xi.

[7] Tertullian, *de exhort. cast.* x; xi; Jerome, *epist.* xlviii. 15.

[8] See 1 Thess. v. 17.

[9] Jerome, *epist.* xxii. 22; *adv. Jov.* i. 7; Ambrose, *de Elia*, lxxix; *stat. eccl. antiq.* xxiv (? and ci); Tertullian, *de exhort. cast.* x.

[10] Jerome, *adv. Jov.*, i. 34.

[11] *De offic.* i. 50.

give heed to devotion—though he maintains that prayer is perfected through continence.[1]

It was inevitable that these notions should find expression in disciplinary requirements such as the prohibition of coitus during penance,[2] while preparing for baptism,[3] and before receiving the Holy Communion.[4] But when Dionysius of Alexandria treats menstruation as a bar to participation in the Lord's Supper,[5] it is probable that he was influenced less by ideological considerations than by the vestiges of sexual taboo with which they are inextricably entangled. On the other hand, he will not be drawn into any pronouncement upon the sinfulness or otherwise of nocturnal emissions, preferring to leave this to the judgement of the individual conscience.[6] Here, John Chrysostom is more definite; such emissions are natural and do not defile—indeed, they show that the sexual impulse is implanted in Man, and is therefore less reprehensible than covetousness and avarice.[7]

These and similar questions are handled at length by Gregory I in a reply to enquiries from Augustine of Canterbury;[8] and his answers are particularly interesting for the light which they throw upon the sexual ideas of his time. He observes that menstruation is simply an infirmity or sickness in woman; it does not disqualify her from entering the church or receiving the Communion, though he allows that if she abstains, she displays a commendable reverence. Likewise, a woman may go to church immediately after childbirth; the Old Testament regulations concerning 'uncleanness' are to be understood mystically and not literally. Her fault lies, not in the pains undergone in delivery, but in the

---

[1] *In epist. I ad Cor.* xix. 3; cf. *Const. Apost.* vi. 28.

[2] Ambrose, *de pœnit.* ii. 10.

[3] Augustine, *de fid. et op.* vi [8].

[4] Jerome, *epist.* xlviii. 15.

[5] *Epist. ad Basilid.* ii; *Const. Apost.* vi, 27, 28, however, takes the opposite view. In certain of the earlier Church Orders menstruous women are required to defer their baptism, cf. *Apost. Trad.* II. xx. 6; *Sahid. Hept.*, Eth. 34, Arab. 33, Sahid. 45; also *Test. Dom.* ii. 6.

[6] *Epist. ad Basilid.* iv.

[7] *In epist. ad Tit.* v. 2.

[8] *Epist.* xi. 64, *resp. ad dec. interrog.*

pleasure enjoyed in coitus—a notion to which we must return shortly. A man, on the other hand, should not enter the church after coitus until he has washed[1]—and then not at once, for his mind is still occupied with lewd feelings of wrong desire and unfit for spiritual things; though if the act were performed solely for the purpose of generation, he may do as his conscience bids— and having made his ablutions, should not be denied the Communion. Finally, discrimination must be used in regard to nocturnal emissions. If the cause is merely superfluity or natural infirmity there is no ground for alarm, and the unfortunate subject merits sympathy rather than reproof. If, on the other hand, it is due to surfeit, a certain measure of guilt is incurred, yet not such as to prohibit from taking the Sacrament or (in the case of a priest) from celebrating the holy mysteries; but if it is the result of deliberate indulgence in foul thoughts when awake, the guilt is patent and unmitigated.[2]

While the Fathers do not conceal, they do not usually explain, their antipathy to coitus and the venereal. Probably they felt that no explanation was needed; they might even have found it difficult to formulate one, and it is unlikely that most of them would have regarded the attempt as congenial or profitable. Nevertheless, it is not difficult to account for their attitude and its acceptance at large in the Church. Without pursuing at the moment its undoubted remoter origins, it is clear that its proximate source is to be found in the oriental-hellenistic dualism in which the age was steeped, and which had infected Christian sexual thought even while under condemnation by the Church for its heretical influence in other directions. Sometimes a sufficient clue is furnished by the contemporary tendency, partly derived from the philosophies, to interpret the quest for the good life in terms of renunciation and ascetical discipline; but occasionally a more specific and personal factor cannot be excluded.

---

[1] Cf. Pseudo-Clement, *Hom.* xi. 28, 30; *recog.* vi. 10, 11. The survival of taboo here is indicated by Gregory's supporting citations from Ex. xix. 15 and 1 Sam. xxi. 4. There is no mention of any need for a woman to purify herself after coitus, which suggests that the 'defilement' was associated with the emission of semen.

[2] *Epist.* xi. 64, *resp. ad undec. interrog.*

Among the authors whose opinions have been cited, none occur more frequently than Tertullian and Jerome, and none (excepting St Paul and Augustine) have left a deeper or more lasting impression upon Christian sexual ideas and attitudes. In both cases confession invests their works with unusual psychological significance; style and manner no less than content suggest that in handling sexual topics the writers were profoundly affected by past experiences to which neither had become fully adjusted, and by repressions which influenced in particular their discussion of coitus.

Tertullian dwells somewhat morbidly upon his pre-eminence in sin prior to conversion,[1] and revealingly contrasts the adultery which he once committed in the flesh with the continence which he now strives to attain in the same flesh.[2] The excesses for which he reproaches himself afford their own explanation of the vehemence with which he repudiates his coital experiences in marriage[3] and equates the chaste use of wedlock with fornication in that both are intrinsically the same.[4] Jerome also led an irregular life at Rome in the days before his baptism,[5] and he, too, deplores the loss of his virginity and the sinful courses of his youth. His extravagant laudation of celibacy and his crude and violent outbursts against marriage, no less than the lascivious thoughts and visions which tormented him in his desert retreat, show that he never succeeded in coming to terms with his own sexuality. Even in the midst of his austerities he burned with desire as the scenes of his student dissipations arose before him, and a feverish imagination filled his cell with bevies of seductive girls.[6] Both his confessions and his controversies proclaim a psychological unfitness to act as a guide in sexual matters, and his influence upon Christian thought in this respect can only be regretted.

---

[1] *De pœnit.* iv.
[2] *De res. carn.* lix.
[3] *Ad ux.* i.
[4] *De exhort. cast.* ix.
[5] Cf. the hints in *epist.* vi. 4; xiv. 6; xlviii. 20.
[6] *Epist.* xxii. 7.

As psychological studies, however, Tertullian and Jerome are less interesting than Augustine, whose sexual thought is likewise more important than theirs. His *Confessions* are the record of a quest for a satisfying philosophy of life, and tell of his progress through Manicheism, Scepticism, and Neo-Platonism to the final assurance of the Christian faith. They also reveal something of the emotional conflict which accompanied this intellectual and spiritual search—a conflict which arose from his inability either to reject sexuality entirely or to integrate it into any scheme of things which commended itself to his mind. Imbued with the spirit of his age, he believed that the highest conception of the good life involved acceptance of the ideal and discipline of continence; but he was conscious, too, of strong venereal impulses, and was loth to surrender the sensual pleasures to which he was attached—even though indulgence only intensified the sense of guilt already engendered by a practice at variance with his principles. He realized that the settlement of his philosophical and religious problems depended partly upon a renunciation which had eventually to be made, but which he wished to defer for as long as possible; hence his constant prayer: "Give me chastity—but not yet."[1]

For thirteen years, as he pursued his quest for a faith that would answer to his needs, Augustine acquiesced uneasily in the partial solution of his sexual problem afforded by concubinage with the mother of his son Adeodatus; but this association only enabled the moment of final decision to be postponed until intellectual certainty was in sight. Then the period of crisis began, in his thirtieth year, and after he had settled with his mother in Italy. She, perceiving that he was attracted to Christianity and anxious to strengthen his moral stability, persuaded him to think seriously of marriage; and with some reluctance he himself seems to have reached the conclusion that the lawful satisfaction of his venereal desires (for such, at this time, was his view of wedlock[2]) might

---

[1] *Conf.* VIII. vii [17].
[2] Ibid, VI. xii [20–22]; cf. *de util. cred.* iii; *de vita beata,* iv.

open a way to the resolution of his remaining difficulties. A suitable engagement was eventually concluded, though the wedding had to be deferred until the bride-to-be reached the age of marriage. Meanwhile, leaving her child behind, Augustine's mistress and illicit but faithful consort was sent back to Africa, so that her presence might not impede the plans now in train. He records his grief at her departure ("My heart, which clave to her, was racked and wounded and bleeding"[1]), and we may not doubt its sincerity; but the episode, as it is related, hardly reflects credit upon anyone save the woman herself (she is never once named), who vowed to remain constant to the lover for the good of whose soul she had been thus callously discarded.[2]

Augustine was still, as he admits,[3] tenaciously held by his sexual desires, and could not resist taking another mistress while he waited unwillingly for the marriage which seemed to promise the only conceivable solution to his dilemma. But the end of the pilgrimage was near, and two incidents formed the prelude to decision. First, from Simplician the tutor of Ambrose, he heard of the conversion of the Roman rhetorician Victorinus, and burned to imitate so distinguished a submission; then, from a fellow African Pontitian, he learnt something of the attractions of monasticism, and lamented his own want of detachment from the sensual pleasures of the world. Reflecting upon these things, he retired in great turmoil of spirit to a secluded part of the garden where he was living, and there for the last time the old struggle between continence and indulgence was renewed.[4] Victory and peace came at length when a voice bade him "Take up and read", and opening a volume of St Paul, his eyes fell upon

---

[1] Ibid, VI. xv [26].

[2] It is never explained why Augustine, having decided upon marriage, did not take what would appear to be the simple and obvious step of regularizing this long and (by his own admission, cf. *Conf.* IV. ii [2]) affectionate union—especially since his mother seems at the beginning of the relationship to have persuaded him then against marrying the woman (*Conf.* II. iii [8]) for fear that his career might be affected. Probably social obstacles now stood in the way—or his mistress may have refused to embrace Christianity.

[3] *Conf.* VIII. i [2].

[4] Ibid, VIII. xi [25–27].

the words: "Not in rioting and drunkenness, not in chambering and wantonness, not in strife and envying; but put ye on the Lord Jesus Christ, and make not provision for the flesh, to fulfil the lusts thereof."[1] In the Apostle's monition, which he interpreted as a call to celibacy, he found the conclusive answer to his quest.

It is plain that Augustine's 'conversion' was, in fact, a decision against both his own proposed marriage and marriage in general. To be more precise, it was a decision against coitus; and without this moral surrender he knew that he could attain neither intellectual nor spiritual certainty. Thus he writes: "Thou didst so convert me unto thyself that I sought neither a wife, nor any other of this world's hopes";[2] and again: "For my soul's freedom I resolved not to desire, nor to seek, nor to marry a wife."[3] Only by embracing continence once for all could he settle the insistent problem of sexuality in a way which harmonized with his own ideals and aspirations, and with the contemporary conception of the good life at its highest—rational, contemplative, moderate, and unruffled by passion. This is not to say that the morality or the propriety of coitus was the principal, much less the only question at issue in his striving towards faith; but it was undoubtedly the critical question,[4] and the one most difficult of solution.

The psychological factors involved in Augustine's conversion are significant for the light which they throw upon his sexual thought as a Christian theologian. His interest in sexual questions, like that of the other Fathers, was never more than incidental and occasional, but they claimed his attention during his controversies with the Manicheans and, more particularly, the Pelagians. The radical dualism of the former branded coitus (and therefore marriage) as unmitigated evils, while the optimistic naturalism of the latter represented both as good, and uncontaminated by the Fall. Neither position, however, was acceptable to Augustine—

---

1 Rom. xiii. 13–14.
2 *Conf.* VIII, xii [30].
3 *Soliloq.* i. 10 [17].
4 Cf. K. E. Kirk, op. cit., p. 324.

the one because it denied that physical sexuality is the gift of God, and as such not wholly corrupt; the other because it failed to allow for the vitiating influence of concupiscence, by which all human acts (and specially the venereal) have been tainted. But the need to steer a middle course between these two errors does not altogether account for the form which his arguments took or the conclusions at which he arrived. His theology can only be fully understood when allowance is made for the emotional attitudes and consequent intellectual presuppositions revealed by the psychological conflict which finally determined his mature view of sexuality. Hence the importance of a biographical preface to any account of his sexual thought and teaching.

The direct connexion between Augustine's personal experience and his theological speculation appears most clearly in his anxiety to attribute the present character of human sexuality to the Fall. He was particularly offended and embarrassed by the act of coitus, with its intensity of venereal emotion and its uncontrollable orgasm, and he blushed to think that even the good work of generation cannot be accomplished without "a certain amount of bestial movement"[1] and a "violent acting of lust".[2] He believed that it could not always have been thus, and that the shameful copulations which men and women now endure in the discharge of their procreative functions are not natural to our kind, but result from the transgression of our first parents.

In Paradise, Augustine maintained, Adam and Eve were naked and unashamed because their genitals, like their other members, were wholly under control and obedient to the dictates of the will,[3] never stirring in opposition to it, or save at its behest.[4] They did not venture upon coitus before their expulsion from Eden, but had they done so, their congress would have been without lascivious heat or unseemly passion:[5] "Away with the

---

[1] *De grat. Chr. et de pecc. orig.* ii. 38 [43].
[2] *De civ. Dei*, xiv. 26.
[3] Ibid, xiv. 17; *de grat. Chr. et de pecc. orig.* ii. 40 [35]; *c. duas epist. Pelag.* i. 35 [17].
[4] *De civ. Dei*, xiv. 19.
[5] Ibid, xiv. 26, also 23, 24; *de nupt. et concup.* ii. 14.

thought", he exclaims, "that there should have been [in the Garden] any unregulated excitement, or the need to resist desire."[1] Libidinous stimulation would have been unnecessary, and ejaculation would have occurred in tranquillity through the acquiescence of the organs in the bidding of the mind[2]—just as now (to quote Augustine's telling but crude comparisons) menstrual blood is discharged,[3] or urine is expelled from the bladder.[4] Whether these placid (not to say dull) exercises would also have been pleasurable, we are not told; but we may perhaps suppose that they would have been attended at least by a certain calm and elevated enjoyment far more rarified, even, than the "gravity of glowing pleasure" attributed by Augustine to coitus in which lust is "tempered by parental affection".[5]

But when pride and self-will led the pair into sin, a new experience befell them: "the eyes of both of them were opened"[6] —that is to say, they became conscious within themselves of a new and destructive impulse, generated (as it were) by their act of rebellion, inordinate and independent of volition, by which they were driven to an insatiable quest for self-satisfaction. This impulse Augustine termed 'concupiscence' (*concupiscentia*) or lust; and although it intrudes into every human concern and relationship, he believed that it operates most powerfully and characteristically in the sexual realm. Proof of this he found in the fact that the first effect of their fall was to make Adam and Eve aware and ashamed of their nakedness. This he interpreted to mean that their own disobedience had immediately recoiled upon them in the disobedience of their genitals,[7] which suddenly lost the docility of innocence; secretly by venereal excitement no less than openly by the tumescence of their organs they discovered that these members were no longer amenable to the will.[8] Shame

---

[1] Cf. *c. duas epist. Pelag.* i. 34 [17].

[2] *De nupt. et concup.* ii. 8, 12, 13, 22.

[3] *De civ. Dei*, xiv. 26.

[4] *De nupt. et concup.* ii. 31.

[5] *De bono conj.* iv [4].   [6] Gen. iii. 7.

[7] *De civ. Dei*, xiii. 13.

[8] *C. duas epist. Pelag.* i. 32 [16].

followed quickly upon this demonstration of unruliness. They could not bear to look upon the manifest consequences of their sin, or to acknowledge that the control of their bodies had been impaired, so "they sewed fig leaves together and made themselves aprons"[1]—their genitals were now *pudenda*,[2] and must be concealed lest they should betray the truth.

Augustine held that the sexual consequences of this original transgression still persist in us, and are shown by the inability of the will to govern the genitals, and by the shame generally aroused by coitus—so that the act is always veiled in secrecy,[3] and even parents blush to think of what they have done together.[4] Concupiscence reveals itself continually in the unbidden motions of the organs;[5] at one time tumescence occurs involuntarily, while at another impotence defies the prompting of the mind and "lust has to be awaited".[6] But above all concupiscence is displayed through the sexual impulses themselves, which are stronger than the other passions and less tractable to the sway of the will, and can only be satisfied in an orgasm which engulfs the rational faculties in violent sensual excitement. This led Augustine to a virtual equation of original sin, concupiscence, and venereal emotion,[7] from which he drew the inference that while coitus in theory is good, every concrete act of coitus performed by fallen Man is intrinsically evil—so that every child can be said literally to have been conceived in the 'sin' of its parents.[8] Venereal desire as implanted by God for the promotion of the increase of mankind is blameless, but the same desire, corrupted by concupiscence, is shameful and sinful;[9] and since generation cannot occur unless the carnal union of husband and wife is motivated and aided by

---

[1] *De civ. Dei*, xiv. 17.

[2] *De pecc. merit. et remiss.* ii. 36 [22].

[3] Cf. *de civ. Dei*, xiv. 18; *de grat. Chr. et de pecc. orig.* ii. 39 [34]; *de nupt. et concup.* 21, 33.

[4] *De nupt. et concup.* ii. 5.

[5] Cf. *de Trin.* xiii. 23 [18]; *de nupt. et concup.* ii. 30.

[6] *De nupt. et concup.* i. 6; cf. *de civ. Dei*, xiv. 16.

[7] See N. P. Williams, op. cit., pp. 366–367.

[8] *De pecc. merit. et remiss.* i. 29 [57].

[9] Cf. *c. duas epist. Pelag.* i. 31 [15].

the seductive stimulus of fleshly lust, neither can it ever occur without at least material fault.[1]

One question still remained; if the coitus of husband and wife, even when performed for the sake of offspring, is thus tainted with sin, can marriage itself be defended as an honourable estate ordained by, and pleasing to God—or must it be regarded, as by the Manicheans, as something *per se* evil? Augustine's answer is clear: a careful distinction must be drawn between the state of matrimony and the carnal acts to which it lends opportunity and sanction. As concupiscence cannot take away the good of marriage,[2] neither can marriage mitigate the evil of concupiscence[3]—but it can serve to moderate venereal desire, and to divert it harmlessly and usefully to the task of procreation. Wedded chastity, in fact, consists in transforming coitus from a satisfaction of lust to a necessary duty,[4] and when the act is employed for generation it is excused of its inherent sinfulness[5]—though it remains none the less the channel by which concupiscence and the concomitant guilt are transmitted from parents to their children. Hence arises the need for baptismal regeneration, by which the guilt (*reatus*) of lust is washed away—though the impulse (*actus*) of lust remains, and with it the sense of sexual shame.[6]

But what if husband and wife have coitus, not because they desire a child, but merely for the relief of their incontinence, or for the enjoyment of venereal pleasure? Augustine refused to tolerate any blurring of the moral distinction (as he conceived it) between generation, sensual gratification, and the alleviation of a regrettable human infirmity; yet he could not condemn outright

---

[1] *De nupt. et concup.* i. 24.

[2] *De grat. Chr. et de pecc. orig.* ii. 38 [33], 42 [37].

[3] *De nupt. et concup.* i. 8 [7]: "We ought not to condemn wedlock because of the evil of lust, nor must we praise lust because of the good of wedlock". This proposition Augustine illustrates by the example of the lame man limping to do good; the evil of the limp does not affect the good object, nor does the latter alter the evil of the limp.

[4] Ibid, i. 8 [9].

[5] Cf. *de bono conj.* x; *serm.* cccli. 5.

[6] Cf. *c. duas epist. Pelag.* i. 27 [13], 30 [15]; also *de nupt. et concup.* i. 19, 25, 26, and *retract.* I. xv. 2.

what St Paul had plainly allowed.[1] He concluded, therefore, that marriage guards all wanton marital indulgence from the grave sinfulness of fornication or adultery[2] so that, although nuptial embraces which are not expressly procreative in intention inevitably involve the commission of sin,[3] that sin is only 'venial'[4] so long as there is no attempt to frustrate the natural consequences of coitus—a practice which Augustine denounces as "abominable debauchery".[5] In other words, what is intrinsically sinful is nevertheless not imputed as sin, but receives forgiveness, as it were, in the very moment of transgression; indeed, it is one of the excellencies of matrimony that it procures pardon even for those sexual acts which are in themselves culpable, in that they are not aimed deliberately at the fulfilment of its primary end as defined in patristic theory. Needless to say, Augustine condemned all fornication between the unmarried; but it is important to observe that he regarded institutional and legal validity as immaterial to the reality of marriage. Thus he held that if a man and a woman come together in coitus "by reason of their incontinence", but preserve mutual fidelity in a permanent relationship and rear

---

[1] Cf. 1 Cor. vii. 5, 9.

[2] *De nupt. et concup.* i. 16; cf. *de bono conj.* iii, iv.

[3] Cf. *de bono conj.* vi, x, xi; *serm.* li. 22; *enchirid.* lxxviii; *c. duas epist. Pelag.* i. 33 [16].

[4] This notion of such coitus as a 'venial' or pardonable sin seems to have been due to a misunderstanding of the Vulgate text of 1 Cor. vii. 6: *Hoc autem dico sicut veniam* . . ., where *venia* (translating the Greek *suggnōmē* [.. here, 'permission' or 'concession']) was interpreted by Augustine to mean 'pardon'— an alternative connotation which the word (and its Greek equivalent) can have, but not in this passage. He inferred that St Paul taught that coitus for the satisfaction of concupiscence, though sinful, may easily be forgiven to the married— ignoring the obvious antithesis: "This I say by way of concession, not of command", and also the fact that the Apostle's concession was not to resume coitus, but to abstain. See *de fid. spe, et carit.* lxxviii.

[5] See, e.g., *de nupt. et concup.* i. 17. It is important to note that here Augustine has in mind, as he makes clear, those who marry for the purpose of indulging their lascivious appetites, and who resort to "evil appliance" or abortion in order that children may not interfere with their pleasures. He does not (and could not) envisage the possibility of responsible family planning, and his strictures are quite irrelevant to the use of contraceptive methods for that purpose.

virtuously and conscientiously such children as they may have, their union is essentially one of true wedlock.[1]

It is unnecessary to labour the point that Augustine's theological speculation upon sexual questions was profoundly influenced by his personal experience with its psychological conflict growing ever more acute until the final crisis of conversion; comparison between the *Confessions* and the arguments which he developed in his other writings affords its own sufficient proof. It is significant that one in whom the pressure of the venereal impulse was unusually strong and persistent should have given coitus a prominent, if not indeed a central place in his thought upon sin and the Fall—that he should have found in sexual passion and the orgasm, and even in the natural and involuntary movements and tumescence of the genitals, evidence of the concupiscence resulting from Man's first transgression. It was entirely consistent with his failure to find any acceptable place for sexuality in the good life to which he aspired that he should picture an Eden in which coitus had yet to occur, and that he should conceive the eventual intercourse of Adam and Eve (had they remained unfallen) as a calculated transaction which would have been accomplished without emotional disturbance. He conceded that this conception of coitus in the state of innocency was entirely speculative and unprovable, but maintained that it was nevertheless reasonably to be assumed from Scripture[2]—though his language betrays the strength of the underlying psychological motivation: "Far be it from us to think that in the marriages which would have taken place in Paradise, the genitals would have been excited by the ardour of lust and not by the bidding of the will."[3] Augustine's theory of true human sexuality, in other words, is founded on no more substantial a basis than what his own attitude compelled him to deem congruous with a condition of original righteousness. The practical consequence of this

---

[1] See *de bono conj.* v. The description applies not inaptly to Augustine's own relationship with his mistress.

[2] *De grat. Chr. et de pecc. orig.* ii. 41 [36].

[3] Ibid, ii. 40 [35].

teaching could only be to establish the assumption that almost all coitus is in some degree culpable, since the act excused of its intrinsic sin by a premeditated purpose of generation, and undisfigured by sensual feelings, is really a grotesque and somewhat repulsive abstraction—not to say a physiological absurdity. Augustine must bear no small measure of responsibility for the insinuation into our culture of the idea, still widely current, that Christianity regards sexuality as something peculiarly tainted with evil.

Gregory the Great introduced a slight modification into the Augustinian theory.[1] In his view the evil element in coitus is to be found, not in the act itself, nor yet (apparently) in the concupiscence by which men and women are now impelled to mate,[2] but in the peculiar sensual pleasure (*voluptas carnis*) which accompanies their congress. Even the lawful intercourse of husband and wife for the purpose of generation cannot occur without a certain incidental delectation which is always sinful; and when the dominant motive in their coming together is not a desire for offspring, but venereal enjoyment, the married have something to mourn over. It is difficult to determine precisely in what way and to what extent Gregory intended to qualify Augustine's view, but it seems that he sought to locate coital evil, not in the inordinate impulse of *concupiscentia* as such, but in the acquiescence of the will in the concomitant excess of sensual emotion, so as to find pleasure therein. For him, the sinfulness of coitus may be said to lie, not in the compulsion of lust by which men and women are moved to copulate, but in the fact that they derive intense enjoyment from the act to which they have been urged by their venereal appetites.

Those who dissented from the general patristic view of coitus

---

[1] The chief statement of Gregory's views occurs in his letter to Augustine of Canterbury, *epist.* xi. 64, *resp. ad dec. interrog.*

[2] I cannot agree with Dr C. S. Lewis (if I have understood him correctly) when he says that for Gregory "the act is innocent, but the desire is morally evil" (*The Allegory of Love*, Oxford, 1938, p. 14), for Gregory states expressly that the *iniquitas* of coitus belongs to the *voluptas admixtionis conjugum*, and not to the *concupiscentia* or desire, as Augustine asserts.

were not slow to point to the examples of the holy men of the Old Testament, who had not one but several wives or concubines, and assiduously begot sons and daughters. Augustine in particular found it necessary in the course of his controversies to explain and defend the polygyny of the patriarchs, and his arguments in justification or excuse thereof are developed in accordance with the theory already described.[1] He maintains at the outset that polygyny is not in itself contrary to the nature of marriage as an institution ordained primarily for the propagation of the human race, since many women can conceive by one man without any danger of *confusio prolis* or neglect of the maternal duty, whereas polyandry stands condemned on the ground that one woman cannot bear the joint child of several men.[2] Polygyny is only to be condemned when it is forbidden by law or custom;[3] it is now rejected by Christians, not because it is inherently immoral, but because it is inconsistent with the *sacramentum* or symbolism of marriage, since the relationship of Christ with the Church can only be truly reflected in a monogamous union. Indeed, the multiple alliances of the patriarchs had their own proleptic sacramentalism, in that they signified "the multitude that should thereafter be made subject to God in all the nations of the earth".[4],

Such being their marriages, what of the patriarchs themselves? Augustine insists that they used the advantage of a plurality of wives solely for the purpose of procreation,[5] and that for this reason alone the concession of polygyny was made.[6] They would

---

[1] For general references, see Augustine: *de bono conj.* xvii f., xxii f., xxv f; *serm.* li. 23 f.; *c. Faust. Manich.* xxii. 6, 30–64, 83–86; *de doctr. Chr.* xviii [27], xix [28], xxi. [31]; John Chrysostom: *in epist. ad Hebr.* xxiv. 2.

[2] *De bono conj.* xvii [20].

[3] *C. Faust. Manich.* xxii. 47.

[4] *De bono conj.* xviii [21]. See also on the 'mystery' of patriarchal polygyny, Origen, *de princ.* IV. i. 9 and *c. Cels.* IV. iv. 44; in *c. Cels.* IV. iv. 45 he explains the conduct of Lot's daughters, which he says "admits not only of a figurative meaning, but also of being defended on its merits", believing as they did that humanity would otherwise perish.

[5] *De cont.* xii; *de bono conj.* xxvi [34].

[6] *Serm.* li. 25.

greatly have preferred to promote the increase of Israel without the need for resorting to coitus,[1] and a Christian ought never to doubt that when they went into their wives they did so, not lustfully, but in the discharge of a necessary but uncongenial duty.[2] It was not because of his incontinence that Abraham married Keturah after the death of Sarah; Isaac, too, was so temperate that he remained content with the single copulation by which his twin sons were conceived, while as for Jacob—how willingly would he have imitated his father's example, had his wives not urged him on to indulgences which he would rather have forgone![3]

In any culture there is usually a close connexion between the prevailing view of marriage and physical sexuality, and the attitude adopted towards woman; but in this respect it is difficult to make an accurate evaluation of the patristic age, for the evidence is both meagre and to some extent conflicting. It is commonly supposed that Christianity effected an immediate and lasting change in woman's personal, matrimonial, and social status, and that this must rank among its finest and most far-reaching achievements. But such a claim is easier to make than to substantiate; it rests chiefly upon the broad and unfounded assumption that the spiritual equality of the sexes demanded by theological principle inevitably led to a corresponding equality in social life. It is clear from such records as we have of the conditions prevailing in the settled life of the Church in the fourth and following centuries that this idealized conception of early Christian sexual relationships has little basis in fact. The legal and, to a large extent, the social position of woman remained virtually unaffected by the spread of the Christian faith, though there is no doubt that her worst personal disabilities were mitigated by the more considerate and respectful treatment which she generally received[4] as a 'sister' in the Lord, and an heir together with man

---

[1] *Serm.* li. 23.   [2] *De nupt. et concup.* i. 8.

[3] *De civ. Dei*, xiv. 34, 36 38; cf. John Chrysostom, *in epist. ad Hebr.* xxiv. 4.

[4] Occasionally, however, cases of ill-treatment are recorded, such as that of which Cyprian accuses the schismatic Novatus, *epist.* xlviii. 2; cf. Pacian, *epist.* ii. 4; iii. 14.

of the grace of Christ. There is no indication that any extra-ordinary liberties or privileges which she may have acquired during the early days of the Church survived by many decades the passing of the first century, and when patristic literature begins to reflect the social patterns and concepts of the Christian world, there is little to distinguish the situation of the believer from that of her female pagan contemporaries.

The writings of the Fathers reveal the same ambiguity of attitude towards woman as towards marriage, though to some extent the views expressed vary according to the author. Thus Clement of Alexandria declares that she is man's equal in every-thing,[1] endowed with precisely the same human nature, though different in sex and therefore in vocation and function,[2] and capable of attaining the same degree of perfection;[3] nevertheless, if they have not become effeminate, men are always better at everything than women.[4] Even his liberalism halts well short of any rejection or even modification of the ingrained androcen-tricity which dominated ancient culture, and which other writers maintain with unyielding insistence.

In marriage, asserts John Chrysostom, the wife must not be considered an equal partner with her husband, for man was ordained to regulate woman and his duty is to mould her and form her while she is yet young and timid; hers, on the other hand, is to submit and obey.[5] Preaching on Eph. v. 33, he expounds this theme to his Christian audience in language which closely resembles that of Isomachus in the *Œconomicus* of Xenophon, reminding us (as does Ambrose[6]) of the youth and personal immaturity of the average fourth-century bride[7] who,

---

[1] *Pæd* i. 4.

[2] *Strom.* iv. 8.

[3] Ibid, iv. 19.

[4] Ibid, iv. 8.

[5] *In epist. ad Eph.*, hom. xiii on iv. 24; hom. xx on v. 33.

[6] Cf. F. Homes Dudden, *The Life and Times of Saint Ambrose* (Oxford, 1935), i, pp. 34 ff.—a valuable section on the life of woman in the fourth century.

[7] Cf. the postponement (already mentioned) of Augustine's proposed marriage until the girl had reached the requisite age; legally this was 12, but customarily girls did not marry until 14.

if she were the daughter of believing parents, would have been kept in strict seclusion until the time of her marriage.[1] It is hardly surprising that the deficiencies in their education and their exclusion from social life should have earned for women the contemptuous epithets of many of the Fathers—weak and frail,[2] slow of understanding,[3] light and unstable in mind,[4] liable to deception,[5] and unsafe to admit to the deliberation of public affairs.[6]

These failings can all, for the most part, be attributed to the various disabilities suffered by the female sex in ancient times; not so, however, certain alleged moral defects commonly attributed to woman—for apart from her supposed incompetence and childishness of temper, she is to be suspected and avoided as a subtle and dangerous temptress, always inclined to beguile man and to inflame him with evil passions.[7] Hence the injunctions of the Fathers against cosmetics and every kind of adornment and dress, on the ground that they are calculated to excite lust in the beholder;[8] men must be protected against the wiles of the sirens who would ensnare them, and draw them into the ways of immorality. Nor is it enough for woman to eschew· these artificial aids to enticement; "even natural beauty", writes Tertullian, "ought to be obliterated by concealment and neglect, since it is dangerous to those who look upon it".[9] In church she must be veiled, lest by uncovering her face she should invite another to sin,[10] while she should avoid banquets, marriage feasts,

---

[1] Cf. Jerome, *epist.* cvii and cxxviii, both describing in detail the education of a girl.

[2] John Chrysostom, *in epist. ad Hebr.*, hom. xxix. 5 (because of their upbringing and sedentary life); Cyril of Alexandria, *in evang. Joh.* xii on xx. 18; Gregory I, *moral.* XI. xlix [65]; Lactantius, *inst.* i. 16; Jerome, *epist.* liv. 13; lxvi. 13; Ambrose, *de fid.* v. 5 [59].

[3] Cyril of Alexandria, *in evang. Joh.* xii on xx. 13–14; cf. ii. 4 on iv. 16.

[4] Gregory I, *moral.* XXVIII. iii [12].

[5] John Chrysostom, *in epist. II ad Cor.* xxiii. 1.

[6] Athanasius, *c. gent.* x. 2.

[7] Cf. Athanasius, *orat. c. Arian.* ii. 69.

[8] Clement of Alexandria, *pæd.* ii. 11; Commodian, *instr.* ii. 19 [No. 60].

[9] *De cult. fem.* ii. 2.

[10] Clement of Alexandria, *pæd.* iii. 11.

the bath, and all other places where her presence and charms might stimulate the desires of men. Doubtless some of these restrictions were imposed in the best interests of women themselves, but they also reflect the unchanging androcentricity of ancient culture with its double standard of morality, and the Church's embarrassment and fear in the face of physical sexuality.

Woman's crowning offence, however, was that she belonged to a guilty sex upon which the sentence of God still abides. "Do you not know", again inveighs Tertullian, "that each of you is also an Eve? . . . you are the devil's gateway, you are the unsealer of that forbidden tree, you are the first deserter of the divine law, you are the one who persuaded him whom the devil was too weak to attack. How easily you destroyed man, the image of God! Because of the death which you brought upon us, even the Son of God had to die . . ."[1] Such misogynic invective is characteristic of its author, but other writers also express similar sentiments, though in less venomous language—for instance: it was woman who expelled the tiller of Paradise from his heritage;[2] she was the occasion of the second calamity which befell mankind as a result of the irregular unions of the "sons of God" with the daughters of men;[3] it is shameful for her even to reflect of what nature she is.[4] Augustine, it is true, supplied a logical refutation of these caluminies when he observed that if woman is dishonoured in Eve, she is correspondingly honoured in Mary,[5] for the birth of Christ enshrines the great mystery that "since through a female death had occurred to us, through a female also life should be born to us";[6] but even this argument did not mitigate the reproach incurred for her sex by the mother of all living.

On the other hand, the examples of such as Gorgonia,[7]

---

[1] *De cult. fem.* i. 1.
[2] Jerome, *epist.* lii. 5.
[3] Augustine, *de civ. Dei*, xv. 22 on Gen. vi. 1–6.
[4] Thus even the mild Clement of Alexandria, *pæd.* ii. 2.
[5] *De fid. et symb.* iv [9].
[6] *De agone Chr.* xxii [24].
[7] The sister of Gregory of Nazianzus, see his *orat.* viii.

Macrina,[1] and Olympias[2] (to name but three out of many) remind us that whatever strictures were passed upon their sex, individual women were highly esteemed for their personal merits and gifts. Many were commemorated as martyrs, and many more won approval by embracing the life of continence, while as 'widows', 'virgins', and deaconesses they were accorded a recognized but subsidiary place in the polity of the Church.[3] The widows were at first simply an object of ministry,[4] and a charge upon the charity of each local Christian community, but in course of time they came also to exercise a ministry of limited proportions, especially in connexion with baptism, one of their duties being the instruction of female converts in the ceremonies of initiation and in the principles of the Christian life.[5] Although at one time they appear to have been superior to the deaconesses,[6] widows never constituted an order of ministry as such,[7] and under the influence of ascetical ideas many of them tended to take vows of continence, and thus to become assimilated to the virgins.

Originally the vows of celibacy taken by virgins were entirely private and individual, and in very early times often secret too,[8] but by the end of the second century Hippolytus seems to regard such persons as already forming a special, distinct class within the Church—a class, however, constituted by voluntary choice,

---

[1] The sister of Gregory of Nyssa, see his *vita S. Macr.* (transl. W. K. L. Clarke, *The Life of Saint Macrina*, London, 1916).

[2] The counsellor of Nectarius and John Chrysostom, see Palladius, *Hist. Laus.* 56; Sozomen, *Hist. Eccl.* viii. 9, 24.

[3] On the ministry of women in general, see *The Ministry of Women* (London, 1919); also F. Zerbst, transl. A. G. Merkens, *The Office of Woman in the Church* (St Louis, Missouri, 1955).

[4] Hermas, *mand.* viii. 10; *sim.* i. 8; v. 3; Ignatius, *epist. ad Polyc.* iv; Polycarp, *epist. ad Phil.* iv; Justin, *I Apol.* lxvii.

[5] Palladius, *Hist. Laus.* 46, 54; *stat. eccl. antiq.* 12.

[6] See *Test. Dom.* i. 40–43; among other tasks, widows are to "prove the deaconesses".

[7] Cf. *Apost. Trad.* I. xi. 1, 4; cf. *Sahid. Hept.*, Eth. 26; Arab. 25; Sahid. 37.

[8] Cf. Ignatius, *epist. ad Polyc.* v; this practice persisted even down to the time of Tertullian, *de virg. vel.* ii, xvi.

possessing no definite function such as that of the widow, but accorded public recognition.[1] Not even in Cyprian's time are virgins treated as an order; they are not, as such, concerned with specific ministrations or liturgical duties, nor are their vows treated as binding for life, should they find them too exacting.[2] By the fourth century, however, virgins are considered virtually as a separate order,[3] and at the beginning of the sixth it is laid down that they are to be consecrated by the bishop[4]—though here the reference is really to something resembling the profession of a nun.

The New Testament bears witness to the antiquity of the office of deaconess,[5] and Pliny[6] attests its existence in the East from a very early date. There is every reason to believe that it continued without intermission at least from the beginning of the second century until the middle of the third, when the *Didascalia*, in an extraordinary metaphor, refers to the deaconess as a type of the Holy Spirit, and worthy of honour accordingly[7]—as do also the *Apostolic Constitutions*[8] somewhat more than a century later,

---

[1] *Apost. Trad.* I. xiii; cf. *Test. Dom.* i. 46; *Sahid. Hept.*, Eth. 27; Arab. 26; Sahid. 38; *Const. Apost.* viii. 24.

[2] Cf. Cyprian, *epist.* lxi. 2. On virgins generally in Africa at this time, and their conduct, see both the letter cited, and the treatise *de hab. virg.*

[3] Cyril of Jerusalem, *cat.* iv. 24, refers to the order (*tagma*) of virgins; cf. also Basil, *epist.* cxcix. 18.

[4] *Stat. eccl. antiq.* 11.

[5] Cf. the reference to the *diakonos* Phœbe, Rom. xvi. 1; also 1 Tim. iii. 11, if Lightfoot is correct in the view that *gunaikas* is really an allusion to *gunaikas diakonous*, 'women-deacons'—see *On a Fresh Revision of the New Testament* (London, 1891), p. 114. Cf. in this connexion the phrases *gunē diakonissa* (or *diakonos*) in *Const. Apost.* iii. 15.

[6] *Epist.* xcvi.

[7] *Didascalia*, xvii, where the bishop is described as a type of the Father, the deacon of Christ, the presbyters of the apostles, and the orphans and widows of the altar, in a passage which is probably derived from Ignatius, *epist. ad Mag.* vi; *epist. ad Trall.* iii; *epist. ad Smyrn.* viii. The idea may owe its origin to the fact that 'spirit' in Hebrew is feminine; in the apocryphal *Gospel according to the Hebrews* the Spirit is mentioned as the feminine element in the Godhead, see M. R. James, op. cit., pp. 2–3. The notion of subordination appears in the requirement that deaconesses shall obey the deacons in everything, as the Spirit obeys Christ.

[8] *Const. Apost.* ii. 26.

though with significant alterations and additions.[1] Fourth-century sources contain many allusions to deaconesses,[2] while in the sixth there is legislation relating to them in the edicts of Justinian.[3] In Egypt it seems that deaconesses were first introduced in the latter part of the third century, but were not regarded as belonging to the ranks of the higher clerics, and were not ordained.[4] In the West, on the other hand, the office was unknown before the end of the fourth century, when a council at Nîmes rejected the pretensions of women immigrants from the East who claimed to exercise the levitical ministry.[5] Nevertheless, ordinations to the female diaconate began to occur, and several councils enacted against this practice,[6] but a provision of the Arlesian *Statuta Ecclesiæ Antiqua*[7] may indicate a capitulation on the part of the authorities, and from the middle of the sixth century deaconesses are several times mentioned as existing in Gaul, while there is also some trace of them in northern Italy.

Whatever the Western practice, however, there is no doubt that deaconesses were regularly ordained in the Eastern Church, and that the nature of their office was not limited by any acknowledged defect of order, but only by a restriction of function due to sex.[8] Thus their ministry was almost exclusively a ministry to women; they acted as intermediaries between them and the

---

[1] See J. Armitage Robinson, 'Deaconesses in the "Apostolic Constitution"', in *The Ministry of Women*, pp. 66–68.

[2] Cf., for example, *Conc. Nic.* (325), xix; Epiphanius, *hær.* lxxix. 4; *expos. fid.* xxi; *epist. ad Joh. episc. Hierusalem.* in Jerome, *epist.* li. 2; Sozomen, *hist. eccl.* viii. 9; John Chrysostom, *epist.* xliii, xciv, ciii; Basil, *epist.* cv.

[3] Cf. *Nov.* iii. 1.

[4] *Sahid. Hept.*, Sahid. 66, 72, 74.

[5] *Conc. Nemaus.* (394), ii.

[6] *Conc. Araus.* (441), xxvi (deaconesses no longer to be ordained, and those already ordained to receive benediction like the laity); *Conc. Epaun.* (517), xxi; *Conc. II Aurelian.* (533), xviii (because of the weakness of their sex).

[7] *Stat. eccl. antiq.* (c. 525), 11.

[8] Cf., in addition to the references given above to deaconesses in the East: *Const. Apost.* viii. 19–20; *Conc. Calc.* (451), xv—only women over 40 to be ordained, and deaconesses marrying to be anathematized; *Conc. in Trullo* (692), xiv, xlviii.

bishop,[1] they assisted them at baptism,[2] visited them when sick,[3] and taught them,[4] besides serving as doorkeepers at the church entrances reserved for females.[5] But they remained subject none the less to the same ecclesiastical disabilities as the rest of their sex. A woman might not offer the oblations nor perform any duty properly belonging to a male,[6] she might not baptize (even in cases of necessity),[7] she might not teach in church[8] or in assemblies of men, regardless of her learning or holiness,[9] she might not pray aloud in church,[10] approach the altar,[11] or pronounce a blessing.[12] The concession of orders to deaconesses did not introduce any modification of these and similar discriminations against the female sex, nor did it imply any relaxation of the Church's androcentricity. The orthodox attitude in this respect presents a curious contrast to that of certain heretical sects, in the cultus and propagation of which women played an active part,[13] and also to pagan religious usage, according to which women frequently exercised hieratic functions. The prohibitions imposed by the Church were probably designed in part both to minimize the risk of confusion between Christianity and its rivals, and to obviate as far as possible the various abuses which were associated in those days with a female ministry.

It is evident that woman's ecclesiastical service during the patristic age was very restricted in its scope, and was determined principally by expediential considerations. This explains the

---

[1] *Const. Apost.* ii. 26.
[2] *Const. Apost.* iii. 16; viii. 28; *Didascalia*, xvi.
[3] *Const. Apost.* iii. 16; Epiphanius, *hær.* lxxix. 3.
[4] Theodoret, *hist. eccl.* iii. 10.
[5] *Const. Apost.* ii. 57; viii. 28.
[6] Tertullian, *de virg. vel.* ix.
[7] Tertullian, *de bapt.* xvii; *de præscr. hær.* xli; *Const. Apost.* iii. 9; *stat. eccl. antiq.* 100; Epiphanius, *hær.* lxx. The question was still debated in the 12th century.
[8] *Const. Apost.* iii. 6; *Test. Dom.* i. 40.
[9] *Stat. eccl. antiq.* 99.
[10] Cyril of Jerusalem, *procat.* 14.
[11] *Conc. Laodic.* (mid 4th cent.), xliv, repeated by *Capit. Theod. episc. Aurelian.* (797), vi, and *Conc. I Aquisgran.* (816), i. 82.
[12] *Const. Apost.* viii. 28.
[13] See the catalogue in Jerome, *epist.* cxxxiii. 4; also F. Zerbst, op. cit., pp. 84 ff.

development of the female diaconate in the East, and its absence in the West. Where women were by custom segregated and confined in their own quarters it was necessary to have ministers such as widows and deaconesses in order to avoid the inconvenience or scandal which might attend the intrusion of clergymen into the˙gynæceum—a need which is frankly admitted in the Church Orders and other sources. In the West, with its greater conventional freedom, this need never arose; and throughout the Church, due to the supersession of adult by infant baptism and to changing ecclesiastical and social patterns, the office of deaconess gradually fell into desuetude. At the same time the sharp distinction made in the ante-Nicene period between the widow, the virgin, and the deaconess became progressively less clearly defined until, in the end, all three were merged in the monastic woman of the Middle Ages.

Like every other society, the Christian Church found it necessary in the common interest to regulate the sexual relationships and behaviour of its members. During the first three centuries, however, there was little positive legislation to this end, although from the earliest times we find precepts inculcating a high standard of moral conduct and threatening the delinquent with ecclesiastical sanctions or divine retribution. Thus the *Didache*, which perhaps reflects opinion and practice in certain parts of the Church towards the close of the second century, enumerates among the commandments pertaining to the 'way of life' the prohibition of adultery, of corruption of boys, of fornication, and of abortion and infanticide.[1] The *Apostolic Tradition* of Hippolytus, a document relating roughly to the same period, lays down rules excluding certain classes of sexual offender from initiation,[2] and these inhibitions are repeated in subsequent

---

[1] *Didache*, ii. 2; cf. the derived *Const. Apost.* vii. 2, 3.

[2] See II. xvi. 10 (procurers); 20 (prostitutes and those who indulge in homosexual practices). Cf. also the rules that a man's concubine is to be accepted for baptism if she has reared her children and has remained faithful to him (23); that a man having a concubine must either marry her legally or be rejected (24a); and that a woman consorting with a slave must either desist or be refused (24b).

Church Orders derived from this source;[1] it also orders the segregation of the sexes during catechetical instruction,[2] and requires the women to wear a scarf over the head as a veil.[3]

A second form of legislation is represented in the 'canonical letters' addressed by Basil of Cæsarea to Amphilochius, bishop of Iconium. These letters set down, among other things, the traditional disciplinary rulings of the Eastern Church upon various kinds of sexual offence, and probably incorporate also several of the author's own decisions. Guidance is supplied upon the appropriate action to be taken in a wide variety of cases, including abortion and fœticide;[4] fornication and adultery;[5] digamy, trigamy, and polygamy;[6] homosexual practices and bestiality;[7] the separation of the married;[8] the fall or marriage of virgins;[9] abduction and rape;[10] bigamy;[11] desertion;[12] and incestuous and other consanguineous unions.[13] It is interesting to observe that in dealing with the fornication of a married man, Basil expresses uneasiness at the double moral standard implied in the legalistic idea that this offence is not technically adultery; yet he acquiesces in the current view that while the wronged wife ought to take back her husband, no such obligation exists in cases where the woman is the sinner, and she may be expelled as 'polluted': "The requirement is not easy", he comments, "but custom has so obtained."[14] Similar instructions are to be found in the early

---

[1] Cf. *Sahid. Hept.*, Eth. 63, 64; Arab. 62, 63; Sahid. 75; *Test. Dom.* ii. 2; *Const. Apost.* viii. 32.

[2] II. xviii. 2.   [3] II. xviii. 5.

[4] Basil of Cæsarea, *epist.* clxxxviii. 2, 8.

[5] *Epist.* clxxxviii, 3, 6; cxcix. 21, 34; ccxvii. 58, 59.

[6] *Epist.* clxxxviii. 4; cxcix. 50; ccxvii. 80.

[7] *Epist.* clxxxviii. 7; ccxvii. 62.

[8] *Epist.* clxxxviii. 9.   [9] *Epist.* cxcix. 18, 20; ccxvii. 60.

[10] *Epist.* cxcix. 21, 25, 27.   [11] *Epist.* cxcix. 31, 36, 46.

[12] *Epist.* cxcix. 35; ccxvii. 78.

[13] *Epist.* clx; ccxvii. 67, 68, 75, 76, 79.

[14] *Epist.* cxcix. 21; cf. clxxxviii. 9 for another reflection of the continuance of this double standard: Jesus' teaching concerning separation (Matt. v. 32) applies equally to men and women, says Basil, but custom ordains that when men fornicate their wives do not reject them—whereas a husband may put away a fornicating wife.

decretals and letters of counsel and direction written by the popes of the fourth and fifth centuries, one of the most notable being that in which Siricius established the rule of clerical celibacy for the West.[1]

The largest volume of material, however, consists of legislation in the narrower sense—that is, of canons and decrees made by the ecumenical, and more particularly the local councils and synods which met with increasing frequency from the beginning of the fourth century; and, to a lesser extent, of imperial laws and edicts. Few of the conciliar assemblies were convened expressly for the reformation of morals or the discipline of the clergy and laity, and many were concerned principally with the suppression of heresy and the regulation of ecclesiastical affairs; but most of them gave at least some incidental attention to sexual topics, and one, the Council of Elvira in 305 or 306, occupied itself extensively with them, to judge by the numerous canons which it promulgated dealing with the relationships between men and women. It would be tedious to set out in full detail the enactments of this and succeeding conclaves, but a general indication can be given of the specifically sexual questions which engaged their attention.

Chief among these matters were the enforcement of clerical continence or celibacy,[2] and the condemnation and punishment of various breaches of the rule of chastity, either by dedicated

---

[1] *Epist.* i *ad Himerium*, 5; cf. ibid, 4 and 8 for other regulations of a sexual interest. See also Innocent I, *epist.* ii *ad Victric.* regarding the marriage of a consecrated virgin; Leo I, *epist.* clix *ad Nicet.*, and clxvii *ad Rustic.* dealing with the permanence of marriage, the celibacy of the clergy, concubinage, and marriage after taking vows of continence; Gregory I, *epist.* xi. 45 *ad Theoct.*, and xi. 50, on the permanence of marriage.

[2] See *Conc. Illib.* (305–306), xviii, xxxiii; *C. Ancyr.* (314), xix; *C. Neocæsar.* (ante 325), i, ix, x; *C. Rom.* (386), iv, v, ix; *C. Hippon.* (393), xviii; *C. Toletan.* (400), i, ii, iii, iv; *C. Rom.* (402), iii; *C. Araus.* (441), xxii, xxiii, xxiv, xxv; *C. Arelat.* (443–452), ii, iii, iv; *C. Andegav.* (453), xi; *C. Turon.* (461), i, ii, iv; *C. Rom.* (465), ii; *C. Agathen.* (506), xvi; *C. II Toletan.* (527–531), i; *C. Arvern.* (535), xii; *C. III Aurelian.* (538), ii; *C. IV Aurelian.* (541), xxix; *C. V Aurelian.* (549) iv; *C. Turon.* (567), xii, xiii; *C. Bracar.* (572), viii; *C. I Matiscon.* (581), xi; *C. III Lugdunen.* (583), i; *C. Autiss.* (578), xx, xxi; *C. III Toletan.* (589), *capit.* v; *C. Oscen.* (598), ii.

virgins[1] and widows,[2] or by Christians at large.[3] Marriages within the forbidden degrees of relationship were frequently prohibited,[4] as were mixed unions of Christians with pagans or Jews,[5] while another recurrent interdiction related to the practice of syneisaktism and the introduction of 'strange women' into clerical establishments as housekeepers or companions.[6] Canons were passed against abortion and infanticide,[7] digamy and trigamy,[8] prostitution,[9] sodomy and bestiality,[10] and self-mutilation,[11] and other measures deal with desertion,[12] the

---

[1] See *C. Illib.* (305–306), xiii; *C. Toletan.* (400), xvi. xix; *C. Rom.* (402), i, ii; *C. Arelat.* (443–452), lii (cf. xxi and xxii); *C. Chalc.* (451), xvi; *C. Andegav.* (453), v; *C. Hibern.* (c. 456), xvii; *C. Turon.* (461), vi; *C. Venet.* (465), iv; *C. Aurelian.* (511), xi; *C. III Paris.* (557), v; *C. Turon.* (567), xx; *C. Barcin.* (599), iv.

[2] See *C. Illib.* (305–306), lxxii; *C. Turon.* (567), xx. Other canons forbid the marriage of widows of the clergy: *C. Aurelian.* (511), xiii; *C. Epaun.* (517), xxxii; *C. II Matiscon.* (585), xvi; *C. Autiss.* (578), xxii.

[3] Against fornication: *C. Illib.* (305–306), vii, xiv, xxxi; against adultery: *C. Illib.* (305–306), xlvii, lxiv, lxv, lxix, lxx, lxxviii; *C. Ancyr.* (314), xx; *C. Neocæsar.* (ante 325), viii; *C. Toletan.* (400), vii; *C. III Aurelian.* (538), ix.

[4] See *C. Illib.* (305–306), lxvi; *C. Arelat.* (314), xi; *C. Neocæsar.* (ante 325), ii; *C. Rom.* (402), ix, xi; *C. Agathen.* (506), lxi; *C. Aurelian.* (511), xviii; *C. Epaun.* (517), xxx; *C. Ilerden.* (524), iv; *C. II Toletan.* (527–531), xi; *C. III Aurelian.* (538), x; *C. Arvern.* (535), xi; *C. IV Aurelian.* (541), xxvii; *C. III Paris.* (557), iv; *C. Turon.* (567), xxi; *C. III Lugdunen.* (583), i; *C. II Matiscon.* (585), xviii; *C. Autiss.* (578), xxvii, xxxii.

[5] See *C. Illib.* (305–306), xvi; *C. Laodic.* (mid-4th cent.), x, xxxi; *C. Hippon.* 393), II. xii; *C. III Toletan.* (589), *capit.* xiv.

[6] See *C. Illib.* (305–306), xxvii; *C. Nic.* (325), iii; *C. Hippon.* (393), II. xvi; *stat. eccl. antiq.* (c. 525), xlvi; *C. Andegav.* (453), iv; *C. Turon.* (461), iii; *C. Agathen.* (506), x, xi; *C. Gerund.* (517), vii; *C. Ilerden.* (524), xv; *C. Arvern.* (535), xv; *C. V. Aurelian.* (549), iii; *C. Bracar.* (563), xv; *C. Turon.* (567), x; *C. I Matiscon.* (581), i; *C. III Lugdunen.* (583), i; *C. III Toletan.* (589), *capit.* v; *C. I Hispalen.* (590), iii.

[7] See *C. Illib.* (305–306), lxiii, lxviii; *C. Ilerden.* (524), ii; *C. III Toletan.* (589), xvii.

[8] See *C. Neocæsar.* (ante 325), iii; *C. Laodic.* (mid-4th cent.), i.

[9] *C. Illib.* (305–306), xii.

[10] *C. Illib.* (305–306), lxxi; *C. Ancyr.* (314), xvi, xvii; cf. *C. Turon.* (567), xiv.

[11] *C. Nic.* (325), i; *C. Arelat.* (443–452), vii. Despite the allegation sometimes made by critics of the Church, such cases were rare, and relatively unimportant. See Justin, *I Apol.* xxix for a proposed self-castration; also the case of Leontius of Antioch (Theodoret, *hist. eccl.* ii. 24; Socrates, *hist. eccl.* ii. 26; Athanasius, *apol. de fuga sua*, xxvi, and *hist. Arian. ad monach.* xxviii). The best-known instance, of course, is that of Origen (Eusebius, *hist. eccl.* vi, 23).

[12] *C. Illib.* (305-306), viii, ix; *C. Hibern.* (c. 456), xix.

abduction[1] or violation[2] of women, and the separation of husband
and wife.[3] There are also a few references to divorce and remarriage,[4] but this particular question appears to have given but
little concern to most councils held at this time. Certain statutes
reflect the sexual attitudes of the age; thus one requires the newly-
married to observe continence on the wedding night out of
respect for the nuptial blessing,[5] and others order women not to
approach the altar,[6] not to receive the Holy Communion with
uncovered hands,[7] not to touch the pall (*palla*),[8] and to wear at
the Eucharist a scarf (*dominicale*) covering the head.[9] Most curious
of all is a macabre direction, due apparently to a mistaken sense
of propriety, that a male corpse is not to be buried beside a
female corpse until the latter has decomposed.[10]

It is evident that from a very early date the Church assumed
and exercised the right to legislate for its members, and
believed that its power to frame regulations appropriate to the
changing needs of the Christian community was inherent, and
was not derived from any external or secular source, such as an
imperial concession. By virtue of this right it not only maintained
the law of Christ appertaining to sexual matters, but extended
and amplified that law as circumstances required. A mere catalogue of conciliar and synodal enactments such as that just given
above reveals at once the range and the limitation of the Church's
concern with the behaviour of men and women. The purpose of
its law-making in this connexion was chiefly to inculcate and
preserve among Christian people a standard of public morality
consistent with the teaching of Jesus and the ethical demands of

---

[1] *C. Ancyr.* (314), xi; *C. Chalc.* (451), xxvii; *C. Aurelian.* (511), ii; *C. III Aurelian.*
(538), xvi.
[2] *C. Ilerden.* (524), vi.
[3] *C. Gangren.* (4th cent.), xiv; *C. Arelat.* (443–452), xxii; *C. Agathen.* (506), xxv.
[4] *C. Illib.* (305–306), ix; cf. x and xi; *C. Arelat.* (314), x; *C. Andegav.* (453), vi;
C. Venet. (465), ii.
[5] *Stat. eccl. antiq.* (c. 525), xiii.   [6] *C. Laodic.* (mid-4th cent.), xliv.
[7] *C. Autiss.* (578), xxxvi.
[8] *C. Autiss.* (578), xxxvii; the *palla* was presumably the altar cloth (*palla
altaris*).
[9] *C. Autiss.* (578), xlii.   [10] *C. II Matiscon.* (585), xvii.

the Gospel, and to impose upon the clergy and the laity the respective personal disciplines which were considered appropriate to each order. Beyond this the canons and epistolary directions rarely go; it was not their object to regulate in any minute detail the private intimacies of married life,[1] nor were they generally framed with any ulterior didactic or hortatory aim. On the other hand, they display no concern with the forensic niceties which were later to complicate the ecclesiastical law; they make no reference to distinctions such as those between nullity and divorce, between prohibitive and diriment impediments to marriage, and between void, voidable, illicit and invalid unions—all of which relate primarily to the institutional aspect of matrimony which was still the concern of the civil law.

One of the earliest regulations pertaining to marriage is that laid down by Ignatius, who says: "It is fitting that when men and women marry they should unite with the consent of the bishop, that the marriage may be according to the Lord, and not for the sake of lust."[2] Neither episcopal approval, however, nor any ecclesiastical rite or blessing was necessary in order to confer validity upon the unions of Christians in the early Church, and it is significant for an understanding of the patristic view of matrimony that the nuptials of the faithful continued to take place with the formalities customary at the time. The traditional ceremonies were not modified, save for the omission of non-essentials which were either unedifying in themselves or redolent

---

[1] Contrast the rabbinical endeavour to ensure that the mutual duty of coitus was not neglected: *Keth.* v. 6: "If a man vowed to have no intercourse with his wife, the school of Shammai say: [She may consent] for two weeks. And the school of Hillel say: For one week [only]. Disciples [of the Sages] may continue absent for thirty days against the will [of their wives] while they occupy themselves in the study of the Law; and labourers for one week. The duty of marriage enjoined in the law (cf. Ex. xxi. 10) is: every day for them that are unoccupied; twice a week for labourers; once a week for ass-drivers; once every thirty days for camel-drivers; and once every six months for sailors. So R. Eliezer"; see H. Danby, *The Mishnah* (Oxford, 1933), p. 252; cf. *Keth.* v. 7 (ibid, p. 252) and *Eduy.* iv. 10 (ibid, p. 430).

[2] *Epist. ad Polyc.* v. 2; the object here is probably to prevent mixed marriages as far as possible.

of pagan superstition, and the substitution of the Eucharist and the benediction for the sacrifice and the other accompanying religious observances. Hence the Church Orders contain no Christian marriage rite, nor is there any reference to one in the literature of the period, while the ancient sacramentaries merely give the prayers of the nuptial Mass and the blessing.[1] Not until the ninth century do we find any detailed account of the rite of Christian matrimony in the West, and even at this late date it proves to be identical with the old nuptial ceremony of pagan Rome in all respects save that already noted—namely, the replacement of the sacrifice and the divinations by the Eucharist; and this is the wedlock which Tertullian, some six hundred years earlier, had extolled as arranged by the Church, confirmed by the oblation, sealed by the blessing, witnessed by the angels, and approved by God the Father.[2]

There is no doubt that the marriage rite which Pope Nicholas I described to the Bulgarians in 866[3] was substantially that used in the Church from the earliest days. It follows closely the pattern of the Roman ceremonies, being divided into two distinct parts. The first, or betrothal (*sponsalia*), consisted of an exchange of consent before witnesses in words constituting *futurarum . . . nuptiarum promissa fœdera*, followed by the gift of a ring from the man to the woman (the *subarrhatio*), and the drawing of a matrimonial contract, accompanied by the delivery of the specified dowry. The second, or marriage proper (*nuptiæ*), comprised a celebration of the Eucharist (in place of the pagan auspication and sacrifice), the benediction of the couple while the veil was held over their heads, and their coronation on leaving the church. The latter part of the nuptials varied somewhat from the pagan rite, in which the woman alone was veiled with the *flammeum* and

---

[1] See C. L. Feltoe, *Sacramentarium Leonianum* (Cambridge, 1896), pp. 140–142; H. A. Wilson, *Liber Sacramentorum Romanæ Ecclesiæ* (*The Gelasian Sacramentary*) (Oxford, 1894), pp. 265 ff; *The Gregorian Sacramentary* (Henry Bradshaw Society, xlix, London, 1915), pp. 120 ff.

[2] *Ad ux.* ii. 8.

[3] *Resp. ad consult. Bulgar.* iii; see L. Duchesne [transl. M. L. McClure], *Christian Worship* (London, 1904), p. 429.

crowned before the ceremony, and in which also the pair exchanged consent in words of present import, and joined their right hands; but the last two items may simply have been omitted by the Pope from his account, since the *consensus per verba de præsenti* would seem to be essential.

Earlier sources confirm, and sometimes supplement, this description given by Nicholas. In regard to the betrothal they specify the free exchange of future consent between the parties,[1] the *subarrhatio* or bestowal of presents,[2] the giving of a ring,[3] the exchange of a kiss[4] and the joining of right hands,[5] the transmission of a dowry,[6] and a ministerial benediction upon the espousals thus concluded.[7] All these formalities were transacted in public before witnesses, who were customarily ten in number;[8] but prior to the time of Justinian, who issued an edict declaring them to be obligatory in the case of men of high rank,[9] the law treated them merely as optional preliminaries to the marriage proper, neither the performance nor the omission of which affected the validity of the subsequent union.[10] In connexion with the nuptial

---

[1] *Lex Julia et Papia Poppæa*, confirmed by Diocletian and adopted by Justinian, *Cod*. V. iv. 12; cf. *Cod. Theod*. III. v. 6.

[2] See the various enactments of Constantine (*Cod. Theod*. III. v. 1, 2, 3, 5), Theodosius II (*Cod. Theod*. III. v. 8), and Justinian (*Cod*. VIII. liv. 34, 36); also Ambrose, *expos. ev. Luc*. vii. 231. Nicholas uses the term *subarrhatio* of the donation of the ring, but it properly applies to the giving of the *arrhæ*, originally the earnest money paid over at betrothal, which the ring may have come to represent.

[3] Tertullian, *apol*. vi and *de idol*. xvi, does not specify the giving of a ring as a Christian ceremony, but regards it as innocent enough. Cf. also Clement of Alexandria, *pæd*. iii. 11.

[4] See enactments by Constantine (*Cod. Theod*. III. v. 5) and Justinian (*Cod*. V. iii. 16); also Ambrose, *epist*. xli. 19.

[5] Tertullian, *de virg. vel*. xi, mentions this, together with the kiss, as a laudable pagan ceremony, and it was doubtless continued by Christians; see also Ambrose, *expos. Ps. cxviii*, i. 16.

[6] See *Cod. Theod*. II. xxi and III. xiii, and *Cod. Justin* V. xi–xv, for the legal regulations concerning dowries.

[7] Siricius, *epist*. i *ad Himer*., iv.

[8] See Niceta of Remesiana [?], *de lapsu virg*. xx.

[9] *Nov*. lxxiv.

[10] Cf. a law of Theodosius II (*Cod. Theod*. III. vii. 3).

ceremony itself, the sources mention the declaration of consent,[1] the benediction,[2] the joining of right hands,[3] the veiling[4] and crowning,[5] and also the loosing or unbinding of the bride's hair.[6] Finally, while sober and decorous celebrations are not disallowed, wanton and riotous behaviour, obscene performances, and lascivious songs (*fescennina*) are denounced as unbecoming at the weddings of Christians.[7]

It is not easy to reduce to a simple and coherent ritual pattern these miscellaneous items of nuptial ceremony, many of which are mentioned only incidentally in passages otherwise quite unrelated to matrimony, but one interesting feature at least stands out. This is the apparent duplication of the bestowal of the ring and the blessing, which are specified in connexion with both the *desponsatio* or betrothal, and the *nuptiæ* or marriage—for although a benediction may often have been pronounced at the espousals as well as at the wedding, it is most unlikely that there was any repetition of the gift of the ring, which at that time took place during the first of the two rites. It is possible, however, that in this instance confusion is due to a loose use of the terminology of the formation of marriage, since in patristic literature *desponsatio* is occasionally employed to denote the wedding (and not the betrothal), and husband and wife are sometimes called *sponsus* and *sponsa*.[8]

---

[1] Ambrose, *de instit. virg.* xli; *expos. ev. Luc.* ii. 5.

[2] Ambrose, *epist.* xix. 7; Siricius, *epist.* i *ad Himer.* iv; *stat. eccl. antiq.* xiii.

[3] Gregory Nazianzen, *epist.* lvii.

[4] Ambrose, *epist.* xix. 7. The pagan nuptial veil was yellow or flame-coloured (hence *flammeum*), and that used by Christians purple or white. While the pagan bride was veiled before the ceremony, the Christian bride was veiled by the priest during the rite (Ambrose, *epist.* xix. 7, cf. *exhort. virg.* xxxiv, and Siricius, *epist.* vii. 3), and afterwards wore her veil when appearing in public (cf. Ambrose, *de pœnit.* i. 69.

[5] John Chrysostom, *in epist. I ad Tim., hom.* ix.

[6] Optatus, *epist. ad Parmen. c. Donat.* vi. 97.

[7] Cf. *Conc. Laodic.* (mid-4th cent.), liii; John Chrysostom, *in Gen., hom.* xlviii, lvi; *in epist. I ad Cor.* xii. 11; etc.

[8] See the supporting citations in G. H. Joyce, *Christian Marriage* (London, 1948), p. 610, from Cyprian, *epist.* lxi; Ambrose, *expos. ev. Luc.* ii. 2; Augustine, *de nupt. et concup.* i. 12 [11]; Jerome, *adv. Helvid.* iv; etc. Reference is also made to Tertullian, *de virg. vel.* vi, but the argument is obscure and the relevance of the passage doubtful.

On the other hand, this usage has prompted the suggestion that the Christians introduced an important change into the traditional marriage rites, by combining the betrothal and the wedding in such a way that the former actually became the ceremony at which the couple were united as husband and wife, the *nuptiæ* being simply the celebrations with which the bride was afterwards conducted to her new home. Hence, it is supposed, there arose a transference of terms, *desponsatio* and *desponsare* being applied to the nuptial rite itself (originally the betrothal), *sponsa* to the bride before the consummation of the union, and *nuptiæ* and *nubere* to the commencement of cohabitation.[1] But this theory, though attractive, is not without its difficulties, and appears to be insufficiently founded. There is nothing to confirm the conjecture that the Christians modified their matrimonial practice to correspond to that of the Jews, among whom the betrothal (*kiddushim*) had the legal effect of marriage; there are many passages in which *desponsatio* clearly retains its original meaning of espousal, and many others in which the sense is indefinite; and there is no evidence that at an early date the placing of a ring on the bride's finger had become the sign that the marriage (as distinct from the betrothal) had been concluded.[2] Furthermore, it is by no means clear that in Nicholas's *Responsa ad Bulgaros* the *sponsalia* have become (as Fr Joyce claims) the actual marriage; the pope makes a plain distinction between the betrothal and the wedding, and assigns the gift of the ring to the former rite, as Duchesne shows in his analysis of this section of the *Responsa*.[3] Whatever deviations in practice may be suggested

---

[1] For a discussion of this theory, see G. H. Joyce, op. cit., pp. 46–47 and 610.

[2] Fr Joyce, op. cit., p. 47 and n. 2, cites Tertullian, *de orat.* xxii, and *de virg. vel.* xi, as indicating that this was the case at the beginning of the third century, but the passages in question do not mention the ring, and clearly relate to the normal ceremony of betrothal.

[3] L. Duchesne, op. cit., p. 429. The relevant passage runs: ". . . we will try to show you the usage which the Holy Roman Church received in ancient time, and still maintains . . . After the espousals (*sponsalia*) are celebrated, which are the promised covenants of future marriage (*futurarum . . . nuptiarum promissa fœdera*) effected by the mutual consent of the couple, and of those under whose authority they are; and when the espouser (*sponsus*) has betrothed (*desponderit*)

by an occasional indeterminate use of the technical terms relating
to the formation of marriage, there can be no doubt that the
Church as a whole adopted and maintained (with suitable
modifications) the normal Roman pattern of two distinct but
closely linked ceremonies—betrothal and the wedding proper.[1]

From at least the beginning of the fourth century, however,
the relative importance of these two rites underwent a gradual
change until eventually the betrothal came to occupy a place of
prominence quite unlike the status accorded to it in the earlier
Roman law. This change was due chiefly to the influence of the
barbarian races which, even before the invasions from the north,
had begun to permeate the Empire, bringing with them laws and
cultural traditions which had a profound effect upon the customs
and the judicial system of the West. The Visigothic and Lombardic codes testify to the significance of the betrothal among the
peoples for whom they were framed;[2] and it is not impossible
that the loose use of *sponsalia* and *desponsatio* already noted, and
the apparent reference of these terms to marriage in certain
sources, may reflect the enhanced consequence of the espousal rite
due to barbarian influence.

This influence may also account for the growing importance
of the ring. One particularly interesting feature of the barbarian
ceremony of betrothal is the emphasis laid upon the *arrhæ* or
earnest-money, symbolizing the primitive practice of wife-
purchase. The Roman law knew nothing of this (though it was
implied in the matrimonial theory and practice of the Jews);

---

himself to his espoused (*sponsa*) by pledges (*arrhis*), [and] by adorning her finger
with a ring of fidelity, and . . . has handed over the agreed dowry, with a
document containing this pledge, in the presence of witnesses for both parties;
then either shortly afterwards (*mox*, which Joyce translates 'immediately', thus
implying a reference to the nuptial Mass) or at some convenient time . . . both
are led to perform the marriage covenant (*nuptialia fœdera*). And first they are set
in the church of the Lord, with offerings which they are due to offer to God by
the hand of the priest; and then they receive the blessing and the heavenly veil
. . . After these ceremonies, as they leave the church, they wear crowns on their
heads . . ."

[1] It is worth observing that Ulpian (3rd cent.) plainly defines *sponsalia* at law
as a transaction preparatory to a future marriage, *Dig.* XXIII. i. 2.

[2] Cf. *Dictionary of Christian Antiquities*, i, pp. 143 and 203.

indeed, the third-century jurist Ulpian expressly states that "bare consent (*nudus consensus*) suffices to constitute betrothal (*sponsalia*)"[1] —a legal principle to which the stage espousals in Plautus add their own confirmation.[2] But it is not difficult to appreciate how this simple procedure gathered accretions with the passage of time and the influence of alien ideas. In the Roman betrothal ceremony the exchange of consent was commonly accompanied by the gift of a ring—at first of iron, and later of gold; and the use of a ring in commercial transactions as an earnest of the purchase money in a contract of sale[3] would naturally suggest its employment for an analogous purpose in the espousal rite when the latter underwent modification in conformity with barbarian practice and the notion of wife-purchase. Hence the close association between the *arrhæ* and the bestowal of the ring in the ninth-century ceremonies described by Pope Nicholas in the *Responsa*. For him, however, the ring is also *annulus fidei*—a "ring of fidelity"; and nearly two centuries earlier it is already evident that the betrothal ring had acquired a sentimental and spiritual significance, for Isidore of Seville writes: "The ring is given by *sponsus* to *sponsa* either for a sign of mutual fidelity, or still more, to join their hearts by this pledge; and therefore the ring is placed on the fourth finger because a certain vein (it is said[4]) flows thence to the heart."[5]

Marriage, then, among Christians and pagans alike, was effected by the successive ceremonies of *sponsalia* or *desponsatio* (the betrothal) and *nuptiæ* (the wedding), both of which the Church adapted to the use of the faithful by the introduction of certain modifications which did not, however, change the basic structure or purpose of these rites. What was the character of the resultant union—especially as regards its permanence or indissolubility? According to Roman law, marriage was simply a contractual relationship established by consent[6] and voidable like any other contract—in this instance, by a mere revocation of the

---

[1] *Dig.* XXIII. i. 4.
[2] Cf. *Aulul.* II. ii. 77–79; *Pœnul.* V. iii. 37–38; *Trinumn.* II. iv. 98–103.
[3] *Dig.* XIX. i. 11, § 6.   [4] See Aulus Gellius, *Noct. Attic.* x. 10.
[5] *De eccl. offic.* ii. 20.
[6] Ulpian, in *Dig.* L. xvii. 30: *nuptias non concubitus sed consensus facit.*

consent,[1] either by mutual agreement (*divortium ex consensu*) or by unilateral action (*repudium*). The latter mode of divorce could be quite arbitrary; but it could also be either *bona gratia* for some reason such as sterility, illness, or insanity which conferred no moral stigma upon the partner repudiated;[2] or for serious misconduct or crime—for example, adultery or attempted murder. In one case, however, no discretion was allowed; the *Lex Julia de adulteriis cœrcendis* (*c.* 17 B.C.) declared a husband to be guilty of the offence of *lenocinium* who knowingly retained an adulterous wife and neglected to prosecute her paramour— though it is doubtful whether this section of the statute was very rigorously enforced. This wide allowance of divorce absolute was restricted by enactments of Constantine,[3] Honorius and Theodosius II,[4] and Theodosius II and Valentinian III,[5] and Justinian also made certain changes in the law,[6] but even so a considerable liberty of repudiation remained to both husband and wife.

In thus introducing legislation to curtail the practice of divorce the Christian emperors were acting in the capacity of secular magistrates. Wisely, they did not attempt to impose a Christian rule of marriage upon the multitudes of their subjects who still adhered to the old religions, but sought to mitigate the worst evils of a system which was nevertheless so much a part of the very fabric of society that it could not be abolished in an instant by a mere imperial fiat. For the Church, however, there was another law than that of the State—a law for whose authority the Fathers pointed to Scripture and to the teaching of Christ, giving to the

---

[1] The act of divorce was entirely private and not juridical, though Augustus stipulated that it should take place in the presence of seven adult Roman citizens, *Dig.* XXIV. ii. 9; court proceedings were only taken if there was need to establish the grounds of divorce by legal process.

[2] *Dig.* XXIV. i. 60, 61, 62; ii. 4; iii. 22 § 7.

[3] *Cod. Just.* V. xvii. 7 (331); for details, see O. D. Watkins, *Holy Matrimony* (London, 1895), p. 291.

[4] *Cod. Theod.* III, xvi. 2 (421); see Watkins, op. cit., p. 292.

[5] *Cod. Just.* V. xvii. 8 (449); see Watkins, op. cit., pp. 292–293.

[6] *Nov.* xxii (536): mutual consent suffices to effect divorce; *nov.* cxvii (542): divorce only allowed on specified grounds; *nov.* cxxxiv (556): *nov.* cxvii confirmed and divorce by consent prohibited.

record of St Matthew no less weight than to those of St Mark, St Luke, and St Paul, and interpreting the first evangelist's qualification: "except for the cause of fornication (*porneia*)", as a reference to adultery.

During the ante-Nicene period there was general agreement that a husband was free to put away an adulterous wife,[1] and some followed the stricter Roman law and Jewish opinion in holding that he ought to dismiss her, particularly if the offence persisted;[2] it was also allowed that a wife might reject an adulterous husband —though she was not compelled to do so.[3] Origen considered it "a matter for enquiry", whether Jesus hinders the putting away of a wife for crimes such as witchcraft, infanticide, and murder,[4] and Hermas appears to argue for separation from an idolatrous wife,[5] but the early Church was not on the whole disposed to extend the meaning of *porneia* beyond its accepted connotation of adultery. The act of putting away thus sanctioned was, in effect, *divortium a mensa et thoro*, or 'separation' as it is now called; it conferred no liberty to enter into a second union such as the law allowed, and remarriage after divorce is frequently and unconditionally forbidden[6]—one of the reasons being that if the

---

[1] Origen, *comm. in Matt.* xiv. 23; Clement of Alexandria, *strom.* ii. 23; Tertullian, *adv. Marc.* v. 7.

[2] Hermas, *mand.* IV. i. 6; Tertullian, *adv. Marc.* iv. 34; *Conc. Illib.* (305–306), lxv, lxx.

[3] Justin, *II apol.* ii; Tertullian, *de monog.* x; *de patient.* xii (though it is possible that these passages merely state the position under Roman law); *Conc. Illib.* (305–306)—probably implied in canon ix.

[4] See *comm. in Matt.* xiv. 23. Origen also observes, when commenting on the clause, "maketh her an adulteress", that a husband can place temptation in his wife's way by allowing her such liberty that she goes beyond what is fitting in her associations with other men; and also by omitting to satisfy her physical desires "under the appearance of greater gravity and self-control"—a neglect which he regards as particularly culpable; ibid, xiv. 24.   [5] *Mand.* IV. i. 6.

[6] Cf. Hermas, *mand.* IV. i. 6; Justin, *I apol.* xv; Athenagoras, *legat.* xxxiii (probably); Clement of Alexandria, *strom.* ii. 23; Tertullian, *de monog.* ix; *Conc. Illib.* (305–306), viii, ix, lxiv; *C. Arelat.* (314), x. Tertullian, *adv. Marc.* iv. 34 is sometimes cited to the contrary; it is certainly an obscurely worded passage, in which the following occurs: "The marriage which is not rightly (*rite*) dissolved remains in existence; to marry, therefore, while a marriage persists is adultery." This could be interpreted as allowing remarriage in cases where a previous union

offending wife should repent, the husband ought to take her back.[1] Nevertheless, Origen states that "some . . . of the rulers [i.e., bishops] of the Church have permitted a woman to marry even when her husband was living",[2] but he acknowledges that this is against the divine law and supposes that it had been sanctioned in certain cases as the lesser of two evils. Watkins[3] suggests that the women in question may well have been wives of pagans who had been divorced by their husbands before conversion. Tertullian also refers to certain women who, on losing their husbands by death or divorce, had not only rejected the opportunity to live a life of continence, but had even remarried, taking non-Christians as partners.[4] These, however, are the only recorded instances of any deviation in practice from the general prohibition of remarriage after divorce during the first three centuries; they are noticed with disapproval, and there is no reason to think that they were other than exceptional.

From the beginning of the fourth century certain differences begin to appear in the disciplinary handling of divorce and remarriage as between the Churches of the East and of the West. Christian opinion, however, remained unanimous in holding that a husband may put away an adulterous wife,[5] and a wife, an adulterous husband.[6] Many authorities took the more rigorous

---

was "rightly dissolved" (as for adultery); but the succeeding sentence brings the argument back to the main point: "Thus if [Jesus] conditionally prohibited the dismissal of a wife, he did not absolutely prohibit it; and what he did not absolutely prohibit, he permitted in other cases where the reason for prohibition does not hold." The matter at issue here is simply whether or not Christ sanctioned divorce; remarriage after divorce is not in question. Marcion had denied that the New Testament allows putting away; Tertullian asserts that it does—and there is no reason to interpret this passage as contradicting his otherwise consistent condemnation of remarriage. Joyce explains it as an instance where the author's addiction to forensic rhetoric has led him to make a dangerous overstatement in his eagerness to strengthen his case, see op. cit., pp. 307–308.

[1] Hermas, *mand.* IV. i. 6.
[2] *Comm. in Matt.* xiv. 23.   [3] Op. cit., pp. 213–214.   [4] *Ad ux.* ii. 1.
[5] The authorities are too numerous to quote.
[6] See Basil, *ethic.* lxxiii. 1; *epist.* clxxxviii. 9; Ambrose, *de Abr.* i. 25; Jerome, *epist.* lxxvii. 3–5; Augustine, *de serm. Dom. in mont.* i. 43.

line and considered that an adulterous wife ought to be dismissed,[1] thus preserving at one point the coincidence of ecclesiastical discipline and the law of the State, but only Jerome ventured to maintain that the same obligation should operate in respect of an adulterous husband.[2] Whereas in the ante-Nicene Church there was a general conviction that the repentant wife should be restored to cohabitation, only Augustine[3] continued to urge this merciful and Christian course in the period now under review and, especially in the East, a harsher attitude developed towards the penitent adulteress. During this time also there was a tendency to enlarge the meaning attached to 'fornication' (*porneia*), with the result that divorce was variously advocated for "fornication, adultery, or any other evil cause",[4] for hindrance to piety,[5] and even for suspicion of fornication.[6] Augustine went furthest when he claimed that divorce was justified for unlawful desires of any kind,[7] but towards the end of his life he retreated from this advanced position to one more conventional, while confessing that he found the significance of *porneia* anything but easy to determine.[8]

Upon the critical question of the lawfulness of remarriage after divorce there is ample proof that both East and West continued to maintain the unequivocal witness of the ante-Nicene age.[9] Nevertheless, there are certain passages in the literature of the period which have been adduced as indications of a disposition to tolerate such unions—and it has been inferred that there was a conflict of opinion in the Church upon this matter. Careful

---

[1] *Conc. Neocæsar.* (ante 325), viii; Asterius of Amasea, *in Matt. xix, hom.* v; Theodoret, *Græc. affect. curat.* ix; Jerome, *comm. in Matt.* on ch. xix. Augustine is undecided in *de serm. Dom. in mont.* i. 43, but revokes the view there expressed in favour of one more definite, in *retract.* I. xix. 6.   [2] *Epist.* lxxvii. 3–5.

[3] *De serm. Dom. in mont.* i. 43.   [4] Epiphanius, *hær.* lix. 4.

[5] Basil, *ethic.* lxxiii. 1.   [6] Jerome, *comm. in Matt.* on ch. xix.

[7] *De serm. Dom. in mont.* i. 46.   [8] *Retract.* I. xix. 6.

[9] See *Conc. Arelat.* [(314)—probably a 5th-cent. council held at Arles], xxiv; *C. XI Carth.* (407), viii; *C. Andegav.* (453), vi; *Can. Apost.* (c. 400), xlvii; Ambrose, *expos. ev. Luc.* viii. 2; Jerome, *epist.* lxxvii, 3–5; lv. 3; *adv. Jov.* i. 10; Augustine, *de serm. Dom. in mont.* i. 39, 43, 46; *de bono conj.* iii, vii; *serm* cccxcii. 2; *de bono vid.* iv; *de conj. adult.* i. 7, etc.; Innocent I, *epist.* ii, *ad Victric.*, xiii; *epist.* vi, *ad Exsuper.*, vi; Basil of Cæsarea, *ethic.* lxxiii. 2; John Chrysostom, *de virg.* xl; *in Joh., hom.* lxiii; *in epist. I ad Thess.* v. 2.

examination of the evidence, however, is sufficient to dispose of this contention. There is, admittedly, one (and only one) express allowance of remarriage after divorce in the post-Nicene writings, but it can hardly be regarded as authoritative. It occurs in the commentary of 'Ambrosiaster' on 1 Corinthians,[1] where it is clear that the unknown author has accommodated his teaching to Roman legal practice; his pronouncement is suspect, not only because it is at variance with the doctrine of all reliable patristic writers, but also because in the same place, contrary to Christian principle and the repeated declarations of the Fathers, he argues for a double moral standard in regard to venereal behaviour. Little weight need be accorded to the testimony of Ambrosiaster.

There remain several less explicit, and sometimes obscurely worded passages to which appeal is made in support of the view that the patristic Church tolerated remarriage after divorce. Lactantius could be interpreted as allowing this concession to the innocent husband of an adulterous wife,[2] but a certain ambiguity which renders his meaning doubtful appears to be due to an unskilful attempt to incorporate the 'Matthæan exception' into a statement as to the lawfulness of putting away. He has no hesitation in terming an adulterer the man who marries a divorcee,[3] and it is most improbable that the passage in question really permits remarriage. A similar endeavour to include the excepting clause undoubtedly explains the clumsy wording of a canon of the Council of Vannes (Brittany) in 456: "Those who have left their wives, saving for the cause of fornication, as the

---

[1] *Comm. in I Cor.* on vii. 11; Joyce, op. cit., pp. 321–322, considers that the passage points to "some local laxity of practice"—where, it is impossible to say.

[2] *Inst.* vi. 23: "Nevertheless, lest anyone should think that he can evade the divine precepts, these provisions are added to remove all misrepresentation and occasion of deceit, that he who marries one who has been divorced by her husband and he who, except for the crime of adultery, puts away his wife in order to marry another, is an adulterer; for it is not God's will that the [one] body (*corpus*) should be severed and parted asunder." Cf. *epit.* lxvi: "He [Christ] commanded that a wife shall not be put away unless convicted of adultery, and that the bond (*vinculum*) of the marriage covenant shall not be dissolved, unless it is broken by infidelity"—here the second clause repeats the sense of the first. In considering the views of Lactantius, it is helpful to recall that he was not a theologian but a layman trained as a rhetorician, and a convert.   [3] *Epit.* lvi.

Gospel says, without furnishing proof of adultery, and have married others are, we decide, to be excommunicated . . ."[1] This does not, as is sometimes alleged, permit remarriage to men who have divorced their wives for adultery; it lays down two rules—(a) wives are not to be put away, except for proved adultery, and (b) men who have dismissed or deserted their wives are not to marry again.

Augustine himself acknowledges the difficulty of interpreting Matt. xix. 9: ". . . in the divine sentences themselves it is so obscure whether he, who is undoubtedly free to dismiss an adulterous wife, is to be held an adulterer should he marry another, that in my judgement anyone who goes astray on this point commits only a venial fault."[2] It has been held on the authority of these words that he does not absolutely refuse remarriage to the innocent husband who puts away an adulterous wife, but this is to place a meaning upon them which their context does not warrant. In the treatise *De Fide et Operibus* Augustine's main concern is to refute the arguments of those who maintained that initiation into the Church should be conditional upon profession of faith only, and not upon amendment of life; and in the passage quoted he is writing, not of Christians, but of those who present themselves for baptism. He confesses that the import of the Matthæan text is so uncertain that, while every effort should be made to prevent the innocent husband remarrying, he is unable to decide whether one who has already contracted a second union should be accepted or rejected for baptism. But this is a special case, and one not relevant to Christians; moreover, it will be observed that Augustine does not approve the taking of a new wife, but merely gives his opinion that in certain circumstances it may be regarded as an excusable error in a convert who seeks to enter the Church. Concerning such unions in general, he has no doubt; they are, as Christ has testified, "not marriages but adulteries"[3], and are condemned by divine law.[4]

[1] *Conc. Venet.* (465), ii.
[2] *De fid. et op.* xix [35]; cf. a similar acknowledgement of the exegetical difficulty in *de conj. adult.* i. 25, and *retract.* ii. 57.
[3] *De fid. et op.* i [2].　　　　　　　　　　　　[4] Ibid, xviii [33].

But he recognizes that where the Scripture itself is obscure a man may well err in good faith, and he would not have such a one treated as a deliberate sinner who knowingly flouts the command of the Lord and merits the Church's condemnation.

Basil of Cæsarea also ventures to mitigate the Church's penitential rule,[1] not because of the ambiguity of Scripture, but in deference to the convention that indulgence should be shown towards male, but not towards female, immorality. He deprecates this double standard, but allows that when a man who has separated from his wife cohabits with another woman, neither the husband nor the mistress should incur the full ecclesiastical penalty of fourteen years penance for adultery, but only that of seven years applied in cases of non-adulterous fornication.[2] If, however, the husband puts away his wife in order to form an illicit connexion, both he and his paramour merit the full punishment for adultery.[3] In giving this decision to Amphilochius in the first of the canonical letters, Basil does not (as it is sometimes alleged) recognize divorce and remarriage; he is concerned solely with the penance applicable to those who enter into irregular unions—for it will be noted that second marriage is actually not in question. Elsewhere he emphatically condemns those who marry again after putting away their wives.[4]

Again, it is claimed that in his *Panarion* or treatise against the heresies,[5] Epiphanius of Salamis condones remarriage after divorce. The passage in question deals with the lawfulness of digamy (remarriage after the death of a partner) for the laity, but a textual amendment introduced by Petavius into his Paris edition of 1622 changed the meaning so as to make it appear that a second union is permissible during the lifetime of a separated

---

[1] *Epist.* clxxxviii. 9.

[2] *Epist.* ccxvii. 58, 59, 77.

[3] See *epist.* cxcix. 21 for a similar case to that discussed.

[4] See *ethic.* lxxiii. 2; also the treatise *de virg.* xli, which may be by Basil.

[5] *Hær.* lix. 4.

partner[1]—and incidentally gives rise to an internal contradiction in the text, for the author plainly declares that the concession of digamy is "not so that [the husband] should have two wives at the same time", indicating that mere separation without the intervention of death does not, in his view, destroy the marriage. Epiphanius, therefore, cannot be cited as a witness to the allowance of remarriage after divorce even in the eastern Church at this time.

There may have been occasional and local instances of laxity in practice, and the relevant pronouncements of the Fathers are not always distinguished for their lucidity; nevertheless, the testimony of the Church, both eastern and western, during the patristic age is conclusive both in its universal allowance of divorce (that is, separation *a mensa et thoro*) for adultery, and in its unconditional condemnation of remarriage during the lifetime of the partner dismissed. When certain authors or councils are alleged[2] to have taught or enacted to the contrary, it is generally because the passages in question have been misinterpreted or a corrupt text has been used; but it should not be overlooked that in dealing with divorce and remarriage the Fathers often use language which, though perfectly intelligible to their contemporaries, is open to misunderstanding when invested with meanings and associations which are derived from mediæval and modern concepts of divorce and indissolubility. Thus, when Theodoret speaks of the loosing of the bond (*zeuglē*) of matrimony;[3] when Asterius of

---

[1] The passage reads thus: "But the man who cannot rest satisfied with his first wife, now dead—from whom [it may be] he was separated on account of fornication or adultery or some other disgraceful cause—should he take a second wife, or should a woman in like case take a second husband, the Scripture does not blame him, nor does it declare him cut off from the Church or from eternal life, but tolerates him because of his frailty: not so that he should have two wives at the same time; but that being cut off from the first, he should lawfully marry another if he chooses." Petavius amended the text to read: "But the man who cannot rest satisfied with his first wife, now dead, or if he should be separated from her on account of fornication . . ."

[2] As, for example, by John Cosin, in his *Argument Proving that Adultery works a Dissolution of the Marriage*; see his *Works* (Oxford, 1843-1855—Library of Anglo-Catholic Theology), iv. pp. 489 ff.

[3] *Græc. affect. curat.* ix.

Amasea declares that "marriages are sundered by nothing save death and adultery", and praises the husband who severs the yoke (*desmos*) which ties him to an adulterous wife;[1] and when Lactantius writes, "[Christ] commanded that . . . the bond (*vinculum*) of the nuptial covenant shall not be dissolved, unless it is broken by infidelity":[2] these authors do not imply, either that an indestructible metaphysical link between man and woman is forged in wedlock, or that adultery so disrupts the union between husband and wife as to permit each to remarry during the lifetime of the other.[3] Such interpretations of their teaching are only possible if an anachronistic significance is read into their words.

What was the patristic view of the nature of marriage and of the effect of divorce? Unfortunately, few of the Fathers afford us much assistance in answering this question, for most of them were content simply to assert the teaching of the Gospels without venturing to embark upon explanations; it was sufficient for them that the Lord (as they understood the records) had permitted divorce for a wife's adultery, and had forbidden the remarriage of either partner thereafter. Augustine, however, has something to say upon the question. In several places he expressly describes marriage as a 'sacrament' (*sacramentum*), and on that account indissoluble except by death;[4] and he defines the substance of this sacrament (*res sacramenti*) as consisting in the requirement that "the man and the woman who are joined together in matrimony should remain inseparable (*inseparabiliter perseverent*) as long as they live."[5] His argument continues: "So enduring, indeed life-long, are the obligations of marriage (*jura nuptiarum*) between those who have contracted them, that the truly married (*conjuges*) are rather those who have separated from one another than those

---

[1] *In Matt. xix, hom. v.*
[2] *Epit.* lxvi.
[3] As Watkins understood Theodoret and Asterius to imply, see op. cit., pp. 309 and 315.
[4] Cf. *de bono conj.* vii [6], xv [17], xxiv [32]; *de nupt. et concup.* i. 19 [17], 23 [21]; etc.
[5] *De nupt. et concup.* i. 11 [10].

who [being divorced] have united with others . . . Thus, during their lifetime, there subsists between husband and wife a certain conjugal relationship (*quiddam conjugale*) which neither separation (*separatio*) nor union with another can cancel."

Augustine goes on to assert that the effect of marriage is, in some sense, like that of baptism—a theme which he elaborates in the treatise, *De Conjugiis Adulterinis*: "Just as the sacrament of regeneration endures, even in one who has been excommunicated because he is guilty of some crime, and just as he does not lack that sacrament even if he is never reconciled to God; so the bond (*vinculum*) of the marriage covenant remains when a wife is dismissed on the ground of fornication, nor does she lack that bond (*vinculum*) even if she is never reconciled to her husband—though she lacks it when her husband dies, whereas the guilty excommunicant never lacks the sacrament of regeneration, even if [he dies] unreconciled, since God never dies. So it remains that if we would think in the same way as the Apostle[1] we may not say that an adulterous husband can be regarded as [virtually] dead, so that his wife is free lawfully to marry another. Even if adultery is a death, not of the body but of the soul, nevertheless it was not of that death that the Apostle spoke when he said: 'But if her husband should die, she may marry whom she will'; he spoke only of the death which happens to the body."[2]

From these passages it might seem that Augustine conceived of the *vinculum* of marriage differently from the other writers whose views have been cited—that while they treated it as capable of absolute severance by adultery, he thought of it as a tie binding husband and wife so firmly during their joint lifetimes as to admit of no dissolution. Any appearance of inconsistency, however, disappears when the patristic idea of the nuptial bond is properly understood. In the first place, it was the unanimous and unquestioned assumption of all Christians (as of ancient law and society everywhere and at all times) that matrimony is a temporal relationship terminated by death. As maintained by the Church,

---

[1] The reference is to Rom. vii. 1–3.
[2] *De conj. adult.* ii. 5.

however, this belief led to an ontological contradiction which Tertullian was not slow to turn to polemical advantage when, as a Montanist, he attacked the catholic acquiescence in digamy. If, he argued, the nuptial *vinculum* is held to persist despite divorce, what rational ground exists for asserting that it is dissolved by death, so as to admit of the remarriage of the surviving partner?[1] But no reply came from the orthodox side; nothing illogical was seen in the prevailing view, for the simple reason that the *vinculum* (both then and later) was regarded as something juridical and contractual rather than spiritual. The idea that marriage might create a metaphysical bond which death itself could not destroy would have been entirely alien to the mind even of Christian antiquity, and in any case was disallowed by the current interpretation of our Lord's answer to the Sadducees concerning the resurrection.[2]

Both Christians and their pagan contemporaries looked upon marriage as a union of man and woman designed principally, if not exclusively, for the procreation of children, and although this narrow conception was greatly enlarged and elevated, notably by Augustine with his theory of the *bona matrimonii*, it always remained basic and dominant. Hence the identity of Church discipline and Roman law at one significant point—namely, the right of a husband to put away an adulterous wife; for adultery on the woman's part, by introducing the risk of *confusio prolis* (confusion of progeny), defeated the chief object of matrimony— the production, not merely of offspring, but of 'legitimate' offspring. It was a matter of cardinal importance that a man should be in no doubt concerning the paternity of the children borne by his wife; but no such consideration restrained a husband from fornication—a factor which contributed to the establishment of the kind of double moral standard that even Basil could only accept and deplore. Christianity, it is true, enlarged the narrow forensic definition of adultery and required from men no less than from women the strictest avoidance of venereal

---

[1] *De monog.* ix.
[2] Mk. xii. 25 = Matt. xxii. 30 and Lk. xx. 34-36.

immorality, but at the same time the Church continued to endorse the old notion of matrimony by approving, and occasionally by requiring, the dismissal of an adulterous wife.

Such divorce, however, was deemed not to affect the status of the couple, between whom there remained, in the words of Augustine, *"quiddam conjugale"*—something of the nature of wedlock, sufficient at least to prohibit the remarriage which the secular law sanctioned. But this "something" was not a spiritual, metaphysical bond; rather, as Augustine clearly states, it was the persistence of certain ineluctable obligations (*jura matrimonii*) which the State regarded as cancelled by divorce—and principally, that deriving from the concession by each partner to the other of "power" over his or her own body.[1] Forbidden to "defraud" one another, no less by fornication or adultery than by unwise asceticism, this mutual surrender of physical sexuality imposed upon husband and wife a moral duty which separation could never annul so long as both were alive and there was a possibility, however remote, that they might resume cohabitation and thus fulfil their matrimonial obligations. But death changed the whole situation; it destroyed the marital status of the couple and terminated the nuptial rights; it severed a relationship which was conceived primarily in carnal terms and, by removing any risk of *confusio prolis*, made remarriage permissible for those who could not endure an enforced continence—for such was the motive commonly imputed to the digamist.

Augustine also insisted that the permanence of the matrimonial *vinculum* was due to the 'sacramental' character of the union—but it is important not to attribute to this term, as it is used in his works, the meaning which it eventually acquired in connexion with marriage and the notion of indissolubility. As employed by the ancient Latin ecclesiastical authors, *sacramentum* had roughly the same significance as the Greek *mustērion* (which it frequently translates), and seems to have been applied more or less indiscriminately to a large variety of religious observances, Church

---

[1] 1 Cor. vii. 4-5.

rites, revealed truths, and pious opinions.[1] With Augustine it is often equivalent to *signum rei sacræ*; the 'sacrament' is a symbol of some sacred verity—and this is certainly its connotation in the passages already considered. Even the plural marriages of the patriarchs could be called *sacramenta* because they represented "the multitude that should eventually be made subject to God in all the nations of the earth"; but Christian monogamy was pre-eminently sacramental since it exemplified not only "the unity of us all made subject to God, which shall be hereafter in one heavenly City",[2] but also (and supremely) the mysteries of the Incarnation[3] and of the union between Christ and the Church—and it is particularly by virtue of the latter that Augustine declares it to be a *sacramentum*.

In so describing marriage, however, it is clear that the notion of its symbolism predominates, and that Augustine does not base his sacramental conception upon an *a priori* attribution of indissoluble character to the union of husband and wife. His argument is not that the bond of matrimony is by its very nature indestructible—therefore wedlock is a fitting *sacramentum* of Christ and the Church; but that matrimony is declared by St Paul to be a *magnum sacramentum* in which Christ and the Church is signified—therefore the nuptial bond, once it has been established between Christians, ought not to be severed, with the result that the symbol of the supernatural union is destroyed. The effect of marriage, like that of baptism or ordination,[4] is permanent—but only in the sense that it creates a status, with corresponding rights and duties, which persists until it is obliterated by death. By accepting and honouring the enduring obligations (Augustine's *jura matrimonii*) belonging to their status, husband and wife set

---

[1] See the extensive list of examples in *Dict. Chr. Ant.*, ii, p. 1831b.

[2] *De bono conj.* xviii [21].

[3] Augustine, *enarr. in Ps. xix*, ii. 6; *in Ps. xlv*, iii; *in Joh.* viii. 4; and cf. Origen, *de princ.* ii. 4; *c. Cels.* vi. 47; Cassian, *de incarn. Dom. c. Nest.* v. 12.

[4] Augustine also compares marriage with ordination in *de bono conj.* xxiv [32].

forth the greater thing (*res major*[1]—that is, the symbolism of Christ and the Church) proleptically latent in the natural institution of marriage, but only made explicit in the nuptial ideal of Christianity. Strangely enough, harmonious and uninterrupted cohabitation was not considered essential to the exhibition of this sacrament of matrimony—though of course it was desirable; it was sufficient that there should be a demonstrable and exclusive adherence of one man to one woman in the conjugal bond. Hence the intrinsic virtue of the *sacramentum* was not vitiated by divorce, so long as the marital unity was not destroyed by remarriage; but death was held to terminate a symbolism which ultimately owed its reality solely to the continuance of a relationship which was legalistic, carnal, and (as it were) quasi-mathematical in conception, rather than spiritual, personal, and metaphysical.[2]

Having considered Augustine's theory of the effect of marriage, it will be evident that any apparent difference between him and other Fathers on this point is due simply to the fact that their conception of the nature of the nuptial *vinculum* was less precisely defined and expressed than his, and consequently more susceptible to anachronistic interpretation. The African doctor represents the *vinculum* as a bond of moral obligation devolving upon husband and wife as a result of the symbolism (*sacramentum*) of their union, and enduring until death dissolves their matrimonial status and renders the discharge of its mutual rights and duties impossible. Lactantius, Theodoret, and Asterius, however, have a more elementary notion of the bond of wedlock. For them, it does not consist in the infrangible moral obligation established by marriage and persistent during the joint lifetime of the couple; it simply

---

[1] See *de bono conj.* vii [7]; Augustine asks, Why is the *vinculum* so strong? and suggests that this can only be explained on the assumption that "out of this weak, mortal, human state [i.e., the natural institution of marriage] there was taken a certain sacrament of some greater thing".

[2] In this connexion it is significant to note that, in *de conj. adult.* ii. 4–5 [4], Augustine bases his argument for the indissolubility of the *vinculum* partly upon St Paul's reference (Rom. vii. 1 ff.) to the effect of death in removing the legal impediment to remarriage.

denotes the tie which joins together a man and a woman as partners in a common domestic life of conjugal responsibility and cohabitation—a signification clearly implied by the use of the Greek words *zeuglē*[1] and *desmos*,[2] both of which suggest the idea of a physical or quasi-physical bond adapted to the fulfilment of some practical end. Hence they speak quite correctly of the severance of the matrimonial *vinculum* by divorce, which disrupts the cohabitation of husband and wife and thus breaks the conjugal harness (as it were) by which both were yoked together; while Augustine, no less correctly according to his view, maintains that the *vinculum* is incapable of fracture since not even discontinuance of cohabitation, but only death, can annul the moral obligations once assumed in marriage. There were thus two different, but to some extent complementary senses in which the term *vinculum*, or bond, and its equivalents were applied to wedlock, and if they are carefully distinguished there is little risk that the teaching of the Fathers will be misrepresented. On one point, however, all the best authorities of the patristic age are agreed—namely, that the remarriage of a divorced Christian during the lifetime of the other partner is forbidden under all circumstances by divine law and ecclesiastical discipline alike.

Confusion between the two different conceptions of the nuptial *vinculum* has been responsible for the attribution[3] to John Chrysostom of the opinion that divorce and remarriage are in certain circumstances permissible to the Christian partner in a mixed union. When a wife is required by her pagan husband to participate in idolatrous worship, or is dismissed by him, Chrysostom says: "It is better that the marriage (*gamos*[4]) should be torn asunder (*diaspasthēnai*)" if it cannot be preserved intact

---

[1] Basically, the loop of the strap used to harness horses together.

[2] A halter, mooring cable, or fetter—from which primary meanings such connotations as 'union' and 'bond' were derived.

[3] For instance, by O. D. Watkins, op. cit., pp. 498–499, and by G. H. Joyce, op. cit., p. 472.

[4] Which Joyce translates "marriage bond"—a meaning less than exact, but better fitted to his argument.

save at the price of apostasy.[1] Fr Joyce interprets this as implying
that if, under such conditions, the Christian partner departs, "the
marriage is altogether dissolved", with the result that she is in no
way hindered from entering into another union.

In the case in question, however, the continuance or otherwise
of the *vinculum* is not actually in doubt. The point at issue is
simply whether, when cohabitation has been rendered intolerable
for religious reasons by the pagan partner, or when the Christian
wife has been put away, she may rightly acquiesce in the disruption of the marriage—that is, of the common domestic life.
Chrysostom, on the authority of St Paul,[2] declares that she may
do so, even though her refusal to compromise her faith, or her
willing acceptance of dismissal by an uncongenial spouse, may
sometimes seem to justify so strong an expression as the 'tearing
asunder' of the union. There is no need whatever to assume that
remarriage is contemplated and, by implication, permitted, if it is
recognized that the phrase *diaspasthēnai ton gamon* refers, not to
the severance of the matrimonial bond, but to the relinquishment
of conjugal cohabitation.

John Chrysostom, therefore, cannot be cited as a witness to the
application by the early Church of the concession later to be
known as the 'Pauline privilege'—though it was mistakenly
derived from the Apostle's words: "Yet if the unbelieving
[partner] departeth, let him depart: the [Christian] brother or the
sister is not under bondage in such cases." There is no evidence
that this saying was interpreted as an allowance of remarriage as
well as of divorce until we come again to the commentary upon
1 Corinthians of the unknown Ambrosiaster.[3] There, however,
it is stated categorically that "the marriage in which God is not
honoured is not indissoluble (*ratum*); and for that reason he who is
dismissed for God's sake does no wrong if he marries another,

---

[1] *In epist. I ad Cor.* xix. 3.

[2] See 1 Cor. vii. 15.

[3] Watkins, op. cit., pp. 463 ff. and 501–502, reads the probability of such a
permission into *Conc. Illib.* (305–306), x (for a discussion of which, see G. H.
Joyce, op. cit., pp. 504 ff.), and Jerome, *adv. Jov.* i. 7, but without sufficient
warrant.

since contempt for the Creator (*contumelia Creatoris*) cancels the obligation (*jus*) of matrimony so far as the deserted partner is concerned, and he is not to be blamed if he forms another union."

Considerable authority has been claimed for this declaration as warranting the exercise of the 'privilege', but there are serious objections to its acceptance. Ambrosiaster's testimony is doubly suspect. In the first place, it will be recalled that alone among the writers of the early Church he advocated a right of remarriage for the husband who had put away an adulterous wife—and that in so doing he appealed incidentally to the customary double moral standard which Christianity had rejected. It will hardly be said that these dubious opinions inspire confidence in his interpretation of St Paul's teaching, especially when he is found once more in direct opposition to the consensus of patristic doctrine. Moreover, Augustine, who treats in some detail of mixed marriages and the position of converts, plainly asserts that even pagan unions, though of an inferior character and inherently less stable than those of Christians, are nevertheless indissoluble according to the natural law; hence the believing partner whose situation is made unbearable is at liberty to separate, but is prohibited from remarriage.[1] Even the harsh and extreme conviction of Ambrose that not only mixed, but also pagan marriages are contrary to the law of God,[2] did not lead him to the conclusion that divorce can be condoned in the case of non-Christians, much less that remarriage thereafter is lawful for them. We may safely infer, therefore, from the evidence available, that during the first five centuries of the Church's existence the 'Pauline privilege' was interpreted as sanctioning only the separation, and never the remarriage of the Christian partner in a mixed union; and that even this concession was made in none but exceptional cases where cohabitation had become unendurable.

---

[1] See *de conj. adult.* i. 13 [14], 21 [25]; *de fid. et op.* i. [2]; and see the discussion in T. A. Lacey, rev. R. C. Mortimer, *Marriage in Church and State* (London, 1947), pp. 16–17.

[2] See *in ev. Luc.* viii. 8.

At the close of the patristic age many typical features of the Christian sexual tradition were already firmly established, though they were to undergo modification in the centuries which followed. On the negative side we have noted the embarrassment, suspicion, antipathy, and abhorrence variously displayed by many of the Fathers towards physical sexuality, and the culmination of this tendency in a virtual identification of coitus with sin or evil in the thought of Augustine. This attitude favoured the growth of an asceticism which set a higher value upon venereal continence than upon other forms of self-discipline, and which made an increasing appeal as the recession of earlier eschatological expectations removed an incentive to detachment, and as the ending of persecution prompted the search for a substitute for martyrdom which could satisfy the demands of heroic idealism.[1] It led also to an excessive exaltation of virginity which encouraged many extravagant and unwholesome notions—among them, the theory that the dedicated female virgin had contracted a special, quasi-nuptial relationship with Christ which gave to her subsequent lawful marriage the character of adultery, and suggested to Jerome the application to the mother of one such woman of the blasphemous appellation, "mother-in-law of God".[2]

Such an attitude, and the double ethical standard which it produced, could not but react unfavourably upon the Christian estimation of marriage, which was not uncommonly represented as a concession to human frailty—indeed, some advocated matrimony at an early age simply in order to avoid entanglement

---

[1] Evidence of this is provided by the use made of the parable of the sower; in the third century it is martyrdom that produces 100-fold and virginity 60-fold (cf. Cyprian, *de hab. virg.* xxi), but in post-Nicene literature virginity takes the place of martyrdom and widowhood that of virginity, leaving marriage still in the lowest category of the 30-fold. Methodius, at the end of the former period, explains that the virgins shall enter first into the rest of the new dispensation because "they were martyrs, not as bearing the pains of the body for a little moment of time, but as enduring them throughout all their life" (*conviv.* vii. 3)— a significant assertion of the pre-eminence of virginity at a time when the Church was about to suffer its most violent trial.

[2] *Epist.* xxii. 20.

in youthful lusts.[1] This depreciation of wedlock, however, was carried to extremes by only a few, such as Tertullian and Jerome; most of the Fathers allowed that it was relatively a good, and not necessarily a hindrance to the devout life, provided that it was used with moderation. Celibates were bidden not to boast,[2] and those who practised asceticism in order to demonstrate their superior spirituality or their contempt for marriage were censured severely.[3] Moreover, not mere venereal continence, but the possession of a spirit of temperance and self-control in all things, was declared to be the test of true virginity; to refrain from sexual indulgence was worthless, if other desires were not held in check.[4] These salutary cautions, however, did not affect the general opinion of matrimony as an inferior state attended by manifold inconveniences, and incompatible with the fullest service of God. Of the joys, privileges, and opportunities of home and family life we find little appreciation, while hardly more than lip-service is paid to the blessing of children.

On the other hand, having thus relegated wedlock to the lowest place in the scale of Christian vocation, the Fathers (and notably Augustine) defended it vigorously and tenaciously against all who denied its relative merit or sought to impugn its moral value. They insisted that the mutual obligations assumed by husband and wife are permanent and binding, severely restricted the right of separation or repudiation, and forbade remarriage after divorce. The conception of marriage between believers as a sacrament or symbol of Christ and the Church not only enhanced the significance of the nuptial union, but also set before the spouses a high ideal of conjugal life. When Pope Callistus approved of marriages between free women and men of servile rank he

---

[1] Cf. *Const. Apost.* iv. 11; Ps.-Clement, *epist. ad Jac.* vii; *Didascalia*, xxiii (and cf. also xvii and xxii); John Chrysostom, *in epist. I ad Tim.* ix. 2.

[2] Cf. Ignatius, *epist. ad Polyc.* v. 2; Clement, *epist. ad Corinth.* xxxviii; Cyril of Jerusalem, *cat.* iv. 24, 25; Augustine, *de bono virg.* xliii [44].

[3] Cf. *Conc. Gangr.* (mid-4th cent.), i, iv, ix, x, xii, xiii, xiv, xv, xvi, xvii; *Conc. Toletan.* (447), xvi; *Conc. Bracar.* (563), xi, xii.

[4] Methodius, *conviv.* xi. 1; Augustine, *de bono virg.* xxi [25]—continence a virtue, not of the body but of the soul.

asserted, in effect, that wedlock which is lawful in the sight of God cannot be rejected by the Church simply because the State deems it invalid;[1] and the same concern to maintain what is true in natural law compelled the Fathers to accept even pagan unions as in principle indissoluble, though of a lower and less stable character than those of the faithful.

A new respect for the sanctity of human life produced forthright denunciations of such ancient and common malpractices as abortion, the exposure of babies, and infanticide. Furthermore, the married and single alike of both sexes were required to observe the strictest morality in their venereal behaviour, although the rapid expansion of the Church during the fourth century and the influx of barbarian elements made it virtually impossible, as we have seen, to eradicate the immemorial notion of a double standard of sexual conduct. Moreover, Christianity itself did little to dispel the general idea of male privilege, for while it made no distinction between the sexes where fornication and adultery were concerned,[2] in most other respects (including that of the status of woman in marriage and society) its innate conservatism in sexual matters conduced rather to the maintenance and even the intensification of androcentricity, than to its abolition.

The Christian attitude to sexuality in all its aspects was profoundly affected by the ascendancy of Hellenistic dualism over Hebraic naturalism during the first great age of the Church. The Jewish conceptions of coitus, marriage, and children, positive and affirmative within their inevitable limits, were almost entirely overlaid by the Græco-oriental tendency to regard the good life as one essentially of *ataraxia* or impassive detachment from all that might impede the rational exercise of contemplation, and to

---

[1] See Hippolytus, *philosoph.* ix. 12 for an account of Callistus' action (strongly prejudiced against the pope); it was probably an expedient necessitated by the fact that free women outnumbered free men among believers, so that it was not always possible for them both to marry within their own rank, and also 'in the Lord'.

[2] For condemnations of the double moral standard in conduct, see Augustine, *serm.* cxxxii. 2; Jerome, *epist.* lxxvii. 3; Gregory Nazianzen., *orat.* xxxvii. 6; also E. O. James, op. cit., pp. 103–104.

look upon sexuality as something not only emotionally disturbing, but also in some sense defiling and tainted with evil. It is futile to speculate how Christian thought might have developed, in this as in other realms of theology, had the early Church clung more closely to its Hebraic roots; the tradition emerged as a natural product of the culture in which it was formed, and faithfully reflects the influences which moulded it. Moreover, in its concern for the integrity of marriage and its abhorrence of venereal licentiousness it preserved some of the best features of the pagan sexual ethic as expounded by the philosophers and moralists of antiquity. Its limitations are manifest, but they were to a large extent those of the age; the Fathers show themselves well acquainted with the best scientific knowledge of their day, and the defects of ancient physiology and psychology must not be held against them, as though Christian thinkers perversely ignored the insights of their contemporaries.

It is relatively easy to extract and compare the views and teaching of the Fathers, and to estimate their influence upon the formation of the Church's sexual tradition, but it is virtually impossible to assess all the other factors which, to a greater or lesser extent, affected Christian thought. There must have been in the early Church at different times and in different localities during what Dr Moffatt calls these "five hundred long years"[1] a great diversity of social custom, ecclesiastical practice, and group attitudes—and concerning these the literature and other records are silent. Such major and obvious differences as that between East and West upon matrimonial questions suggest that at the popular and local level there were probably numerous and marked variations, at least in matters of detail; and it was part of the Church's task in this field to impose upon this diversity an adequate uniformity of teaching and discipline. In the West, this task was accomplished with striking success, though hardly without suppressing healthy divergencies of opinion and stifling some salutary criticism. Jovinian, Helvidius, and Vigilantius (for

---

[1] J. Moffatt, *The First Five Centuries of the Church* (London, 1938), p. ix.

example) must have spoken for a large number of their contemporaries, and it would have been to the ultimate profit of the Church had their criticisms been heeded instead of ridiculed and condemned out of hand. Again, there is evidence even at this early date (and it grows ever more abundant with the passage of the centuries) that the rule of clerical celibacy was impossible to enforce, and was widely evaded or openly defied. Nevertheless, the achievement of the Fathers and Doctors of the early Church in the realm of sexual relationship must be measured by the fact that most of the basic presuppositions of the tradition which they developed (such as the superiority of virginity to marriage, the binding force and spiritual symbolism of matrimony, the incompatibility of wedlock and holy orders, and the contamination of coitus with a certain taint of evil) were never challenged in principle, and underwent only minor modification, during the succeeding millennium.

IV

THE MEDIÆVAL WESTERN CHURCH

DURING the earlier centuries of the mediæval era (the so-called 'Dark Ages') the question of divorce and remarriage assumed a larger and more practical importance than it had occupied in the age of the Fathers. For a time the witness of western Christendom lost its original unanimity under the stress of alien influences and the lax standards of barbarian society, and it is chiefly upon the evidence furnished by this period that the allegation is sometimes made that the Church has never consistently maintained the indissolubility of marriage. None the less, the traditional teaching was also upheld with undiminished strictness, not only in Italy[1] but also north of the Alps,[2] and the looser discipline which temporarily prevailed in the Frankish and German lands had no influence upon the doctrine of the mediæval Church as it was finally expounded by the great canonists and scholastic theologians.

---

[1] Cf. the following papal pronouncements: Gregory I, *epist.* xi. 45 *ad Theoctistam*, forbidding unilateral divorce for the purpose of entering the monastic life (cf. also *epist.* xi. 50 and vi. 48)—a form of *repudium* allowed by the civil law, with permission of remarriage to the partner dismissed, *nov.* xxii. 5; Gregory II's instructions to legates for Bavaria (716), see *addit. ad leg. Baiuwar.* in *Monumenta Germaniæ Historica, Leges,* iii, p. 453; Zacharias, *epist.* vii *ad Pipin.* (747), M.G.H., *Epist.* iii, p. 480; Stephen III, *epist. ad monast. Brittann.* v (754); also *Conc. Forojulien.* (791), x.

[2] Cf. *Conc. Nannet.* (dated 658, but probably late 8th cent.), x; *C. Toletan.* (681), viii; *C. Suession.* (744), ix; a synod at Aachen (789)—see *Capit. Carol. Mag.*: *capit. eccl.,* ann. 789, xliii; *C. VI Paris.* (829), iii. 2 (repeated verbatim by *C. Vormat.* (829); see *M.G.H., Leg.* i, p. 345); *C. Remense* (1049), xii; *C. Turon.* (1060), ix; *C. Rotomag.* (1072), xvi, xvii, xviii.

As in the patristic age, there are in this period a few instances of rulings so uncertain in their meaning that some have claimed them as permitting remarriage. Thus Watkins presumes that such an allowance is implied by the Council of Bourges in 1031,[1] but it would seem rather that we have here yet another example of the confusion not infrequently caused by a clumsy attempt to incorporate the Matthæan exception into an otherwise straight-forward prohibition of repudiation.[2] To the same cause must be attributed the obscurity of a canon passed at a council held in Rome in 826, and confirmed by another held there in 853.[3] More perplexing, however, is the remarkable decision given by Gregory II in 726 to one of several enquiries from Boniface of Maintz,[4] the precise significance of which it is impossible now to determine. The particulars of the case submitted are not known, and cannot be inferred from the pope's letter; but these are his words: "Regarding your question as to what a husband is to do, if his wife has been attacked by an infirmity (*infirmitate correpta*) rendering her incapable of coitus: it would be good if he were to remain as he is, and practise abstinence; but since this is a hard thing to do (*hoc magnorum est*), he who cannot contain had better marry. Furthermore, since the woman is kept from married life by infirmity, and is not excluded because of some detestable offence, let him not fail to support her."

---

[1] Op. cit., pp. 389–390.

[2] *C. Bituric.* (1031), xvi: "Those who dismiss their lawful wives without the fault of fornication are not to take others while the former are living, nor are wives to take other husbands, but let them be reconciled to each other." As in other cases, the prohibition thus compressed into an ambiguous form is twofold: (a) wives are not to be dismissed unless they have committed fornication; (b) neither those who thus dismiss their wives nor the wives so dismissed may remarry.

[3] *C. Rom.* (826), xxxvi: "No man, except for the cause of fornication, may leave the wife who is joined to him, and then unite with another. In other cases it is expedient that the offender be united in his former wedlock." This canon enacts (a) that a wife is not to be dismissed, except for fornication; (b) that no man who has dismissed his wife for any cause may remarry; (c) that in other cases than that of fornication by the wife, it is fitting that the parties should be reconciled.

[4] *Epist.* iv, *Ad varias Bonifatii consultationes*, M.G.H., *Epist.* iii, p. 276.

Some modern authorities approve the solution suggested by the canonist Roland Bandinelli, who supposed that prior to the consummation of her union the bride had been rendered unfit for coitus by disease[1]—a circumstance by no means impossible in an age when child marriages were customary, at least in the upper classes. In such an event the papal decision would amount to the dissolution of an unconsummated union—a form of dispensation employed later, but apparently not at this time. Gratian included Gregory's reply in the *Decretum*,[2] observing however that "it is found contrary to the sacred canons, and even more, to the doctrine of the evangelists and apostles", and that it seems to have been in the nature of a temporary concession to the English.[3] Watkins considered that the pope had been influenced by the indulgent provisions of Theodore's Penitential, and had actually sanctioned divorce and remarriage;[4] but Dr Mortimer, with more reason, regards Gregory's ruling as one of several instances of "dispensations from the impediment of an existing bond, permitting a modified polygamy".[5] Both this explanation and that of Roland are plausible; but it is difficult to suppose that in this one case the pope ventured to go against the settled teaching of the Roman Church, the decrees of his predecessors, and his own express directions to the legates for Bavaria, so as to allow the complete dissolution of the bond effected by a lawful and consummated marriage.

The first clear departure from the traditional doctrine of the western Church is to be found in the Penitential attributed to Theodore of Canterbury, a collection of his disciplinary rulings composed not long after his death, during the first half of the eighth century. In it the dissolution of wedlock with the right of remarriage is allowed in a variety of circumstances, many of

---

[1] *Summa Rolandi*, C. xxxii. 5 (cf. C. xxxii. 7); see G. H. Joyce, op. cit., p. 333 and n. 1.

[2] C. XXXII, q. vii, c. 18.

[3] Dictum to C. XXXII, q. vii, c. 24. Actually, of course, Gregory's reply had no reference whatever to England.

[4] Op. cit., pp. 377–378.

[5] Op. cit., p. 110, n. 1; also p. 12, n. 1.

which reflect the unsettled and turbulent conditions of the time.[1] The marked affinity between these provisions[2] and the practice of the eastern Church as influenced by the legislation of Justinian shows that upon matrimonial questions the Archbishop, himself an Eastern, held views which were at variance with those of the Church of his adoption.[3] They conflict with the enactments of the contemporary Council of Hertford convened in 673 under his presidency,[4] and are ignored in the penitentials of Bede and Egbert which are dependent upon his own. Only two documents of this period contain any concessions comparable to those made by Theodore—the *Judicium Clementis* (probably the work of Willibrord), which allows a husband to remarry when a year has elapsed after the capture of his wife by the enemy,[5] and the *Dialogue of Egbert*, which contains a tortuous statement suspending judgement in cases of supervenient impotency where there has been divorce and remarriage thereafter.[6] Otherwise, the

---

[1] *Pœnit. Theod.* II. xii. 5, 8, 12, 19–24: see A. W. Haddan and W. Stubbs, *Councils and Ecclesiastical Documents* . . . (Oxford, 3 vols. 1869–1878), iii, pp. 199–200.

[2] The cases mentioned are: (5) adultery of a first wife (the husband may remarry forthwith, and the divorced wife after 5 years penance); (8)—(a) entry into the monastic life with the other partner's consent (the latter may remarry); (b) reduction of a man to slavery for theft or fornication (his wife, if this was her first marriage, may remarry); (12) supervention of incapacity for coitus (the marriage may be dissolved by mutual consent); (19) desertion by a wife (the husband, with the bishop's approval, may remarry after 5 years); (20) capture of a wife with violence, and with no possibility of redemption (the husband may remarry after a year); (21) capture of husband or wife without violence, redemption not being impossible—apparently a reference to acts of brigandage (the remaining partner may remarry after 5 years; but [22] if the captured partner returns subsequently, the second marriage must be dissolved); (23–24) capture of a wife—apparently in war, or by pirates from beyond the seas (the husband may remarry forthwith, and if the wife returns, the second marriage nevertheless stands—capture of this kind being deemed equivalent to death).

[3] See the interesting tabular comparison in O. D. Watkins, op. cit., p. 418.

[4] *Conc. Herudford.* (673), x; see Haddan and Stubbs, op. cit., iii, p. 118.

[5] *Judic. Clem.* (693), xix; xiv, however, penalizes divorce and remarriage in the case of a man, even if his wife consents; and xv allows separation only by mutual consent with a view to remaining unmarried; see Haddan and Stubbs, op. cit., iii, p. 227.

[6] See *resp. ad interrog. XIII*, in Haddan and Stubbs, op. cit., iii, p. 409.

English Church during the pre-Conquest era remained loyal to the teaching of the Fathers in the matter of the bond of wedlock,[1] while the abbots of Iona, Cummean[2] and Adamnan,[3] the one prior to, and the other contemporary with ,Theodore, bear witness to Scottish practice; but the evidence from Wales[4] and from Ireland[5] is conflicting and uncertain, though of little significance for its influence upon the thought of the Church.

During the eighth century the influence of Theodore's Penitential began to spread beyond the coasts of England, affecting first the practice of the Frankish Church, and then the provisions of certain early compilations of canon law. The conditions which favoured acceptance of the Penitential's regulations on divorce and remarriage were not due, as it has sometimes been alleged, to an easygoing accommodation of Christian discipline to the licence of the secular law in the transalpine lands which had recently come under the sway of the Church. Both the legal codes based upon the customs of the Teutonic invaders, and those which preserved so much of the Roman law as had survived among the

---

[1] Cf. Bede, *comm. in Mk. x*; *Leg. Presb. Northumb.* (950), xxxv and liv (see J. Johnson, *A Collection of the Laws and Canons of the Church of England* [Oxford, Lib. of Anglo-Cath. Theol., 1850], i, pp. 377 and 380); a penitential attributed to Dunstan (963), xxvi and xxvii (see Johnson, op. cit., i, pp. 433–434); *Conc. Ænham.* (1009), viii; Canute's *Laws Ecclesiastical* (1017), vii.

[2] See *Pœnit. Cummeani, de fornicatione*, xxviii, xxix.

[3] See Watkins, op. cit., pp. 421–422.

[4] The *Canones Wallici* (? 7th cent.), xxvii [*Cod. Bigot.* xvii] and *Cod. Bigot.* lx punish adultery with death and treat marriage even with a female slave as indissoluble (see Haddan and Stubbs, op. cit., i, pp. 131 and 137); but the ecclesiastical *Laws of Howel the Good* (c. 928), VIII (of Women), recognize trial marriage for seven years, with a bilateral right of separation and remarriage, subject to certain forfeits (Haddan and Stubbs, op. cit., i, pp. 247–251).

[5] The so-called 'second synod of Patrick' (a convention of unknown date but considerable antiquity) allows the remarriage of an innocent husband in the case of divorce of a wife for fornication (see *Conc. II. Hibern.*, xxvi, xxviii, in Haddan and Stubbs, op. cit., ii, p. 337), but the 'first synod of Patrick' (8th cent.), simply excommunicates an adulterous wife (*C. I Hibern.*, xix; Haddan and Stubbs, op. cit., ii, p 329), while the Penitential of Finian disallows remarriage after divorce (*pœnit. Vinn.* [end of 5th cent.], xliii).

provincials,[1] allowed considerable liberty of divorce, either
unilaterally for the commission of specified offences,[2] or by
mutual consent;[3] but there is nothing to indicate that the Church
condoned what the civil statutes permitted.[4] By the time that
Theodore's Penitential was becoming known, however, the
Frankish clergy had grown lax and demoralized, and were
naturally disposed to welcome so authoritative a warrant for
tolerating what the law sanctioned and public opinion approved.
This undoubtedly explains the concessions made by various
canons enacted in the year 756 by councils[5] held at Verberies

---

[1] After the invasions the system of 'personal law' prevailed, everyone being
judged according to the law of his own race. Later the various laws of the several
barbarian kingdoms were codified and promulgated in two forms: the *Lex
Barbara*, founded upon the original Teutonic law, and the *Lex Romana*. Of the
latter there were three main codes: the *Lex Romana Visigothorum* (506), the *Lex
Romana Burgundiorum* (506–516), and the *Edictum Theodorici* (? c. 500), which was
in force among the Italian Ostrogoths.

[2] See *Lex Rom. Burg.* xxi. 1, 2, 3 (*M.G.H., Leg.* iii, p. 609) and *Lex Rom.
Visigoth.* iii. 16: a husband may divorce his wife for adultery, poisoning, and
procuring, and a wife her husband for homicide, poisoning, and tomb-robbery
(cf. the legislation of Constantine, *Cod. Justin.* V. xvii. 7 [331], and of Honorius
and Theodosius II, *Cod. Theod.* III. xvi. 2 [421]; *Lex Barb. Visigoth.* III, vi. 2
(*M.G.H., Leg.*, sect. I [i], p. 167): a wife may divorce her husband for homosexual
practices, or if he forces her to commit adultery; *Lex Barb. Langobardorum*,
Rotharis, 195–197 (*M.G.H., Leg.* iv, p. 47): a wife became free to divorce her
husband if he attempted to kill her, if he accused her falsely of adultery or witchcraft, or if he permitted another man to do her violence; *Lex Barb. Lang.*,
Grimoald, 6 (*M.G.H., Leg.*, iv, p. 94): a wife gained her liberty of divorce if her
husband kept a concubine in his house. In the case of both Lombardic laws, the
wife secured a right to divorce through the husband's forfeiture of *mundium* or
authoritative guardianship over her.

[3] Roman law (as we have seen) allowed divorce by consent; so did the follow-
ing barbarian codes: *Pactus Alamannorum* (c. 600), iii. 2 (*M.G.H., Leg.* iii, p. 38);
Lex Gundabati (Burgundian, c. 517), xxxiv. 3 (*M.G.H., Leg.* iii, p. 546); also
Formula Marculfi, ii. 30 (*M.G.H., Leg.*, sect. V, p. 94); *Formula (Sirmondi)
Turonensis*, xix (ibid, p. 145); *Formula Andegavensis*, lvii (ibid, p. 24).

[4] On the contrary we have, for example, the action of Germanus of Paris, who
excommunicated King Charibert for an illicit consanguineous marriage, Gregory
of Tours, *Hist. Franc.* iv. 26.

[5] The convention at Verberies consisted of laity as well as ecclesiastics, and it
has been debated whether this assembly can properly be regarded as a Church
synod; its decrees, and those of Compiègne too, were enforced as royal capitu-
laries, and not as canons.

(Vernon-sur-Seine)[1] and at Compiègne,[2] specifying certain contingencies in which divorce and remarriage were permitted.[3] It is interesting to note that no reference was made in these canons to the repudiation of an adulterous wife, or to the innocent husband's right of remarriage; the omission may be due to the fact that a decision of the Council of Soissons in 744 was interpreted as bearing upon such cases—though actually its relevance is questionable.

Within the Frankish Church these measures were for some time regarded as authoritative, and they were also received elsewhere with a respect which procured for several of them a place in certain canonical collections and penitentials which enjoyed a considerable unofficial reputation.[4] The Carlovingian renaissance, however, marked the beginning of an attempt to reaffirm the traditional teaching; Charles the Great[5] and Louis the Pious[6] saw

---

[1] *Conc. Verner.* ii, v, ix–xii, xviii: in cases of incest between a married man and his step-daughter (ii and xi), stepmother (x), sister-in-law (xi, cf. xii), and wife's first cousin (xviii), conjugal life must cease and the wife may remarry; if a wife conspires against her husband's life, he may divorce her and remarry, but she may not remarry (v); if a man is compelled to emigrate and his wife refuses to accompany him, he may remarry when he settles, but she may not remarry (ix)— at the Council of Compiègne (*C. Compend.* xxi), however, remarriage was not allowed to the man in such a case.

[2] *Conc. Compend.* ix, xvi, xix: in the case of incest between a man's wife and his brother, the marriage must be dissolved and the husband may remarry (ix); when one partner, by mutual agreement, enters the monastic life, the other may remarry (xvi); if one partner contracts leprosy the union may be dissolved by mutual consent, and the other partner may remarry (xix).

[3] Dr Mortimer, op. cit., p. 110, n. 1, suggests that these canons are really, in effect, dispensations similar to that given, in his view, by Gregory II (see above, p. 105). This interpretation would certainly fit some of the cases covered by the canons, but it seems doubtful whether the intention of those who put them forth was actually to dispense so as to allow a modified polygamy; having regard to their context and probable origin, they are better regarded as relaxations of the Church's discipline.

[4] E.g., Regino of Prüm, *de eccl. discipl.* (906), ii.118, 124, 127, 213, 214, 216; Burchard of Worms, *Decretum* (1007–1014), vi. 41, ix. 54, xvii. 10, 11, 17 (he holds, however, that marriage is in principle indissoluble, *Decret.* ix. 62–64); *Petri Except. Leg. Rom.* (c. 1050), i. 37.

[5] See *capit. eccl.* (789), xliii, and *capit. miss.* (802), xx, forbidding remarriage.

[6] See *Conc. VI Paris.* (829), iii. 2, repeated in the document *De his quæ populo annuntianda sunt* (*M.G.H., Leg.* i, p. 345).

that steps were taken to secure the observance of a stricter law, erroneous penitentials were condemned and confiscated,[1] and new manuals of discipline were composed which clearly assert the indissolubility of marriage.[2] Not long afterwards the celebrated divorce case of Lothair II of Lorraine and his wife Teutberga[3] afforded Nicholas I an opportunity to declare Rome's uncompromising opposition to remarriage, regardless of provincial abberrations, and the pope was ably supported in his resistance to the king's demands by the distinguished Frankish bishop, Hincmar of Rheims. But the spirit of Theodore's Penitential and the decrees of Verberies and Compiègne continued to influence ecclesiastical practice in the Frankish and German Churches, principally through the *Decretum* of Burchard of Worms, until in the latter half of the eleventh century the reforming movement inspired by Hildebrand (Gregory VII) finally placed the whole question beyond controversy for the next four centuries. New collections of canons were made in which no exception was allowed to the universal prohibition of divorce and remarriage,[4] and Gratian's *Decretum* states with final authority the settled and unconditional adherence of the western Church to the principle that lawful and consummated Christian marriage is absolutely indissoluble.[5]

---

[1] *Conc. II Cabill.* (813), xxxviii; cf. *Capit. Rodolf. archiepisc. Bituric.* (850), xxxiii (in J. Mansi, *Sacrorum Conciliorum . . . Collectio* [Venice, 1759 ff.; facsimile reproduction, Paris and Leipzig, 1901 ff.], xiv, col. 948); *Conc. VI Paris.* (829), xxxii.

[2] E.g., Rabanus Maurus, *Lib. Pœnit.* iii, and *Pœnit.* xxi; Halitgar of Cambray, *de Pœnit.* iv. 10–11.

[3] For details of this case, see the account in G. H. Joyce, op. cit., pp. 351–354.

[4] See, e.g., the *Collectio LXXIV Titulorum* (c. 1050), the *Collectio* of Anselm of Lucca, and the *Decretum* (c. 1095) and the *Panormia* (c. 1100 ?) of Ivo of Chartres (who alters his citation of canons v and ix of Verberies so as to omit the clause permitting remarriage—see *Decret.* x. 169, and *Decret.* viii. 189 and *Pan.* vi. 91 respectively).

[5] The *vinculum* established by consummated marriage cannot be dissolved by imprisonment (*Decret.*, C. XXXIV, q. i, c. 1, 2), absence (C. XXXIV, q. i, c. 4), entry into monastic life (C. XXVII, q. ii, c. 19–23; C. XXXIII, q. v), slavery (dictum to C. XXIX, q. ii, c. 6), apostasy (C. XXVIII, q. ii, c. 2), or supervenient impotence (C. XXXII, q. vii, c. 25, 26), so as to allow of remarriage by one partner during the lifetime of the other. C. XXXII, q. vii contains many assertions of this doctrine, including that of c. 16: ". . . whosoever shall have put

The qualifying adjectives are significant, for it was during this period that the 'Pauline privilege' was first interpreted in the West as permitting not only the separation, but also the re-marriage of a wedded convert, the implication being that unions of non-Christians were not inherently indissoluble. Prior to the turn of the millennium, however, only Theodore's Penitential granted this concession;[1] Hincmar of Rheims, in line with ancient tradition, allowed divorce but did not hint at the possibility of any subsequent remarriage,[2] and the Council of Tribur in 895 plainly declared that pagan wedlock is permanent: "In baptism offences are abolished, but not lawful marriages."[3] But Hugh of St Victor and Robert Pullen introduced a new interpretation of St Paul's words. Relying upon a version of Ambrosiaster's text (the authorship of which he attributed to Gregory I), Hugh held that the *jus matrimonium* was cancelled, and the convert set at liberty to contract another union, wherever there was *injuria*[4] *Creatoris*; and this he defined very widely to include, not only the dismissal of the Christian spouse on God's account, but also the refusal of the Christian spouse to live with the pagan, even if the latter (though unwilling to embrace Christianity) was prepared to continue cohabitation.[5] This view, with which Robert Pullen concurred,[6] departed from the letter of the Apostle's permission both in sanctioning remarriage, and in allowing a convert to repudiate an infidel partner, and it failed to gain the full assent of the canonists and decretists.

Gratian maintained that when the unbeliever is willing to abide the union cannot be dissolved, but that the departure of the pagan partner severs the nuptial bond so as to permit the re-marriage of the convert;[7] and this was also the opinion of Peter

---

away his wife for the cause of fornication cannot marry another during his lifetime, and if he shall have so married, he is guilty of adultery."

[1] *Pœnit. Theod.* I. xii. 17, 18 (Haddan and Stubbs, op. cit., iii, p. 200).

[2] *De divort. Loth., interrog.* xxi (cf. xix).

[3] *Conc. Tribur.* (895), xxxix.

[4] Sic, not *contumelia*, as in the original text, see *de sacr.* II. ix. 11.

[5] *De sacr.* II. ix. 13.   [6] *Sent.* vii. 29.

[7] *Decret.*, C. XXVIII, q. ii and the dictum following.

Lombard.[1] Gratian's teaching was refined and expanded by Roland Bandinelli and by Innocent III, the final conclusion being that pagan and mixed marriages are not *per se* absolutely indissoluble, but that on conversion the Christian spouse, though free to separate, may only remarry if the unbeliever refuses cohabitation, blasphemes the Deity, or incites the convert to sin[2]—and with this decision both Aquinas[3] and Bonaventura[4] agreed. Thus one of Hugh's determinations was confirmed; but the other was reversed, making the operation of the privilege as now defined contingent, in effect, upon the caprice of the non-Christian partner, and so creating possibilities of hardship or malicious retaliation.

In developing a theological rationale for this novel conception of the *privilegium Paulinum* the mediævals had to take account of the tradition received from the early Church that the unions of infidels, though inferior to those of Christians in character and stability, were nevertheless in some sense indissoluble—a tradition apparently contradicted by the new doctrine. They readily allowed that marriage in the natural order was an estate invested by God at its institution with dignity and moral worth; and some went so far as to hold that it had then been constituted a sacrament[5] and endowed with a certain quality of permanence.[6] So binding did Innocent III regard non-Christian matrimony that he directed divorced converts to resume cohabitation with the spouses whom they had repudiated before baptism, whenever circumstances permitted such a course.[7] Both John Duns Scotus[8]

---

[1] *Sent.* IV. xxxix. 7.

[2] *Decret. Greg. IX* (the 'extravagantes', abbreviated 'X'), IV. xix. 7; the conversion of the unbelieving partner, however, before the Christian partner (having separated) effects a second union, estops the latter from remarriage, X, IV. xix. 8.   [3] *Summa Theol.* III Suppl., lxix. 5.

[4] *In Sent.* IV. xxxix. 2 q. I.   [5] Cf. Ivo of Chartres, *epist.* clv.

[6] Cf. Boniface VIII, *Decret. Sext.* III. xv. I; Aquinas, *Summa Theol.* III Suppl. lxvii I *sed contra*; John Duns Scotus, *Report. Paris.* XXXI. i. 11.

[7] X, IV. xix. 8; but certain glossarists maintained that in such cases the original union had been dissolved, and that the convert was in fact being required to enter into a new marriage with the former partner, see Richard of Middleton, *in Sent.* IV. xxxix, q. 2, a. 2, and the glosses cited by G. H. Joyce, op. cit., p. 479, n. 2.

[8] *In Sent.* IV. xxvi. I concl. I.

and Aquinas[1] considered that the natural law prescribed the immutability of wedlock on account of the good of the family and of society.[2] Furthermore, the latter argued that severance of the matrimonial bond is contrary to equity, since the divorced wife is at a disadvantage in procuring another husband; to social order, because woman needs man for governance no less than for procreation; and to the principle of friendship which attains its highest expression in marriage, for the closer and more intimate a relationship, the more stable and enduring it becomes.[3]

But if natural marriage possessed such a lasting character, how could its dissolution be justified, even *in favorem fidei?* Several solutions were proposed to this problem. Hugh of St Victor seems to have considered that the wedlock of non-Christians was in itself permanent, but that the conversion of one of the partners effected an ontological change in the whole relationship, as a result of which it lost its original indissolubility, thus permitting at least the remarriage of the convert.[4] Gratian, however, broke with the tradition in concluding that matrimony among infidels, although legitimate and subject to the obligations of the natural law, is not in any real sense indissoluble (*ratum*); but he adduces in support of this view an empirical argument which is hardly convincing—namely, that such matrimony is demonstrably not *firmum et inviolabile* because divorce is practised under heathen and Jewish law.[5] Aquinas reasons more cogently that while all marriage possesses a certain *vinculum* which conduces to permanence, that which is established between believers is stronger than that which is established between unbelievers; wherefore, since the

---

[1] *Summa Theol.* III Suppl., lxvii. 1.

[2] In *Summa c. Gent.* iii. 123, however, he so far modifies this view as to admit that since the making of provision for children is only a subordinate end of marriage, belonging to the secondary and not to the primary precepts of the natural law, dispensation from its obligations is not absolutely hindered.

[3] *Summa c. Gent.* iii. 123.

[4] *De sacr.* II. ix. 13; Watkins, however, with less probability, holds that Hugh regarded pagan marriage as essentially dissoluble, see op. cit., p. 553.

[5] *Decret.*, dictum to C. XXVIII, q. i, c. 17.

supervention of the stronger bond abolishes the weaker, the re-marriage of a convert automatically cancels his previous union.[1] But what entitles none but the convert to repudiate an existing lawful marriage in order to contract another? Panormitanus[2] answered that non-Christian wedlock, lacking the signification of Christ and the Church, admits of dispensation; this, it is true, cannot be effected by any human agency—but in one particular instance God himself, through St Paul, has granted such a concession in favour of those who, having abjured infidelity, desire to remarry 'in the Lord'.[3]

Thus the qualitative difference between natural and Christian marriage was finally ascribed to the latter's unique sacramental character. Augustine, it will be remembered, had already defined the indissolubility of wedlock in the City of God in terms of the moral obligation devolving upon the believing husband and wife in consequence of the *sacramentum* or symbolism of their union, and traces of this notion survived in mediæval thought.[4] During the twelfth and thirteenth centuries, however, a new theory of the nuptial sacrament gained favour, according to which Christian matrimony was not only a *signum rei sacræ*, but also (and pre-eminently) one of seven efficacious signs expressly instituted by Christ whereby sanctifying grace is conveyed to the faithful. This led to the development of a new conception of the matrimonial *vinculum*. Whereas Augustine had regarded it as an indefeasible bond between the spouses arising from the ethical imperative of the *sacramentum*, the Scholastic theologians envisaged it as a mystical and inviolable nexus attached to the

---

[1] *In Sent.* IV. xxxix, q. i, a. 5, ad. 1.

[2] Probably Nicholas de Tudeschis, Archbishop of Palermo, who died in 1445.

[3] *In X*, IV. xix. 7.

[4] Panormitanus, *in X*, IV. xix. 7, states that since Christian marriage prefigures the perpetual union between Christ and the Church, it *ought* to be indissoluble (*figuram debet esse indissolubile*); he clearly treats its permanence as an obligation resulting from its symbolism. Earlier, Ivo of Chartres had implied that a similar kind of obligation existed in the case of natural marriage, *epist.* clv: since God approved wedlock and willed it to be immutable, it *ought* not to be severed (*non debet disjungi*) by any human agency.

consummated marriages of the baptized by virtue of a divine ratification which invested them with unique metaphysical significance. Such unions not only exemplified the perpetual marriage of Christ with the Church but also partook of its very character; being likewise effected by grace, they acquired immediately and for ever the inviolability of their supernatural antitype. No longer was it held that matrimony *ought not* to be dissolved; it was simply asserted that it *could not* be dissolved. Thus a profound theological distinction was established between Christian and non-Christian wedlock, for the latter, not possessing the sacramental meaning which could only belong to the unions of believers, necessarily lacked their immutability.

This new interpretation of the Pauline privilege posed one final question: at precisely what point does the convert's original marriage cease to exist? The determinative text of Ambrosiaster suggested that anything which could be construed as *contumelia Creatoris* on the part of the pagan spouse sufficed to sever the bond. Some, however, considered that a formal sentence of divorce was necessary in order to release the believer; but in the end the opinion prevailed that the first union continued in being until it was terminated by the convert's remarriage. This solution was supported by the teaching of Aquinas that the stronger *vinculum* of Christian matrimony automatically cancels the weaker tie of natural wedlock, but no express decision on the point was formulated during the Middle Ages.

Circumstances compelled the mediæval divines to devote their attention first to the indissolubility of marriage and the problems connected therewith, but this was not the dominant issue of the time in the realm of sexual theology. More urgent and fundamental was the question of the formation of matrimony, for while its permanence was an established point of doctrine needing only elucidation and enforcement, the means by which the relationship came into existence had never been discussed during the patristic period. Various factors now combined to give it prominence and to make it a matter of cardinal importance for the Church.

Under the Roman system, marriage suits were at first handled exclusively by the civil courts, but legislation by the Christian emperors[1] brought them also within the cognizance of the bishop, to whom was conceded a quasi-judicial authority to hear and determine any cause (matrimonial or otherwise) which litigants might agree to submit to his arbitration. Upon the dissolution of the western Empire this episcopal prerogative seems to have fallen into abeyance, although the bishops were able to exercise a considerable measure of control over the marital affairs of the faithful through the enactments of provincial and other synods, and the barbarian sovereigns not infrequently enforced the spiritual sanctions of the canons by the penalties of the secular law. During the eighth and ninth centuries ecclesiastical jurisdiction was gradually recovered, especially by the Frankish Church through the growing practice of submitting matrimonial cases to the bishop's synod for decision; but there was no means of compelling the execution of any sentence pronounced until statutes passed by councils at Meaux in 845 and at Kiersy in 858[2] assured the support of the civil power to enforce the episcopal verdicts.

The enfeeblement of the royal authority in France, the concession by the Emperor to certain north Italian prelates of the dignity and function of count, and in general the political conditions which produced the feudal system, all hastened the recognition of the competence of the ecclesiastical courts in most western lands except those where the Lombard law prevailed—and these, too, fell into line before the end of the eleventh century. Only in England was the establishment of the new system delayed—and the situation there was exceptional. Under the Anglo-Saxons, spiritual and temporal jurisdiction were not clearly distinguished, and offences against the canons and the civil laws alike were tried by a common tribunal on which both the bishop and the secular

---

[1] Cf. enactments of Arcadius and Honorius (398), and of Honorius and Theodosius II (408), *Cod. Justin.* I. iv. 7, 8 (confirming an earlier constitution of Constantine).

[2] See *Conc. Meld.* (845), lxxi, and *M.G.H., Leg.*, Sect. II (ii), p. 431.

magistrates sat. Yet it seems to have been felt that matrimonial affairs were peculiarly an ecclesiastical concern, for even in pre-Conquest days certain cases of adultery had been assigned to the episcopal tribunal for judgement.[1] When William I separated the secular from the spiritual judicature[2] there was nothing to hinder the Church from gaining control of marriage in England as it had already done on the Continent, and by the beginning of the twelfth century its authority was virtually uncontested.[3]

Having achieved exclusive jurisdiction in matrimonial causes, the Church was inevitably confronted with the problem of the formation of marriage, for as a necessary preliminary to adjudication it must be established in every case that a valid union exists. What, then, constitutes marriage? In attempting to answer this question, the theologians and canonists were faced at the outset by the confusion resulting from the currency in western Christendom of two different systems of law, the Roman and the Teutonic each of which had its own theory and practice governing the formation no less than the dissolution of wedlock. According to Roman jurisprudence, consent alone sufficed to create the union, but among the Germanic peoples the bond seems to have been effected by the transmission of *mundium* or authoritative guardianship of the bride from her father to her husband; and even when an exchange of consent took place, it usually had to be confirmed by some act such as the taking of an oath or the payment of *arrhæ*. In a matter of such critical importance it was essential that uniformity should prevail in Christendom, and the Church showed no hesitation in preferring the Roman to the Teutonic conception of the formation of marriage; but legislative unification was not immediately achieved, and vestiges of the Germanic

---

[1] See the *Laws of Canute*, liv and lv, relating to cases where an accusation of adultery is made by a husband against his wife, or where a married man has coitus with a maid-servant.

[2] See the Ordinance printed in W. Stubbs, *Select Charters* (Oxford, 1948), pp. 99–100.

[3] See F. Pollock and F. W. Maitland, *The History of the English Law before the time of Edward I* (Cambridge, 2 vols., 1898), i, p. 106; ii, pp. 364 ff.

system survived for several centuries as part of local customary law.

The attainment of legal uniformity was aided by the work of the canonists in developing and codifying the ecclesiastical law—a task which received a great impetus from the revival of interest in Roman jurisprudence at the end of the eleventh century. Searching in libraries for ancient texts to sanction the reform of abuses in the Church, scholars discovered the half-forgotten compilations of Justinian, and found therein numerous references to marriage. These served, among other things, to strengthen the growing conviction that the constitutive element in matrimony is essentially the consent exchanged by the parties; but this did not immediately become an accepted principle of the canon law, mainly because the simple theory of the Roman-Byzantine code had first to be adapted to, and then interpreted in terms of, the Christian conception of marriage as a sacrament—a task which was complicated by the fact that at this time the notion of sacrament was itself beginning to change.

Indeed, the sacramental character of Christian matrimony proved at first something of an embarrassment to those who were concerned to define the formation of marriage. It had never been disputed that the unions of the baptized acquired their signification of Christ and the Church and their consequent indissolubility only as a result of consummation. This could not but suggest that the efficient cause of Christian wedlock is not consent alone, but consent and coitus—with the corollary that coitus is intrinsic to marriage. But mediæval theologians, as inheritors of the patristic view of sex, were generally reluctant to attribute such importance to consummation as to allow that it could determine the existence no less than the symbolism of matrimony. On the other hand, the Church was committed to the doctrine that the one-flesh alone possesses the sign of the supernatural marriage; and it was commonly held that the *sacramentum* belonged to the union from the moment of its inauguration—either actually or proleptically. Hence the question, What makes a marriage? was seen to be ultimately dependent upon a prior question—namely, Is coitus an essential or merely an accessory element in marriage? Thus the problem of physical sexuality which had troubled the Fathers now confronted the mediævals in a new form.

Upon the essentiality of coitus Christian opinion had been divided. St Paul plainly taught that it is the specific act by means of which man and woman become one-flesh,[1] and that it must be regarded as a normal and not unimportant feature of married life;[2] and the general tenor of Scripture endorses this typically Hebraic view. Clement of Alexandria voiced the common conviction of the early Church in his dictum that the *skopos* of marriage is procreation, and its *telos* the virtuous education of children[3]—a conviction which implies no disapproval at least of the minimal incidence of coitus necessary to produce a family. Although the more ascetically inclined among the Fathers expressed approval of nuptial continence, the patristic approach to matrimony is governed (even if sometimes regretfully) by the assumption that in the average marriage there will be cohabitation and physical relations. Indeed, so firmly rooted was the acceptance of coitus as essential to normal wedlock that certain Doctors considered the term 'wife' to be misapplied to Mary in the Gospels, since her union with Joseph (by this time regarded by Christian piety as unconsummated) could not be described as a true marriage.[4]

The only dissentient opinion is that of Augustine, whose consideration of sin and sexuality led him to a conclusion more consonant with jurisprudence than with theology. He held that man and woman can be *conjuges* without the *commixtio corporum*,[5] and that Joseph and Mary, therefore, were in every material sense

---

[1] I Cor. vi. 16.

[2] I Cor. vii. 3-5.

[3] *Pæd.* ii. 10; cf. *strom.* ii. 23.

[4] Cf. Ambrose, *de inst. virg.* i. 7; John Chrysostom, *in Matt.*, *hom.* v. 5; Jerome, *in Matt.* i. 17. The first two argue that if Mary had known the *usus* of the marriage bed, and had truly possessed the status of wife, our Lord would not have committed her to the care of St John, but to that of her husband and rightful protector, Joseph.

[5] Cf. *c. Jul. Pelag.* v. 16; *de consensu evang.* ii. 1 [2].

husband and wife, having exchanged a valid consent to matrimony.[1] But while the consensus of the Fathers (with the exception of Augustine) is that coitus is integral to the life of marriage, its part in the formation of marriage is not mentioned—unless, perhaps, an uncertain and indirect allusion is to be seen in a statement by Ambrose implying that the nuptial relationship is established by the *copula carnalis*.[2] Elsewhere, however, he declares that the *pactio conjugalis*, and not the *defloratio virginitatis*, effects the union,[3] meaning that the sexual act alone and without consent does not constitute matrimony; there must be both pact and coitus.[4]

During the early Middle Ages conflicting views are found. Isidore of Seville[5] in the seventh century and Nicholas I[6] in the ninth both treat consent as the efficient cause of marriage, while Hincmar of Rheims maintains the necessity for consummation. In an opinion on the case of a certain Stephen, an Aquitanian nobleman, the latter cites an anonymous saying (attributed to Augustine) to the effect that the unconsummated union lacks the symbolism of Christ and the Church,[7] and in support of this he appeals to a letter of Leo I, interpreting the pope's reference to

---

[1] *De nupt. et concup.* i. 12 [11]; cf. *serm.* li. 13.

[2] *Epist.* lx (*ad Patern.*), 1: "If anyone has coitus with a woman betrothed and handed over to him, he calls it marriage"—such seems to be the sense of the passage.·   [3] *De inst. virg.* i. 6.

[4] This interpretation is supported by Gratian's dictum on the text, see *Decret.* C. XXVII, q. ii, c. 45.

[5] *Etymol.* ix. 7: "The name of *conjuges* is most correctly given to people in view of the initial plighting of their troth, even though *concubitus conjugalis* has not taken place."

[6] *Resp. ad consult. Bulgar.* iii: "Let the consent of those whose unions are in question [i.e., by the Greeks, because of formal or ceremonial irregularities] be sufficient by itself, as the [civil] laws prescribe. If this consent is alone wanting in marriage, all other celebrations, and even coitus itself, are rendered void, as the great doctor John Chrysostom bears witness when he says: 'Consent (*voluntas*), not coitus, makes a marriage.'" This dictum is erroneously ascribed to Chrysostom, and occurs in the anonymous work, *opus imperfect. in Matt.*, hom. xxxii, generally printed with his works.

[7] *Epist.* xxii, *de nupt. Steph.*: "Marriage lacks the symbolism of Christ and the Church if it is not treated as marriage (*si se [nuptiæ] nuptialiter non utuntur*), that is, if there is no *commixtio sexuum*."

the "nuptial mystery" as an allusion to coitus.[1] Hincmar does not explain the precise connexion between consent and consummation, though undoubtedly he presupposes some kind of link between them, and various constructions have been placed upon his arguments. He seems to imply that the consent in the wedding ceremony establishes certain mutual obligations which cannot be repudiated (though in exceptional circumstances, such as the husband's impotence, they may be cancelled by ecclesiastical dispensation), whereas the consummation completes and cements the union so as to render it indissoluble. On the other hand, however, it has been suggested that he anticipated the canonists of Bologna by distinguishing between 'marriage', which consent suffices to effect, and the sacrament of matrimony, for which consummation is required.[2] No final conclusion upon his views appears to be possible from the evidence available.

Ivo of Chartres proposed an intermediate theory which enjoyed some success, but his thought and terminology are far from clear and consistent. Thus he deduced from Genesis that true marriage is initiated by coitus,[3] yet he held also that a sworn engagement is

---

[1] See Leo I, *epist.* clxvii (*ad Rustic.*), 3 (resp. ad q. 4). The pope was asked whether a quasi-conjugal union between a free man and a slave should be reckoned as a marriage. He replied that since the Bride of Christ is not a bond-woman, but free (Gal. iv. 31), the symbolism (*nuptiale mysterium*) of Christian matrimony cannot be realized when a free man is joined to a woman of servile status: "Since marriage was so constituted from the beginning that, over and above the union of the sexes (*præter sexuum conjunctionem*) it should have the symbolism of Christ and the Church, that woman is undoubtedly not married, in whom it is stated that the nuptial mystery is not present." At a later date this text was converted into an assertion that consummation is necessary, by the addition of the word '*non*'. It then read: ". . . marriage was so constituted that apart from the union of the sexes (= coitus) it should *not* have the symbolism . . . etc." In more or less this form (but attributed to Augustine) it is cited by Ivo of Chartres, *Panorm.* vi. 22, and passed into Gratian's *Decretum*, C. XXVII, q. ii, c. 16. Anselm of Laon, in his treatise on marriage, quotes a variant of this forgery: "That woman cannot be regarded as married, of whom it is stated that she has not had coitus (*commixtio sexuum*)."

[2] See *de divort. Loth.*, *interrog.* xiii; also the discussion in G. H. Joyce, op. cit., p. 56 and n. 1.

[3] *Epist.* xcix.

irrevocable, and that matrimony therefore acquires its indissolubility before consummation.[1] His ultimate conclusion was that consent (*desponsatio* or *pactum conjugale*) inaugurates a relationship which is in a certain sense marriage,[2] and possesses its own signification,[3] but that until consummation has occurred the union lacks the fulness of matrimony.[4] Coitus gives to consent a necessary completion—though how, Ivo does not explain.

The treatises and collections of 'sentences' belonging to the first half of the twelfth century reflect the hesitations and divergent views of the canonists and theologians, and show that the Church was still only groping towards a solution of its problem. Some continued to emphasize the importance of coitus as integral to the perfection of matrimony;[5] others, among whom it is not surprising to find that Jerome of his age, Peter Damiani,[6] resolutely rejected the idea that consummation can either effect or perfect a marriage. There is evidence, too, of growing interest in a question which was later to become one of some consequence —namely, the exact definition of the nature of matrimonial consent. Anselm of Laon proposed and William of Champeaux developed a distinction between *fides pactionis*, which can be broken (though penance must be done), and *fides conjugii*, which is indestructible;[7] and William's pupil Abelard likewise differentiated between two kinds of pledge which he termed *fœderatio de conjugio contrahendo* and *fœderatio conjugii*.[8] These early analyses of consent already contained the germ of the more precise discrimination made by Peter Lombard between *sponsalia de futuro* and *sponsalia de præsenti* which was greatly to assist elucidation of the

---

[1] *Epist.* xcix, cxlvii, clxvii, clxi, ccxlvi.

[2] *Pan.* vi 14 (rubric); vi. 15; consummation is unnecessary, *Pan.* vi. 16, 29.

[3] Cf. *epist.* ccxlii: consent effects a union of souls and wills no less important than that of the bodies; coitus alone does not realize the symbolism of Christ and the Church, for the one-flesh relationship so established lacks charity (until consent has been exchanged?).

[4] *Pan.* vi. 23.

[5] Cf. *Sent. Mag. A.* (? Alger of Liège), lx; Honorius of Autun, *elucidarium*, ii. 16.

[6] *Opusc.* xli: *de temp. celebr. nupt.*

[7] See William of Champeaux, *Sent.*, § *de conjugiis.*

[8] *Epit. theol. Chr.* xxxi.

formation of marriage by clarifying the difference between betrothal and matrimony proper. About this time too, it should be noted that the famous maxim of Ulpian, *nuptias non concubitus sed consensus facit* ("consent, not coitus, makes marriage"),[1] which eventually won universal acceptance as a concise expression of the Church's doctrine, made its first appearance in a theological context, in the Roman collection entitled *Polycarpus*.[2]

Pre-eminent among the writers of this period who devoted themselves to matrimonial questions was the Parisian theologian, Hugh of St Victor, from whom we have the first full and general discussion of the theology of marriage in Christian literature. Hugh emphatically rejected the *copula* theory; in his view, wedlock is simply a lawful society of man and woman established by free, spontaneous consent expressive of a present intention[3]—and he carefully distinguished such consent from the sworn engagement or *desponsatio* of betrothal, which to him is only a *pactio et promissio futuri consensus*:[4] "to promise and to perform are two different things". Consummation, on the other hand, he held to be unnecessary for the validity of marriage; it is merely an accompaniment to the conjugal pact, *comes et non effector conjugii, officium et non vinculum*—indeed, continence actually increases the merit of the spouses and the truth and sanctity of their union.[5] Had Hugh taken his teaching to a logical conclusion, he could hardly have escaped a breach with the hitherto unchallenged tradition of Christendom that the consummated marriage alone possesses the nuptial *sacramentum*.[6] He avoided any such radical

---

[1] *Cod. Just., Dig.* L. xvii. 30; cf. *nov.* xxii. 3.

[2] It occurs also in a singular form in the *Cæsaraugustana* collection: *nuptias non concubitus sed affectus facit*—the *affectus* being the will of the parties to comport themselves in everything as husband and wife.

[3] *De beat. Mariæ virginitate*, i; cf. *de sacr.* II. xi. 4.

[4] *De sacr.* II. xi. 5.

[5] *De sacr.* II. xi. 4; *de b. Mar. virg.* i.

[6] Logically, too, his view would have allowed homosexual 'marriage', for it defined matrimony as a relationship effected by consent and consisting in *societas*; offspring he regarded as belonging, not to marriage but to the *officium conjugii*. Against this possibility Hugh could only argue that Gen. ii. 24 envisages only the association of male and female, *de b. Mar. virg.* iv.

departure, however, by propounding a theory of the double signification of matrimony which allowed him to affirm that "there cannot be the symbolism of Christ and the Church where there has been no *commercium carnale*", and at the same time to maintain that consent establishes forthwith a state of sacramental marriage to which consummation can add nothing essential.[1]

The basic proposition of this theory was that coitus and consent represent two entirely different spiritual realities. Coitus certainly effects the *magnum sacramentum* of Christ and the Church, but it is nevertheless only a sacrament derived from the use of marriage (*sacramentum conjugalis officii*) and invested with a carnal symbolism. Consent, however, is an expression of the inward bond of mutual affection (*fœdus dilectionis*) between man and woman which belongs to the essence (as opposed to the use) of matrimony; therefore it effects the greater sacrament (*sacramentum majus*) which signifies the love of God for the soul, and constitutes the true sacrament of marriage (*sacramentum conjugii*).[2] Hugh even attempted a further refinement of his theory by describing the greater as the interior, and the lesser as the exterior sacrament,[3] but his primary distinction had the most influence upon the thought of the Church in the debate which was shortly to begin.

By the middle of the twelfth century considerable progress had been made towards an understanding of the formation of marriage; the nature of the problem itself had been clarified, and the main issues had been defined. Already it was evident that a sharp cleavage of opinion existed between the canonists and the theologians. The former, guided by their texts and more appreciative, perhaps, of practical considerations and of the realities of life, maintained that coitus is essential, either to the establishment or to the perfection of matrimony. The latter, less dependent upon authorities and more inclined to speculation, anxious to emphasize the sacramental significance of wedlock, and disposed to regard the example of Joseph and Mary as determinative of the whole

---

[1] *De sacr.* II. xi. 5.

[2] *De b. Mar. virg.* i, iv.

[3] *De sacr.* II. xi. 8.

question, resolutely upheld the consensual view. Both conceptions were now to be fully and systematically formulated, the one by Gratian in his *Decretum*, the other by Peter Lombard in the *Book of the Sentences*.

Gratian, following his usual plan, listed the relevant authorities on both sides and examined in detail the various points under discussion. He then attempted to reconcile them by proposing yet another distinction—this time, between two forms of nuptial relationship. He did not deny that consent is the efficient cause of marriage,[1] but he went on to distinguish between the union so realized, and that which comes into existence as a result of consummation; the first he termed *conjugium initiatum* and the second *conjugium ratum*[2]—and he concluded that the latter alone has the properties of indissolubility and sacrament which belong to the *matrimonium perfectum*.[3]

Peter Lombard, on the contrary, not only adhered to the view that marriage is effected solely by mutual consent,[4] but claimed for the consensual no less than for the carnal relationship the symbolism of Christ and the Church. Thus he developed a stage further the theory of a double sacramentalism in matrimony which had already been advanced by Hugh of St Victor. From consent, Peter held, there ensues a union which signifies the joining of Christ to the Church in charity, and from consummation a union representing that whereby, through the Incarnation, the members of Christ's Body are joined to their Head.[5] Strictly speaking, these are not separate sacraments, but one sacrament exhibited in two complementary aspects—first, as established by

---

[1] Exposition to C. XXVII, q. ii; cf. dictum to C. XXIX, q. i.

[2] Dictum following C. XXVII, q. ii, c. 34: ". . . marriage is initiated by espousal (*desponsatio*) and completed by consummation (*commistio*). Hence, between *sponsus* and *sponsa* there is marriage, but it is *conjugium initiatum*; between those who have consummated their union (*copulatos*), however, there is a *conjugium ratum*."

[3] See the texts cited in C. XXVII, q. ii, cc. 35–39, and the dictum to c. 39; cf. C. XXXII, q. vii: *matrimonium ratum et consummatum* is indissoluble.

[4] *Sent*. IV. xxvi. 6; xxvii. 2, 3; xxviii. 2.

[5] *Sent*. IV. xxvi. 7.

consent so as to lack nothing intrinsic to its symbolism, and secondly, as given a more complete signification by coitus.

This dual conception of the nuptial *sacramentum* reinforced Peter's contention that by mutual consent everything essential to Christian marriage is realized, but the theologians seem generally to have preferred Hugh's treatment of the matter, according to which consent was accorded its own characteristic symbolism. In one respect, however, they were indebted to Peter. William of Champeaux, as we have seen, had already perceived the difference between *fides pactionis* and *fides conjugii*,[1] and Peter developed this idea by formulating an important distinction between the different kinds of promise made at betrothal and at marriage, thus clarifying considerably the problems connected with the formation of the bond. In both ceremonies, he said, the parties consent to take one another as husband and wife, but in the one their pledge has a future reference—it is *consensus per verba de futuro*, while in the other it has a present reference, being *per verba de præsenti*;[2] and only the latter form of *desponsatio* can bind upon the couple the *vinculum* of indissoluble wedlock.

The two great syntheses of Gratian and of Peter Lombard immediately rendered all preceding works more or less obsolete; but they themselves were far from perfect and soon began likewise to grow out of date as new material accumulated. Numerous commentators annotated the *Decretum* and expounded the *Liber Sententiarum*, while the great lawyer-popes of the late twelfth and early thirteenth centuries enlarged the Church's case law by their decretals, many decisions from which were gathered into the five collections known as the *Compilations*, whence they passed eventually into the official *Compilatio Decretalium* of Gregory IX. In these various sources there can be traced the course of the controversy which now developed around the question of the

---

[1] *Sent.*, § *de conjugiis*; see above, p. 122.

[2] *Sent.* IV, xxvii. 9. Innocent II, about this time, employs a similar differentiation in one of his decretals, see *Compil. I*, IV. i. 10, and G. H. Joyce, op. cit., p. 63, n. 2.

formation of marriage—a controversy in which the initial protagonists were the canonists of Bologna, who supported Gratian,
and the dialecticians of Paris, who maintained the arguments of
Hugh of St Victor and Peter Lombard.

Most of the decretists and theologians were content to work
along the lines laid down by their respective masters, with the
result that they contributed little to the debate but elaborations of
the doctrines already propounded in the two syntheses. Two
writers, however, displayed some originality, and deserve mention. Gandulph, an eclectic, attempted in his *Sententiæ* to harmonize the conflicting tenets of the schools by accepting 'present'
consent as the efficient cause of marriage,[1] but insisting that
consummation is necessary in order to perfect the union thus
established.[2] He also proposed a useful distinction by suggesting
that coitus produces the symbolism of Christ and the Church only
when it is directed to procreation or to the payment of the
debitum carnalis—the latter, in his view, signifying the obedience
due to Christ by the Church.

Vacarius, on the other hand, following a hint by the disciple of
Gratian who composed the *Summa Coloniensis*, ignored the main
points at issue in the current dispute, and propounded in his
Summa de Matrimonio the theory that marriage really comes into
being at the moment when bridegroom and bride actually
commit themselves one to another as husband and wife. This
traditio constitutes them one-flesh by a *vinculum juris*, and their
union is then valid (*ratum*) and, even if they are infidels, sacramental of Christ and the Church. This conception of its formation
brought wedlock into the same category as the conveyance of
property, but it had obvious affinities with Teutonic custom, and
it also recalls the stress laid by the Romans upon the *deductio in
domum*. Maitland saw in it "a civilian's protest against the mess
that [was] being made of the law of marriage by canonists and
divines"[3]—which probably explains why Vacarius seems to have
found favour with neither side.

---

[1] *Sent.,* §§ 235, 238, 241.   [2] *Sent.,* § 241.
[3] F. W. Maitland, *Collected Papers* (Cambridge, 1911), iii. p. 101.

The controversies of the schools had undoubtedly brought chaos into the administration of the ecclesiastical law. In Italy the courts accepted the principles of Gratian, and in France those of Peter Lombard, with the result that a marriage might be set aside in Rome on grounds which would not be admitted in Paris. Nearly three centuries of argument seemed to have brought Christendom no nearer the unification of its matrimonial legislation and juridical practice, but merely to have substituted one problem for another, and a solution was imperative. It emerged in the end, not from the disputes of the scholars, but from the day-to-day legal activities of the popes as they pronounced judgement upon the marriage cases submitted to them for final decision. Rome was the highest court of appeal and the fount of the Church's legislative authority, and it was fortunate at this juncture that several of the incumbents of the Holy See (notably Alexander III and Innocent III) were lawyers of more than ordinary ability who had received a thorough training as canonists. The Papacy alone proved competent to restrain the exuberant logic of the schools and curb their more extravagant speculations, and between the legists and the theologians it stood for common sense and aimed at a workable compromise.

The problem was still to determine the precise moment at which the bond of marriage is forged, and to its solution the most important individual contribution was made by the eminent canonist Roland Bandinelli, who in 1159 ascended the papal throne as Alexander III. He adopted and clarified Peter Lombard's distinction between *desponsatio de futuro* and *desponsatio de præsenti*, but he seems for some time to have been uncertain as to the conditions upon which the validity of consent depends. However, after holding at first that either the presence of a priest or a notary,[1] or the observance of the customary solemnities[2] is required, he eventually reached the conclusion that nothing more

---

[1] X, IV, iv. 3.
[2] X, IV. xvi. 2.

is needed to establish a marriage than the exchange of lawful mutual consent in words of the present.[1]

Nevertheless, Alexander did not reject Gratian's teaching that matrimony, though effected by consent, is completed and rendered indissoluble only by coitus;[2] nor did he deny the traditional doctrine that the consummated union alone signifies Christ and the Church—though by implication he did not disallow the possibility that another symbolism might be attached to the unconsummated marriage.[3] Indeed, he took the principles of the school of Bologna to their logical conclusion. On the one hand, he declared that coitus following betrothal is sufficient to create a valid matrimonial union;[4] on the other, he acted on the assumption that where there had been no consummation, there was no indissolubility. Hence dispensation from the effects of consent which had not been sealed by coitus was, in his view, permissible when either spouse (with or without the agreement of the other) elected to retire into the monastic life,[5] or when equity demanded redress in cases such as those of *affinitas superveniens*—that is to say, affinity resulting from coitus with a relative of the partner in marriage.[6]

---

[1] *Compil. I*, IV. iv. 6 [8]: "*ego te recipio in meum, et ego te recipio in meam*" is sufficient to declare the intention of the parties.

[2] *Compil. I*, IV. i. 2: "Man and woman are not one-flesh unless they have united in coitus (*nisi cohæserint copula maritali*)."

[3] X, I. xxi. 5: "The marriage which is not consummated by *commixtione corporum* cannot claim to represent that marriage which was contracted between Christ and the Church by the mystery of the Incarnation"—which does not exclude the theory advanced by Hugh of St Victor that the unconsummated union signifies the union of God with the soul.

[4] X, IV. v. 3, a decision followed by Innocent III (X, IV. v. 6) and Gregory IX (X, IV. i. 30). The theory was that coitus between the betrothed was equivalent to consent *per verba de præsenti*; and Gregory insisted that this presumption was *juris et de jure*—that is, one which did not admit of rebuttal. The effect of coitus in such cases depended, of course, upon the existence of a genuine interior consent to conjugal union.

[5] X, III. xxxii. 2, 7. This must sometimes have been the only way in which a woman could escape from a repulsive marriage of convenience.

[6] See X, IV. xiii. 2, where a man had refrained from consummating his marriage but had had coitus with his mother-in-law; Alexander judged that if the matter were public knowledge, the man must do penance but might then receive a dispensation to remarry, while the wife regained her liberty.

Alexander's successors completed the work which he had begun. First, it was necessary to modify the conclusions which he had reached concerning the permanence of an unconsummated marriage; while Celestine III confirmed his decision in the case of solemn religious profession,[1] Innocent III disallowed it in regard to supervenient affinity.[2] There then remained the relatively easier task of defining the nature and conditions of valid consent; it might, for instance, be conditional so long as the stipulations imposed did not affect the essence of marriage,[3] but it must be lucid,[4] free from error,[5] and from any threat of violence.[6] It could be exchanged by duly authorized proxies in the absence of the parties,[7] and might be expressed in signs[8] as well as in words; the former, however, must be intelligible and unambiguous, and the latter must be interpreted according to their common sense as significant of a sincere intention.[9] Finally, it was not necessary for valid matrimony that consent should have been

---

[1] Cf. X, III. xxxii. 14.   [2] Cf. X, IV. xiii. 6: the marriage must stand.

[3] Thus even immoral or illicit conditions, if not contrary to the essence of marriage, did not invalidate consent, X, IV. v. 7 (Gregory IX); it could be stipulated that one partner should pay the other a sum of money, X, IV. v. 3 (Alexander III), or that the marriage should depend upon the consent of a third person, X, IV. v. 5 (Urban III) and 6 (Innocent III). But if conditions were imposed which were contrary to the essence of marriage, the consent was void, X, IV. v. 7 (Gregory IX). Conditional marriage became marriage pure and simple upon fulfilment of the conditions, or the exchange of *consensus de præsenti* (i.e., without any stipulation attached), or engagement in coitus, X, IV. v. 5, 6 (see above).

[4] X, IV. i. 24, madness renders consent void.

[5] A marriage became voidable through *error conditionis*, such as ignorance on the part of one party concerning the servile status of the other, X, IV. ix. 2 (Alexander III), 3 (Urban III), and 4 (Innocent III).

[6] But a marriage effected under duress might be confirmed by the establishment or the continuance of free conjugal relationships, X, IV. i. 28 (Honorius III); ix. 2 (Alexander III); to render the union invalid, the fear must be such as would cause even a firm man (*vir constans*) to falter, X, IV. i. 15 (Alexander III).

[7] X, III. xxxii. 14 (Innocent III); if the principal withdrew his consent prior to the marriage, the ceremony is invalid, see *Decret. Sext.* I. xix. 9 (Boniface VIII).

[8] X, IV. i. 23 (Innocent III); this would be necessary in the case of the deaf or dumb.

[9] X, IV. i. 7 (Alexander III)—and cf. Peter Lombard, *Sent.* IV. xxvii, and Aquinas, *in Sent.* IV. xxvii. 1, art. 2, q. 1a. 4.

exchanged *in facie Ecclesiæ* or with the usual solemnities or formalities,[1] though all were agreed in condemning clandestine alliances. Thus a second marriage contracted openly after entering into a secret union was branded as sinful,[2] and despite its ratification *in foro externo*, was not allowed to continue. Both the ecclesiastical and the civil authorities[3] took stringent measures to prevent clandestinity, which had become a serious problem in mediæval times, but the simple solution of declaring such unions invalid was never contemplated—in fact, it was excluded by the new theory of the nuptial *sacramentum* which has already been mentioned. When two competent persons exchanged free mutual consent *de præsenti*, it was held that they had satisfied the conditions which (so it was believed) Christ himself had laid down as necessary to the sacrament of marriage, so that the Church was powerless to prevent the realization of the sacrament; consequently the secret union became indissoluble and fully symbolic.

The Church's acceptance of the principle, *consensus facit matrimonium*, and its endorsement of the corollary that unconsummated marriage is in all essential respects true and complete marriage, established beyond controversy a conclusion towards which Christian thought had been gradually moving for many centuries—namely, that coitus (though a normal feature of marital life) is merely an accessory, and not an intrinsic element in matrimony itself. Consequently the one-flesh *henosis* was at last displaced from its proper centrality in the theological conception of sexual relationship, and in its place there was set a purely consensual union—an innovation quite alien to the teaching and the spirit of the Scriptures. Not even the recognition that consummation is necessary in order to give wedlock its indissolubility

---

[1] *Compil. I*, IV. vi. 6, 8; *Compil. II*, IV. iii. 1; X, IV. iii. 2 (Alexander III); but in one case Alexander ordered the Bishop of Padua to excommunicate the offenders, *Compil. I*, IV. iv.

[2] Hugh of St Victor, *de sacr.* II. xi. 6, and Peter Lombard, *Sent.* IV. xxviii, held otherwise, but later opinion was against them: cf. Aquinas, *in Sent.* IV. xxxviii, *expos. text.*: "It is better for a man to die excommunicate [on account of the sin of his second (open) marriage] than married to her who is not his wife."

[3] For details, see G. H. Joyce, op. cit., pp. 112–115.

and the symbolism of Christ and the Church could compensate for this radical change of emphasis, for the *matrimonium ratum* effected by consent had also its sacramental character and even, in the view of some theologians, its own signification of the super-natural marriage; indeed, it was by comparison the *majus sacramentum*, and could be annulled only by solemn religious profession or (so some canonists thought) by papal dispensation.[1] What factors were responsible for this particular conclusion to the dispute concerning the formation of matrimony?

The obvious and immediate reason for the triumph of the consensual theory was that, better than any other, it served to provide the ecclesiastical courts with a simple and effective test by which the existence, and sometimes the validity, of a marriage could be ascertained. Having acquired and consolidated its exclusive jurisdiction in matrimonial causes, it was imperative that the Church should devise some such method of verification, for mediæval unions were not infrequently formed in circumstances which could later give rise to genuine or feigned doubt concerning their integrity. In an age when child betrothal and marriage were common and clandestinity a scandal, when two legal systems had to be reconciled and local customs proved inconveniently persistent, when many years might separate the exchange of 'future' and 'present' consent, and when alliances were often dictated by expediency and sometimes contracted under duress, the only practicable criterion of the truth of wedlock was lawful, valid, free, and mutual *consensus per verba de præsenti*. Consent before witnesses had an indisputable evidential value greatly superior to coitus, which could not readily be proved or disproved, especially where there had been collusion or malicious allegations of misconduct. Thus legal requirements and the promotion of justice helped to establish the principle, *consensus facit matrimonium*, as a doctrine of the Church—though it should not be forgotten that Christians had long been familiar

---

[1] The greatest of the schoolmen, however, disapproved of the dissolution of marriage by papal dispensation; it is now allowed, nevertheless, by the canon law of the Roman Church for a "just cause", *Cod. Jur. Can.* (1917), § 1119.

with it as an axiom of Roman jurisprudence, and appear to have accepted it without question as determinative of marriage *in foro externo.*

But underlying the forensic factor there was an emotional attitude favourable to any conception of wedlock which minimized the importance of coitus. Though happily free from the absurd and violent prejudice which disfigures some patristic writing, the work of the Scholastics nevertheless reveals in a slighter degree the same fundamental antipathy or indifference to the carnal intercourse of the sexes that is displayed in the literature of the early Church, and it is evident that they found the sexual act a source of theological embarrassment. Gregory I, it will be recalled, had so far qualified the teaching of Augustine as to locate the evil imputed to coitus in the pleasure concomitant with the act, rather than in the concupiscence by which (so it was alleged) men and women were impelled to copulate. During the early Middle Ages interest in the question died down, but revived again under the stimulus of the controversy over the efficient cause of marriage, and led to a subsidiary debate which grew somewhat lively towards the end of the twelfth century.

Hugh of Pisa shows that the pleasurable emotions which were reprehensible to Gregory still continued to offend the mediæval theologian,[1] and the tradition seems to have persisted that coitus is shameful and can never take place without sin.[2] So suspicious of any carnal delectation were some moralists that they counselled a rule of abstinence which, if strictly observed, would have condemned devout married Christians to an almost perpetual continence;[3] but more liberal divines such as the Cistercian Peter

---

[1] See, e.g., *in Sent.* IV. xxxii, q. 2, c. 4 *ad verbum non datur*: "There is a certain passion (*fervor*), a certain pleasure (*voluptas*), which is always sinful . . . hence it is expressly held that coitus can never occur without sin"—though in the case of union for legitimate ends, the fault is of course only venial.

[2] Cf. Robert Pullen, *Sent.* vii. 30; Innocent III, *De contemptu mundi,* i. 4; *Comm. in Ps. sept. pænit.,* on Ps. iv.

[3] Thus, abstinence was recommended during the seasons of fasting, and on certain festivals; and also on Thursday in memory of Christ's arrest, on Friday in memory of his death, on Saturday in honour of the Virgin Mary, on Sunday in honour of the Resurrection and on Monday in commemoration of the departed.

the Chanter in his *Summa de Sacramentis*, and Robert de Courson in his treatise *De Matrimonio*, attacked the rigorists as semi-heretics who aimed to destroy marriage by indirect means, and even went so far as to propose that all lawful coitus should be regarded as meritorious. Their teaching fortunately proved more acceptable than that of the moralists whom they had denounced, and it was affirmed and elaborated by the great Schoolmen who brought the debate virtually to an end by the middle of the thirteenth century.

Peter Lombard had already perceived that the key to a solution of the problem of coitus lay in the distinction between sin and evil. He rejected the idea that venereal intercourse is sinful, either in itself or in its accompanying pleasure—thus repudiating the theories of Augustine and of Gregory;[1] but he maintained never-theless that it always contains an element of evil, the origin and nature of which, however, he did not explain.[2] Albert the Great carried the discussion a stage further with the important sugges-tion that the evil in coitus has nothing to do with venereal pleasure, which would actually have been more intense in Paradise;[3] in his view it was due to fallen Man's weakness of reason, in consequence of which he cannot now enjoy any pleasure without momentarily losing sight of the first Good.[4] This theory found in coital experience a delectation which is evil, not because of its intensity, but because it effectively distracts the mind from contemplation of God; such, thought Albert, was one of the ways in which we were punished for the original transgression of our race.

Doubtless it was supposed that a few free Tuesdays or Wednesdays would occur during the lifetime of a married couple! Much earlier, similar prohibitions are found. B. Thorpe, *Ancient Laws and Institutes of England* (London, 2 vols., 1840), ii, p. 81, cites Regino of Prüm, *de eccl. discipl.* i. 329: the married must abstain for 40 days before Easter, Pentecost, and Christmas; each Sunday night, and on Wednesdays and Fridays; and from the manifestation of conception until after the child's birth; also i. 331: every man to abstain from his wife for 7, 5, or 3 days before Communion.

[1] He explains that Gregory intended only to impute blame to coitus which was non-procreative in intention.   [2] *Sent.* IV. xxvi. 8–9.

[3] Aquinas makes the same point, *Summa Theol.* I. xcviii. 2 ad 3.

[4] *In Sent.* IV. xxvi. 7.

Aquinas both developed and qualified this idea. He denied that coitus has been so corrupted by the Fall that it now contains no trace of goodness, for since a good God created Man's bodily nature, nothing appertaining to that nature, or to which it properly inclines, can be wholly or universally bad; hence it is impossible that the sexual act "should be so entirely unlawful (*illicitus*) that nothing conducive to virtue can be found therein".[1] Indeed, it is sufficiently excused by the matrimonial blessings,[2] and is meritorious when performed by married persons in a state of grace, either with the motive of justice (the discharge of the marriage debt), or with that of religion (the procreation of children to worship God). Nevertheless, while the *bona matrimonii* exempt the coition of husband and wife from blame, they cannot (according to Aquinas) relieve it of the intrinsic taint of evil by which every act of venereal intercourse is now supposedly contaminated—though this taint, it is important to note, is one, not of *moral* evil, but only of evil *proceeding from* moral evil.

To understand this subtle distinction it is necessary to bear in mind the high value attached by the Scholastics to reason. Just as Augustine, influenced by Platonic dualism, had viewed with suspicion anything calculated to deflect the mind from its calm contemplation of the eternal, so Aquinas, equally inspired by Aristotle's doctrine of *sōphrosunē* or the 'golden mean', found an element of evil in all that disturbed the exercise of the rational faculty.[3] Both alike saw in the intensity of venereal emotion and the culminating orgasm of the sexual act a potent and effective hindrance to Man's pursuit of the good life, and both attributed this defect in human nature to the Fall; but they advanced slightly different theories to account for its particular character and mode of operation.

The bishop of Hippo taught that the transgression of Adam and Eve had caused an inordinate and compulsive desire for self-

---

[1] *In Sent.* IV. xxvi, q. 1, a. 3, *sol.*

[2] *Summa Theol.* III Suppl. xlix. 4 *resp.*, 5 *resp.*; cf. *Summa c. Gent.* iii. 124: coitus is not sinful if it is according to reason, for it is the natural end of certain bodily members and a necessary condition of preserving the species.

[3] *Summa Theol.*, III Suppl. xlix. 1 *resp.*, referring to Aristotle, *ethic.* vii. 11.

satisfaction which he termed concupiscence, and which found its typical and least resistible expression in the venereal impulse. The Angelic Doctor, however, argued that the effect of the first sin was rather to be seen in a weakening of the will which is revealed most strikingly in Man's impotence to bring his sexual emotions and actions under rational control. Hence coitus is now impossible without the ardent desire and mental agitation which mark the rebellion of concupiscence against volition, and cause a "fettering of the reason" (*ligamentum rationis*)[1] such as would never have been experienced in the state of innocence, when carnal intercourse would have been attended by greater sensual delight while remaining always amenable to the bidding and governance of the will.[2] In other words, Aquinas located the seat of coital evil, not in the act itself, nor in concupiscence, nor yet in venereal pleasure, but in what he regarded as the inevitable irrationality of the *copula* in fallen humanity; but for this defect husband and wife could not be held morally responsible—it was simply a punishment which had come to rest upon the race in consequence of its initial rebellion against the Creator.

Although, in the final determination of the Schoolmen, coital pleasure was not sinful *per se*, it could not be pursued for its own sake without sin; if it was sought within marriage the offence was always venial, and if outside marriage, it was mortal.[3] The act itself, however, was acquitted of fault if the sensual enjoyment was accepted as something incidental to generation, to the payment of the nuptial *debitum*, or to the recollection of the sacramental blessing of marriage (*rememoratio boni sacramenti*)—that is, of its symbolism and attendant grace; and it was only a venial sin if the seeking of pleasure was simply by way of a remedy against concupiscence.[4] But the Scholastics required moderation above all else, even in things lawful, and referred approvingly[5] to a saying of Xystus, an unknown philosopher twice quoted by

---

[1] Ibid, II–I, xxxiv. 1 ad 1.   [2] Ibid, I. xcviii. 2 ad 3.

[3] Ibid, III Suppl. xlix. 6 resp.

[4] See Albert, *in Sent*. IV. xxvi, a. 12.

[5] Cf. Peter Lombard, *Sent*. IV. xxxi. 6; Albert, *in Sent*. IV. xxvi, a. 8; and cf. Aquinas, *Summa Theol*. III Suppl. xlix. 6 *resp*.

Jerome:[1] "He who loves his own wife too ardently is an adult-erer."[2] The man thus denounced is not, apparently, he who entertains too warm an affection for his wife, but he whose *amor* (that is, his desire for venereal pleasure—the word here does not mean 'love', as we understand it) is so vehement that it impels him to abandon the restraint which pays careful regard to the *bona matrimonii*, and incites him to treat her as if she were merely, like any other woman, a means of lustful gratification.

The thought of the Schoolmen upon physical sexuality shows a great advance upon that of the early Fathers in its realism and comparative moderation, but beneath the subtle distinctions with which it was elaborated we still perceive something of the old emotional antipathy. Although coitus is no longer branded as sinful, and is acknowledged to be meritorious when performed according to reason and in furtherance of the ends of matrimony, it is regarded nevertheless as belonging only to the secondary perfection, or operation, of marriage, and not to its first perfec-tion or essence[3]—a differentiation which over-simplifies the very complex nature of the nuptial *henosis*, and of existence as one-flesh. While the matrimonial consent was held to be an implicit (but not explicit) consent to coitus,[4] it was also maintained that marriage only requires the ability for the sexual act, and not its performance,[5] since it neither establishes nor perfects the union;[6] even the capacity for generation is unnecessary, for the aged, who can copulate but cannot produce offspring, are notwithstanding competent to marry.[7] The spirit of primitive syneisaktism survives in the view of Peter Lombard[8] and of Aquinas[9] that wedlock without carnal intercourse is holier; and the latter's justification of clerical celibacy on the ground that continence not

---

[1] *Adv. Jov.* i. 49; *comm. in Ezech.* vi. 18.

[2] Xystus, *Sent.* ccxxxi: "*Omnis ardentior amator propriæ uxoris adulter est*".

[3] Aquinas, *Summa Theol.* III Suppl. xlii. 4 ad 2.

[4] Ibid, III Suppl. xlviii. 1 *resp.*   [5] Ibid, III Suppl. lviii. 1 ad 1.

[6] Ibid, III Suppl. li. 1 ad 4; coitus following betrothal (*consensus de futuro*), however, effects marriage, unless there is evidence of fraud, ibid, xlvi. 2 *resp.*; cf. xli. 4.   [7] Ibid, III Suppl. lviii. 1 ad 3.   [8] *Sent.* IV. xxvi. 7.

[9] *Summa Theol.* III Suppl. xlii. 4 *sed contra*; cf. III. xxix. 2.

only encourages the devotion of the mind to divine things,[1] but also ensures the bodily purity of those who have to handle the sacred vessels,[2] shows that even Scholastic rationalism was not proof against the influence of vestiges of sexual taboo which had survived from an earlier age.

The attitude of mediæval theologians to coitus undoubtedly created a climate of opinion favourable to the consent theory of the formation of marriage, but it also had a more direct and obvious influence upon the development of this doctrine. It is evident to the student of their writings upon matrimony that one of the problems which exercised the divines of the Middle Ages was that of giving, to quote Maitland, "the name of marriage to such union as the Christian legend would allow St Joseph to contract with the Blessed Virgin".[3] Religious sentiment shrank from the thought that the mother of Jesus, after his birth, had endured the contamination of carnal intercourse or the degrading pleasures of the conjugal bed. Since at least the beginning of the fifth century the perpetual virginity of Mary had been something nearer a dogma than a pious opinion,[4] and propriety had long represented her spouse as an aged man whose rôle was that of guardian rather than husband. Yet their union must needs be depicted as normal and complete in all material respects, and the principle, *consensus facit matrimonium*, conveyed an assurance that it was indubitably a true marriage. Augustine had allayed any doubt as to Mary's title to the style of 'wife' by invoking the consensual theory of Roman matrimonial jurisprudence, and Aquinas affirmed without hesitation that she and Joseph had "consented to the nuptial bond, but not expressly to the carnal

---

[1] *Summa c. Gent.* iii. 137.

[2] *Summa Theol.* III Suppl. liii. 3 *resp.*, and ad 1.

[3] F. W. Maitland, op. cit., iii, p. 91.

[4] *Summa Theol.* III. xxix. 2 *resp.*; an account of the development of this notion, with a critical examination, will be found in the excursus on the term, 'Brethren of the Lord', in J. B. Mayor, *The Epistle of St James* (London, 3rd ed., 1913), pp. vi–lv. It should be unnecessary to observe that the perpetual virginity of Mary and the virgin birth of Christ are two quite different matters; the credal statement: "Born of the Virgin Mary", affirms the latter, but bears no reference to the former.

bond, save on the condition that it was pleasing to God".[1] Thus their marriage, as conceived by the devout imagination, became the pattern to which all Christian marriage must conform; consequently it was inevitable that consent should be regarded as the essential, and consummation an incidental, element in the formation of matrimony.

A third reason for the triumph of the consent theory was that concurrent with the dispute concerning the efficient cause of marriage there went the development and application to wedlock of the new conception of sacrament. According to Augustine, the *sacramentum* of marriage consists in its symbolism of certain mysteries of the Christian faith, and chiefly that of the union between Christ and the Church. Hugh of St Victor and Peter Lombard, as we have seen, elaborated and extended this idea, with particular reference to the double sacramentalism of wedlock by which both consent and consummation were given their appropriate signification. But the latter part of the twelfth century saw the emergence of a distinction between sacred symbols as such, and those special symbols (or 'sacraments' technically so-called) which were deemed to be efficient causes of the grace which they signified. There was at first some uncertainty as to the number of such *sacramenta*, but it was eventually fixed at seven, each of which was embodied in an ecclesiastical rite having its proper 'sacramental moment' identified with the bestowal of the grace symbolized—whence the rites themselves were also termed sacraments.

Among these seven rites marriage was included—mainly, it seems, on the strength of its symbolism and its traditional status as a *sacramentum*, for it was regarded at first as an exception to the general rule that sacraments cause grace, and the question of its supernatural efficacy was for some time in debate. Some, including Peter Lombard,[2] Alexander of Hales,[3] and Peter the Chanter[4] followed the earlier opinion of Abelard,[5] and treated matrimony

---

[1] *Summa Theol.* III. xxix. 2 *resp.*; cf. III Suppl. xlii. 4 ad 2.
[2] *Sent.* IV. ii.   [3] *Summa Theol.* II. clxvii. 4 art. 1.
[4] *Verb. Abbreviatum*, xxxvii.   [5] *Epit. Theol.* xxxi.

solely as a remedy against sin. Others, and among them certain
canonists of the school of Bologna,[1] argued that in view of the
pecuniary conditions commonly attached to the contract, the
supposition that marriage is a sacrament in the new sense might
often involve the parties in a transaction which was virtually
simoniacal, since grace would be bought and sold; and inevitably
there arose the question: How can the initiation of a relationship
which authorizes and encourages acts stained with turpitude be
attended and blessed by the divine favour? On the other hand,
there were those who maintained that wedlock is nevertheless
something more than a mere symbol or a necessary remedy—
that it does in fact possess the virtues of the reality which it
signifies; but even they were uncertain as to the nature of the
assistance bestowed from above upon the couple.

Various intermediate solutions were proposed: that marriage
conserves, but does not confer grace;[2] that the gift is one, not of
sanctifying but of remedial grace;[3] that sanctifying grace is
probably given.[4] But theological opinion in general eventually
endorsed the mature conclusion of Aquinas that sanctifying grace
is certainly bestowed in matrimony,[5] and this determination,
which had been anticipated in a decretal of Lucius III in 1184,
received official confirmation in the *Decretum pro Armenis* issued
by the council of Florence in 1439. Nevertheless, there was still a
little uncertainty about the matter, and the debate continued to
smoulder. Peter John Olivi was required in 1283, and again in
1311, to defend his assertion that marriage is not a sacrament in
the same sense as the other six *sacramenta*; Hugh of Strasbourg, at
the end of the thirteenth century, maintained that it is simply a
preservative medicine against concupiscence; Duns Scotus
hesitated to allow that matrimony is truly an efficacious sign when

---

[1] See G. H. Joyce, op. cit., p. 173, with citations from the glossarist Bernard of
Parma and the decretist Hostiensis.

[2] Cf. William of Auxerre, quoted by Joyce, op. cit., p. 174, n. 4; also Alan of
Lille, *Theol. Reg.* cxiv; *Summa de fid. cath.* i. 65.

[3] Cf. Bonaventura, *in Sent.* IV. xxvi. 2, q. 2.

[4] Cf. Aquinas, *in Sent.* IV. xxvi. 2, art. 3; this was also the view of Albert.

[5] *Summa c. Gent.* iv. 78.

virginity is admittedly not; and Durand of St Pourcain continued to uphold the doubts of the canonists. But the verdict of the mediæval Church was never seriously challenged; the rite of matrimony was acknowledged as one by means of which grace is conveyed to the contracting parties, and only one question remained to be settled—by what agency and at what moment is the supernatural gift bestowed?

This, at least, occasioned no great controversy. A few thought that the nuptial benediction was the source of grace,[1] but it was soon established that this is a ceremonial accessory, and is not essential to the efficacy of the union; the ministers of the sacrament of marriage are the bride and bridegroom themselves, and the form of the sacrament is their reciprocal consent.[2] The fact that the 'sacramental moment' in the nuptial rite was thus identified with the mutual exchange of *consensus per verba de præsenti* undoubtedly facilitated recognition of the latter as the moment at which the marriage was believed to come into existence.

The final condition for the establishment of a *matrimonium ratum* was that the union should be lawful, and in this connexion reference must be made to those impediments to marriage which were termed diriment—that is, prohibitive or destructive of the nuptial bond itself. Such impediments derived partly from the natural law, partly from divine law, and partly from the theological principles or the rules of ecclesiastical discipline by which matrimony is defined or regulated. They are sufficiently (but not fully) stated in a verse by the canonist Tancred which is quoted, with several omissions, in the Supplement to the *Summa Theologica*.[3] Certain of the impediments enumerated therein have already been mentioned—namely, those arising from defective consent due to fear, violence, or fraud, or to error regarding the

---

[1] Cf. William of Auvergne, *de sacr. matr.* vi, ix; the *gloss. ord.* on X, V. iii. 9, *cum in eccles.*; Bonaventura, *in Sent.* IV. xxvi, a. 2, q. 2.

[2] Cf. Aquinas, *in Sent.* IV. xxvi. 2, art. 1, ad 1.

[3] See l. 1 *resp.*; the full list is given in Watkins, op. cit., p. 136, and in *The Church and the Law of Nullity of Marriage* (London, 1955), pp. 14 and 57.

identity or condition of one of the contracting parties. Of the rest, that of an already subsistent union (*ligamen*) followed naturally from the Church's prohibition of remarriage after divorce, and of polygamy in either form; that of impotence, from the fact that incapacity for coitus prevented the realization of the *magnum sacramentum* and the generation of offspring; and that of age, both from the two last-mentioned factors, and from the necessity for a valid consent. The common good required that abduction (*raptus*), crime (*crimen*),[1] and gross disregard of public propriety (*honestas*)[2] should hinder marriage; but the impediments of holy order (*ordo*), solemn religious profession (*votum*), and even difference of faith (*cultus disparitas*) were simply prohibitions of a disciplinary kind. Tancred's list also included clandestinity, which was not (as we have seen) considered by the canonists as in itself an invalidation of matrimony.

More complicated in theory and application than most of these impediments was that of consanguinity. Its basis lay in the prohibitions of Leviticus against the union of close relatives,[3] but it was not long before the rule: "None of you shall approach to any that is near of kin to him, to uncover their nakedness",[4] was interpreted as warranting a greater strictness than the Mosaic law had required. Augustine had forbidden the marriage of first cousins,[5] and Ambrose that of uncle and niece,[6] though neither

---

[1] *Crimen* in this context denoted adultery of a spouse with a third party, which precluded any subsequent marriage between them, especially if there had been attached to the illicit connexion a promise to murder or attempt the murder of the innocent spouse.

[2] The impediment of *honestas* arose when betrothal between two persons set up between one of them and a third person a relationship which transgressed the limits of affinity; or in any other case of marriage involving an offence against public decency or decorum.

[3] A man might not marry his mother (xviii. 7), sister (xviii. 9; xx. 17; cf. Deut. xxvii. 22), father's sister (xviii. 12; xx. 19), mother's sister (xviii. 13; xx. 19), son's daughter (xviii. 10), daughter's daughter (xviii. 10).

[4] Lev. xviii. 6.

[5] *De civ. Dei*, xv. 16. Such unions were forbidden in 384, but were again allowed in the East by Arcadius in 405 (*Cod. Justin.* V. iv. 19), while Honorius mitigated the penalties applicable in the West. Justinian made the marriage of first cousins permissible by *civil* law throughout the Empire (*Inst.* I. x. 4; *Cod.* V. iv. 19).

[6] *Epist.* lx; Ambrose appears to have thought that the marriage of first cousins

is condemned by the Sinaitic code, and subsequent legislation widened considerably the range of interdiction. Gradually the Scriptural impediments were extended until the prohibited degrees of relationship coincided with those governing the rules of inheritance, with the result that none more closely akin than third cousins might marry. Such persons, according to the Roman system of computation, were related in the eighth degree, but the Germans, by their different method of calculation, would have related them in the fourth degree—a divergence which renders the enactments of certain councils somewhat ambiguous. At first there was considerable diversity in practice, but eventually the Germanic reckoning replaced the Roman, and the prohibition of marriage was extended to sixth cousinship, or the seventh degree. The inconveniences of such a rigorous law, however, proved to be so great that during the eleventh and twelfth centuries the demand for some relaxation grew ever more insistent until, in 1215, Innocent III limited the impediment from consanguinity to relationships within the fourth degree of the *computatio canonica* or Germanic system of calculation.[1]

The thirteenth and fourteenth centuries saw further discussion of the matter, in the course of which a necessary distinction was drawn between the Levitical prohibitions and the extensions thereof which had been multiplied by ecclesiastical legislation. At first it was held that the Scriptural impediments were part of the divine law, and were consequently immutable and of universal obligation, while the others admitted of dispensation by the spiritual power under which they had been constituted. But Duns Scotus[2] contended that this view gave to the Mosaic code a sanction which it did not inherently possess; it was not, he argued, binding *per se* upon Christians, and any force conceded to it under the new Dispensation derived from the authority of the Church by which its provisions had been endorsed. Eventually the con-

---

was prohibited by the *lex divina*.

[1] See X, IV. xiv. 8; and for a more detailed discussion, with authorities, G. H. Joyce, op. cit., pp. 511–522.

[2] *In Sent*. IV. xl. 1.

clusion was reached that the natural law, as apprehended by the enlightened reason, only forbids marriage between those most closely bound by ties of blood—a category restricted by the earlier Schoolmen to parent and child, and enlarged by their successors to include brother and sister also; but that the unions of near kinsfolk were to be deprecated as inordinate and should be restrained by ecclesiastical law, under which impediments might rightly be constituted and enforced for the well-being of the Christian society. In practice, the prohibition of marriages within the fourth degree remained.

Even more involved than the impediments due to consanguinity were those held to arise from affinity, or relationship determined otherwise than by the tie of blood. Here, too, the interdictions of the Levitical code[1] governed the Church's law and practice—though again, ecclesiastical legislation soon went beyond that of Moses in its strictness, particularly in the prohibition of marriage with a deceased wife's sister,[2] and with the widow of a maternal uncle.[3] Originally the intention underlying the impediment of affinity seems to have been the avoidance of domestic discord by precluding the possibility of wedlock between persons likely to be members of the same household; but the prohibitions were necessarily somewhat arbitrary and variable in accordance with social custom, and it was inevitable sooner or later that a determining principle should be sought, and a more logical system evolved.

The seventh century saw the emergence of the principle,[4] as

---

[1] A man might not marry his step-mother (Lev. xviii. 8; xx. 11; Deut. xxii. 30; xxvii. 20), wife's mother (Lev. xviii. 17; xx. 14; Deut. xxvii. 23), son's wife (Lev. xviii. 15; xx. 12), wife's daughter (Lev. xviii. 17), wife's son's daughter (Lev. xviii. 17), wife's daughter's daughter (Lev. xviii. 17), father's brother's wife (Lev. xviii. 14), brother's wife (Lev. xviii. 16; xx. 21), or step-sister (Lev. xviii. 11).

[2] Cf. *Conc. Illib.* (305–306), lxi; Basil of Cæsarea, *epist.* clx; Pope Damasus, *epist. ad Gallos Episcopos.*

[3] Cf. *Conc. I Aurelian.* (511), xviii; *C. Epaun.* (517), xxx; *C. I Arvern.* (535), xii; *C. III Aurelian.* (538), x; *C. II Turon.* (567); *C. Autiss.* (578), xxvii, xxxii, which also forbids, *inter alia*, marriage with a deceased wife's sister.

[4] It had already been hinted at by Basil, *epist.* clx, and by Augustine, *c. Faust.*

the opinion began to gain currency that affinity is consequent upon coitus. Because a man and woman thereby become one-flesh, it was argued that carnal intercourse immediately and automatically unites their respective kindred in a quasi-consanguineous relationship which inhibits marriage to the same extent as true consanguinity.[1] To such relationships it was natural to apply the rules already controlling the alliances between persons of the same blood, with the result that matrimony was prohibited within the seventh degree of affinity, reckoned according to the *computatio canonica*.[2]

But the application of the principle did not stop here. St Paul had expressly taught that union in one-flesh could arise otherwise than from the consummating coitus of husband and wife, and this suggested that affinity is established, not only by lawful coitus, but also *ex copula illicita*. Certain canons enacted by the councils of Verberies[3] and Compiègne[4] show that this idea had won acceptance in the Frankish Church before the close of the eighth century; it received further support from one of the pseudo-Isidorian decretals,[5] and by the end of the ninth century seems to have been generally recognized north of the Alps. Italian canonists, however, strongly influenced by Roman jurisprudence which did not acknowledge affinity *ex copula illicita*, were slower to adopt it, but during the eleventh century they too fell into line, and Gratian and his successors[6] entertained no doubt as to its soundness.

Manich. xxii. 61, but it is first expressed clearly by Gregory I, *epist.* xi. 64 *resp. ad sext. interrog.*, and in Theodore's Penitential, II. xii. 27.

[1] Cf. *Conc. Rom.* (721), ix; Pope Zacharias, *epist. ad Pipin.* (747), see *M.G.H.*, *Epist.* iii, p. 485; *C. Mogunt.* (847), xxx; *C. Vormat.* (868), xxxii=*Decret. Grat.*, C. XXXV, q. ii, c. 18.

[2] Cf. Benedict Levita, *Capit. Coll.*, add. iv. 2; Hincmar of Rheims, *de nupt. Steph.*; *Conc. Bituric.* (1031), xvii, xviii; *C. Rotomag.* (1072), xiv; Gratian, *Decret.*, C. XXXV, q. ii, c. 7 tit.; Peter Lombard, *Sent.* IV. xli.

[3] *Conc. Vermer.* (756), ii, x, xi, xii, xviii.   [4] *Conc. Compend.* (756), vii, x, xiv, xv.

[5] See Gratian, *Decret.*, C. XXXV, q. ii, and q. iii, c. 10 citing a passage attributed to Gregory I, from *epist. ad Felicem, Messan. civ. episc.*

[6] Cf. Roland, *Summa Rol.* XXXV. 2, 3; Tancred, *Summa de Matr.* xxix *de affinitate et ejus generibus*; Alexander III, X, IV. xiii; Bernard of Pavia, *Summa Decret.* IV. xiv *de consang. et affin.*, 16.

The new theory afforded wide scope for the exercise of scholastic ingenuity, and from the simple affinity caused by the coitus of husband and wife the canonists proceeded to evolve two further kinds—*affinitas secundi generis*, linking a man with any person married to a relative of his wife;[1] and *affinitas tertii generis*, linking a man with any person married to the relict of a relative of his wife.[2] Furthermore, if a widow remarried, the children of her second union were regarded as *affines* to the relatives of her first husband.[3] Finally, a distinction was drawn between 'occult' affinity and affinity of a 'public' or 'notorious' sort; the former, having in one case existed for ten years, might be dealt with by the imposition of penance, but the latter required the separation of the couple and perpetual continence on the part of the offender.[4] It is doubtful whether some of the more far-fetched of these impediments were ever recognized in practice, and they did not remain in force for long. Innocent III, in 1215, greatly reduced their number[5] to give the canon law on affinity a narrower range even than that of the Roman law,[6] and further simplifications were effected by Gregory IX;[7] but despite these reforms, the principle of *affinitas ex copula illicita* remained throughout the Middle Ages to hinder reasonable freedom of marriage.

We have not yet done with affinity, however, for another form of this impediment, impossible outside Christendom and unknown to the early Church, still further complicated mediæval matrimony. It was first made the subject of legislation when Justinian forbade wedlock between a man and the woman (whether bond or free) for whom he had stood sponsor at baptism;[8] and this enactment originated the complex fabric of law by which spiritual affinity (*cognatio, affinitas, proximitas,* or

---

[1] Cf. Bernard of Pavia, *Summa Decret.* IV. xiv. 12; also Gratian, *Decret.*, C. XXXV, q. ii, c. 12 citing a spurious decretal attributed to Julius I (337–352).

[2] Cf. Bernard of Pavia, as previous note; also Gratian, *Decret.*, C. XXXV, q. ii, c. 22 citing a decretal of Pascal II (1099–1118).

[3] Cf. Bernard of Pavia, *Summa Decret.* IV. xv; Gratian, *Decret.*, C. XXXV, q. x, c. 1, 2, 4.

[4] See a decretal of Alexander III in *Compil. I*, IV. xiii. 4.   [5] X, IV. xiv. 8.

[6] Cf. *Dig.* XXIII. ii. 15; XXXVIII. x. 4 § 6–7.

[7] X, IV. xiv. 9.   [8] *Cod.* V, iv. 26.

germanitas spiritualis) was defined and regulated.[1] This impediment arose directly from the notion that sponsorship at Christian initiation sets up a new metaphysical relationship between the godparent and the baptized which is not only comparable to, but also higher than, that of natural parenthood.[2] Here again we perceive the consequence of a defective attitude to physical sexuality; Augustine had contrasted generation and its carnal pleasure with regeneration and its spiritual delectation,[3] and it was soon felt that the sinful associations of the former disqualified a person for the godly privilege of the latter—on which account parents were eventually prohibited from assuming the responsibilities which (as Augustine himself had declared) were theirs by obligation and right.

The theory that a quasi-parental relationship is contracted at the font inevitably gave rise to the idea that sponsorship is the cause of an affinity which prevents the marriage of a godparent, either with the person baptized, or with one of his parents;[4] and it was not long before the multiplication of impediments due to *cognatio spiritualis* began to produce a set of prohibitions as complicated as that derived from consanguinity or from affinity proper. Since more than one sponsor was customary at baptism, it was held that co-sponsorship (*compaternitas* or *commaternitas*) created a bar to marriage between a child's otherwise unrelated godparents; while if the sponsors in question were already husband and wife, they were required to cease cohabitation or at least to live continently together, since their joint discharge of the sponsorial office had caused an affinity which superseded the natural bond of marriage, and rendered their coitus incestuous.[5] The full range of the interdictions arising from spiritual relationship is indicated by a canon of the council of Prague in 1346, which recognizes no less than ten such connexions as constituting

---

[1] For a detailed study of this subject, see my *Sponsors at Baptism and Confirmation* (London, 1952), pp. 79–94.

[2] Cf. *Conc. in Trullo* (692), liii, for the earliest mention of this idea.

[3] *Epist.* xcviii. 1.

[4] *Conc. I Mogunt.* '813), lv, is perhaps the first enactment on the latter point.

[5] First mentioned by Walafrid Strabo, *de rebus eccl.*, xxvi.

prohibitive or diriment impediments to wedlock.[1] Moreover, precisely the same effect was attributed to confirmation as to baptism, resulting in ten further obstructions to matrimony;[2] and it will be observed that even the minister of these sacraments became involved in the mesh of affinities arising from their performance.

Although baptism could, in an emergency, be given by a layman, it was normally administered by the priest, while confirmation belonged to the episcopal office; the application, therefore, of the impediment of *cognatio spiritualis* both to the ministers of these rites and to their wives and children is proof in itself of the relative ineffectiveness of the rule of clerical celibacy during the greater part of the Middle Ages, and of its infringement by all grades of the sacerdotal hierarchy. During the four centuries following the pontificate of Gregory I, councils and synods enacted against the marriage or concubinage of the clergy with a monotonous regularity which testifies both to the extent of the so-called abuse, and to the apparent impotence or disinclination of the ecclesiastical authorities to prevent or contain it. Yet the abandonment of a principle so congenial to the mediæval religious mind as the celibacy of the sacred ministry was unthinkable, and the tenth century saw the beginning of a campaign during which the papacy strove by every possible means to reduce a reluctant and often rebellious clergy to obedient continence.

A renewal of the spirit of asceticism, due in the first instance partly to the Cluniac revival and partly to the reformatory zeal of Peter Damiani, found expression in a series of enactments

---

[1] *Conc. Pragen.* (1346), *de cog. spirit.* = *Conc. Pragen.* (1355), li; the relationships are as follows: between the baptized and the sponsor, the sponsor's spouse, and the sponsor's children; between the baptized and the minister of baptism, the minister's spouse, and the minister's children; and between the parents of the baptized and the sponsor, the sponsor's spouse, the minister of baptism, and the minister's spouse.

[2] The impediments arising from confirmation are parallel to those, enumerated in the previous note, arising from baptism, and involve the person confirmed, his parents, the sponsor and his or her spouse and children, and the minister of confirmation and his wife and children.

reasserting the old prohibitions and penalizing all who should infringe them;[1] clerics were ordered to banish their wives or concubines and thereafter to remain separated from women, while the children of their unfortunate consorts thus turned adrift were declared to be slaves of the Church. Nicholas II followed up these initial measures in 1059 with a new sanction of unprecedented severity and Donatistical spirit forbidding Christians to attend Mass celebrated by any priest known to keep in his dwelling a concubine or *mulier subintroducta*[2]—a step which aroused fierce resistance, and marked the commencement of a bitter struggle between the rigorists and the advocates of clerical liberty. The conflict produced its anti-pope in the person of Cadalus, bishop of Parma, who claimed the title of Honorius II, and to whose cause the city of Milan rallied. There the strife was particularly intense and protracted, for the Milanese clergy had from of old enjoyed the privilege of marriage, and papal attempts to suppress it were regarded as a blow to civic prestige and independence; but the question of celibacy became inextricably entangled with various causes of municipal faction which were assiduously fomented by pope and emperor for their own ends, and eventually rigorism triumphed.

The papal victory was due largely to the unfaltering resolution and energy of Hildebrand who, as Gregory VII, made clerical celibacy part of his programme for the reformation of the Church.[3] The enforcement of discipline, however, proved difficult and was attended with but partial success, despite the assiduity with which the pope urged its application, and the stringent measures by which he sought to prosecute his aims, even to the extent of absolving the laity from their obedience to incontinent prelates and priests.[4] Many of the clergy continued to resist the demands of authority, and a further effort to reduce them

---

[1] See *Conc. Ticinen.* (1022), i, ii, iii, iv; *Conc. Bituric.* (1031), v, vi, viii, x; *Conc. Mogunt.* (1049); *Conc. Rom.* (1051).

[2] *Conc. Rom.* (1059), iii.

[3] *Conc. Rom.* (1074), xi, xiii ; Gregory VII, *epist. extrav.* iv.

[4] See *epist. extrav.* xiv, which also applied to simonaical clerics.

to submission resulted in legislation in 1123 by the first Lateran council under Calixtus II, and in 1139 by the second Lateran council under Innocent II, which was calculated to undermine the sanctity and permanence of the matrimonial bond itself. Hitherto, while the monastics and persons in holy orders had been commanded to put away their wives, the reality of their wedlock had never been called in question; now, however, not only were offenders again required to conform to the laws of the Church (a rule which reversed the patristic teaching that matrimony could not be dissolved by religious vows, and that separation for the purpose of entering the monastic life was not permissible except by the mutual consent of the parties[1]), but any union contracted in defiance of the canons was declared to be no marriage.[2] These statutes effected no immediate or impressive change in the general situation, and their principles were but reluctantly accepted even by many who favoured their purpose; nevertheless, papal persistence ensured their eventual success, and in 1215 the fourth Lateran council under Innocent III crowned two centuries of unremitting effort with enactments[3] which proclaimed the triumph of Hildebrand's policy. Thenceforth little is heard of clerical marriage, except in the remoter and more barbarous parts of Europe, where the Church's jurisdiction was less firmly established.

It is not easy to disentangle the motives underlying this strenuous promotion of sacerdotal celibacy. The arguments expressly advanced in its favour were virtually those which had characterized the patristic polemic against clerical marriage; they

---

[1] Cf. Augustine, *de bono vid.* x; Gregory I, *epist.* xi. 45.

[2] See *Conc. I Lateran.* (1123), xxi, and *Conc. II Lateran.* (1139). H. C. Lea, *An Historical Sketch of Sacerdotal Celibacy in the Christian Church* (Boston, 2nd ed., 1884), pp. 313–314, interprets the former council's ". . . *contracta . . . matrimonia ab hujusmodi personis disjungi . . . judicamus*" as meaning that clerical marriages were to be dissolved, but the phrase may signify nothing more than similar ones discussed earlier, which only authorize separation. However this may be, there can be no dubiety about the latter council's ". . . *copulationem, quam contra ecclesiasticam regulam constat esse contractam, matrimonium non esse censemus.*"

[3] *Conc. IV Lateran.* (1215), xiv, xxxi.

were based upon the assumption that coitus is in some sense evil and defiling, and therefore incompatible with the priestly or other ministerial functions. But it is significant that the pontiffs who enforced this discipline most energetically were also those who asserted most vigorously the temporal as well as the spiritual supremacy of the Church. It is impossible to avoid the conclusion that in forbidding marriage to the clergy, Gregory VII and his successors were bent upon forging an instrument by means of which the dominance of the ecclesiastical power in the West could be established and consolidated. Nothing could aid their cause more effectively than the creation of a body of men set apart from the world and its life, entirely bound to the Church, sub-servient to the will of its rulers, and owning no secular ties or obligations.[1] Yet if this was their real object, it was never openly avowed; the ostensible purpose of reform was always the 'purity' of the sacred ministry, and it is an eloquent comment upon the sexual attitudes of western Christendom that they thus lent themselves to exploitation for the aggrandizement of the spiritual power and the furtherance of papal policy.

Unless their true significance is appreciated, the numerous enactments of mediæval councils against clerical 'incontinence' are likely to convey an unwarranted impression of widespread and incorrigible libertinism among the priesthood—and indeed, writers unfavourable to the Church have not infrequently drawn such a conclusion from their misreading of the evidence. In an age coarse and barbarous in many respects when judged by the politer standards of modern times, it is not surprising that the incidence of venereal immorality among the clergy sometimes caused scandal, especially during periods of decadence such as that which marked the decline and dissolution of the Carlovingian empire. But this is not the whole picture, and the general situation takes on a different and less alarming appearance when it is realized that

---

[1] There were, of course, other practical considerations; the rule of celibacy was also designed to prevent the transmission of benefices and church property from father to son, and to check ecclesiastical alliances founded upon inter-marriage and family interest.

many of the priests who were stigmatized as 'incontinent' were merely offenders against canon law who otherwise lived blamelessly, either as duly married men (*uxorati*), or more often as *concubinarii*, cohabiting under conditions of normal matrimony with hearth-mates (*focariæ*) who were wives in all but name.

The clergy cannot, of course, be entirely absolved of the charge of licentious behaviour—but again, it helps to preserve a due perspective if account is taken of the contemporary situation. Whereas today in England (counting all religious denominations) there is one minister or priest for every thousand of the total population, in the thirteenth century approximately one in every twelve adult males was a cleric. Of this large number, many had no definite call to the Church's ministry, but had sought ordination because it was the normal thing for a man to do if he wished to follow a professional career; consequently the yoke of celibacy was often laid upon those who had no vocation thereto, and who succumbed all too easily to temptation. Paradoxically, the enforcement of continence tended to produce an increase in immoral living, and it must be confessed that the reformers often seem to have been more concerned that the clergy should be unmarried than that they should be chaste—an attitude which could not but affect adversely both morality in general, and the common estimation of marriage. Nor was the law always applied in its true spirit, for while priests were forbidden honourable wedlock, it was not long before their ecclesiastical superiors discovered that connivance at the weakness of the flesh could be turned to financial advantage by the taxation of *concubinarii* in respect of their women, and of the children born to them.[1]

---

[1] I have been sparing in my citation of references to clerical celibacy and concubinage during the Middle Ages, chiefly because the wealth of material makes full documentation tedious and selection difficult; but ample quotation of sources will be found in G. Cross, 'Celibacy (Christian)', and D. S. Schaff, 'Concubinage (Christian)', in *Encycl. Rel. and Eth.*, iii, pp. 273 ff., and 817 ff., and above all, in H. C. Lea, op. cit. The latter is a monument of erudition, but rather an encyclopædia than a history; the author's extensive documentation adds up to a formidable indictment of the policy of the mediæval Church, and the sources speak for themselves, but the resultant picture, though accurate as far as it goes, lacks the balance which a more sensitive and critical treatment would have given.

The sexual interests of the mediæval Church were at once narrower and deeper than those of the patristic age, and its contribution to the development of the tradition must be assessed accordingly. Of the many and varied questions to which reference was made in our survey of the early Church, some find little or no place in the discussions and controversies of theologians and canonists. Digamy, for instance, now hardly presents any problem; it is true that the eleventh-century canonical collection, the *Collection in Nine Books* (*Vaticanus* 1349), denounces second marriages as *stupra et adulteria*,[1] and that Anselm of Lucca regards a third marriage as "superfluous",[2] but most authors treat second, third, and even fourth unions as permissible,[3] and Aquinas maintains that every such alliance bears the significance of Christ and the Church.[4] Nor is the superiority of the virgin or the widowed state to the wedded any longer a matter for argument; the double ethical standard is now accepted and is openly proclaimed in the enforcement of clerical celibacy, in the exaltation of the monastic life, in the prominence given to the example of Joseph and Mary (who were represented as combining in their union the excellence of virginity with the good of matrimony), and indeed, in the whole ethos of mediæval Christianity.

On the other hand, marriage and the problems connected therewith assumed an altogether greater importance as a result of the new responsibilities which devolved upon the Church in

---

As a collection of material bearing upon the subject, however, Lea's book is invaluable, and should be consulted in connexion with the foregoing paragraphs.

[1] Lib. ix, c. 9—due probably to the influence of the theory of *unitas carnis*.

[2] *Collect. Canon.* x. 4.

[3] Cf. Peter Lombard, *Sent.* IV. xlii. 7; Aquinas, *Summa Theol.* III Suppl. lxiii. 1 resp.—though a digamist (presumably after the death of his second wife) cannot be considered for admission to the priesthood, for he must conform to Christ's example: "*vir unius sponsæ . . . qui procul dubio virgo est*", see Peter Damiani, *Liber qui dicitur Dominus vobiscum*, xii.

[4] Cf. *Summa Theol.* III Suppl. lxiii. 2 (of second marriage explicitly, but the argument applies equally to further unions), thus reversing the earlier conclusion of Hugh of Amiens, *c, hær.* iii. 4; second marriage, however, though a perfect sacrament (symbol) in itself, is defective in its signification when considered with reference to the preceding union—hence the omission of the blessing from the marriage rite in cases of digamy, cf. X, IV. xxi. 1, 3.

consequence of its gaining sole jurisdiction in matrimonial causes
—a factor which, as we have seen, largely determined the theological developments of the twelfth and thirteenth centuries,
during which the doctrines of consent and sacrament were
elaborated, and the nature of the nuptial contract was elucidated.
The latter question only came to the fore as the debate on the
formation of marriage was nearing its close, and at first it was
approached with a certain hesitancy—mainly because of some
doubt as to the propriety of applying the term 'contract' to the
union, though the Franciscan theologians seem to have adopted
it without difficulty.[1] The eventual conclusion was in line with
established teaching—namely, that marriage is a consensual, not
a solemn contract between husband and wife, consisting of "the
mutual handing over of their bodies, each for the perpetual use
of the other for the procreation and proper education of children".[2]
This contract was concluded by the parties themselves, either in
person, or by letter,[3] or by proxy,[4] and was expressed by consent
exchanged *in facie ecclesiæ*, not tacitly, but by words or intelligible
signs.

In attempting to estimate the influence of mediæval thought
upon the evolution of the western Christian sexual tradition, it is
necessary to emphasize the profound effect of this concentration
upon the formal and legal aspects of matrimony. Circumstances
compelled the Church to work out a theory of marriage which
was adapted rather to the business of the ecclesiastical courts than
to the needs of the pastoral ministry. Consequently its conception
of the nuptial union was cast in an institutional mould which took
little account of the metaphysical and personal aspects of the
relationship between husband and wife, and was expressed in
juridical or forensic categories alien alike from the Scriptural and
from the patristic views of marriage. Inevitably the development
of a theology of wedlock was conditioned and controlled by this
predominantly legal and institutional concern; granted certain

---

[1] Cf. Bonaventura, *in Sent.* IV. xxviii. 1, q. 3 and q. 5; xxix. 1, q. 3.
[2] John Duns Scotus, *Opus Oxon.* xxvi. 1 § 17.
[3] See *gloss. ord.* on *Decret. Grat.*, C. XXX, q. v, c. 8.
[4] See *Decret. Sext.* I. xix. 9.

basic Christian principles such as those of indissolubility and sacrament, the tendency of the Schoolmen was always to follow the general pattern and spirit of classical jurisprudence, modifying and extending it as need required, and employing the Bible and the writings of the Fathers rather as repositories of proof-texts than as the material out of which a true theology of marriage might be constructed. Thus Peter Lombard extracted from his sources (mainly patristic) a wealth of *sententia* illustrating, among other things, the efficient power of consent and the factors which vitiate it, the persons who may contract, and the impediments diriment of matrimony; he does, it is true, deal also with the *bona matrimonii* and with divorce and indissolubility, but his whole approach is determined by the concept of wedlock as an institution rather than essentially an unique personal relation.

Nor was the legal orientation of the Church's interests the only thing which restricted its theological view of marriage. The Schoolmen of the late thirteenth and the fourteenth centuries, who were no longer engrossed with the problem of the formation of the nuptial union, were none the less cramped when treating of matrimony by the now established convention of expounding its meaning, either in terms of the new sacramentalism, or within the apparently flexible yet ultimately limiting framework prescribed by the philosophical method of Aristotelianism. Thus they discussed the matter, form, and grace of the sacrament of marriage, and analysed its formal, efficient, material, and final causes according to one or another of the several current schemes of classification;[1] but these exercises hardly conduced to an understanding of the interior and metaphysical character of the marital *henosis*. Although some, such as Aquinas, were evidently not unaware of the personal factors in wedlock, they clearly regarded them as lying outside the realm of legitimate theological study—a conclusion undoubtedly due in part to their own inexperience of a relation, the inner significance of which can

---

[1] According to Albert and Bonaventura, the formal cause related to the institution of marriage, the efficient cause to consent, the material cause to impediments, and the final cause to the *bona matrimonii*.

only be known existentially. Hence it is not surprising that the tradition which they did so much to develop should have represented matrimony as little more than an ecclesiastical or social institution, and that Dr Karl Barth should have denounced the Church's doctrine of matrimony as nothing but a doctrine of the wedding ceremony[1]—one, that is, which finds its centre in the legal-sacramental moment at which present consent is exchanged.

This narrow view seems at first the more remarkable when we reflect that the eleventh century, which saw the beginning of the debate about the efficient cause of marriage, saw also the emergence of the concept of romantic love as a cultural factor destined to affect almost every aspect of the life of western society. But it is easy to over-estimate the influence of this new idea upon mediæval Christendom; for a long time it appears to have been little more than a literary convention current among the upper classes, principally in the south of France, and only very gradually did it bring about a transformation of European sexual attitudes. There is abundant evidence to show how slightly the common notion of matrimony and the general pattern of conjugal life during the Middle Ages were touched by any 'romantic' conception of the relationship between husband and wife. In ignoring love, therefore, and with it the personal aspect of wedlock, the Scholastics were simply treating their subject with characteristic realism—though their approach may also reflect an understandable suspicion of an idea which had emanated from a region tainted with heresy and which, in certain of its manifestations, betrays traces of Manichæan influence.[2]

---

[1] See K. Barth, *Die kirchliche Dogmatik* (Zurich, 1947 ff.), III/4, p. 253.

[2] On romantic love, see Charles Williams, *He Came Down from Heaven* (London, 1938), pp. 83 ff.; *The Descent of the Dove* (London, 1939), pp. 128 ff.; C. S. Lewis, *The Allegory of Love* (Oxford, 1938), pp. 1 ff.; D. de Rougement, *Passion and Society* (London, 1956); D. S. Bailey, *The Mystery of Love and Marriage* (London, 1952), pp. 3–6; J. Langdon-Davies, *Sex, Sin, and Sanctity* (London, 1954)—the last being a criticism of the thesis maintained by Dr Lewis and M. de Rougement—see pp. 203–262.

A critical historical test of the quality of sexual relationship in any age is provided by the status accorded to woman, and by the current notions about her—and even a superficial examination of the sources reveals a marked contrast between the romantic idealization of the 'lady' in troubadour verse, and the actual position which she enjoyed or endured in mediæval life. The age of the Schoolmen was just as androcentric as that of the early Fathers, though the former express themselves less crudely, and hardly display any emotional prejudice against woman as a temptress supposed to incite man to commit venereal sins. Aquinas, for example, holds that her mythological origin signifies that she was destined for social union with man; being made from his rib, she is neither to exercise authority over him, nor to exist in a servile condition.[1] Yet he rejects the idea that she was created to be man's helper in the broad and general sense of partner in all the affairs and enterprises pertaining to human life, for in these he can be aided more effectively by another man; woman is his collaborator simply in that for which she is biologically indispensible—the work of generation.[2] Her subjection to him as her 'head' is ontological, because in him "the discretion of reason predominates";[3] his superiority is demonstrated even by the act of coitus wherein he bears the more active, and therefore the nobler part, while she is passive and submissive.[4] Aristotle's anthropology is still dominant;[5] the male is the perfect human being, and the female is defective or misbegotten (*mas occasionatus*) as regards her individual nature—though this intrinsic deformity does not hinder the part which she has been appointed to play in the natural economy as it is directed to the continuation of the race.[6]

---

[1] *Summa Theol.* I. xcii. 3 *resp.*

[2] Ibid, I. xcii. 1 *resp.*   [3] Ibid, I. xcii. 1 ad 2.

[4] Ibid, III Suppl. lxvi. 5. Aquinas (or his editor) does not argue, like Sanchez several centuries later, that the so-called 'normal' position for coitus, with the woman succumbent, is the only natural mode of copulation, since it signifies the superordinate status of the male—any deviation from this position being against nature, *de matr.* IX. xvi. 1.

[5] *De gen. animal.* ii. 3.

[6] *Summa Theol.* I. xcii. 1 ad 1.

During the Middle Ages marriage and sexual morality were threatened from two sides. As always, there were the satirists, such as the authors of the *fabliaux* (early French metrical tales) who ridiculed wedlock, and writers such as Mattheolus of Boulogne and Eustace Deschamps showed that the vituperative and pessimistic spirit of such as Jerome and Tertullian was still abroad. But the greater danger came from a recrudescence of the Manichæan heresy, which assumed a particularly threatening form in the doctrines of Catharism, especially as professed in Albigensia. Its adherents maintained that all carnal pleasure is sinful, and regarded marriage as nothing but an organized debauch; generation was condemned as a diabolical work causing the imprisonment of the soul in the body, but promiscuous venereal indulgence (including, there is good reason to suspect, homosexual practices[1]) was certainly condoned by the Catharist authorities—even though the élite (the *Perfecti* or Initiates) were themselves irreproachable in their conduct. Against this subversive teaching the Church marshalled all its resources of traditional teaching in defence of matrimony,[2] but the resultant apologetic, relying overmuch upon an assertion of ecclesiastical authority against the heretics, contributed little to the development of theological thought.

Although the Fathers of the early Church were careful to define the circumstances which rendered coitus blameless or culpable, they do not appear to have been greatly concerned with the intrinsic morality of venereal acts and its determinative principles. In mediæval times, however, this question received some attention, and in connexion therewith the penitentials are significant because they represent the first serious attempt (albeit somewhat crude and unsystematic) to differentiate between the various kinds of sexual act for the purpose of apportioning

---

[1] See my *Homosexuality and the Western Christian Tradition* (London, 1955), pp. 137–140 for a discussion of this point.

[2] Among the treatises produced by the orthodox side were Eberhard of Bethune, *Antihæresis*, vii; Eckert of Schönau, *Serm. c. Cathar.*; Alan of Lille, *c. hær.* i. 64; Moneta of Cremona, *adv. Valdenses et Cathar.* iv. 7; Gregory of Florence, *disput. inter Cathol. et paterin. hær.*

penances commensurate with the assumed gravity of those deemed to be sinful. The method and scope of these disciplinary manuals is sufficiently illustrated by Theodore's Penitential, which records the decisions given from time to time by the archbishop in answer to enquiries concerning the treatment of offenders against Christian morality. Due punishment is assigned, not only to various male and female homosexual acts,[1] to fornication and adultery,[2] and to incest,[3] bestiality,[4] and masturbation,[5] but also to certain forms of physical gratification sometimes practised by the married;[6] yet there is no indication of any rationale underlying the different penalties imposed, and for the purpose of this survey the importance of this and the other penitentials lies chiefly in their minute classification of venereal transgressions, and in their interesting scaling of the appropriate penances.

For the fullest treatment of this subject, however, we must turn to the *Summa Theologica* of Thomas Aquinas, who deals with it in that part of his treatise which is devoted to a discussion of the cardinal virtue of temperance and the contrary vice of lust (*luxuria*). Sin, he argues, is that which contravenes the order of reason by which everything is fittingly directed to its proper end;[7] lust, therefore, being chiefly concerned with the venereal pleasures which above all others debauch the mind,[8] consists in exceeding the order of reason in regard to venereal acts. Now right reason declares that the appointed end of such acts is procreation;

---

[1] For a detailed account of the treatment of homosexual practices in the penitentials, see my *Homosexuality and the Western Christian Tradition*, pp. 100–110.

[2] *Pœnit. Theod.* I. ii. 1, 18; vii. 1; viii. 6; xiv. 9, 10, 11, 12, 14, 15; II. xii. 11.

[3] *Ibid*, I. ii. 16, 17, 20.

[4] Ibid. I. ii. 2, 3; vii. 1.

[5] Ibid, I. ii. 9 (male); 13 (female, presumably with the aid of an artificial penis: *Si sola cum se ipsa coitum habet*); viii. 4, 9, 11.

[6] Ibid. I. ii. 15 (? *fellatio*); xiv. 22 (anal coitus); 23 (coitus during menstruation). I. xiv. 21 even penalizes coitus *retro*—that is, apparently, with penetration from behind (the method recommended by Lucretius as particularly apt for promoting conception, *de rerum nat.* iv. 1264–1267).

[7] II–II. cliii. 2.

[8] II–II. cliii. 1.

consequently they are discordant with reason, either when they are in themselves inconsistent with that end, or when they are performed inordinately with respect to the woman concerned.[1] The first category includes the vice against nature (*vitium contra naturam*) which renders generation impossible, and simple fornication which hinders the proper education of the child conceived, by depriving it of a father's care;[2] the second embraces such sins as incest (where the woman is related to the man by consanguinity or affinity), adultery (where she is under the authority of a husband), and seduction or rape (when she is under the authority of a father).

Kisses, touches, and caresses, continues the Angelic Doctor, are *per se* innocent and can occur without lustful delectation; but they become mortally sinful by reason of their motive, as when they are done for the purpose of enjoying forbidden pleasure.[3] Nocturnal emission, too (significantly termed 'nocturnal pollution'— *pollutio nocturna*), is never in itself sinful, though it is sometimes the result of a previous sin such as intemperance in eating or drinking, or the deliberate entertainment of lascivious thoughts.[4]

Most serious, however, of all the species of lust is the *vitium contra naturam*, which is contrary not only to right reason, but also to "the natural order of the venereal act as becoming to the human race".[5] It can occur in four ways: by procuring ejaculation (*pollutio*) without coitus, or masturbation; by copulation with non-human creatures, or bestiality; by *concubitus ad non debitum sexum*—that is, by coital or (presumably) other venereal acts of a homosexual character, male with male or female with female; and by deviation from the "natural manner of [heterosexual] coitus (*naturalis modus concumbendi*), either in the employment of undue means (*instrumentum non debitum*), or by resorting to other

---

[1] II-II. cliv. 1.

[2] II-II. cliv. 2.

[3] II-II. cliv. 4.

[4] II-II. cliv. 5: emissions consequent upon speculative thoughts about carnal acts, such as necessarily engage the moral theologian from time to time, are not sinful as to their cause.

[5] II-II. cliv. 11.

monstrous and bestial modes of intercourse".[1] Of these various sins against nature, the gravest is bestiality; next come sodomy (which no doubt includes other homosexual practices), and the non-observance of the *debitus modus concumbendi*, while masturbation is held to be the least serious, consisting as it does simply in the omission of copulation.[2] But even masturbation is a more grievous offence than any of the venereal sins not classified as *peccata contra naturam*—though these, too, have their own order of gravity, the most heinous transgression being incest, next adultery and then seduction (both aggravated by the use of violence), and lastly simple fornication committed without inflicting injustice upon another.[3]

It is instructive to compare with this confident determination of the morality of venereal acts the somewhat equivocal attitude displayed by Aquinas towards prostitution—a vice involving at least fornication, if not also adultery and certain of the sins against nature. Although Christian opinion consistently denounced all breaches of the rule of chastity, it had always tended nevertheless to acquiesce uneasily in the view that the present condition of human society made prostitution a necessary evil, and theologians found it difficult not to concede that the harlot was in some sense indispensable to the well-being of the body politic. Thus Augustine affirmed that "no Church, not even the most careless", admitted "public prostitutes, continuing in their most shameful profession";[4] but he did not hesitate also to maintain that they fulfil a useful purpose: "What", he asks, "can be called more sordid, more void of modesty, more full of shame than prostitutes, brothels, and every other evil of this kind? Yet remove prostitutes from human affairs, and you will pollute all things

---

[1] Unfortunately Aquinas does not define the *naturalis modus concumbendi*, though in his view it would only include acts apt for generation—and would involve use only of the *vas debitum*, cf. II–II, cliv. 12 ad 4.

[2] II–II. cliv. 12 ad 4.

[3] II–II. cliv. 12 *resp.*

[4] *De fid. et op.* xv [25].

with lust; set them among honest matrons, and you will dishonour all things with disgrace and turpitude."[1]

Aquinas takes the same view; while insisting that every kind of fornication is sinful,[2] he yet finds it impossible to disallow prostitution entirely.

"Human government," he argues, "is derived from the Divine government, and should imitate it. Now although God is omnipotent and supremely good, nevertheless he allows certain evils to take place in the universe, which he might prevent, lest without them greater goods might be forfeited, or greater evils ensue. Accordingly in human government also, those who are in authority rightly tolerate certain evils, lest certain goods be lost or certain greater evils be incurred." He refers to the passage from Augustine already quoted,[3] and elsewhere, too, he calls Augustine to witness on the same point—namely, that the toleration of necessary evils "makes prostitution in the world like the filth in the sea, or the sewer in a palace. Take away the sewer, and you will fill the palace with pollution; and likewise with the filth [in the sea].[4] Take away prostitutes from the world, and you will fill it with sodomy. Wherefore Augustine says, in Book XIII of *De Civitate Dei*, that the earthly city has made the use of harlots a lawful immorality (*licitam turpitudinem*)."[5] And in discussing the problem of restitution, Aquinas expresses the opinion that payment made to a prostitute constitutes unlawful giving, in that the payment is made for an unlawful purpose; but that the giving itself is not unlawful, and the woman is entitled to keep what she has received. Only if she had extorted an excessive payment by fraud or deceit would she be bound to make restitution to her client.[6]

This reluctant and embarrassed tolerance of prostitution (at least in large cities) as the ineluctable price of social 'purity' and

---

[1] *De ordine*, ii. 4 [12].

[2] Cf., in addition to the references given above, *Summa c. Gent.* iii. 122.

[3] *Summa Theol.* II–II. x. 11.

[4] Because if it is not voided into the sea, it remains to pollute the land.

[5] *Opuscula*, xvi (enumeration of Paris ed. of 1875, iv), 14. The reference to *de civ. Dei* appears to be in error.

[6] *Summa Theol.* II–II. lx. 5 and 2.

the preservation of feminine 'virtue', intensified the already ingrained androcentricity of the Christian tradition, and gave a semblance of qualified approval to the very double standard of venereal morality which the New Testament and the Fathers had condemned. Nothing could demonstrate more clearly the strange and often perplexing ambivalence and confusion of mediæval sexual thought. For more than eight centuries the Church had striven to inculcate a relatively high ideal of marriage as a relationship instituted and blessed by God; yet its defence of the holy estate against the detractions of heretics and cynics, and its teaching on the sacramental and indissoluble character of the marital union, were in fact largely vitiated by other factors which could not but conduce to an opposite conception of wedlock.

Some of the more obviously influential of these factors only require enumeration—the exaltation of virginity as the supreme and truly 'religious' state of life; the refusal of marriage to the clergy; the continual insinuation or asseveration that coitus is a defilement and a hindrance to the service of God; the emphasis placed upon the remedial function of matrimony, and the neglect of its relational aspects; and the persistence of a comparatively low view of woman. The multiplication of artificial and fanciful diriment impediments due to fictions such as *cognatio spiritualis* and *affinitas illegitima* made wedlock at once more difficult to contract, and more precarious, for those who dwelt in the closely-knit, rigidly stratified, and often isolated communities of mediæval society; and although the allegations of corruption levelled against the ecclesiastical courts have doubtless been much exaggerated,[1] it cannot be gainsaid that the intricacy and stringency of the canon law relating to these prohibitions, the practice (and sometimes the abuse) of dispensation, and the premium set upon perjury by the distinction between *verba de futuro* and *verba de præsenti*, all tended to throw into relief the inconsistency between ideal and reality in the matrimonial realm. Moreover, this inconsistency was further stressed by another fiction—the so-called

---

[1] See the judicious appraisal by Dr Mortimer in his revision of T. A. Lacey, op. cit. (cf. the original ed. of 1912, p. 159, with that of 1947, pp. 138–139).

Pauline privilege; denial that marriage in the order of nature is indissoluble cannot ultimately have been without its effect upon the conception of Christian wedlock as a permanent union.

Similarly, the Church's assiduous defence of venereal morality was weakened by other factors than its attitude to prostitution. The indiscriminate enforcement of the rule of celibacy fastened upon the clergy a burden which many were quite unfitted and unable to bear, with the result that the lives of those who should have upheld a high standard of chastity often demonstrated rather the frailty of the flesh. The allowance or encouragement of vows of continence taken unadvisedly, in youthful ignorance or under virtual compulsion, by many who had no vocation thereto, was responsible for not a little scandalous behaviour by monastics of both sexes—though these lapses were magnified by the Reformers for polemical reasons. Outward conformity with ecclesiastical discipline was not always an expression of inward 'purity', and even sincere professions could mask an unconscious rejection of the celibate state; it is impossible to misunderstand the psychological significance of the carnal imagery in which some mystics clothed their vividly suggestive experiences of the spiritual marriage, or the underlying causes of the *minne*-piety which was enthusiastically cultivated in the nunneries.

Probably, however, the most powerful of all these negative influences was the continual disparagement of coitus as something polluted or inherently evil. It is most unlikely that ordinary mediæval men and women appreciated, or were even aware of, the subtle arguments by which the Schoolmen defined the act as evil, but not always morally evil. Though they were doubtless nstructed that its generative and remedial uses were not blameworthy, the general impression left by the Church's teaching upon simple and unlearned people can only have been that the physical relationship of the sexes was regarded by religion as unworthy, if not as shameless and obscene. The effect of such teaching must necessarily have been grave; it caused a distortion of principles and values which has left an indelible mark upon

Christian sexual thought, and we can only guess at the psychological disturbances and conflicts which it produced in the lives of individuals.

The extent to which this dualistic antipathy to coitus controlled the theological conception of matrimony is well illustrated by the lectures on the first epistle to the Corinthians which John Colet delivered in the University of Oxford at the close of the fifteenth century, and with which this part of our historical survey may fittingly end. His handling of the seventh chapter is interesting, for it shows how little the thought of the Church had advanced during the Middle Ages in what relates to the essence of marriage and sexual relationship. Here, expressed in the gentle, urbane, persuasive words of the great humanist are, at bottom, the same sentiments that Jerome, Peter Damiani, and others of that sort had clothed in coarser and more violent language. Colet takes some time to reach the heart of his subject, for he approaches it gradually and cautiously by way of a long dissertation upon the difference between precept (that which must be done to ensure salvation), counsel (that which is not of obligation, but which all ought to desire to do), and indulgence (that which is permitted simply as a concession to individual weakness); and in this context he discusses the life of marriage, treating it as belonging to the third category of indulgence.

St Paul, explains Colet, commends singleness, but suffers those who are too weak to endure continence to take a wife in lawful wedlock as a remedy against passion.[1] Marriage, however, is but a second best, having nothing good in itself, save only in so far as it provides a remedy for a necessary evil; its sole value is that it restrains and confines the lawlessness of venereal desire. Colet follows Augustine in teaching that although wedlock was originally useful for generation, it now lacks even this justification; since Christ has fulfilled the truth of spiritual marriage, it is no longer necessary either as a symbol prefiguring what was to come, or as a means for increasing mankind.[2] Man's weakness has

---

[1] J. Colet (transl. and ed. J. H. Lupton), *Exposition of St Paul's First Epistle to the Corinthians* (London, 1874), p. 90. [2] Ibid, p. 91.

extorted from an indulgent God the use of wives and matrimony, but the true ideal is that of masculine continence.[1] Indeed, all Christians, both men and women, should strive after angelic chastity, both as single and as married, for in coitus they show themselves in no way superior to the beasts, and fall far below God and the life of heaven which they ought to imitate.[2] It is significant that one so critical of Scholastic sophistry and so open-minded and liberal in his devotion to the New Learning should have entertained this narrow and distorted conception of marriage, but nothing could illustrate better than Colet's exposition the beliefs and prejudices which determined the attitude to sexual matters even of the best minds of the age.

---

[1] Ibid, p. 94.

[2] Ibid, p. 95; cf. p. 48: the source of venereal sin (and equally, it must be presumed, of lawful coitus) is to be found in the remotest and lowest faculty of the body—the sense of touch.

V

THE REFORMATION AND
SEVENTEENTH-CENTURY ANGLICANISM

MATRIMONIAL and sexual questions do not figure largely in the controversies and literature of the sixteenth century, for the Reformers, like the Fathers and the Schoolmen, were essentially practical and therefore, despite the urgent need for a reconsideration of the Church's teaching and a reformation of doctrinal error in this field, more disposed to correct the abuses and defects of the existing institutional system than to venture upon any deep investigation of the theology of sexual relationship. Moreover, they were restrained from speculation, partly by their own conservatism in regard to sexual matters, and partly by their appeal to Scripture, which often produced an attitude as reactionary in this respect as it was radical in others.

The first and principal sexual topics to engage the Reformers were clerical celibacy and obligatory vows of continence. Both were regarded as contrary to divine law and as badges of papal servitude, and most of the Reformation confessions and formularies proclaim the honesty of wedlock and the iniquity of irrevocable monastic vows.[1] Individual divines emphasized and

---

[1] Cf. the *Ten Theses of Berne* (1528), ix; the *Augsburg Confession* (1530), ii. 2, vi; the *First Helvetic Confession* (1536), xxviii; the *Second Helvetic Confession* (1566), xxix; the *Second Scots Confession* or *National Covenant* (1580). Two other formularies, while not specifically mentioning clerical celibacy and vows of continence, condemn the laws introduced by men into the Church, by which they bind the conscience: the French *Confession of Faith* (1559), xxxiii; the *Belgic Confession* (1561), xxxii—all in P. Schaff, *The Creeds of Christendom* (New York, 1877–1884), iii, pp. 210, 2, 230–231, 304–305, 482–483, 378, and 423. Cf. also the Danish *Ordinances of the Diet of Odense* (1527), ii; the Bernese *Edict of Reformation* (1536), v;

elaborated these official pronouncements, calling Scripture and history to witness against a system which had led to much immorality, and had brought discredit upon the Christian religion. Thus Zwingli declared that since God had ordained marriage and had nowhere forbidden it, it is lawful for all without exception; he denounced compulsory vows of chastity, and roundly asserted that it was sinful for clerics and monastics to refuse matrimony if they knew that they had been denied the gift of continence.[1]

Almost from the beginning of his revolt, Luther attacked clerical celibacy and monastic vows, advising those about to be ordained never to swear continence,[2] and boldly counselling any dutiful priest who had succumbed to the frailty of the flesh to cohabit with the woman if she were willing, disregarding with a clear conscience the pope's pleasure or displeasure, the canon law, and public opinion—for in God's sight they are already espoused.[3] Vows of chastity, he held, originate in the delusion that the divine favour can be won by performing self-imposed disciplines[4]—in other words, that salvation depends upon works, not upon faith; whereas continence is as little in our power as are God's other wonders and graces. All, however, are made for marriage, and the divine law that man's desire is towards woman cannot be restrained by oaths and regulations; whoever attempts to live single presumptuously undertakes the impossible, and such temptation of God brings its own reward in uncleanness of thought and life.[5]

---

and the *Genevan Confession* (1537), xvii—all in B. J. Kidd, *Documents of the Continental Reformation* (Oxford, 1911), pp. 234, 557, and 570.

[1] See the *Sixty-seven Articles* (1523), xxviii–xxx, in P. Schaff, op. cit., iii, p. 202. These Articles were never accepted as having credal authority. Zwingli had already joined with others in petitioning the bishop of Constance to allow the marriage of the clergy in 1522, see B. J. Kidd, op. cit., p. 400.

[2] *Appeal to the Ruling Classes*, tr. B. L. Woolf, *Reformation Writings of Martin Luther* (London, 1952), i. p. 160.   [3] *Appeal to the Ruling Classes*, ibid, p. 161.

[4] *Predigt vom ehelichen Leben*, in *sämmtliche Werke* (Erlangen ed., cited hereafter as E), xvi, p. 531.

[5] Letter to Wolfgang Reissenbusch (*Letters of Spiritual Counsel*, ed. and transl. T. G. Tappert [London, 1955]—cited hereafter as LSC—p. 273).

Calvin argued in much the same strain, though he was more cautious than Luther, and made it clear that he disapproved only of vows of celibacy which are improperly regarded as acts of religious service, and are rashly undertaken by those who cannot keep them.[1] Continence is not in everyone's power; let none, therefore, say that nothing is possible with God's help, for he aids only those who obey his call. They do not show obedience who despise his remedies and struggle vainly and arrogantly to overcome their natural and proper feelings—and whose outward abstinence may conceal a lack of inward chastity.[2] In particular, the imposition of celibacy upon the clergy is to be condemned; the Scriptures show that men have no right to forbid what God has left free.[3]

On the question of the intrinsic merit of virginity Luther and Calvin were divided. The former regarded it as something to be shunned, and thought that it should be so praised that men are repelled rather than attracted.[4] Both personal experience and consideration of the natural order of things convinced him that continence, far from being normal, is an idiosyncrasy of 'peculiar' (*seltzam*) persons,[5] and possessed only by one in several thousands;[6] and he, too, emphasized the fact that beneath a semblance of chastity there often fester an incontinent spirit, evil desires in the heart, and an everlasting burning.[7] Calvin, on the other hand, while fully alive to these arguments, held nevertheless that virginity is essentially superior to marriage,[8] and that if given by God as a virtue and not embraced under compulsion, it should not be despised.[9]

---

[1] *Institutes*, IV. xiii. 18.   [2] Ibid, II. vii. 42–43.

[3] Ibid, IV. xiii. 23.

[4] Letter to John Luther, see LSC; p. 261.

[5] *Predigt vom ehelichen Leben*, *Werke* (E), xvi, p. 512.

[6] Letter to three Nuns, LSC, p. 271.

[7] *Grosser Katechismus*, *Werke* (E), xxi, p. 71.

[8] *In Epist. I ad Cor.*, on vii. 7–8, *Opera* (Amsterdam, 1667), vii, pp. 150–151; cf. the *Second Helvetic Confession*, xxix. 1: celibacy, for those who have the gift, is a state peculiarly fitted for the pursuit of divine things, on account of the freedom it affords from distractions, see P. Schaff, op. cit., iii, p. 304.

[9] *Inst.* II. vii. 42.

Both the great Reformers held marriage in high esteem; but while Luther, though eulogistic, is somewhat conventional in certain of his views, Calvin, after his sober fashion, reveals a more profound and original conception of the relation between husband and wife. For Luther, wedlock is God's gift to mankind —a state of life approved by him (in contrast to celibacy, which is not commanded) and possessing the authority of his word;[1] it was implanted in our nature,[2] instituted in Paradise, confirmed by the fifth commandment, and safeguarded by the seventh.[3] It is a "true, heavenly, spiritual, and divine estate", a "school" of faith and love, because men and women learn both therein;[4] therefore matrimony, and not the *vita contemplativa* extolled by the Church, is the true way to the attainment of life everlasting. It may be used with a good conscience, for God himself brings husband and wife together, and all the menial tasks, hardships, and troubles of marriage become of incomparable value because he has sanctioned and approved them.[5] Therefore Luther urges Wolfgang Reissenbusch, who was hesitating to embark upon wedlock, to set aside his scruples: "Why should you delay . . .? It must, should, and will happen in any case. Stop thinking about it and go to it right merrily. Your body demands it. God wills it and drives you to it. There is nothing you can do about it."[6]

But these forthright arguments reveal something of Luther's conservatism, and of his conventional and fundamentally defective attitude to physical sexuality. Marriage certainly inculcates a chaster disposition than virginity, because it permits expression of the natural carnal desires, which must otherwise be suppressed;[7]

---

[1] See the *Predigt vom ehelichen Leben*, *Werke* (E), xvi, p. 531, and a *Hochzeitpredigt* on Heb. xiii. 4, *Werke* (E), xviii, p. 90.

[2] See another *Hochzeitpredigt* on Heb. xiii. 4, *Werke* (E), iii, p. 526.

[3] *Grosser Katechismus*, *Werke* (E), xxi, p. 70.

[4] *Das siebente Kap. S. Pauli an die Korinthern ausgelegt*, *Werke* (E), li, pp. 22 ff.; 520 ff.; cf. *Table Talk*, recorder unknown, where Luther speaks of mutual love as the *substantia matrimonii*, the foundation of the relationship, see LSC, p. 286.

[5] See the *Predigt vom ehelichen Leben*, *Werke* (E), xvi, pp. 531, and the *Hochzeitpredigt* on Heb. xiii. 4 in *Werke* (E), xviii, pp. 90 ff.

[6] See LSC, p. 274.

[7] *Grosser Katechismus*, *Werke* (E), xxi, p. 71.

but this does not mean that coitus is intrinsically good and pure. In his treatment of sexual acts Luther follows Augustine and Aquinas, and ascribes our present experience of the venereal impulse to the Fall.[1] The effects of sin are all-pervasive, and we continue to bear the penalties accruing from the original transgression of Adam and Eve. Consequently coitus cannot now be performed entirely in the knowledge and worship of God, but is accompanied by a sense of shame due to loss of trust in him;[2] somehow it is always unclean, but for most of mankind it remains nevertheless a regrettable yet imperative necessity.[3]

This attitude, which extends even to the lawful venereal desires and acts of husband and wife, colours Luther's notion of wedlock. Fully sensitive to, and warmly appreciative of, its honesty and advantages, he still retains in large measure the negative outlook of the Fathers and the Schoolmen: "No matter what praise is given to marriage", he protests, "I will not concede it to nature that it is no sin."[4] It is a "medicine" and a "hospital for the sick"[5] —the only effective antidote against, or cure for, the incontinence which troubles every man; for the human male, to take a wife is just as much a necessity of nature as are eating and drinking.[6] Nevertheless, the remedy gives no licence to the wanton and lascivious; matrimony must be used with becoming moderation, and must not be made a pigsty in which the lecherous and sensual can wallow.[7]

Calvin, on the contrary, took a less pessimistic, more positive view. He repudiated Jerome's interpretation[8] of St Paul's words: "It is good for a man not to touch a woman",[9] and affirmed that

---

[1] *Predigt von dem ehelichen Stand, Werke* (E), xvi, pp. 59 ff.

[2] Luther apparently would not (or could not) consider the possibility that trust in God can be restored through grace, and that the coitus of the redeemed might in consequence be relieved to a great extent of its shame and guilt.

[3] Cf. *Grosser Katechismus, Werke* (E), xxi, p. 72.

[4] *Predigt vom ehelichen Leben, Werke* (E), xvi, p. 541.

[5] *Hochzeitpredigt* on Heb. xiii. 4, *Werke* (E), iii, p. 520.

[6] Letter to Wolfgang Reissenbusch, LSC, p. 274.

[7] *Grosser Katechismus, Werke* (E), xxi, p. 72.

[8] *Adv. Jov.* i. 7: "If it is good not to touch a woman, it is bad to touch one".

[9] I Cor. vii. 1.

coitus is undefiled, honourable, and holy, because it is a pure institution of God.[1] The reason why it has been disparaged as something unclean is that "Satan dazzles us with an appearance of what is right, in order that we may be led to imagine that we are polluted by intercourse with our wives."[2] Yet even Calvin was somewhat uneasy—characteristically, on account of the pleasure concomitant with coitus. This pleasure, he held, must inevitably be attended by a certain element of evil due to the immoderate desire resulting from the corruption of human nature by the Fall; yet God does not treat it as sinful when it is sought or accepted as incidental to procreation and the building of society. He covers it with the veil of matrimony, and allows husband and wife to enjoy themselves,[3] so long as they do so with modesty and propriety[4]—but he gives them no licence to indulge intemperately, and their behaviour should always be sober and appropriate to the dignity of their state.[5]

Marriage, for Calvin, was a high calling. He deprecated the unmeasured praise of virginity as a covert attack upon wedlock,[6] and condemned the "petulant reproaches" of detractors such as Jerome,[7] who had the effrontery to brand as unclean what Christ had honoured as the symbol of his union with the Church.[8] But he recognized none the less that the arch-defamer of matrimony was, in fact, the Devil, who had first attached odium to it by tempting the married to lasciviousness, and had then further degraded it by causing the introduction of the "pestilential law of celibacy".[9]

---

[1] *In Epist. I ad Cor.*, on vii. 6, *Opera*, vii, p. 150.

[2] Ibid, on vii. 5, *Opera*, vii, p. 149.

[3] *In Quattuor Reliq. Lib. Mos.*, on Deut. xxiv. 5, *Opera*, i, p. 515.

[4] Ibid, on Lev. xx. 18, *Opera*, i. p. 518.

[5] *Inst.* II. vii. 44.

[6] *Inst.* IV. xii. 27.

[7] *In Gen.*, on ii. 18, *Opera*, i, p. 14; there are similar criticisms of Jerome in the commentary on 1 Cor. vii, see, e.g., *Opera*, vii, pp. 150 and 151. Tyndale's opinion is apposite here; he condemned this Father as not less perverse and dangerous to morality than Ovid, *Prologue to the Book of Numbers*, *Works* (Parker Soc.), i, p. 438.

[8] *Inst.* IV. xii. 24.   [9] *In Gen.*, on ii. 22, *Opera*, i, p. 15.

In several respects Calvin's conception of marriage, and therefore of woman, was more original and affirmative than that of Luther. Although he allowed that propagation of the species is a special and characteristic end (*proprius finis*) of matrimony,[1] he taught also that its primary purpose is rather social than generative.[2] Woman was not ordained simply to be man's helper in procreation, nor was she necessary because of the corruption of human nature by the Fall—that is, as a 'remedy'; she was created, not to be merely the companion of his chamber, but rather the inseparable associate of his whole life.[3] Luther, on the other hand, saw woman chiefly as a bearer of children[4] and a divinely appointed means of venereal relief for the male; and he emphasized more strongly her subordination in wedlock.[5]

Although they accepted woman's subjection to man (however it might be modified in practice) as part of God's law, both Reformers seem to have thought that this did not in theory incapacitate her for the ministry of the Church, since the universal priesthood of believers takes no account of sexual differences. None the less, they would not admit her to spiritual functions, and particularly the proclamation of the Word, for this was not only forbidden in Scripture, but also liable to cause inconveniences. Luther considered that woman's exclusion from ministry was warranted by the need for preserving order and decency, and by her inferior aptitude—though an exception might be made in times of necessity.[6] Calvin likewise held that within the *politia ecclesiastica* her subordinate status deprived her of authority to preach publicly; rather, her specific ministry is that of motherhood.[7]

---

[1] *In Gen.*, on xxiv. 59, *Opera*, i, p. 129.

[2] *In Gen.*, on ii. 18, *Opera*, i. p. 14.

[3] *In Gen.*, on ii. 18, *Opera*, i, p. 14.

[4] Cf. the letter to three Nuns, LSC, p. 271.

[5] Cf. his advice to Stephen Roth (the letter begins: "Grace and peace in Christ, and authority over your wife"!) see LSC, pp. 277–278.

[6] Cf. *Vom Miszbrauch der Messe*, quoted by F. Zerbst, op. cit., pp. 96–97; also *Werke* (E), xii, pp. 375 ff.

[7] Cf. *In Epist. I ad Cor.*, on xi. 3, *Opera*, vii, p. 177, and on xiv. 35, *Opera*, vii, p. 200; *In Epist. I ad Tim.*, on ii. 12, *Opera*, vii, p. 448.

It is typical of their different attitudes that Calvin regarded polygyny as repugnant to God's ordinance of marriage,[1] and that he took the very unusual view (for a Christian apologist) that the plural unions of the patriarchs were indefensible,[2] whereas Luther adopted a more liberal standpoint. He certainly stated clearly in a letter to Joseph Levin Metsch that the example of the Old Testament is not to be followed by Christians "because there is no necessity for it, no benefit in it, and no special word of God commanding it"—but neither was there any divine injunction prohibiting polygyny, and he allowed that God might command an individual to go "beyond the liberty which is conditioned by love",[3] should need so require. Therefore he was prepared to exercise a power of dispensation such as he believed had always been possessed by the Church for use in extreme cases; hence the reluctant permission of bigamy to Philip of Hesse,[4] and other concessions of like effect which he made from time to time.[5]

Luther's assumption of dispensatory rights in the matter of bigamy did not imply the substitution of his own or some other ecclesiastical jurisdiction for that formerly enjoyed by the mediæval Church. For him, marriage in its social aspect was essentially a secular and civil affair, subject to the authority of the magistrate, who in turn was subject to the laws of God and of reason.[6] But the transference of jurisdiction was not absolute; Consistories replaced the old episcopal courts, and in practice the administration of the law in matrimonial causes depended upon the harmonious co-operation of Church and State. The theologians proclaimed the principles upon which such causes should be judged, and advised the rulers accordingly; and the retention of a *forum ecclesiasticum* for the trial of marriage cases was justified

---

[1] *In Gen.*, on ii. 24, *Opera*, i. p. 15.

[2] *In Gen.*, on xvi. 1, *Opera*, i. p. 82.

[3] See LSC, p. 276.

[4] See, in this connexion, the explanatory letter to John Frederick of Saxony, LSC, pp. 288–291; and in general, T. M. Lindsay, *History of the Reformation*, i, pp. 380 ff.

[5] See G. H. Joyce, op. cit., p. 581.

[6] *Werke* (E), xliii, p. 116.

on the ground that these were substantially cases of conscience, and thus fell to be dealt with by the spirituality.[1] Calvin, too, ceded to the secular courts all jurisdiction in matters pertaining to marriage; but (unlike Luther) conceiving the State as a theocracy, he insisted that the magistrates must handle all suits strictly in accordance with the principles of the New Testament as interpreted by the divines of the reformed Church.[2]

This conception of the respective jurisdictions of the spiritual and temporal authorities naturally affected, in particular, the question of divorce and remarriage. So long as matrimonial causes were tried exclusively by the ecclesiastical courts, the principle of indissolubility obtained—though it was preserved, as we have seen, only at the expense of the anomaly of Pauline privilege, and of the many abuses accruing from impediments of consanguinity and affinity needlessly and artificially elaborated. But the transference of marriage cases to the civil power, and the different theological idea of matrimony developed by the Reformers, inevitably created a new attitude to the permanence of the union.

Luther, indeed, professed such a hatred of divorce that he owned he would even prefer bigamy! He recognized that Christ had sanctioned nothing but separation (and that, only in the case of fornication), and had required the innocent husband to remain unmarried;[3] yet he did not forget also that St Paul had preferred marriage to burning, and he concluded that the teaching of the Gospels was intended less as a directive to rulers than as a guide for the individual conscience.[4] Legislation, therefore, must be adapted to the general needs of the community in conformity with the law of nature. The severance of the matrimonial bond, he believed, is effected automatically by adultery, so that the office

---

[1] Cf. M. Chemnitz, *Examen Conc. Trident.* (Frankfurt, 1578), ii. p. 268 (on sess. xxiv *de matr.*, xii).

[2] *Les Ordonnances Ecclésiastiques de l'Église de Genèvre* (1541), vii, *du mariage*, see B. J. Kidd, op. cit., pp. 598–599.

[3] *Pagan Servitude* (*De Captivitate Babylonica*), in B. L. Woolf, op. cit., i, p. 306.

[4] *Brief an den Rath zu Danzig, Werke* (E), liii, p. 296.

of the magistrate (who acts with the authority of God's vice-gerent) is simply to legalize the resultant dissolution of the union, and to sanction remarriage.[1]

Upon these principles Luther's practice was based. He explains, for example, that in order to curb infidelity the usage in Witten-berg was to banish the offender and to allow the innocent party the privilege of remarriage.[2] But adultery was not the only cause for which he granted relief. He extended the Pauline privilege to all cases of desertion[3]—an offence which he construed very widely as embracing refusal by a wife of her conjugal duties,[4] hindrance on the part of one spouse to the living by the other of a godly life, and rejection of reconciliation following separation on account of domestic dissention.[5] Melanchthon would have further enlarged the grounds of divorce so as to include brutality and attempted murder. Having repudiated the traditional doctrine of indissolubility and the discipline dependent thereon, Lutheran divines and lawyers in general could find no satisfactory halting-place short of the provisions of the Roman-Byzantine code[6]—though not all of them were disposed to accept in full the some-what liberal enactments of Theodosius and Justinian.[7]

Calvin also regarded adultery as a ground of divorce authorized in Scripture, but he was, as usual, more conservative in his outlook and less inclined than Luther to admit innovations. Thus in 1556 he gave it as his opinion that the Pauline privilege related exclu-sively to refusal of cohabitation by the pagan husband of a convert;[8] but five years later the Genevan Ordinances of 1561 show some relaxation, permitting the dissolution of wedlock, not

---

[1] *Tischreden (Table Talk)*, 2256, *Werke* (E), lxi, p. 241.

[2] Letter to Simon Wolferinus, LSC, p. 348.

[3] Cf. Letter to John Wickmann, LSC, p. 284—seven years desertion dissolves the marriage; see also *Pagan Servitude*, in B. L. Woolf, op. cit., i, p. 307.

[4] *Predigt vom ehelichen Leben*, *Werke* (E), xx, p. 72.

[5] *Das siebente Kap. S. Pauli an die Korinthern ausgelegt*, *Werke* (E), li, pp. 39 and 443.   [6] See *Cod. Justin.* V. xvii. 8 (449); *Nov.* xxii.

[7] M. Chemnitz, op. cit., ii, p. 261 (on *de matr.* vi) would recognize only adultery and desertion; for a discussion of post-Reformation Lutheran opinion, see G. H. Joyce, op. cit., pp. 412 ff.

[8] *In Epist. I ad Cor.*, on vii. 15, *Opera*, vii, p. 153.

only for desertion of any kind, but for incorrigible vagabondage on the part of a husband and for strong presumption of adultery on the part of a wife. Calvinist theologians and jurists, however, went no further, but limited divorce strictly to the grounds sanctioned (as they believed) by the New Testament—though they agreed in construing the Pauline privilege as applicable no less to the case of the Christian deserter than to that of the pagan.

If these changes inevitably produced a number of divorce suits, drastic simplification of the complex system of impediments by means of which the mediæval Church sought to control the formation of marriage certainly effected a considerable reduction in the volume of actions for nullity. Both the great Reformers were unsparing in their denunciation of the prohibitions imposed by the canon law. To Luther, these were nothing but so many traps set to catch the simple Christian, and because of them people avoided marriage and resorted to illegal cohabitation. Nor was this the worst evil, for many hindrances to wedlock were not diriment or absolute, and dispensations could always be purchased —a traffic in *pudenda* (as he bluntly termed it) no less disgraceful than the traffic in indulgences. God's joining, he asserted, holds good in spite of men's laws; the impediment of spiritual affinity is sheer nonsense, and likewise that of disparity of religion—why should a Christian not marry an unbeliever, if the latter agrees not to interfere in religious matters?[1]

Luther and Calvin both took as the basis of their own systems the prohibitions of Leviticus, which they believed to be derived from the natural law, and therefore to be of universal and perpetual obligation;[2] but they, too, found it necessary to make certain additions. Parity of reasoning, argued Calvin, justified an extension of the Scriptural impediments to parallel cases not specified in the Mosaic law;[3] thus, if a man may not marry his

---

[1] See *Pagan Servitude*, in B. L. Woolf, op. cit., i, pp. 277 ff.; cf. Calvin, *Inst.* IV. xix. 31, etc.

[2] Calvin, *In Quattuor Reliq. Lib. Mos.*, on Lev. xviii. 1-8, *Opera*, i, p. 520; Luther, *Predigt vom ehelichen Leben*, *Werke* (E), xx, p. 63; *Pagan Servitude*, in B. L. Woolf, op. cit., i, pp. 298-299.

[3] *In Quattuor Reliq. Lib. Mos.*, on Lev. xviii. 1-18, *Opera*, i, p. 521.

father's sister,[1] logic forbids a woman to marry her father's brother—a union not proscribed in the Old Testament code. Luther, on the other hand, considered that whatever Leviticus does not expressly exclude is lawful, though it may be desirable for the common good to admit certain obstructions to matrimony which lack Biblical sanction,[2] such as impotence[3] or a vow of continence taken before wedlock[4]—and of course, an existing marriage is a bar absolute, save when dispensation in favour of bigamy is indicated!

One of the principal factors to determine the views of the Reformers on marriage was their rejection of the mediæval innovation that the rite of matrimony is a sacramental rite. Calvin insisted that wedlock was a good, holy, and divine ordinance, but that God had appointed no external ceremony of a special grace-bearing character by means of which to confirm his promise. The *mustērion* to which St Paul alludes is Christ and the Church, not the union of husband and wife—and he pertinently asks: if the latter is indeed a sacrament, how at the same time can it be unclean, polluted, and carnally defiling—as writers of high repute in the Church have asserted?[5] Luther, too, maintained that the idea of the sacrament of marriage is unfounded, and was introduced into the Church through ignorance; it has no Scriptural warrant, for the Bible nowhere says that people shall receive the grace of God by exchanging nuptial vows. He even goes so far as to doubt whether wedlock may rightly be termed a

---

[1] Lev. xviii. 12; xx. 19.

[2] See *Pagan Servitude*, in B. L. Woolf, op. cit., i, p. 303.

[3] Luther considers in some detail the case of a woman married to an impotent man. Although she could seek relief by means of divorce (which would amount to annulment), she may be reluctant to do so because of the publicity involved; but why should she struggle to resist her natural emotions which have no outlet? Let her husband consent to her secretly having coitus with another man. Anyway, he is not really her husband if they have not become one-flesh, and ought to concede this right if her desires are strong; but if he refuses, then let her marry someone else and move to a remote part. Such a remedy is justified if he persists in defrauding her; ibid, B. L. Woolf, op. cit., i, pp. 304 ff.

[4] Luther is uncertain at what age a vow of this kind can be taken responsibly, and can therefore be held valid.

[5] *Inst.* IV. xix. 34-35.

sacramentum in the Augustinian sense, for there is no evidence that God instituted it expressly to be symbolic of anything; but he is prepared to concede that it is a sort of natural allegory of Christ and the Church.[1]

Denial by the Protestants that marriage is a sacrament called forth the first of the anathemas pronounced by the Council of Trent at its twenty-fourth session, when matrimonial and cognate questions were discussed. Subsequent canons denounced other doctrines, opinions, and concessions of the Reformers. They affirm that polygamy is unlawful; that the Church can create or dispense from diriment and other impediments; that consummated wedlock is inviolable, but that *matrimonium ratum non consummatum* may be dissolved by solemn religious profession, and that separation *a mensa et thoro* is permissible; that vows of chastity may not be set aside; that virginity is a higher and more blessed state than marriage; and that jurisdiction in matrimonial causes belongs by right to the ecclesiastical authority. Furthermore, various decrees were passed relating to the reformation of abuses. Among other matters, the Protestant teaching, that clandestine unions and those effected by minors without parental consent are invalid, was rejected, and steps were taken to ensure due publicity for all weddings (this was the important decree known as *Tametsi*); the impediments resulting from *cognatio spiritualis*, public honesty, and *affinitas illegitima* were revised and restricted; and conditions were laid down for granting dispensations from certain prohibited degrees.[2]

In effect the Council of Trent affirmed, with certain modifications and additions, the chief features of the mediæval Church's matrimonial doctrine and discipline, while the Reformers sought their principles and standards from Scripture, the natural law, and the practice of the primitive Church. This, however, does not mean that from the middle of the sixteenth century we have to reckon with two conflicting sexual traditions, one 'Catholic' and the other 'Protestant'. Since national and cultural as well as

---

[1] *Pagan Servitude*, in B. L. Woolf, op. cit., i, pp. 292–296.
[2] For the relevant canons and decrees, see P. Schaff, op. cit., ii, pp. 292–296.

religious factors played their part in the fragmentation of the western Church, it was all the more inevitable that Christians should find themselves in disagreement about marital and sexual matters; yet beneath even the most pronounced theological and political cleavages there remained common convictions and emotional attitudes which were too deeply rooted in the past to be eradicated or easily changed in a few decades. Judged in terms of its immediate results, the Reformation proved to be, not the point of departure of a new sexual tradition but the source of fresh differences within that which already existed. Only after the lapse of four centuries is it becoming apparent that the achievements of Luther and Calvin had deeper implications than are suggested by their actual teaching.

Of the Reformed contributions to the development of thought upon sexual relationship, those most productive of positive gain were the rejection of the double ethical standard which exalted virginity above marriage, and the consequent repudiation of the rule of clerical celibacy. In those Churches where ministers were allowed to marry "at their own discretion, as they shall judge the same to serve better to godliness",[1] the benefit has far outweighed the inconveniences sometimes alleged. Not only has it been displayed in a higher moral responsibility, a more effective personal ministry, and an invaluable witness to the Christian ideal of wedlock and family life, but it has also borne fruit in an increasingly profound theological understanding of the relational aspects of sex and marriage, such as could come only from reflection upon the inner meaning of an experience hitherto denied to the clergy.

It is hardly surprising that the Reformers were enthusiastic about the blessings of matrimony, and sensible of the consolations and the salutary disciplines of the home. In particular, they esteemed very highly the privilege and responsibility of parenthood. Luther considered that the procreation and training of children is the chief end of marriage, and he did not hesitate to describe parents as "apostle, bishop, and priest" to their offspring.[2]

---

[1] The XXXIX Articles, XXXII.

[2] *Predigt vom ehelichen Leben, Werke* (E), xvi, p. 538.

Their work of education, he said, is most honourable and valuable to society,[1] and they could render no better service to God, to Christianity, and to the whole world.[2]

Yet despite this elevated idea of the parental office, a retrogressive tendency can also be discerned in the Reformed attitude to the family. Just as the great kings of Israel and Judah furnished the type of the 'godly prince' to which rulers were exhorted to conform, so the patriarchal households provided the model for the home life of the devout Protestant. But the inculcation of this Semitic ideal of domesticity, though doubtless not unedifying, was also not without its adverse effects; it intensified the existing androcentricity of society, justified the continued subordination of woman, established the father in a quasi-magisterial rôle, and stringently subjugated children to the wills of their parents. This last was especially true in the matter of marriage[3]—though Luther insisted that while parents might prohibit an unwise union, they have no authority to compel a son or daughter to marry where love is wanting.[4]

The liberating potential of the Reformation in the sexual realm was to some extent neutralized by a certain 'puritanism' in venereal matters which lurks even behind Luther's robust and earthy realism. Doubtless this tendency was encouraged by excesses such as those of the Münster Anabaptists, but it seems also to have characterized the revulsion of the sixteenth century from past licentiousness—especially that of Renaissance Italy. Thus little more than fifty years after the decease of Alexander VI, Paul IV implemented the Tridentine decree against paintings calculated to excite lustful feelings[5] by having Michaelangelo's nudes in the Sistine Chapel paintings clothed with decent

---

[1] *Predigt von dem ehelichen Stand, Werke* (E), xvi, p. 64.

[2] Ibid, *Werke* (E), p. 65; *Hochzeitpredigt* on Heb. xiii. 4, *Werke* (E), iii, p. 522.

[3] Cf. Calvin, *in Gen.*, on xxi. 21; xxiv. 3; and xxxiv. 4, *Opera*, i, pp. 115, 126, 177.

[4] See LSC, pp. 264–270; and cf. pp. 282–283 and 287–288.

[5] *Conc. Trid.*, sess. xxv, *de invocatione, veneratione, et reliquiis sanctorum, et sacris imaginibus*, see P. Schaff, op. cit., ii, p. 203.

draperies. This prudishness showed itself in the Protestant disposition to regard venereal sins with a severity which was intensified
by the Reformers' lively sense of the divine providence which had
appointed marriage as the remedy for man's incontinence. Thus
Luther opposed the restoration of brothels in Saxony, and argued
that wedlock or the hope of wedlock is the proper solution to the
problem of prostitution[1]—though when giving advice about the
closing of houses of ill fame in Halle, he counselled caution on the
ground that premature eradication of the evil might do more
harm than good.[2]

The sexual teaching of the continental Reformers naturally
influenced developments in England, though its effect is to be
seen rather in the thought of the Anglican divines of the sixteenth,
and more particularly the seventeenth centuries, than in the
formularies of the Church of England, which on the whole
preserved a remarkably conservative attitude. Thus while Luther
and Calvin both assigned to the civil magistrates all jurisdiction in
matrimonial causes, differing only the one from the other as to
the source of the law so to be administered, in England the spiritual
courts remained and continued to deal with suits for nullity,
divorce *a mensa et thoro*, restitution of conjugal rights, jactitation,
and so forth until deprived of their powers by the Matrimonial
Causes Act of 1857.

The only substantial change in the legal position was that
occasioned by the establishment of the royal supremacy. Appeals
to Rome in marriage cases were forbidden,[3] but the jurisdiction
of the national ecclesiastical authorities was confirmed[4]—with
one significant qualification. Archbishops, bishops, and arch-
deacons had now to share their judicial functions with such
Doctors of civil law as had been duly commissioned to serve the

---

[1] See the letter to Jerome Weller, LSC, p. 292.
[2] Ibid, p. 204. Luther's attitude to prostitution is forcibly expressed in an
admonition to the students at Wittenberg on the evils and hygienic dangers
of resorting to whores, see ibid, pp. 292–294.
[3] 24 Henry VIII, c. 12, s. 2. See E. Gibson, *Codex Juris Ecclesiastici Anglicani*
(Oxford, 1761), i. p. 84. Cf. also 24 Henry VIII, c. 22, s. 5, ibid, i, p. 409.
[4] Cf. 24 Henry VIII, c. 22, s. 5, E. Gibson, op. cit., i, p. 409.

spiritual courts; and they exercised those functions, not in their own right, but "by, under, and from" the sovereign,[1] to whom pertained (in the words of the Articles of 1562) "the chief government of all estates of this realm, whether they be ecclesiastical or not".[2] Moreover, subject to the limitations specified in the Act for the Submission of the Clergy,[3] and to subsequent modification or abrogation by statute, the canon law continued in force as part of the customary law of the kingdom, except where its provisions were embodied in later legislation; and the principles of the Church's traditional jurisprudence influenced not a little the practice of the ecclesiastical law for the next three hundred years.[4]

Again, the Form of Solemnization of Matrimony followed without any significant deviation the mediæval marriage rite—principally that of the Sarum Manual. The doctrine expressed therein is that traditionally taught by the western Church, and apart from the use of the vernacular, the influence of the continental Reformation is to be seen only in certain uncontroversial additions from Hermann's *Consultation*—namely, the statement of the three "causes for which matrimony was ordained"; the joining of hands, with its accompanying formula and declaration; and two passages of Scripture in the address. The interpolation of a collect, representing the benediction which occurred after the Canon in the nuptial Mass, certainly deprived that blessing of its special significance; but both the 1549 and the 1552 rites direct that the couple must receive the sacrament on the day of the wedding—an obligation only modified in 1661. In transferring the prayer of benediction from the Mass to the marriage

---

[1] 37 Henry VIII, c. 17, E. Gibson, op. cit., i pp. 442–443.

[2] Article, 'Of Civil Magistrates', see E. Cardwell, *Synodalia* (Oxford, 1842), i, pp. 50 (Latin) and 71; cf. the XXXIX Articles of 1571, Article XXXVII, ibid, i, pp. 88 (Latin) and 104–105.

[3] 25 Henry VIII, c. 19, s. 7: canons not contrary to the laws or the royal prerogative are to continue in force until otherwise ordered. 35 Henry VIII, c. 16 extended the provisional validity of the old canon law during Henry's lifetime—but arrangements had been made for the appointment of a revision commission, see below, on the *Reformatio Legum Ecclesiasticarum*, pp. 212 ff.

[4] See the Report, *The Canon Law of the Church of England* (London, 1947), pp. 45–68.

service, however, a commendable change was effected by introducing a reference to the bridegroom; the mediæval ceremony (both *Sponsalia* and Mass) followed the pagan Roman *Velatio nuptialis* in placing the whole emphasis upon the bride alone—though the original veiling had so far been modified that the veil or canopy was held over the bridegroom as well.[1]

On the other hand, the Church of England broke with the tradition of western Christendom on several important points. One of the first questions to engage the attention of our divines was that of prohibitive degrees and diriment impediments; but here the spur to reformation was rather the exigencies of the 'King's matter' than any desire to remove the mischiefs consequent upon artificial and needless hindrances to marriage. The Convocations of 1533, whose opinion had been sought upon the validity or otherwise of union with a deceased brother's wife, gave their suffrages to the royal cause by an overwhelming majority, declaring that such an alliance is contrary to divine law and does not admit of dispensation.[2] Their verdict clearly influenced the legislature, for an Act[3] passed in the same year went far towards endorsing the Lutheran teaching that no impediments to wedlock are admissible but those stated in Leviticus—an opinion maintained by many of the English Reformers,[4] and supported by the two formularies, *The Institution of a Christian Man*, or 'Bishops' Book' (1537),[5] and *A Necessary Doctrine and Erudition for any Christian Man*, or 'King's Book' (1543).[6]

---

[1] See F. Proctor and W. H. Frere, *A New History of the Book of Common Prayer* (London, 1907), p. 618.

[2] See D. Wilkins, *Concilia Magnæ Britanniæ et Hiberniæ* (London, 1737), iii, pp. 756–758, 767.

[3] 25 Henry VIII, c. 22, ss. 3, 4, E. Gibson, op. cit., i, p. 409.

[4] Cf. Tyndale, *The Obedience of a Christian Man*, *Works* (Parker Society—hereafter abbreviated PS), i, p. 245; Becon, *A Comfortable Epistle to the Afflicted People of God*, pref., *Works* (PS), iii, p. 199; *The Acts of Christ and Antichrist*, doctr. 70, *Works* (PS), iii, p. 532; etc.

[5] 'Of the Sacrament of Matrimony', see C. Lloyd, *Formularies of Faith* (Oxford, 1825), pp. 83–84; cf. 'Declaration of the Seventh Commandment', ibid, p. 160.

[6] 'The Sacrament of Matrimony', see C. Lloyd, op. cit., pp. 270–271 cf. 'Exposition of the Seventh Commandment', ibid, p. 326.

Cranmer, however, saw that the Mosaic code was incomplete for practical purposes,[1] and circumstances soon moved the Supreme Head to a like conclusion, for in order to invalidate his marriage with Anne Boleyn he revived the old impediment *ex copula illicita*.[2] Next, to facilitate his alliance with Catherine Howard, he procured the passage of an Act in 1540[3] which provided that matrimony duly solemnized and consummated annuls an unconsummated pre-contract; that the union of cousins and of others "not prohibited by God's law" is valid;[4] and that "no reservation or prohibition, God's law except, shall trouble or impeach any marriage without the Levitical degrees". The Henrician statutes were all repealed during the next two reigns,[5] but Elizabeth re-enacted that portion of the measure of 1540 which declared lawful all unions (not more exactly specified) which did not infringe the Scriptural impediments.[6] But the prohibitions eventually laid down by canon XCIX of the code of 1604 were based upon a table published by Archbishop Parker in his *Admonition* of 1563[7]—and the latter, in turn, reproduced the provisions of the abortive *Reformatio Legum Ecclesiasticarum*, in which the Levitical law was treated as having the same force as the Decalogue, and the principle of parity of reasoning was invoked to extend the range of that law to parallel cases, including those arising *ex copula illicita*.[8] Thus the Anglican Church found itself, in effect, with a Calvinistic table of kindred and affinity, to

---

[1] *Letters*, clxxviii, *Works* (PS), ii, p. 329.

[2] 28 Henry VIII, c. 7; Henry had had coitus with Anne's elder sister, Mary.

[3] 32 Henry VIII, c. 38, s. 2, E. Gibson, op. cit., i, p. 416.

[4] This, it has been held, was so framed with the object of abolishing the impediment of *cognatio spiritualis*.

[5] See 2 & 3 Edward VI, c. 23, ss. 1, 2, 3 (excepting the application of the Levitical degrees, s. 4); 1 Mary, sess. 2, c. 1, s. 3; 1 & 2 Philip and Mary, c. 8, ss. 18, 19. See E. Gibson, op. cit., i, pp. 409, 410, 417, 418.

[6] 1 Elizabeth I, c. 1, s. 13, E. Gibson, op. cit., i, p. 418.

[7] See E. Cardwell, *Synodalia*, i, p. 130; for comment upon certain anomalies consequent upon this canon, see R. Haw, *The State of Matrimony* (London, 1952), pp. 72–73.

[8] See *De grad. in matr. prohib.*, iv, v, vi, in *Reformatio Legum Ecclesiasticarum*, ed. E. Cardwell (Oxford, 1850), pp. 47 ff.

which various modifications were subsequently made, chiefly during the present century, with the object of adjusting it to the scope of the civil law.[1]

Although the English Reformers followed those of the Continent in rejecting the mediæval conception of marriage as a rite instituted by Christ, causing the grace which it signifies, they and their seventeenth-century successors not only maintained the earlier doctrine that wedlock is a holy symbol, but also continued generally to use the term 'sacrament' in this sense—a practice which has somewhat confused the idea of the theological character of matrimony commonly entertained by Anglicans. The development of thought within the Church of England is already apparent in the 'Bishops' Book' of 1537. Marriage is still included among the seven sacraments and is held worthy of this name and dignity, but it is expressly distinguished from baptism, penance, and the Lord's Supper on the grounds that it was not instituted by Christ as an instrument or remedy necessary for salvation and the attainment of everlasting life; that it was not commanded by Christ to be ministered and received under any specific outward and visible sign; and that it does not convey any spiritual grace whereby sin is remitted, and regeneration and justification are effected.[2] Nevertheless, the rite of matrimony is still regarded as a sacramental rite of some kind. Its outward and visible sign is the exchange of consent, and its inward and spiritual grace the sanctification of coitus and the attainment of everlasting life through the education of children in the true faith and observance of Christianity[3]—but the sacrament itself (the symbol)

---

[1] Cf. Lord Lyndhurst's Act of 1835 (5 & 6 William IV, c. 54)—any marriages already contracted within the prohibited degrees to remain valid, but all such unions in the future to be null and void; the Deceased Wife's Sister's Marriage Act, 1907; the Deceased Brother's Widow's Marriage Act, 1921; the Marriage (Prohibited Degrees of Relationship) Act, 1931—removing certain impediments due to affinity affecting the unions of aunts or nieces with nephews or uncles by marriage. The last three statutes were repealed and re-enacted by the Marriage Act of 1949, ss. 1, 79, and Schedules 1 and 5.

[2] See C. Lloyd, op. cit., pp. 128–129.

[3] Ibid, pp. 88–89.

consists in the union of man and woman as one—flesh to signify Christ and the Church.[1]

The 'King's Book' of 1543, though conservative and reactionary in its general tendency, does not attempt any definition of the sacrament of matrimony, but is content to affirm that being a state honourable and acceptable to God, it receives his assistance.[2] The Homily, 'Of Common Prayer and the Sacraments', however, is more precise, and records a further stage in the development of Anglican thought. It affirms that since marriage (it is not clear whether this means the rite, or the state, or both) signifies a holy thing, it may in that sense properly be termed a sacrament; nevertheless, it is not a sacrament technically so called, for it is not one of "the visible signs, expressly commanded in the New Testament, whereunto is annexed the promise of free forgiveness of our sin, and of our holiness and joining in Christ".[3] No mention is made of the bestowal of any special grace, though the Homily, 'Of the State of Matrimony', assures husband and wife of God's favour and assistance in their endeavours to use rightly his singular gift and benefit.

In the light of these pronouncements and of the teaching of the Prayer Book the meaning of Article XXV of the XXXIX Articles becomes clear. It declares that there are only two sacraments proper ordained by Christ in the Gospels, and that these are not to be confused with "those five commonly called sacraments (*vulgo nominata sacramenta*)", among which matrimony figures as a state of life allowed (*probatus*—better, approved or commended) in the Scriptures. It is not a sacrament in the 'technical' sense, because it has no "visible sign or ceremony ordained of God"—in other words, the Article rejects the mediæval innovation which declared, in effect, that the exchange of consent in the nuptial rite is a sacramental act procuring an immediate outpouring of specific grace upon bride and bridegroom. Nothing is said, however, of matrimony as a sacrament

---

[1] Ibid, p. 85.　　　　　　　　　　　　　　　　[2] Ibid, p. 293.

[3] See *Certain Sermons or Homilies appointed to be read in Churches* (London, 1843), pp. 376–377. There are many different editions of the Homilies.

in the ancient meaning of the word, both because the Article is not concerned with sacraments in that sense, and because the teaching of the Church of England as set forth in its formularies, and above all in its liturgy, is quite unequivocal; wedlock is "such an excellent mystery, that in it is signified and represented the spiritual marriage and unity betwixt Christ and his Church". Their treatment of this question plainly demonstrates the determination of the English Reformers to reinstate the doctrine of the "ancient Fathers".

Once the true import of Article XXV is understood, it is not difficult to appreciate the reason for the opinions expressed by individual divines. When they inveighed, as they did with much vigour, against the sacramental tenets of the Papists,[1] it was not because they entertained a low view of wedlock,[2] nor was their attack directed against the symbolism of marriage. It was aimed simply and solely at the idea, contrary to the New Testament and to the teaching of the Fathers of the early Church, that the due reception of the grace of matrimony depends upon the performance of a special ecclesiastical rite, and not upon the free gift of God[3]—a notion wholly inconsistent, in their eyes, with the divine institution of marriage in Paradise, and with its character of a natural ordinance pertaining to all men, Christian and pagan alike.[4] This concern to emphasize that God's approval and blessing of wedlock does not depend upon the observance of any particular liturgical form explains, no doubt, why the Reformers

---

[1] Cf. Calfhill, *Answer to the Treatise of the Cross*, iv, *Works* (PS), pp. 235–241; Rogers, *The Catholic Doctrine of the Church of England*, art. xxv, prop. 8, *Works* (PS), pp. 260–261; Tyndale, *Answer to More's Dialogue*, *Works* (PS), iii, p. 175; *The Obedience of a Christian Man*, *Works* (PS), i, p. 254; Fulke, *Defence of the English Translation of the Bible*, xvi. 2, *Works* (PS), i, p. 493; *A Discovery of the Dangerous Rock of the Popish Church*, xiii, *Works* (PS), ii, p. 229; Whitaker, *Disputation on Holy Scripture*, contr. I, q. 2, ch. xii, *Works* (PS), p. 197.

[2] Cf. Fulke, *Defence of the English Translation*, xvi. 2, *Works* (PS), i, p. 492: it is a "devilish slander" to impute to the Anglicans the view that marriage is a mere civil contract.

[3] Cf. Fulke, *Rejoinder to Martial's Reply to Calfhill*, art. iv, *Works* (PS), ii, pp. 169–170.

[4] And contrary, let it be said, to mediæval theory, which did not deny the sacramental character even of clandestine unions, if otherwise valid.

never struck expressly at the doctrine that the bestowal of nuptial grace occurs precisely at the moment when consent is exchanged —an idea supported (as we have seen) by the 'Bishops' Book' and never repudiated in any subsequent formulary. It probably explains, too, why they continued to affirm the principle bound up with the mediæval conception of the matrimonial sacrament— namely, that the union of husband and wife is effected, in all that is essential, by consent alone.

In view of the deep cleavage between the Anglican and the Roman Churches on the question of the sacramental nature of marriage, especially as touching the spiritual efficacy expressly or implicitly imputed to the moment of consent, it is hardly surprising that Andrewes dismissed the dispute about the use of the *word* 'sacrament' as nothing but an argument about terminology—"a mere *logomachia*". "If the thing were agreed upon", he said, "we should not strive for the name";[1] but it was precisely the "thing"—the mediæval and Tridentine doctrine that matrimony is a sacramental rite instituted by Christ himself and conveying to bride and bridegroom the grace which it signifies, that precluded any possibility of agreement. Thorndike, it is true, did attempt to show that Anglicans could also regard the nuptial rite as sacramental. St Paul, he observed, certainly did not say that the marriage of Christians is a *magnum sacramentum*, but only that the union of Adam and Eve was a great mystery. Nevertheless, the equivocation might be allowed, because Christian wedlock is peculiar in that it is celebrated with a blessing, which is the expression of the Church's authority in permitting its members to marry; the solemnity of blessed matrimony, therefore, might well be termed a sacrament, "as containing a ceremony signifying that spiritual grace of living like Christians in the state of wedlock, for which it signifies the parties to be qualified".[2] But even this

---

[1] *Answer to Cardinal Perron (I)*, xvi, *Works* (Library of Anglo-Catholic Theology—hereafter abbreviated LACT), xi, pp. 25–26. The notion still persists, however, that the difference between Canterbury and Rome in this matter is simply a verbal quibble, cf. E. J. Bicknell, *A Theological Introduction to the Thirty-nine Articles of the Church of England* (London, 1936), p. 453.

[2] *Of the Laws of the Church*, iii. 30, *Works* (LACT), iv (2), pp. 742–745.

ingenious subtlety fails to meet the objection that according to the Roman theory grace is conveyed, not merely signified or promised; the gulf still remained, and no other seventeenth-century theologian made any attempt to bridge it.[1]

In another matter—namely, that of clerical celibacy, the Anglicans followed the continental Reformers; but here, too, there was some diversity of opinion, and the wedded minister was not accepted in England with quite the same alacrity and unanimity as he had been in Germany and Switzerland. The sixteenth-century divines themselves advocated and defended as with one voice the clergyman's right to marry,[2] supporting their claim with every argument which truth or rumour could supply from the lives of mediæval priests and monastics. Tyndale even thought that clerical marriage should be compulsory, both as a moral safeguard, and because experience in ruling a household is the best preparation for the exercise of pastoral oversight;[3] moreover, the union of the priest and his wife stands as a living exemplification of the marriage of Christ and the Church.[4] But approval, particularly that of the Crown, was conceded only gradually and reluctantly, and the relevant statutes and official formularies reflect the fluctuations of opinion and practice which accompanied the vicissitudes of the English Reformation.

It is evident that as early as 1521 a few of the clergy had taken wives on their own authority, for a royal proclamation in that year inhibited and deprived those who had done so, and threatened severe penalties upon any subsequent infringement of the canon law.[5] Eleven years later, however, on the eve of his elevation to Canterbury, Cranmer himself married a second time,

---

[1] Cf. Hall, *The Old Religion*, xi, §§ 2, 3, *Works* (Oxford, 12 vols, 1837–1839), ix, pp. 370 ff.; Gee, *The Texts Examined which the Papists cite* . . . (Oxford 1837), i, p. 460; Beveridge, *Discourse on the XXXIX Articles*, *Works* (LACT), vii, pp. 436–443.

[2] The references are too numerous, and the matter too monotonous, to justify citation in detail; a good number of passages is supplied by the index volume to the Parker Society's edition of the English Reformers.

[3] *The Obedience of a Christian Man*, *Works* (PS), i, p. 230.

[4] *Answer to More's Dialogue*, iii. 13, *Works* (PS), iii, pp. 153–155.

[5] See J. Strype, *Memorials of Thomas Cranmer* (Oxford, 1840), ii, p. 691.

and the absence of any reference to celibacy in the 'Bishops' Book' of 1537 no doubt indicates that its abolition was part of the general programme of reform. It was believed that the King eventually intended to sanction the marriage of the clergy,[1] but a royal proclamation of 1538,[2] and the Act of the Six Articles in the following year,[3] afforded little evidence of any such liberal purpose; unions contracted by priests were invalidated, those who refused to put away their wives forfeited goods and benefices, and any who presumed to marry in the future were declared to be felons—though these penalties were subsequently modified by a statute of 1540.[4]

With the accession of Edward VI, however, the situation changed. In the eighth session of the Convocation of 1547 all canons, laws, and customs forbidding the marriage of priests and monastics were abolished,[5] and the Commons enacted that married men might be ordained[6]—though the measure reached the Lords too late to be passed before Parliament rose. But an Act of 1549[7] granted to the ministry the liberty which its proctors

---

[1] See J. Strype, ibid, i, p. 99, referring to a defence of priests' marriage ascribed to Ponet.

[2] Ibid, i, p. 98.

[3] See 31 Henry VIII, c. 14, E. Gibson, op. cit., i, p. 437.

[4] 32 Henry VIII, c. 10. J. Ayliffe, *Parergon Juris Canonici Anglicani* (London, 1726), p. 367, states that the statute 32 Henry VIII, c. 38, abolished these sanctions when it declared that all marriages are lawful which are not prohibited by God's law—but this, as we have seen, related solely to prohibited degrees; there was no implied intent to permit clerical marriage—though the wording could be so construed outwith the context. The 'King's Book' of 1543 expressly says that bishops, priests, and deacons are to be "continent", and no mention of their being husbands of one wife is included in the catalogue of qualifications taken from 1 Tim. iii and Tit. iii; it is also stated that the liberty of marriage accorded to all men does not apply to "priests, and to others which of their free liberty, by vow advisedly made, have chosen the state of continency". They "must freely and willingly continue in the same"; see C. Lloyd, op. cit., pp. 289 and 293.

[5] See E. Cardwell, *Synodalia*, ii, p. 424. Becon records a discussion on the subject which took place at this time at Cranmer's table, *The Book of Matrimony, Works* (London, 1560–1564), i, fol. Dcvi recto and verso; see my *Thomas Becon and the Reformation of the Church in England* (Edinburgh, 1952), pp. 57–58.

[6] But not that the clergy might marry.

[7] 2 & 3 Edward VI, c. 21, E. Gibson, op. cit., i, pp. 438–439.

had desired, and another in 1552[1] relieved the unions of the clergy from any stigma still attaching to them, and legitimated their issue—though it is to be noted that the preamble to the first of these statutes sounded a conservative note, declaring that "it were most to be wished that [the clergy] would willingly and of their selves endeavour themselves to a perpetual chastity", and somewhat reluctantly sanctioning wedlock on account of "uncleanness of living, and other great inconveniences, not meet to be rehearsed".

The Marian reaction brought a repeal of this legislation,[2] and it was not restored during Elizabeth's reign, though the Queen's Injunctions of 1559 permitted priests and bishops to marry under certain conditions—the former, after the match had been approved by the diocesan, two justices of the peace, and the bride's parents, kinsfolk, or master; and the latter, after similar permission had been obtained from the metropolitan and such royal commissioners as her majesty might appoint for the purpose. Masters, deans, and heads of colleges might only take wives with the consent of the Visitor.[3] Elizabeth's antipathy towards clerical marriage is well known, and is attested by contemporary records,[4] but it would seem that the clergy themselves had not commended their cause by reason of certain indiscretions; and although the thirty-second of the XXXIX Articles of 1562[5] grants that ministers, like all other Christian men, may "marry at their own discretion, as they shall judge the same to serve better to godliness", it was not until the following reign that the law of the land

---

[1] 5 & 6 Edward VI, c. 12, E. Gibson, op. cit., i, p. 439.

[2] 1 Mary, sess. 2, c. 2 (1553), E. Gibson, op. cit., i, p. 439.

[3] Injunction 29, see E. Cardwell, *Documentary Annals of the Reformed Church of England* (Oxford, 1844), i, p. 225.

[4] Cf. Parker, *Works* (PS). p. 148; *Original Letters* (PS), i, pp. 164 and 358; ii, pp. 129–130.

[5] Article XXXI of 1552 simply states that "Bishops, priests, and deacons are not commanded to vow the single life without marriage, neither by God's law are they compelled to abstain from matrimony"; see E. Cardwell, *Synodalia*, i, pp. 29–30 (and for Article XXXII of 1562, ibid, pp. 48 and 68–69).

expressly sanctioned their use of this liberty by reviving the Edwardine statutes repealed under Mary.[1]

With the final legalization of clerical marriage at the beginning of the seventeenth century the question ceased to be of practical and domestic interest to the Anglican Church, though the Jacobean and Caroline divines were assiduous and learned in their defence of this privilege against the polemic of the papists.[2] Some, however, regretted that there was no ecclesiastical recognition even for voluntary celibacy in the Church of England. Thus Thorndike said that it was "a blot in the Reformation which we profess, that we are without it". He maintained that it had two clear advantages—one financial, and the other the facilitation of an unhindered life of prayer; and although he allowed that compulsory continence can impose a great strain upon those who are unfitted to bear it, he nevertheless advocated a compromise under which the parish clergy should marry if they so desired, while those in cathedral and collegiate churches might be bound to continence.[3] On the other hand George Herbert, himself married, would prefer his Country Parson to be single, for the ministry "requires the best and highest things".[4] But none, at this time or later, opposed clerical marriage on principle save William Law in the next century, who condemned it in unmeasured terms, instancing the impropriety of "reverend Doctors in sacerdotal robes making love to women", and the shamefulness of a clergyman's looking for a wife.[5]

Their appreciation of virginity again distinguishes the Anglican Reformers from those of the Continent. There were, it is true,

---

[1] I James I, c. 25, s. 49, see E. Gibson, op. cit. i, p. 439.

[2] Cf., among many others, Davenant, *Determinations*, xliii, in *Disputatio de Justitia*, transl. J. Allport (London, 1846), ii, pp. 448 ff.; Hall, *The Honour of the Married Clergy Maintained*, *Works*, ix, pp. 158 ff.

[3] *The Reformation of the Church of England*, xxxviii, 2–6, *Works* (LACT), v, pp. 574–576; cf. *The Due Way of Composing the Differences on Foot, Preserving the Church*, 31, *Works* (LACT), v, p. 51.

[4] *A Priest to the Temple*, ix: 'The Parson's State of Life'.

[5] See *Some Animadversions upon Dr Trapp's late Reply*, in *Works* (London, 1762, reprinted 1892–1893), vi, pp. 175 ff.

some like Becon who regarded the married state as in every respect superior to the single,[1] but for the most part the divines of the sixteenth century did not doubt that the latter is the more honourable.[2] Some qualified this judgement so far as to allow that virginity is not always and absolutely better than wedlock, but only at some times and in some places, for those who have not the gift of continence—and that in view of the late examples, such as are thus endowed should be encouraged to persevere in their calling, but not to the extent of taking monastic vows, which are superfluous.[3] Among seventeenth-century writers, Hall went so far as to assert that virginity is "the most excellent estate of life which is incident to frail humanity",[4] and Davenant considered that "the extraordinary gift of virginal continence is greater and more perfect than the ordinary gift of conjugal chastity"—though celibacy is not, on this account, a counsel of perfection.[5] Bramhall condemned Henry VIII's suppression of the monasteries, and considered that a reformed monasticism was consistent with the principles of a reformed religion;[6] and Thorndike, too, would have a pure sort of religious life restored to the Church of England, as "agreeable with Christianity and expedient to the intent of it"—provided that no irrevocable vows were exacted.[7]

---

[1] See *The Book of Matrimony*, *Works* (1560–1564), i, fol. Dcxvi verso; also fol. ccccclxii recto; those who elect to live celibate reject the higher in favour of the lower state, *Catechism, Works* (PS), ii, p. 103.

[2] Cf. Latimer, *Sermon V on the Lord's Prayer, Sermons* (PS), pp. 393–394; Hutchinson, *The Image of God*, xxv, *Works* (PS), p. 148; Fulke, *Defence of the Translation*, xvi, *Works* (PS), i, p. 492; Hooker, *Laws of Ecclesiastical Polity*, V. lxxiii. 1: the single life is " a thing more angelical and divine" than marriage.

[3] Fulke, *A Discovery of the Dangerous Rock of the Popish Church, Works* (PS), ii, pp. 228, 383–384; cf. *Stapleton's Fortress Overthrown*, ii. 5, ibid, pp. 99–101; also Tyndale, *Prologue to the Book of Numbers, Works* (PS), i, pp. 438–439.

[4] *The Honour of the Married Clergy Maintained*, i. 7, *Works*, ix, pp. 179–180.

[5] *Disputatio de Justitia*, xlv. 5, in Allport, op. cit., i, p. 492; cf. xli. 10 and xliv. 1, op. cit., i, pp. 416 and 452.

[6] *A Just Vindication of the Church of England*, I. ii, *Works* (LACT), i, p. 120.

[7] *The Laws of the Church*, III. xxxii. 16, *Works* (LACT), iv (2), p. 815; cf. *The Reformation of the Church of England*, xxxvii, ibid, v, p. 571.

Taylor, however, after a judicious and realistic examination of the respective merits and advantages of virginity and marriage unhesitatingly concludes that the latter is the more to be commended. He repeatedly affirms that neither state in itself is more acceptable to God than the other; each is indifferent alike to piety or impiety, and each may equally be used well or abused.[1] In particular, virginity is not a 'purer' condition—it is not holier than chaste marriage, nor does it more advance the Christian cause, save by accident, in certain circumstances, and as an instrument convenient for the occasion.[2] It may be useful in some times, to some persons, and for some purpose—but *per se* it is no act of religion and no service to God.[3] Nevertheless, if it is "chosen and voluntary in order to the conveniences of religion and separation from worldly encumbrances", it may be better than the married life—though it will not possess greater sanctity;[4] but compulsory celibacy is unreasonable, mischievous, and futile—it is contrary to common sense, Scripture, and human experience to contend that all men have, or can have continence simply by labouring and praying for it.[5]

There is, of course, St Paul's argument that the unmarried cares for the things of the Lord and the married for the things of the world—the basis of the Church's double ethical standard; but Taylor contends that far from destroying his case, the text actually supports it. There is nothing, he says, in the Apostle's words to imply any disparagement of wedlock or to suggest that it unfits a person for ecclesiastical office or dignity—but rather the contrary. Although the married may of necessity be more deeply involved in the world than the celibate, he is at least free from one of the most pressing anxieties—that caused by carnal desires and acts; for God has given him a remedy which is denied to the single

---

[1] *Ductor Dubitantium*, II. iii. 11. § 10, *Works* (London, 10 vols., 1847–1856), ix, pp. 562–563.

[2] Ibid, III. iv. 20. § 19, *Works*, x, pp. 423–424; cf. II. iii. 12. § 10, *Works*, ix, p. 573.

[3] Ibid, III. iv. 20. § 17, *Works*, x, p. 423.

[4] *Holy Living*, ii. 3, *Works*, iii, p. 56.

[5] *Ductor Dubitantium*, III. iv. 20. §§ 17–18, *Works*, x, pp. 420, 423.

person. The latter, on this account, has greater and more dangerous spiritual worries, and cannot always serve God with the same freedom, despite the fact that he may have fewer material cares.[1] The married person, therefore, is at an advantage, and the contention of Clement of Alexandria still stands: if the single life affords more privacy and opportunity for devotion, marriage has more necessities, calls forth a more varied piety, and requires the exercise of more graces—it is indeed a "nursery of heaven". "Single life makes men in one instance to be like angels, but marriage in very many things makes the chaste pair to be like Christ", for it is nothing less than "the symbolical and sacramental representment of the greatest mysteries of our religion".[2]

No Anglican divine of the sixteenth or seventeenth centuries, except perhaps Becon, shows so deep an understanding as does Taylor of marriage as a personal relationship of sexual love—and it is not unlikely that the eloquent and heartfelt testimony borne by both men to the blessing of wedlock owed much to the faithful companionship and sympathetic support of their wives during the vicissitudes and adversities which each endured in more than due measure. Through their writings on matrimony there breathes a new spirit, and their counsel to husbands and wives has the added authority which comes of knowing not only what marriage ought to be, but also what it is. In Taylor's case we are especially conscious of an attempt to work out the meaning of Christian discipleship in terms of the circumstances and concepts of married life which obtained in his age. Becon repudiates the idea that matrimony is a matter of fortune or chance, and declares that it is a true vocation to which men and women are called by God's singular providence and wisdom, through the work of the Holy Spirit;[3] and he paints a touchingly attractive picture, as seen

---

[1] Ibid, III. iv. 20. § 20, *Works*, x, pp. 425–426.

[2] *Sermons*, xvii—'The Marriage Ring' (1), *Works*, iv, pp. 211–212; "chaste", here and elsewhere in the literature, does not of course mean 'continent', but describes that proper attitude of mind in which the couple should approach their coital relationship.

[3] *The Book of Matrimony, Works* (1560–1564), i, fol. ccccclxix recto; cf. ccccclxii verso; also the *Catechism, Works* (PS), ii, p. 341.

from the husband's side, of the "sweet fellowship" of wedded life in which "everything is common".[1] Taylor maintains that marriage is the queen of friendships, and husband and wife the best of all friends;[2] the love which binds them together is "a union of all things excellent: it contains in it proportion and satisfaction and rest and confidence; and I could wish that this were so much proceeded in, that the heathen themselves could not go beyond us in this virtue, and its proper and appendent happiness".[3]

This changing conception of the relationship between husband and wife was responsible, no doubt, for the emergence of a different view of the purposes of wedlock. Patristic and mediæval theologians generally emphasized the blessings annexed to marriage rather than the ends for which it was instituted, and the *bona matrimonii* (faith, offspring, and sacrament) appear in more or less their conventional form in the sections on wedlock in the 'Bishops' Book' of 1537 and the 'King's Book' of 1543;[4] but the Prayer Book of 1549 introduced the three "causes for which matrimony was ordained", and these have usually been regarded as an authoritative statement of the purposes of marriage as received in the Anglican Church. Moreover, it has been commonly assumed that the order in which they are set forth (procreation, remedy, mutual society) indicates their relative importance—so that the principal end of wedlock is the generative, and the common life ranks last. But this assumption, though apparently supported by the *Reformatio Legum Ecclesiasticarum* (? 1552),[5] is not confirmed by the teaching of the divines in whose time, and in many cases by whose labours, the various Prayer Books were compiled; the consensus of their opinions, therefore, may not unreasonably be taken to interpret the sense of the liturgy with sufficient accuracy.

---

[1] *The Book of Matrimony*, op. cit., i, fol. Dcl; the passage in question is printed in full in my books, *The Mystery of Love and Marriage*, pp. 6–7, and *Thomas Becon and the Reformation of the Church of England*, p. 114.

[2] *A Discourse of the Nature and Offices of Friendship*, *Works*, I, pp. 90–91.

[3] *Sermons*, xviii—'The Marriage Ring' (2), *Works*, iv, p. 224.

[4] See C. Lloyd, op. cit., pp. 89–92 and 275–277.

[5] *De matr.* i, see E. Cardwell, op. cit., p. 39.

At first, Lutheran influence is apparent; marriage is a remedy appointed by God, whereby man may "avoid a dissolute, common, and libidinous life, with other uncleanness".[1] Even the seventeenth-century divines did not cease to urge its medicinal value;[2] and Donne actually placed avoidance of fornication first among the purposes of wedlock on the ground that it was so ordained by God, who anticipated the disease by furnishing its cure—though he conceded that to use one's wife *in medicinam* is the lowest of all employments of matrimony.[3] In the view of a majority of the Reformers and Carolines, however, if we may judge by the order in which the purposes are stated, mutual society is primary, followed by procreation, and then remedy.[4] Cosin, commenting on Bucer's suggestion in the *Censura*,[5] that the third cause ought to be placed first, says that mutual society was "the chiefest and most general cause for which matrimony was ordained, even in paradise, *Faciamus in adjutorium*; but they[6] thought it better to let it stand as it was; for society and help may be had without marriage . . . but procreation of children cannot lawfully be had without it".[7] Taylor, too, expressly defined mutual society as the first purpose of wedlock, being first in the Creator's design ("It is not good that man should be alone"); then followed procreation, but "the avoiding fornication came in by the superfœtation of the evil accidents of the world".[8] Comber

---

[1] J. Hooper, *A Declaration of the Ten Commandments*, x, *Works* (PS), i, p. 375; cf. Becon, *Catechism*, iii, *Works* (PS), ii, p. 103.

[2] Cf. Andrewes, *A Pattern of Catechetical Doctrine*, iv (on the 7th commandment), *Works* (LACT), vi, p. 233.

[3] *Sermons*, lxxxiii, *Works* (London, 1839), iv, pp. 33–34. Cf. earlier, Tyndale, *The Obedience of a Christian Man*, *Works* (PS), i, p. 254.

[4] See, e.g., the Homily, 'Of the State of Matrimony', *Homilies*, op. cit., p. 534; Taverner, Postil: 'On the Day of Wedding', in E. Cardwell (ed.), *Postils on the Epistles and Gospels* (Oxford, 1841), p. 594; Becon, *The Book of Matrimony*, *Works* (1560–1564), i, fol. Dcxlviii recto ff.; Sandys, *Sermons*, xvi, *Works* (PS), i, p. 380.

[5] See C. Hopf, *Martin Bucer and the English Reformation* (Oxford, 1946), p. 72.

[6] Sc. the compilers of the Prayer Books of 1549 and 1552.

[7] *Notes on the Book of Common Prayer*, series III, *Works* (LACT), v, p. 492.

[8] *Sermons*, xvii—'The Marriage Ring' (1), *Works*, iv, p. 215.

seems to have treated the first and third causes as equal in importance; procreation, he states, appears to have been "the prime
intention of Almighty God" in his institution of marriage, but
mutual society, despite its being placed third in order by the
Prayer Book, is "one of the principal ends" of matrimony.[1]

The testimony of the Reformers and of the seventeenth-century
divines thus suggests that the Prayer Book merely enumerates the
causes without intending to place them in any order of relative
importance or priority;[2] and that of the three, mutual society is
by consent of the majority the chief. Indeed, it is doubtful
whether the causes should be regarded simply as 'ends' of
marriage; rather, they seem to bring together into a single
formula the traditional conception of the purposes of wedlock
and the *bona matrimonii* of Augustinian and Thomist thought,
preserving the substance of the latter in the form of 'causes' and
not blessings. Thus the *henosis* or union of husband and wife in
one-flesh is blessed by the mutual society, help, and comfort
which they enjoy as one of the benefits of the common life
through which the symbolism or *sacramentum* of their relationship
is exhibited. Their marriage is also blessed by the coitus in which
the venereal impulses are expended creatively in relational acts
which assist the preservation of fidelity (*fides*), and may lead to the
begetting of children (*proles*).

The three causes, then, may be said to state the nature of wedlock, considered in terms of its blessings, and of the effects to
which it tends and the objects which husband and wife ought to
pursue; but do they so well define the essential character and ends
of marriage? Unfortunately the ontological question was ignored
almost completely by Anglican theologians as it had been by
their predecessors. Nevertheless, the Prayer Book itself may
contain a clue, for the opening exhortation added to the nuptial
rite of the Sarum Manual by the compilers of the Book of 1549

---

[1] *A Companion to the Temple, Works* (Oxford, 1841), iv, pp. 38, 46.

[2] This is supported by the wording of the Books of 1549 and 1552: "One
[cause] was . . . secondly . . . thirdly", which has every mark of an enumeration rather than a graded order.

directs attention first to the signification of matrimony—a signification which depends entirely upon the belief that husband and wife realize together an unique kind of unity, at first formally, and then in an ever-growing measure actually, as they address themselves to the task of their common life. This suggests, as does Scripture itself,[1] that the true and primary purpose of wedlock is simply that the two shall become one; and that upon this *henosis*, constituted responsibly in consideration of God's will, and built up by perseverance through grace, the blessings implied by the causes may rightly be expected. The priority of the unitive over other ends of marriage is certainly to be inferred from Ralph Cudworth's treatise, *The Union of Christ and the Church*, in which he argued that the mystical symbolism of wedlock is no mere accidental likeness or "bare similitude", but that the *henosis* of husband and wife is a divinely appointed image of the heavenly, spiritual union—the couple are *sponsus et sponsa ectypi*, as the celestial Bride and Bridegroom are *sponsus et sponsa archetypi*.[2]

From their emphasis upon the primacy of mutual society, help, and comfort, and from their lively appreciation of marriage, it might be expected that the Anglicans would have displayed a liberal attitude towards woman. Certain writers, indeed, do acknowledge her qualities, though not always consistently; Tyndale, for example, insists upon her subordination in marriage, observing that she is put under her husband in order that he may "rule her lusts and wanton appetites",[3] yet when apologetic requires it, he is prepared to make the highest claims—she may, in circumstances of necessity, not only baptize but also preach and administer the Lord's Supper.[4] Becon pays tribute to woman's wisdom and prudence, and to her competence to give sound

---

[1] Gen. ii. 24.

[2] See J. Tulloch, *Rational Theology and Christian Philosophy in England in the Seventeenth Century* (Edinburgh and London, 1874), ii, pp. 200–201.

[3] *The Obedience of a Christian Man, Works* (PS), i, p. 171.

[4] *Answer to More's Dialogue, Works* (PS), iii, pp. 18, 30, cf. 98, 176; see also on the ministering of women, Whitgift, *Defence of the Answer . . ., Works* (PS), ii, pp. 495 ff., and *Original Letters* (PS), i, p. 164.

counsel,[1] and Taylor dissociates himself from the morose cynics who deem her unfit for man's friendship—though the discriminations of that age are doubtless responsible for his conclusion that her offices are better suited to times of prosperity than to those of adversity.[2] Nevertheless, the old androcentricity remained, and is reflected in numerous admonitions to the married concerning their duties and obligations.

The relationship of husband and wife is uniformly and monotonously expounded in accordance with the injunctions delivered in the epistles to the Colossians and to the Ephesians, supported by appropriate *exempla* culled from the Old Testament —and occasionally, too, from classical literature and ancient history, Christian and pagan. The basic principle of sexual relationship is that of male headship; men in general are credited with superior understanding and a prerogative of reason and government,[3] while women are alleged to be so constituted as to require guidance, control, and protection. They are intrinsically inferior in excellence, imbecile by sex and nature, weak in body, inconstant in mind, and imperfect and infirm in character;[4] yet in spiritual capacity it is allowed that they are equal to their lords, having "as good an interest in the promises of God, and as fair a title to that eternal life which the divine grace bestows upon us".[5]

---

[1] *Catechism, Works* (PS), ii, pp. 338–339; cf. *The Book of Matrimony, Works* (1560–1564), i, fol. ccccclxix recto.

[2] *Discourse of the Nature and Offices of Friendship, Works*, i, pp. 94–95.

[3] Cf. Taylor, *Ductor Dubitantium*, II. iii. 20. § 11, *Works*, ix, p. 703. The exception to this, of course, was that of sovereignty—and of female rule, Anglicans had had a varied experience. Protestant polemic had made much of the subordination argument in its attack upon the "monstrous regiment of women" as exemplified in the two Marys of England and Scotland (cf. in addition to Knox's treatise, Ponet, *A Short Treatise of Politick Power*; Goodman, *How Superior Powers ought to be Obeyed* . . .; Traheron, *A Warning to England to Repent* . . .; Becon, *An Humble Supplication unto God* . . .; and generally, S. R. Maitland, *Essays on* . . . *the Reformation in England* [London, 1849], pp. 126–149); but the accession of Elizabeth caused them to retract hastily and somewhat ignominiously, see Maitland, ibid, Essay X.

[4] Cf. Hooker, *Eccl. Pol.*, V. lxiii. 2, 5; 'Of the State of Matrimony', *Homilies*, op. cit., p. 537; Davenant, *Exposition of the Epistle to the Colossians*, transl. J. Allport (London, 1832), ii, p. 152.

[5] Comber, *A Companion to the Temple, Works*, iv, p. 165.

Their subordination, however, is no mere accident of circumstances, nor is it the result of a certain incidental or temporary immaturity and inexperience. It is inherent in the very nature of things and integral to the divine hierarchical ordering of the universe. Many proofs of this, claims Davenant, can be adduced—the feminine defects just listed; the express sanction of God himself, who is the author of peace and not confusion; the creation of woman after, out of, and for the benefit of, man; and the fact that she first fell into sin, and then allured him to transgression.[1] If this divinely appointed (and male-centred) order were disturbed, Davenant confidently predicts that serious domestic and social inconveniences would ensue.[2]

This presumptive ontological relationship of male and female determines the respective offices and dispositions of husband and wife. She must be studious to conform to his wishes and to please him, and diligent in the discharge of those duties incumbent upon her; her demeanour must be compliant, her interests strictly domestic, and her obedience ready and good-humoured. He, on the other hand, must comport himself towards her as a father towards a child;[3] and his rule must be like that of the soul over the body, "obnoxious to the same sufferings, and bound by the same affections, and doing or suffering by the permissions and interests of each other".[4] The husband's power, says Taylor, is one of advice, "paternal and friendly, not magisterial and despotic". The wife's obedience is hers to pay, but never his to exact; it should be displayed in her submission and humility, in her opinion of his wisdom, and in her acknowledgement of his rightful privilege and pre-eminence in the family. Her own authority, real enough in its own limited and subordinate sphere, is properly exhibited "*in gynæceo*, in the nursery and offices of domestic employment".[5]

---

[1] Cf. also Thomas Jackson, *Works* (Oxford, 1844), vi, p. 235; and earlier, Latimer, *Sermons*, xxxiv, *Works* (PS), ii, p. 92.

[2] *Exposition of Colossians*, op. cit., ii, pp. 152–155.

[3] Becon, *Catechism*, *Works* (PS), ii, p. 338.

[4] Taylor, *Holy Living*, iii. 2, *Works*, iii, p. 129.

[5] *Sermons*, xviii—'The Marriage Ring' (2), *Works*, iv, pp. 219, 221, 227.

These tedious and jejune admonitions are recorded simply as typical of the attitude of the Anglican divines towards sexual relationship as expressed in their formal expositions of marital duty. They contain nothing original or theologically significant, and their spirit contrasts so markedly with that of the eulogies by Becon and Taylor upon love and conjugal happiness that we may take leave to doubt whether the precepts thus excogitated in the study were fully and consistently put into practice in every-day life. Indeed, the evident disparity between theory and experience suggests that while the relationship between husband and wife was still formally conceived in traditional terms, something of a new understanding of the meaning of wedlock was beginning to emerge, perhaps as a result of delayed 'romantic' influences and the humanism of the Renaissance—though it is clear that the consequent tension was not easily or immediately resolved.

A similar inconsistency appears in regard to the family. Again, the duties of parents and children are expounded conventionally in strongly authoritarian and paternalistic terms; yet here, too, there are signs of a new attitude towards the child—or at least, one which is never reflected in patristic or mediæval literature. Thus Becon, in his homely fashion, bids Wotton look forward to the time when "some little young babe shall play in your hall . . . which with a mild lisping or amiable stammering shall call you Dad".[1] Taylor naturally has something to say of family life. He reminds parents to be tender-hearted, pitiful, and gentle, "complying with all the infirmities of the children, and in their several ages proportioning to them several usages, according to their needs and capacities"; they must give good examples, and must express towards them "sweetness of conversation, affability, frequent monitions, all significations of love and tenderness, care and watchfulness . . ."[2] No man, he declares, can tell "but he that loves children, how many delicious accents make a man's heart dance in the pretty conversation of those dear pledges; their

---

[1] *The Book of Matrimony, Works* (1560–1564), i, fol. Dcl.

[2] *Holy Living*, iii. 2, *Works*, iii, p. 126.

childishness, their stammering, their little angers, their imperfections, their necessities, are so many little emanations of joy and comfort to him that delights in their persons and society".[1] These are notes scarcely sounded hitherto in theological literature.

The Church of England, like the reformed Churches of the Continent, strenuously discouraged the marriage of minors without parental consent being first obtained,[2] and alliances of this sort were generally reprobated in the strongest terms—though on the other hand, the right of the boy or girl to refuse an uncongenial match was upheld, and all forms of compulsion were condemned.[3] Opinion was divided as to whether such unions, once entered, held good despite the absence of parental approval. Taylor took the unusual and dubious view that they are naturally invalid, since persons under age are in no circumstances competent to contract for their good[4]; but Hall's is the more probable conclusion, that although marriages of this kind are unlawful they are none the less valid and, if consummated, are indissoluble.[5]

Closely allied to this question was that of clandestinity, in regard to which England maintained in substance the law of pre-Reformation times—save for the brief period during which a statute of Henry VIII[6] (as we have already seen) deprived an unconsummated pre-contract of its force against a subsequent marriage duly celebrated and consummated. With the repeal of this enactment in the following reign[7] the old common law was

---

[1] *Sermons*, xviii—'The Marriage Ring' (2), *Works*, iv, pp. 169–170.

[2] See Becon, *Catechism*, iv, *Works* (PS), ii, pp. 355, 358, 371–372; Tyndale, *The Obedience of a Christian Man*, *Works* (PS), i, pp. 169–170; Sandys, *Sermons*, xiv. 32 and xvi. 15, *Works* (PS), pp. 281, 325–326; Davenant, *Exposition of Colossians*, ii, p. 187; Comber, *A Companion to the Temple*, *Works*, iv, pp. 65–68; Constitutions and Canons Ecclesiastical (1604), C; 4 & 5 Philip and Mary, c. 8; 39 Elizabeth, c. 9.

[3] Cf. Hall, *Cases of Conscience*, iv. 4, *Works*, vii, pp. 475–477; etc.

[4] *Ductor Dubitantium*, III. v. 8. § 16, *Works*, x, p. 487.

[5] *Cases of Conscience*, iv. 2, *Works*, vii, p. 466; cf. Comber, op. cit., *Works*, iv. pp. 68–69.

[6] 32 Henry VIII, c. 38.

[7] 2 & 3 Edward VI, c. 23.

revived, and both ecclesiastical formularies[1] and legal opinion[2] and practice[3] confirmed the binding nature of unions effected *per verba de præsenti*.[4] Grave evils and inconveniences, however, attended this adherence to canonical principle, and during the latter part of the seventeenth and the first half of the eighteenth centuries irregular marriages, commonly solemnized at churches exempt from episcopal jurisdiction, or by criminous clerics imprisoned in Newgate and the Fleet, attained the proportions of a major social scandal.[5] Several laws were passed in a vain attempt to curb the abuse,[6] but it was not until 1754 that Lord Hardwick's Act[7] rendered invalid all unions not celebrated in the parish church of one of the parties after due publication of banns, and laid down various safeguards relating to licences, the marriages of minors, and so forth.[8] By this measure Church and State in England achieved what the Council of Trent had already accomplished for Roman Catholic countries by the decree *Tametsi*.

Concerning venereal behaviour and coitus, little of interest is said in the sixteenth century. No more than passing reference need be made to the repeated condemnations of fornication and adultery which are to be found in the writings of the Reformers,

---

[1] See the Articles of 1585, and the Canons of 1604 (canon C), in E. Cardwell, *Synodalia*, i, pp. 143, 152, 223, and 305.

[2] Cf. H. Swinburn, *Treatise of Spousals or Matrimonial Contracts* (London, 1686), xi. 19: even secret contracts without witnesses are valid in the eyes of God; also J. Ayliffe, *Parergon*, p. 364.

[3] Cf. Holt, *C. J.*, in Collins *v* Jesset (1703): "If a contract be *per verba de præsenti* . . . it is as much a marriage in the sight of God, as if it had been *in facie Ecclesiæ*: with this difference, that if they cohabit before marriage *in facie Ecclesiæ*, they are for that punishable by ecclesiastical censure", see in E. Gibson, op. cit., i, p. 417.

[4] See also the interesting case resolved by Sanderson, 'The Case of a Matrimonial Contract', *Works* (Oxford, 1854), v, pp. 122–126.

[5] For details, see R. Haw, op. cit., pp. 142–148; G. H. Joyce, op. cit., pp. 141–142.

[6] See 6 & 7 William III, c. 6; 7 & 8 William III, c. 35; 9 & 10 William III, c. 35; 10 Anne, c. 19.

[7] 26 George II, c. 33.

[8] The steps leading up to the passing of this Act are succinctly stated in R. Haw, op. cit., pp. 148 ff., and its provisions are summarized on p. 150.

but it is significant of their strict moral attitude that the *Reformatio Legum Ecclesiasticarum* would have made all such offences, including incest and prostitution, punishable by excommunication and perpetual exile, or by some other condign penalty.[1] The traditional attitude to coitus persists in its most extreme form in the 'Bishops' Book', where it is not merely forbidden as wrong outside marriage, but is described as being "of itself and of his own nature damnable"—an unequivocal assertion of its intrinsically evil or sinful character, which is neutralized, however, by the sanctifying power of the word of God and the sacrament of matrimony, whereby it is made "pure, clean, without spot of sin, and honourable".[2] This view is considerably softened in the 'King's Book', which simply states that coitus is unlawful unless sanctioned by wedlock;[3] it finds no support whatever in later formularies and theological literature.

From the age which produced casuists like Taylor, Hall, and Sanderson we might have expected a thorough and extensive treatment of such topics as the morality of venereal acts, as well as many resolutions of cases of conscience relating to matrimonial and allied questions,[4] but unfortunately the material bearing upon

---

[1] See *de matr.* iii and *de adult. et divort.* i, ii, iii, iv, xviii, xx, in E. Cardwell, op. cit., pp. 40, 49–50, 51, 57–58.   [2] See C. Lloyd, op. cit., p. 89.   [3] Ibid, p. 274.

[4] There are, of course, a number of such resolutions to be found in the works of the Caroline divines. Reference has already been made to some of these, and others will be cited later, but many of them do not further illuminate the questions already discussed adequately in this study. Of the fifty Determinations made by Davenant, only one—on the necessity of celibacy to Holy Orders—concerns us (see *Disputatio de Justitia*, J. Allport, op. cit, ii, pp. 448 ff.). Of Sanderson's eleven Cases, three are relevant, but add nothing significant to what has already been said—namely, those on marrying with a recusant; on unlawful love (dealing with the effect of a vow made by two married persons with a view to a future union, should both be freed by the deaths of their respective partners); and on the validity of a matrimonial contract *de præsenti* (*Works*, v, pp. 75 ff., 88 ff., and 122 ff.). Hall's forty-three *Cases of Conscience* include no less than thirteen on the following problems of marriage: parental consent and authority (1, 4); divorce and remarriage (2, 3); unions of near of kin (5, and Add. 1, 2, 3); betrothal (6); seasonal prohibition of wedlock (7); conditions of validity (8, 9); nullity (10); see *Works*, vii, pp. 463–506. To certain of these, as to instances given by Taylor, reference has been, or will be made. Hammond has a consideration of divorce in *A Letter of Resolution to Six Quæres*, iii. 2, *Works* (London, 1653), pp. 84 ff.

sexual relationship is comparatively small in volume and often disappointing in interest.[1] The most detailed discussions of venereal behaviour are to be found in Taylor's two works, *The Rule and Exercises of Holy Living* and *Ductor Dubitantium*, the former of which contains a section entitled 'Rules for Married Persons, or Matrimonial Chastity', wherein the author discusses the principles which ought to guide husband and wife in their coital relationships.[2] They should indulge in their permitted endearments, he says, with that measure of detachment which sets God highest in their affections, and should use such modesty and decency that they "never force themselves into high and violent lusts with arts and unbecoming devices, always remembering that those mixtures are most innocent which are most simple and most natural . . ." He will not lay down any universal rule as to what constitutes temperance in coitus, but suggests that it should be "moderate, so as to consist with health", "so ordered as not to be too expensive of time", and "without violent transporting desires, or too sensual applications". According to the counsel of St Paul, abstinence by the married from their "mutual entertainments" is approved "at solemn times of devotion"; and in self-examination a careful scrutiny of their "undecencies and more passionate applications of themselves in the offices of marriage" is recommended.

The most interesting passage in these rules, however, is that in which Taylor considers the sensual delectation and satisfaction

---

[1] Taylor hoped to deal with a "heap of matrimonial cases, which I design in a book by itself, if God shall give me opportunity, and fit me with circumstances accordingly" (*Ductor Dubitantium*, III. v. 35 ad fin., *Works*, x, p. 500); and Ralph Cudworth, Senr. had begun "a long work, The Cases of Conscience, in the three societies, of family, Church, and commonwealth", in which he proposed to handle "the perplexed questions concerning marriage, contracts, divorce, etc." (letter to James Ussher, *The Whole Works of . . . James Ussher* [Dublin, 17 vols., 1847–1864], xvi, p. 347). Taylor's project was not realized, but Hall (*Works*, vii, p. 507) reports that "my ancient and worthy colleague, Dr Ralph Cudworth, told me that he had with much labour furnished that lack [of a casuistry of marriage], and devoted it to the press; which yet sleeps in some private hands"; it has never come to light, however.

[2] *Holy Living*, ii. 3, *Works*, iii, pp. 62–64; cf. with this passage the observations by Comber in *A Companion to the Temple*, *Works*, iv, pp. 45–46.

which accompanies coitus. In their "permission and licences", he says, husband and wife must so observe "the order of nature and the ends of God" that they never seek or enjoy venereal pleasure apart from one or more of the ends which hallow it, and to the attainment of which it has been appointed as an inducement. These ends he defines as "a desire of children, or to avoid fornication, or to lighten and ease the cares and sadnesses of household affairs, or to endear each other"—and this is probably the first express recognition in theological literature of what may be termed the relational purpose of coitus. Taylor does not indicate whether any one of these ends takes precedence over the others, but it is likely that he would have set the generative before the rest. His concluding censure of Onan, who "did separate his act from its proper end", may suggest that he would have disapproved of any selection against procreation; though it is to be observed that the reluctant brother in this case sought none of the ends of coitus—there was no selection, properly speaking.

One practical question arises in this connexion: is coitus during menstruation consistent with matrimonial chastity? Such intercourse had been penalized by the Levitical code,[1] and had been condemned at various times by the Fathers and the Schoolmen—though Aquinas (or his editor) considered that in certain circumstances it might be permissible.[2] More recently, the 'Bishops' Book' and the 'King's Book' had treated it as a transgression of the seventh commandment,[3] and Andrewes had included it among the sins of incontinence.[4] Taylor, however, determined that coitus during menstruation was merely prohibited by the Mosaic law for ceremonial and judicial reasons which are no longer relevant, and that there is no moral issue involved; its interdiction is one of

---

[1] Lev. xv. 24; xviii. 19; xx. 18.

[2] A woman may not ask for coitus during normal menstruation, but she is not forbidden to do so if the discharge is not strictly menstrual, but is due to sickness, *Summa Theol.* III Suppl. lxiv. 3; on the other hand, if the husband insists on coitus at such a time, his wife (after due but not prohibitive admonition) may consent, ibid, 4.

[3] See C. Lloyd, op. cit., pp. 163 and 326.

[4] *Pattern of Catechetical Doctrine*, iv, *Works* (LACT), vi, p. 244.

those ordinances to which the Christian is not now subject, and it is superstitious to think that abstinence at such times is any service to God. The Apostle enjoined that husband and wife were not to defraud one another; therefore they may lawfully come together during menstruation—but only when their congress is ordinarily and probably necessary, and can take place without scandal or reproach.[1] Likewise Taylor refuted Jerome's argument that as the beasts abstain from copulation while the female is with young, so men and women ought to refrain from coitus during pregnancy. We are not mere animals, he observed,, and obey other laws than those of instinct; any such prohibition would expose husbands to the temptation of fornication, and would deprive both spouses of the proper endearments and comforts of married life.[2]

Unfortunately the Caroline moralists did not concern themselves specifically with the ethical (as distinct from the casuistical) aspect of venereal behaviour, and showed no disposition to explore more thoroughly the ground already surveyed by Aquinas. Again, Taylor is the only one to touch upon the subject, and that briefly; but he did suggest a departure from the strict gradation of unnatural offences proposed in the *Summa Theologica*. Sins *contra naturam*, he contended, are not intrinsically worse than other sins, for all alike are committed against God; therefore, even if they are venereal, they should not be assessed according to a predetermined scale fixing immutably the relative gravity of different acts, but regard ought to be paid to such relevant factors as motive, occasion, and consequences. Thus, although all voluntary 'pollutions' (he retains the traditional term) are materially sins against nature, Taylor argued that they are not necessarily or in every case worse than adultery or fornication. Unlike some 'unnatural' acts, fornication is expressly forbidden by divine command; moreover, it always involves two in the transgression, and is commonly aggravated by being

---

[1] *Ductor Dubitantium*, II. ii. 3 §§ 3–16, *Works*, ix, pp. 363–370.

[2] Ibid, II. i. 1 § 11, *Works*, ix, p. 285.

"acted with more vile circumstances and follies, and loss of time, and other foul appendages".[1]

It was, perhaps, this application to moral problems of common sense and a regard for proportion which led the Carolines to a view of prostitution different from that of Romish casuists such as Liguori who, while modifying the more extreme permissiveness of the schools of Salamanca and Alcala, followed Aquinas in approving as the lesser of two evils the toleration of harlots and brothels in large cities.[2] Davenant condemns the teaching of the Angelic Doctor, and takes the contrary view; it is worse, he says, for a whole city to be polluted with houses of ill-fame than for a few honest wives and maidens to run the risk of violation, for such establishments, far from reducing the evil, create habits of lust and encourage rather than prevent attacks upon virtuous women.[3] Taylor, too, makes the same point:[4] it is certainly lawful to suffer evils which cannot be abated, but not to promote and practice wrongdoing; the permission of brothels does not curb lust, but simply ensnares young men and adds to their temptations. He also attacks vigorously the immemorial notion that the male nature demands a ready venereal safety-valve: prostitution is a scandal to law and religion, and the need for it "is but phantastic, accidental, and inferred by evil customs, or some secular interest, or weaker regard; for there is no necessity that men must either debauch matrons or be fornicators; let them marry, for that is the remedy which God hath appointed. . . ." He allows that the obstruction of lawful wedlock by convention and by worldly and improper laws undoubtedly aggravates the evil, but he has no hesitation in placing his finger upon its source—and no one has ever stated more tersely and penetratingly the real cause of prostitution: "men make necessities of their own, and then find ways to satisfy them".

---

[1] Ibid, II. i. 6 § 3, *Works*, ix, pp. 327.

[2] See for details my book, *Sexual Offenders and Social Punishment* (London, 1956), pp. 54–55.

[3] *Exposition of Colossians*, op. cit., ii, pp. 40 ff.

[4] *Ductor Dubitantium*, I. v. 8 § 17, *Works*, ix, p. 246–247.

No sexual question has aroused more discussion or revealed greater differences of opinion among Anglicans than that of divorce and remarriage. To its inherent theological and legal complexities there were added from the beginning the intricate problems consequent upon the intimate and peculiar relationship between Church and State in England; furthermore, the evidence has been variously interpreted by historians and by interested parties, with the result that it is difficult to ascertain and evaluate the true position during the sixteenth and seventeenth centuries.

First, it is clear that in this as in other respects the old canon law was not abrogated. Its continuance after the breach with Rome is attested by the 'Bishops' Book'[1] and the 'King's Book';[2] and its acceptance in the reformed Anglican Church is confirmed by Parker's Admonition of 1563,[3] by the Constitutions of 1597[4] which were designed to check (among other abuses) "divorces lightly passed",[5] and by the Canons of 1604. The latter enjoin the use of good circumspection in taking evidence in matrimonial cases;[6] the pronouncement of all decrees of separation *a mensa et thoro* in open court;[7] and the insertion into every such sentence of a caution and restraint, prohibiting either party from re-

---

[1] ". . . the bond of lawful marriage is of such sort, that it cannot be dissolved or broken, but by death only", see C. Lloyd, op. cit., p. 88; cf. pp. 91–92.

[2] ". . . in marriage lawfully made, and according to the ordinance of matrimony prescribed by God and the laws of every realm, the bond cannot be dissolved, during the lives of the parties between whom such matrimony is made", ibid, pp. 276–277.

[3] See E. Cardwell, *Documentary Annals of the Reformed Church of England* (Oxford, 1854), i, p. 318. The wording is a little obscure: "That they contract not anew with any other, upon divorce and separation made by the judge for a time; the laws yet standing to the contrary". The significance of the words "for a time" is not clear; and no laws are known "standing to the contrary"—unless the reference is to the precedent, established in the Northampton case, of divorce absolute by Act of Parliament.

[4] See E. Cardwell, *Synodalia*, i, p. 154: divorces, expressly termed *sententia separationis a thoro et mensa*, are not lightly to be granted, and only upon security being given that there will be no remarriage.

[5] See the proceedings at the fourth session of the Convocation of 1597, held on November 18th, in E. Cardwell, *Synodalia*, ii, p. 580.

[6] Canon CV, E. Cardwell, ibid, i, pp. 224–225, 307.

[7] Canon CVI, ibid, i, pp. 225, 307.

marriage during the lifetime of the other, and requiring security[1] against transgression of this undertaking.[2] These enactments, the plain sense of the Marriage Service, and the confirmatory interpretations of the canonists Edmund Gibson[3] and John Ayliffe,[4] establish beyond any reasonable doubt the adherence of Anglican canon law to the principle that no form of 'divorce' is consistent with Christian principle but separation from bed and board.

It has been argued, however, that the canon law as it stands represents neither the convictions of the English Reformers in regard to divorce and remarriage, nor the practice of Church and State during the latter half of the sixteenth century; and in support of this claim the section *De Adulteriis et Divortiis* of the *Reformatio Legum Ecclesiasticarum* is commonly alleged. This would have sanctioned the absolute dissolution of the nuptial bond, with the consequent right to contract a second union, in the following cases—adultery, desertion, prolonged absence without news, deadly enmity, and incorrigible maltreatment;[5] in other words, it would have framed the Anglican law of marriage after the pattern already established among the more advanced continental Protestants. Have we here, rather than in the Canons of 1604, the true mind of the Church in England? Before this question can be answered, a brief account of the origin and fortunes of the document is necessary.[6]

---

[1] The bond was to be in a sum of £100.

[2] Canon CVII, E. Cardwell, *Synodalia*, i, pp. 225, 307–308.

[3] See op. cit., i, pp. 445–447.

[4] See op. cit., p. 229, on divorce (i.e., separation) *ex causa subsequenti*: ". . . the marriage being once good, it can never be dissolved *a vinculo*, because such subsequent cause cannot affect the bond of matrimony, though it is sufficient to separate the parties *a mensa et thoro* . . . and if either of the parties shall marry again in the lifetime of the other, such marriage is void . . ."

[5] *De adult. et divort.* v, viii, ix, x, xi, see E. Cardwell's edition of the text, op. cit., pp. 51–55. Minor contentions, incurable illness, instigation of one party by the other to commit adultery, and adultery by both parties, do not qualify for divorce, ibid, xii, xiii, xiv, xvii; see E. Cardwell, op. cit., pp. 55–57. Separation *a mensa et thoro* was to be abolished, xix, ibid, p. 58.

[6] For detailed accounts of the history of the *Reformatio Legum*, see R. Haw, op. cit., pp. 74–89; L. Dibdin and C. E. H. Chadwyck Healey, *English Church*

The Act of 1534 for the submission of the clergy[1] provided for the appointment of a commission of thirty-two persons to revise the canon law, and subsequent statutes[2] renewed this provision from time to time without implementing it. In 1551, however, a commission was at last nominated, and the preparation of a preliminary draft of the revised code was remitted to a sub-committee of eight; but less than three weeks later a new commission was empanelled, several changes in membership being made. By this time the Act under which the commission had been constituted was on the point of expiry, its powers being limited to three years from enactment in 1549. A new list of thirty-two was drawn up, incorporating further changes, but although the necessary Bill passed the Commons, Parliament was dissolved before it could be read a third time in the Lords. The commission now lacked authority to proceed with its business, and it was never revived; a 'Bill for making Ecclesiastical Laws by 32 Persons' was rejected by the Upper House in 1559,[3] and although Convocation urged in 1562 that action should be taken,[4] no attempt was made to resume the work thus interrupted.

Meanwhile, something had been accomplished—though how, we can only guess. It seems probable that the sub-committee of eight (or some of them) produced a rough draft; that Dr Haddon, Master of Trinity Hall, Cambridge, was asked to frame the Latin clearly and elegantly; and that Cranmer and Peter Martyr undertook to cast the document into its final form.[5] So much is suggested by a manuscript now in the Harleian collection in the British Museum, bearing alterations by Haddon and Peter

---

Law and Divorce (London, 1912), Part I; D. S. Bailey, Memorandum on the *Reformatio Legum Eccl.* appended to the Minutes of Evidence (Day 6) given before the Royal Commission on Marriage and Divorce, 1951–1955, and reprinted in *The Church and Marriage* (London, 1954—a Church of England Moral Welfare Council publication), pp. 50–55.

[1] 25 Henry VIII, c. 19, E. Gibson, op. cit., ii, p. 932.
[2] 27 Henry VIII, c. 15; 35 Henry VIII, c. 16; 3 and 4 Edward VI, c. 11.
[3] *Journal of the House of Lords*, i, pp. 566, 568.
[4] See E. Cardwell, *Synodalia*, ii, pp. 499–500.
[5] See E. Cardwell's edition of the text, op. cit., pp. vi–viii.

Martyr, and annotations by the Archbishop himself; but it seems that their task was never completed.

Another manuscript of the draft, however, containing eight sections missing from that upon which Cranmer had worked, was in the hands of Matthew Parker, who had been one of the commissioners. In 1571 it was apparent that the question of ecclesiastical reform would be raised in Parliament, and Parker (now Archbishop) allowed this document to be published by the martyrologist John Foxe, having first corrected it to ensure its accuracy. Doubtless his purpose was simply to ensure that a true version should be available for discussion, as well as to make public the results of the commission's labours; but in the event nothing more was done than to remit the code to a committee of the House for translation into English—after which it lapsed into the obscurity which is not seldom the fate of such 'historical documents'.[1]

It will be clear from this summary account that the *Reformatio Legum Ecclesiasticarum* never possessed the slightest legal or canonical authority; nor is there any evidence whatsoever, judicial or historical, that the ecclesiastical courts acted upon its proposals in dealing with matrimonial causes during the period between its compilation or publication, and the promulgation of the Constitutions of 1597 or the Canons of 1604.[2] There remains, however, the question of its theological authority; how far does it represent the mind of the Church of England at this time, in the matter of divorce and remarriage? The following considerations will suggest an answer.

The code, as we have it, was substantially the work, not of a royal commission, but of a small group of more or less like-minded men, among whom the influence of native extremists like Hooper and of foreign refugees like Laski and Peter Martyr was dominant—indeed, there is reason to think that throughout the process of drafting, the Italian was the moving and guiding

---

[1] There seems to be no evidence that the translation was completed—if, indeed, it was ever begun.

[2] See R. Haw, op. cit., pp. 87-88 and 133-134.

spirit. It is often alleged that the section *De Adulteriis et Divortiis* reflects Cranmer's own ideas, but in fact it conflicts both with the conception of marriage implied in the Prayer Book for which he was so largely responsible, and with that expressly stated in the Archbishop's *Collectiones de Divortio*;[1] moreover, there are other parts of the code which are inconsistent with his known teaching.[2] There is no warrant for the assumption that Cranmer himself favoured the enactment of the *Reformatio Legum* in its extant form as the canon law of the Anglican Church.

Other things must not be overlooked. It took no less than sixteen years to secure the appointment of a commission for which statutory sanction had been obtained in 1534, and Cranmer was among the prelates who opposed the continuing Act under which it was belatedly constituted. The short history of the commission is one of frequent changes in membership, suggesting dissensions and difficulty in reaching an agreed version of the new canons[3]— and it must be remembered that the draft eventually produced never received the official approval of the thirty-two, nor even in its entirety the scrutiny of Cranmer and Peter Martyr. Upon the expiry in 1552 of its authorizing Act, no steps were taken to renew the commission, and both Northumberland and the bishops of London and Ely were known to be against any extension of its life—a sufficient refutation in itself of Foxe's sanguine assertion that only Edward's untimely death prevented the enactment of the code.[4] Nor were circumstances more propitious under Elizabeth; the Bill of 1559 failed, Convocation's petition

---

[1] Lambeth MSS, No. 1108; see L. Dibdin and C. E. H. Chadwyck Healey, op. cit., pp. 104–121.

[2] Cf., for example, the section on the Lord's Supper, *de sacr.* xl, E. Cardwell, op. cit., p. 31, which implicitly runs counter to Cranmer's views as expressed in the 'Black Rubric' which he insisted on being inserted in the Prayer Book of 1552.

[3] See Cox's letter to Bullinger on October 5th, 1552, stating that although the revision of the Prayer Book had been successful, "the severe institution of Christian discipline we most utterly abominate"—suggesting that the proposals for amending the canons were in some particulars too drastic for the more moderate Anglicans; see *Original Letters* (PS), i, p. 123.

[4] Cf. J. Strype, *The Life and Acts of Matthew Parker* (Oxford, 1821), ii, p. 63.

in 1562 was ignored, and Foxe's edition of 1571 had a very poor circulation and aroused almost no interest in the country.[1]

This inconclusive record hardly lends conviction to the allegation that the section *De Adulteriis et Divortiis* of the *Reformatio Legum Ecclesiasticarum* represents the settled mind of the Anglican Church at this time. Had the bishops and Convocation been really enthusiastic about the cause of matrimonial reform (as is often maintained), it is inconceivable that they would have shown themselves so lukewarm and dilatory in the business of revising the canons. Doubtless not a few individual partisans of advanced reform were anxious to see the doctrine and practice of England brought more closely into harmony with that of Protestant Germany and Switzerland, and were active in pressing their views upon the authorities;[2] but although they may have been heard sympathetically, they were never allowed to influence official teaching or ecclesiastical policy. Mr Haw has pronounced the only possible verdict upon this obscure but intriguing passage of sixteenth-century history: ". . . the evidence shows that the *Reformatio* registers the high-water mark of continental Protestant advice to the Church of England in respect of marriage and divorce, and that, after much deliberation, that advice was finally and absolutely rejected".[3]

Nevertheless, it is clear that many in the country, from motives of self-interest if not of religion, would have welcomed a relaxation of the Church's marriage discipline, and were attracted by the Lutheran theory that adultery automatically dissolves the nuptial bond. Such persons, no doubt, were mainly responsible for the attempts which were made soon after Edward's accession to procure by statutory means the relief that the ecclesiastical courts were impotent to grant. Thus the Commons rejected in 1549 two Bills which would have allowed divorce absolute for

---

[1] See E. Cardwell's ed., op. cit., pp. xii, and xiii n. *m*.

[2] Cf. Hooper, *A Declaration of the Ten Commandments*, x, *Works* (PS), i, pp. 379, 382, 385; also earlier, Tyndale, *Exposition of Matt. v, vi, and vii, Works* (PS), ii, pp. 51, 54.

[3] Op. cit., p. 89.

adultery,[1] and threw out in 1551 a Bill which had already passed the Lords, and would have given to a sentence of divorce *a mensa et thoro* delivered by the spiritual tribunal the legal and civil effect of a divorce *a vinculo matrimonii*.[2]

What general legislation could not achieve, however, a private process might secure, and Parliament in the latter year supplied a regrettable precedent by passing an Act which retrospectively validated the second marriage of the Marquess of Northampton, who had divorced his first wife *a mensa et thoro* in 1542 on account of her adultery. This accommodation of a powerful nobleman, who was too impatient to await the verdict of a commission appointed to adjudicate upon his cause, encouraged others to think that even without statutory sanction they might treat similar sentences by the Church courts as permissions to remarry, with the result that during Edward's reign (if Becon[3] and Strype[4] are to be credited) this practice reached scandalous proportions among the wealthy classes.[5] Visitation articles and Injunctions show that it still continued in Elizabeth's time, and that the episcopate was determined to check it,[6] while its illegality was confirmed in 1602 by the civil court, on the advice of Archbishop Whitgift, in the case of Rye *v* Fuliambe, when marriage subsequent to a divorce *a mensa et thoro* was declared to be null and void.

Even though such marriages were unlawful, an Act in the year following this judgement exempted them from the penalties

---

[1] *Journal of the House of Commons*, i, pp. 6, 9.

[2] Ibid, i, p. 23; *Journal of the House of Lords*, i, p. 409.

[3] See his sermon 'Against Whoredom and Uncleanness', *Homilies*, op. cit., p. 132.

[4] *Ecclesiastical Memorials* (Oxford, 1822), ii (2), p. 138.

[5] This state of affairs, too, may help to explain why the mandate to the commission of thirty-two was allowed to lapse in 1552; it may have been thought by those in authority inexpedient to proceed with the drafting of a canon law which would (*inter alia*) have encouraged rather than restrained this licence.

[6] See R. Haw, op. cit., p. 141; also E. Cardwell, *Documentary Annals*, i, pp. 361, 414; ii. p. 35. There seems to be little record (only three possible cases) of such irregular marriages being celebrated by the clergy in parish churches, see R. Haw, op. cit., p. 134; doubtless the irregular ceremonies were conducted in private chapels.

attached to bigamy[1]—a concession which could not but suggest
a measure of condonation, and certainly points to the persistence
of this abuse. Moreover, certain bishops permitted themselves to
act contrary to the canon law. In the case of Archbishop Abbot
the charge is based on hearsay: Thorndike alleges that he was at
first "tender" in imposing the caution or restraint stipulated by
canon CVII of 1604, but became convinced of its necessity after
"experience of adultery designed upon collusion to free the parties
from wedlock".[2] In other instances the offence is more specific:
Parker granted a licence for the remarriage of Sir John Stawell,
who had divorced his wife *a mensa et thoro* for adultery;[3] Laud
assisted at the remarriage of Lady Rich to the Earl of Devon—an
act which he bitterly regretted to the end of his days;[4] and John
Thornborough, when bishop of Limerick, himself contracted
such a union—but these were obviously isolated breaches of
the canons to which it would be improper to attach undue
importance.

That there was, however, a body of opinion in the Church
favourable to remarriage after divorce for adultery, is evident
from the support accorded by John Cosin, the erudite bishop of
Durham, to a Bill introduced into Parliament by Lord Ross in
1670 for permission to contract a second union following a decree
of separation *a mensa et thoro* secured by that nobleman in the

---

[1] I James I, c. 11, s. 3, E. Gibson, op. cit., i, p. 422.

[2] *Of the Laws of the Church*, iii. 14. § 24, *Works* (LACT), iv (1), p. 321. No
example of his leniency is cited, nor is it expressly stated that he allowed or
condoned remarriage. A footnote in the ed. cited relates this change of practice
to the Archbishop's experience in the Essex case of 1613, though this was actually
a nullity suit (in fact, it seems to have been a matter of wilful refusal to con-
summate).

[3] See L. Dibdin and C. E. H. Chadwyck Healey, op. cit., pp. 83 ff. Writing to
Parker, Bishop Berkeley of Bath and Wells says that Stawell admits that "the
common laws and the laws of the realm" are against him, but that "the best
learned in Oxford" have advised him that under the circumstances it is lawful for
him to "take his remedy". Parker granted the licence on April 26th, 1572.

[4] See Laud's diary, with its reference to "my cross about the Earl of Devon's
marriage", *Works* (LACT), iii, p. 132—also the allusion in 'Anniversaria', p. 80.
Laud kept the day of this lapse as one of solemn fast ever after, and strove to
bring the Earl to repentance.

ecclesiastical court against his wife on account of her infidelity. Cosin, and Wilkins of Chester who took a like view,[1] were in a minority among the peers spiritual, but their opinion commended itself to a sufficient number of members to procure the passage of the Bill through both Houses. This measure, like that obtained by the Marquess of Northampton, was probably regarded by most of those concerned, not as a declaration of principle, but (to quote Lord Essex) as "an act of grace, that is to say, a mere dispensation, which no other person could demand *ex debito justo*".[2] Nevertheless, it initiated a stream of such processes, which slowly increased in volume with the passage of the years until, when rendered unnecessary by the Matrimonial Causes Act of 1857, no less than three hundred and seventeen such private Acts had been secured.[3]

Even the convention of obtaining a prior sentence from the ecclesiastical court was set aside in 1697 by the Earl of Macclesfield, who took his case to Parliament in the first instance, and still gained the Act he desired. This created a further precedent and encouraged collusion and fraud, but no steps were taken to control such proceedings until towards the end of the eighteenth century, when orders laid down that before a divorce Bill could be introduced, damages must be obtained against the adulterer in an action for 'criminal conversation', and that a decree of separation *a mensa et thoro* must be obtained from the Church courts. The whole system, however, was manifestly unsatisfactory, and inequitable in that it operated only in favour of the rich, and it was at last terminated by the legislation of 1857 which transferred from the spiritual to the secular tribunal all jurisdiction in matrimonial causes, and laid the foundation for the present statute law of divorce and nullity.[4]

---

[1] Some add Reynolds of Norwich, but it is uncertain which side he took.

[2] See T. A. Lacey-R. C. Mortimer, op. cit., p. 163.

[3] See R. Haw, op. cit., p. 137: ". . . for the first forty-five years after the [Ross] Act was passed there were only five similar private Acts. The next fifty years produced sixty more, and in the following half-century the number increased to about one hundred and sixty, whilst the ensuing period up to the legislation of 1857 . . . brought the total up to three hundred and seventeen."

[4] For details, see R. Haw, op. cit., pp. 158 ff.

Although the history of the *Reformatio Legum Ecclesiasticarum* shows that the divines of the sixteenth century were, on the whole, strongly disinclined to allow excessive liberties in the matter of the dissolution of wedlock, it is none the less probable that the majority was of the opinion that adultery dissolves the matrimonial bond, and that the remarriage of the innocent husband (some added, the innocent wife too) is permissible—a view which they believed to be based upon the law of God as declared in Scripture.[1] Unfortunately, however, the literature of the period contains very little discussion of the theological, as distinct from the practical and more especially, the polemical issues involved. It is not until we reach the Jacobean and Caroline Doctors that we find any serious consideration of the principles underlying divorce and remarriage—and it is then immediately apparent that there is a clear division of opinion upon the matter, with authorities of weight on both sides.

Thus Andrewes asserts that adultery cannot dissolve the bond, for if it did, reconciliation thereafter would necessitate another wedding. He finds that remarriage is not warranted by God's word, in the interpretation of which he anticipates the source critics in maintaining that the consentient testimony of Mark and Luke must prevail against Matthew—though he admits (as did Augustine, it will be remembered) that the latter is "not clear and plain", and acknowledges that "divines differ about it" (that is, the 'excepting clause'). Further, he argues logically enough that if the act of adultery does in fact dissolve the union, then the continued cohabitation of the innocent with the guilty spouse thereafter is itself adulterous—which is nonsense.[2] Donne, however, considering the same point, will not express a definite opinion because the Church has never pronounced expressly upon it; but he goes so far as to allow that if adultery does not

[1] Thorndike condemns the Reformers for what he holds to be their chief mistake in this field, viz. that the marriages of Christians stand by Moses' law and not Christ's—hence their toleration of divorce and remarriage; see *Just Weights and Measures*, xviii. 9, *Works* (LACT), v, pp. 205–206: but the Reformers deduced their doctrine principally from the permission they derived from Matt. xix. 9.

[2] *Discourse against Second Marriage*, *Works* (LACT), xi, pp. 106–110.

effect the death of the relationship, "surely it is a deadly wound" —a conclusion which brings us no nearer a solution of the problem.[1]

Though they do not discuss this specific question, other divines are of Andrewes's persuasion in the matter of remarriage. Edmund Bunny, writing at about the same time, defends the indissolubility of wedlock, and reveals the interesting fact that Whitgift was also of this mind, but would not allow publication of Bunny's views lest they should stir up controversy.[2] Another contemporary, John Howson,[3] takes the same view, as do the later authors John Prideaux,[4] and Thomas Comber,[5] while Edward Stillingfleet maintains that Church and State can regulate the contraction and annulment of matrimony, but neither "can null the contract as to conscience, so as to make it lawful for such persons [i.e., as are divorced] to marry others".[6]

Robert Sanderson, in a Visitation sermon of 1634, expresses himself with less conviction. Second marriage after divorce, he says, is one of those "doubtful cases in moral divinity" regarding which "reasons seem to be probable both *pro* and *contra*, and there are learned men as well of the one opinion as of the other". Hence, if there should be any doubt as to its lawfulness, the proper course is to refrain; to contract a second union in such circumstances would be sinful—but not, presumably, if such a marriage were thought to be right in conscience.[7] On the other hand, the casuist is more decided than the preacher. In 'The Case of the Validity of a Matrimonial Contract *in verbis de præsenti*' Sanderson concludes that the bond of matrimony cannot be dissolved either "by the consent of both parties or by the release of one . . . because the obligation of matrimony ariseth from

---

[1] *Sermons*, lxxxiii, *Works*, iv, pp. 38–39.
[2] See the treatise, *Of Divorce for Adultery, and Marrying Again* (Oxford, 1610).
[3] *Tertia Thesis Theologica* (Oxford, 1606), p. 35.
[4] *Fasciculus Controv. Theol.* (Oxford, 1649), pp. 299 ff.
[5] *A Companion to the Temple*, *Works*, iv, pp. 121–122.
[6] 'Of Divorcing a Contract *de præsenti*', in *Ecclesiastical Cases* (London, 1735), iii, p. 73.
Visitation Sermons, iv, *Works* (Oxford, 1854), ii, p. 132.

the ordinance of God as well as from the consent of parties. And therefore those whom God by his ordinance hath joined together, neither themselves nor any other have power to separate."[1]

Thorndike takes a different view. Christ taught, he says, and the Church has maintained that matrimony is in principle indissoluble—but what precisely does this mean? Marriage is indeed indissoluble in point of right, for it is (as Augustine and other Fathers believed) "the profession of an obligation upon the parties to hold it indissoluble"; but is it so, too, in point of fact? To this question Thorndike is compelled to return a negative answer; our Lord, he observes, clearly made an exception in the case of fornication—and who, moreover, can say that for its effectual operation in sexual relationship the law of God may not presuppose the conditions of a civil contract, so that transgression of the obligation renders void (or voidable) the union founded thereon? It follows, therefore, that in the case of divorce for adultery the innocent party is not forbidden by divine law to remarry; but the ecclesiastical law, the purpose of which is to regulate "that which God's law hath left indefinite", may in certain circumstances impose a restraint—as when the allowance of what is *per se* lawful may lead to "inconveniences . . . both visible and horrible".[2]

According to Thorndike, therefore, canon CVII of 1604 is a disciplinary measure designed to prevent collusive divorces, and not an expression of theological principle. In a later treatise, however, he suggests that this rule is not imposed simply on the authority of the Church's *magisterium*, but that Jesus himself had clearly signified "that the innocent party should remain tied, when the trust is dissolved"—although at the time his hearers did not comprehend his intention. Thus remarriage after divorce is prohibited, not because it is wrong in itself, but because a regulation to this effect was made by our Lord for the good of the

---

[1] *Works*, v, p. 126.
[2] *Of the Laws of the Church*, iii. 13, 14, *Works* (LACT), iv (1), pp. 281–331; I have given the substance of a long and closely reasoned argument, which includes citation and examination of numerous authorities.

Christian society.[1] In commenting upon the Ross case, Thorndike expresses regret that Parliament, in permitting the remarriage of the innocent party, did not at the same time inflict an appropriate punishment upon the guilty.[2]

Hammond follows Thorndike in his interpretation of the canon.[3] The right to put away an adulterous wife, he claims, was an exception implied in the institution of marriage itself; the only question in doubt is whether he who divorces an adulteress can remarry—or whether she, being put away, may take another husband. On this point, he observes, the New Testament is not clear; therefore Mark and Luke, who appear to be against such remarriage, must be expounded by Matthew, whose account is both fuller and primary. Two considerations thus arise: on the one hand, it seems probable that in the case of putting away for adultery, which is "allowed both in the first institution, and by Christ himself, there lies no interdict or hindrance against . . . [the innocent husband] marrying again . . .";[4] yet on the other, the canon law allows no such liberty, and it is arguable on two counts that adultery does not dissolve the bond—namely, because a wife may not put away an adulterous husband, and because continued cohabitation with an adulterous wife is not itself adultery, as it would be if the *vinculum* were severed.[5] What, then, must we conclude?

After weighing both sides, Hammond proceeds to the following resolutions:[6] first, he who remarries, having put away his wife for another cause than fornication, "doth commit an unchristian sin"; secondly, it is nevertheless probable that when a wife is divorced for adultery, the subsequent remarriage of the

---

[1] *The Reformation of the Church of England*, xxxvi, § 7, *Works* (LACT), v, pp. 568–569.

[2] Ibid, v, p. 579.

[3] For Hammond's argument, which again I have given only in summary form, see *A Letter of Resolution to Six Quæres of Present Use in the Church of England* (London, 1653), pp. 84 ff.

[4] Ibid, p. 109.

[5] Ibid, p. 110.

[6] Ibid, p. 113.

innocent husband is lawful and not adulterous; yet thirdly, Mark, Luke, and St Paul in 1 Cor. vii. 39 are so opposed to such re-marriage that the Anglican Church's law forbids it on disciplinary grounds. Hence the meaning of the canons is clear: the require-ment of a bond when a decree of separation is pronounced shows that remarriage is regarded, not as adulterous, but rather "as a matter of dangerous consequence if it should be permitted".[1]

Hall determines the question of remarriage after divorce in one of his 'Cases of Conscience', and has no hesitation in affirming its lawfulness. At the outset he states a point of some importance —namely, that to consider the bond *in vacuo*, without reference to the duties and common life of bed and board, is "merely chimerical, nothing but fantasy". He goes on to argue that when a just divorce (that is, one for adultery) intervenes, the *vinculum* is sundered and all ties are as if they had never been. If a marriage ceases at death, then (he contends) it surely ceases equally at divorce, which is a judicial death severing all obligations. What then of remarriage? Continence after divorce is certainly com-mendable—but if it is impossible, then God never leaves man at a loss. So Hall concludes: "I doubt not but I may, notwithstanding great authorities to the contrary, safely resolve that in the case of divorce it is lawful for the innocent person to marry." Since, however, the Church of England is "somewhat tender on the point", and remarriage, though not sinful, is often frowned upon socially, he counsels continence if reconciliation should prove impossible—"but", he adds, "I dare not lay a load upon any man's conscience which God hath not burthened, I dare not enslave those whom God will have free."[2]

In the Ross case, Cosin was one of the two bishops who sup-ported the divorce, and the arguments which he used are set out

---

[1] Ibid, p. 114. It is with reference to these resolutions that other passages in Hammond's writings must be interpreted, which might at first sight appear to disallow remarriage, e.g., *Practical Catechism*, ii. 7, LACT, pp. 139–140; and *A Paraphrase and Annotations upon the New Testament* (London, 1653), p. 102.

[2] *Cases of Conscience*, iv. 3, *Works*, vii, pp. 471–474; cf. iv. 2, on the question of remarriage after desertion: ". . . it never was the intention of the holy and wise God, by virtue of that which was ordained for man's comfort and remedy of sin, to bind him to a remediless misery", ibid, vii, p. 471.

in note form in a paper "proving that adultery works a dissolution of the marriage".[1] He first considers the Scriptural evidence, and arrives at the same conclusion as Thorndike: Mark and Luke must be supplemented by Matthew, who clearly records Jesus as having made an exception to the principle of indissolubility in the case of the husband of an adulterous wife. Cosin then comes to the question of the nature of the matrimonial *vinculum*. Like Hall, he regards bed and board, or cohabitation, as pertaining "to the essence and substance of matrimony"; therefore it is merely fanciful to attempt to distinguish between divorce *a mensa et thoro* and divorce absolute, for the bond consists in part of the obligation to live together. Hence "the promise of constancy and mutual forbearance, if it hinders divorce as to the bond, hinders it also as to bed and board; because the same bed and the same table were promised in the marriage contract: but the promise does not extend even to tolerating adultery, or malicious desertion, which according to God's ordinance dissolves the marriage."

But Cosin weakens his case by citing an array of patristic and conciliar references, most of which prove on examination to be either irrelevant or contrary to his argument; he seems not to have appreciated that to the Fathers 'divorce' did not usually imply more than separation *a mensa et thoro*.[2] He also appeals to the questionable testimony of the *Reformatio Legum Ecclesiasticarum*, and to the dubious precedent created by the few private Acts of divorce which had then passed through Parliament. As for canon CVII of 1604, he maintains somewhat sophistically that it does not speak "of such separations, wherein the bond itself is broken, as it is by fornication"—though there is more substance in his observation that the canon does not pronounce remarriage void, but only requires forfeiture of the caution.

One of the divines whom Cosin enlists on his side is Taylor, but Taylor's writings yield very little that bears upon the subject of divorce and remarriage, and only a few scattered and mainly

---

[1] See *Works* (LACT), iv, pp. 489 ff.

[2] See above, p. 88.

incidental references can be regarded as at all relevant.[1] In discussing whether a woman married to an adulterous husband should refuse cohabitation, he first states the argument advanced in favour of this course—namely, that the husband's coitus with the harlot has made them one-flesh, and has consequently dissolved the union with his wife. Then he rejoins as follows: the adulterer is one with the paramour in a certain sense (which he describes as spiritual and legal), but not naturally; the act of infidelity has broken the marital union, and the offending husband has imparted to another some of the rights which belong to his wife—but not so as to create a relationship with the harlot which cannot and ought not to be severed. Therefore the innocent wife's maintenance of cohabitation is not only lawful, but may be also an act of piety and charity calculated to promote repentance and reconciliation; yet if the marriage becomes intolerable, there is always the extreme remedy of separation—but Taylor says nothing of divorce, let alone remarriage.[2]

For the rest, there are only isolated sentences of illustration or comment to reveal Taylor's possible opinion. Thus, in comparing similar sins one with the other, he says: ". . . polygamy is like adultery, and marrying after divorce (except only in the case of fornication) is like polygamy",[3] which may imply that despite the persistence in some sort of the bond (as argued above), marriage in such a case is none the less lawful. A curious explanation of the quality required in a bishop by the Pastoral Epistles (that he must be "the husband of one wife"[4]) also suggests a tolerance of remarriage: "If a person was divorced before [sc. ordination] and married again, he may accept of a bishopric: but if he do so afterwards he is guilty of the breach of the commandment".[5] On the other hand, a reference (admittedly somewhat

---

[1] In the LACT edition of Cosin's *Works* the editor (J. Samson) supplies a footnote referring to *Ductor Dubitantium*, I. v. 15 § 6, but there is no such place, and it is impossible to locate the passage to which attention is directed; it may be I. v. 8 §§ 6 ff.—see below, n. 2.

[2] *Ductor Dubitantium*, I. v. 8 §§ 6–14, *Works*, ix, pp. 240–245.

[3] Ibid, II. iii. 3 § 1 (4), *Works*, ix, p. 506.   [4] 1 Tim. iii. 2.

[5] *Ductor Dubitantium*, II. iii. 18 § 3 (2), *Works*, ix, p. 691.

obscure) to the unlawfulness of polygamy could be construed as an expression of the contrary view: ". . . our blessed Saviour said, 'He that puts away his wife unless it be for fornication, and marries another, committeth adultery': therefore he much more is an adulterer who marries another when his wife is not put away, and hath not committed fornication".[1] On the whole, the evidence as to Taylor's opinion is inconclusive, though it suggests that he may have been inclined rather to allow than to disallow remarriage after divorce; certainly Cosin cites him as a favourable witness, while none claim his support on the other side.

At first sight, the position of the seventeenth-century Anglican Church in regard to divorce seems confused and inconsistent. The canons of 1604 permitted separation from bed and board, but required the parties so divorced to remain single during each other's life; certain divines held that by its very nature and according to God's ordinance, matrimony is a union dissoluble only by death; others, no less learned and authoritative, while maintaining that wedlock is in principle permanent, would have allowed remarriage of the innocent party in cases of adultery, as a concession warranted on grounds of equity and sanctioned by our Lord himself. Thus the theologians were divided, and some taught contrary to the ecclesiastical law—a remarkable situation, if that law did indeed enunciate the matrimonial doctrine which the Church of England was pledged to uphold. What, then, did the canons really mean, and how were they understood by the Carolines?

It is interesting, first, to note that while the more liberal divines appear unconcerned at the want of harmony between their teaching and the canons, the rigorists (as we may call them) seek to base their argument upon God's will and ordinance as declared in Scripture, and rarely rely for support on the authority of the Church's law. Neither side, in other words, seems to have regarded that law as determinative in itself—and careful examination of the canons suggests why. Although they are entirely consonant with the doctrine of indissolubility, they nowhere

---

[1] Ibid, II. iii. 3 § 7, *Works*, ix, pp. 510–511.

adduce that doctrine as the reason for their caution against re-marriage, nor is it anywhere stated specifically during this period that they were framed expressly to declare it. Consequently the canons are open to the interpretation which Thorndike and Hammond did in fact place upon them—namely, that they are disciplinary, and simply prohibit what is not in itself unlawful, but only in certain circumstances inexpedient or dangerous to the Christian commonwealth.

If the Doctors of the seventeenth century did indeed so regard the canons, then their attitudes are immediately intelligible. Appeal to a mere disciplinary law would have afforded the rigorists somewhat dubious support for the doctrine which they desired to maintain; hence they preferred to ground their teaching upon the surer foundation of Scripture, and the divine command which they deduced therefrom. The more liberal, on the other hand, arguing from the same biblical source to an opposite con-clusion, would hardly be much concerned that their theological principles conflicted with, and required the revision of, the current rule prohibiting remarriage; whereas they might well have hesitated to advance proposals contrary to a law expressive of the Church's official doctrine.

It is possible, of course, that the liberals and the rigorists did not concur in their view of the canons—that there were in existence at this time two conflicting interpretations, the former regarding them as disciplinary, and the latter as declaratory of the indis-solubility of marriage. But whatever conclusion is drawn from the evidence, the fact itself is indisputable: in the seventeenth-century Church of England there was a clear division of opinion upon the question of divorce and remarriage, which could not be resolved by invoking the canons—either because they were by common consent thought to be disciplinary, and not declaratory of doctrine, or because there was no agreement as to their meaning and authority. It would be quite unrealistic to mini-mize this conflict of principle, or to dismiss either rigorists or liberals as dissident factions whose opinions were (and are) of no ultimate consequence. The Reformers, on the whole, favoured a controlled and restricted permission of divorce and remarriage; the Jacobeans and the Carolines were more equally divided upon the point—and the division still persists within Anglicanism.

In conclusion, two matters must briefly be mentioned. First, the Reformation led in England to a considerable simplification of the grounds upon which a marriage might be annulled. The impediments arising from consanguinity and affinity were (as we have seen) restricted, and those of *cognatio spiritualis*, crime, disparity of religion, Holy Orders, and monastic vows were abolished; the bar of *error de conditione* had already become obsolete, while that of *ligamen*, though affirmed by the canons and the statute law, was modified in practice by granting private Parliamentary Acts of divorce. Thus the causes of nullity were reduced to *error de persona*, fear, violence or duress, abduction, insanity, impotence, and non-age; in recent years the last has been modified, and new grounds have been created by the Matrimonial Causes Act of 1937.[1]

Secondly, there is the question of the remarriage of deserted Christian converts on the authority of the Pauline privilege. This was one of no practical importance in the reformed Church of England, for the ban excluding Jews was not lifted until the time of the Commonwealth, and colonization had made but little progress. Hence there is no reference to the subject in the canons and other formularies; but mention ought to be made of Hammond's original but undoubtedly accurate exegesis of 1 Cor. vii. 15—the text upon which the theory of the privilege rests. Rejecting the traditional interpretation, he maintained that the phrase "not under bondage", means that the believer is not "so far enslaved or subjected, that he or she should do acts prejudicial to their true religion, for that end that she may continue with her husband, or he with his wife".[2] In other words, the Apostle (as Hammond reads him) simply refused to insist upon the duty to

---

[1] For the mediæval canon law, see pp. 130 and 141 ff.; and for a comprehensive account of the law of nullity since the Reformation, see *The Church and the Law of Nullity of Marriage*.

[2] *Practical Catechism* (LACT), ii. 7, p. 141.

continue cohabitation, but did not permit dissolution of the marriage and the contraction of another union.

During the sixteenth and seventeenth centuries the hitherto undifferentiated sexual tradition of the western Church underwent various local modifications. In England its development was influenced by the particular tendencies and circumstances of the national Reformation, by native characteristics and attitudes, and by the distinctive method of Anglican divinity—the application of a threefold criterion of Scripture, tradition, and reason to the discussion of theological questions. Continuity with the past was maintained in the Marriage Service of the Book of Common Prayer, which preserved the essential features and teaching of the mediæval Sarum rite; in the canon law which, despite curtailment and the introduction of certain changes, departed in very few respects from that of the Church of the Middle Ages; and in the consensual theory of the formation of marriage to which both civil and ecclesiastical jurisprudence adhered. Anglican conservatism is also to be seen in the persistence of a high regard for virginity (expressed, however, with typical moderation and sanity, and without any depreciation of matrimony), as well as in the androcentric bias of theological thought, which still proclaimed the subordination of woman, and a low view of her nature and capacities. On the other hand, the reforming spirit is clearly discernible in the radical simplification of the law of marriage relative to diriment impediments, and in the rejection of clerical celibacy and perpetual vows of continence.

The allowance of wedlock to the clergy undoubtedly helped to stimulate theological reflection upon the nature of matrimony and of sexual love, with the result that signs began to appear of a new and deeper comprehension of the relationship between husband and wife, prompting a majority of the Reformers and the Carolines to rate mutual society, help, and comfort as the principal end of marriage. Taylor's casuistry reveals a more rational approach to the morality of venereal acts and to problems of sexual behaviour; the Anglican attitude to prostitution is sounder and more uncompromising than that of the Middle Ages or the Counter-reformation, and seventeenth-century divinity no longer dwells (like that of the Schoolmen, and even of Luther) upon the inherent evil or sinfulness of coitus. Respect for tradition, interpreted as the doctrine and practice of the 'undivided' Church of the early centuries, is expressed in a return to the patristic conception of the matrimonial *sacramentum* and *vinculum*. But although English marriage discipline, as defined by the canons, conformed to the usage and witness of primitive times, there was a marked diversity of opinion as to the theological significance of the ecclesiastical law, and a conviction on the part of not a few divines of weight that Christ in the Scriptures permitted at least the divorce and remarriage of the innocent party in the case of adultery.

VI

THE TRADITION TODAY

We have now taken this survey of sexual thought in the western Church from the first century to the end of the Caroline period in Anglican history. During the next one hundred and fifty years English theological interest in the relationship of man and woman was negligible, and the few Churchmen, such as Paley,[1] who dealt with the subject contributed nothing worthy of special record; hence modern Anglicanism received its particular form of the western sexual tradition virtually as that tradition had left the hands of the divines of the seventeenth century. We may usefully pause here, therefore, in order to recapitulate very briefly the principal features of Christian sexual thought in the West, noting how they have influenced theological and emotional attitudes within the Church of England.

Almost from the beginning, we discern a markedly negative reaction to everything venereal which has profoundly and adversely affected the character and development of Christian sexual ideas—a reaction expressed with every degree of intensity from mild suspicion or apathy to violent hostility or revulsion. The causes of this attitude do not concern us here, though they undoubtedly lie deep in the remote history of the race; but the various channels by means of which it infiltrated into Christianity can be traced clearly enough—and of these the chief were Hebrew

---

[1] See *The Principles of Moral and Political Philosophy*, III. iii, 'Of the Relative Duties which result from the Constitution of the Sexes' (London, 1806), i, pp. 325 ff., with its complacent androcentricity, its contractual conception of marriage, and its acceptance of divorce *a vinculo* by Act of Parliament as consistent with Christ's teaching.

speculation upon sin and the Fall, Greek philosophical asceticism, and the oriental dualism which so profoundly infected the religious life of the Hellenistic world. Due to these convergent influences the conviction rapidly gained ground and became firmly entrenched in the early Church, that coitus is not only in some indefinable sense unclean and defiling, but also intrinsically evil or sinful, either on account of the concupiscence by which men and women are supposedly impelled thereto, or because of the sensual pleasure involved in the act. Although modified by the subtle qualifications of the Schoolmen, the views of Augustine and Gregory I survived unaltered in substance in the teaching of Luther, and thus passed into the reformed tradition. Although the Anglican divines are silent upon the question of the evil reputedly inherent in sexuality, and exhibit a more healthy conception of coitus, the prejudices of the past have none the less affected English attitudes. Clerical opinion and ecclesiastical pronouncements still sometimes betray a certain uneasiness about physical sexuality, while there is abroad a vague and almost unformulated popular notion that the Church regards 'sex' as a regrettable and unmentionable necessity, and venereal sin as the worst of all transgressions.

Closely connected with, and partly derived from this negative view of the venereal was the sexual asceticism which has always controlled and dominated the Church's conception of sanctity, the good life, and the pursuit of perfection. Originating from the same sources as the antipathy often displayed towards coitus, it encouraged a dualistic idea of human nature in which the body was opposed to the mind or the soul, and sexuality was associated with the 'flesh' as something carnal which must be subjugated to the rule of the spirit. Hence continence was represented, either explicitly or implicitly, as the highest and most meritorious form of self-discipline, and an obligation of perpetual celibacy was eventually imposed upon a reluctant and often rebellious clergy. St Paul's contrast between the worldly involvement of the married and the other-worldly detachment of the unmarried led to the exaltation of singleness devoted to God as the noblest kind of Christianity and the 'religious' life *par excellence*; and the cult of virginity which proliferated so remarkably in the congenial climate of the patristic age continued thereafter to exercise a deep influence upon the character of Christian spirituality. Even after the abolition of compulsory clerical celibacy and life-long monastic vows at the Reformation, the single state remained for many Anglicans the most exalted of all possible ways of life, and Tractarianism encouraged the realization of this ideal in the revival of religious communities in the Church of England.

Again, the tradition is fundamentally androcentric. Although the Church proclaimed the spiritual equality of the sexes, it nevertheless perpetuated the Aristotelian view that the male is the norm of humanity and the female a deviation therefrom. Its sexual thought was masculine in origin and in character, reflecting the typical arrogance of the male. It upheld and provided elaborate theological justification for the unqualified subordination of woman which was a prominent feature alike of Jewish religion and social custom, and of Roman jurisprudence. In its laws, its teaching, and its institutions it maintained the position of privilege to which men believed that they were entitled by natural endowment, immemorial right, and divine appointment. This deeply ingrained androcentricity had serious consequences for the Church and for society—and not least in the venereal realm. Although Christianity consistently denounced fornication as a sin equally grave in both sexes, its view of woman tended to encourage an attitude which condoned or advocated evils such as prostitution. Language is significant here, and one instance will suffice: in the literature of patristic and mediæval times dealing with questions of sexual relationship and marriage, the act of coitus is repeatedly designated by the disgusting phrase, 'the use of the woman'. Nothing reveals more clearly and succinctly than these words the false attitudes and wrong assumptions which have governed so much of Christian sexual thought.

Woman's utility (in the venereal sense) was conceived as of two kinds. She was useful to man in the work of generation in which, as the 'seed'-producer, he was regarded as playing the principal rôle—indeed, this was the only human activity for which her co-operation was indispensible; and she was useful as a 'remedy' —that is, as a means whereby his imperious venereal impulses could be directed creatively, or at least expended harmlessly. Colet the enlightened humanist and Luther the Reformer both testify to the persistence in Christian thought, after fifteen centuries, of the belief upon which prostitution thrives—namely, that the male cannot contain without harm or that abstinence is an intolerable strain, and that the female has been ordained to afford him legitimate relief from the importunities of desire. Such a view of woman could not but degrade her to the level, as it were, of a 'venereal being'.

Not only was woman to be used, however, she was also to be feared, for in her (it was thought) sex and sin were peculiarly associated. Primitive Christian teaching[1] endorsed the Jewish belief that she was the original transgressor, and the author of all human ills: "From a woman was the beginning of sin; and because of her we all die".[2] Certain misogynists among the Fathers not only assigned to every woman individually a share in the guilt for Eve's fall, but actually regarded each member of the feminine sex as herself in some sense another Eve—a temptress by nature, always seeking to ensnare men by her wiles and to destroy them. They felt that in her sexuality there resided a 'dæmonic' quality, and failed to realize that the emotional disturbance which she appeared to provoke was in fact due, not to her seductive influence, but to the male's susceptibility to venereal stimuli, heightened as it often was by hostility to, or fear of physical sex, and by the unwise disciplines of a morbid asceticism.

When such attitudes to woman, to coitus, and to virginity are dominant, they are hardly calculated to produce other than a low and unbalanced conception of marriage. Although the Fathers recognized its divine institution, its social and procreative value, and its characteristic blessings, it was nevertheless for most of them a state of life less to be approved or commended than to be

---

[1] 1 Tim. ii. 14.
[2] Ecclus. xxv. 24.

tolerated as an indulgence to human infirmity. They found it difficult to see in matrimony anything more than a hindrance to the ideal of the *vita contemplativa*; it was, they allowed, a way for those who were incapable of high spiritual attainment and had not been endowed with the gift of continence requisite for the life of perfection—but it was one attended by many inconveniences, and able only to bring forth fruit thirtyfold.

Mediæval theologians, however, were generally less pessimistic than their predecessors in their view of wedlock. They continued, of course, to regard it as a state inferior to virginity and to emphasize its remedial function, but they also showed a keener appreciation of its value, and of its place in the supernatural as well as the natural order. The new concept of the nuptial sacrament elevated marriage as a state of life endowed with its own appropriate grace, and the very fact of the Church's acquisition of jurisdiction in matrimonial causes it lent an additional importance and dignity. Unfortunately the latter development had also its adverse effects. At a critical stage in its evolution the Church's theology of marriage became very closely involved with the working out of a theory of the formation of marriage, and with the practice and the needs of the ecclesiastical courts, with the result that it assumed a legal and institutional character which has clung to it ever since. Furthermore, the influence of the Aristotelian philosophical method later imparted to nuptial theology an extra formalism, and tended to prescribe the study of sexual relationship. Nor did the innovation and extension of impediments conduce to the greater stability of wedlock, while the mediæval Church's acceptance of Ambrosiaster's erroneous conception of the Pauline privilege implicitly weakened its witness to the indissolubility of the *vinculum matrimonii* by denying the permanence of marriage in the natural order.

One of the most regrettable consequences of the exaltation of virginity and the relegation of matrimony to the lowest place in the scale of Christian vocation, was that marriage and family life was never presented as itself a way of sanctification through what Charles Williams called the 'affirmation of images'. Christian spirituality was worked out almost exclusively in terms of the celibate life and the cloister—that is, of the 'negation of images'. Its exponents started from the assumption of Augustine and the Greek philosophical tradition, that the pursuit of perfection and the good life demands a measure of detachment from the world and its concerns which the married can never achieve, being involved in secular and domestic affairs and distracted by recurrent venereal excitements from following after higher and holier things. For husband and wife, therefore, certain minimal precepts were thought sufficient, together with an assurance of grace adequate to their simpler needs and lower status; the home was never set forth as a school of sanctity until Luther vindicated it as a place where the religious life can be led no less than in the monastery. Even the lay pietistic movements of the Middle Ages were content in the main to imitate the monk's way of devotion.

Yet despite these and other negative features in its sexual thought, and the evident shortcomings of its practice, the Church in the West strove consistently to maintain in its teaching certain positive principles and ideals, and to enforce them so far as circumstances allowed. Although its attitude to physical sexuality was often unsatisfactory, it nevertheless opposed any discrimination between man and woman which would perpetuate the old double moral standard in venereal behaviour. From the first it employed its authority in defence of the integrity and honesty of marriage against those who attacked the union of husband and wife as something wholly evil or impure—even though the force of its apologetic was frequently impaired by an uncertain or reactionary view of the relationship of the sexes. Thus the conviction that wedlock is a holy and honourable estate ordained of God, and not merely a secular institution, impelled Callistus to uphold the ecclesiastical validity of illegal unions between Christian slaves and free women, and found expression also in the mediæval view that clandestinity · cannot affect the authentic character of an otherwise regular marriage. And although the Reformers and the more liberal of the Carolines found in their reading of the Scriptures a limited concession of divorce and re-marriage, they nevertheless held tenaciously to the belief that God wills matrimony to be permanent, and that its dissolution is tolerable only for the avoidance of greater or more scandalous evils.

Upon this summary review of the western Church's sexual tradition two general comments must be made, the first of which concerns its predominantly negative character. The convenient classification of its outstanding features as 'negative' or 'positive' must not be taken to imply a tradition of simple and clear-cut contrasts; indeed, the foregoing chapters will have revealed it as one of considerable variety and complexity—although the broad pattern stands out clearly enough. Nor must the preponderant negative elements be seen in isolation from their true historical and cultural context, or in a false perspective. Features which, when evaluated in terms of modern standards and knowledge, appear to be negative in themselves or in their tendencies, were not necessarily so regarded by those who in centuries past helped to shape Christian sexual thought. The divines of the patristic or the mediæval eras did not twist or deform an originally positive and wholesome conception of sexuality inherited from some past golden age, nor did they deliberately and perversely contrive to perpetuate within the Church views which were quite out of harmony with the mood of the time. On the contrary (as has been already emphasized more than once) the Fathers and the Schoolmen were children of their age whose thought was inevitably conditioned by current attitudes, and who simply moulded the tradition unconsciously, as it were, in conformity with the contemporary climate of opinion. They cannot, of course, be exonerated of responsibility for the form and content of the western Church's thought on sexual relationship, but their contribution to its development was rather by way of the modification and transmission of ideas than of innovation; the negative features which they accepted, endorsed, and passed on emanated not from the Gospel, but from Hebrew Fall-speculation, from oriental and Hellenistic dualism, and not least, from survivals of primitive taboo.

Secondly, the tradition was always a living one; however persistent its dominant features and rigid its theological framework, it certainly did not become petrified either in the fifth or in the thirteenth century. It took roughly three hundred years to settle the relative merits of virginity and marriage, and during that time the literature reflects an unmistakable tension between a liberal and a rigorist view of the question. The disciplinary rule of clerical celibacy was slow in winning assent in the West, and was followed by the East only in a modified form; throughout the Merovingian age it was virtually ignored, and after the Hildebrandine reform it was accepted only with considerable reluctance by the clerical rank and file. The notion that matrimony is a sacrament in the Tridentine sense was of very gradual growth, as was the complementary idea that exchange of consent is the efficient cause of wedlock; and discussion of the significance and morality of coitus continued long after it had been decided that consummation is not essential for the formation of marriage. The closing centuries of the Middle Ages witnessed a continual debate upon the nature and effect of the nuptial contract and sacrament, in the course of which many points of theological detail were elucidated and defined. The sixteenth and seventeenth centuries, on the other hand, provide several instances of a reversion to earlier principles or modes of thought; thus the Reformers repudiated the novel mediæval doctrine of the matrimonial sacrament, and certain of the Carolines, discarding the Scholastic conception of indissolubility, revived the Augustinian idea of the *vinculum* of wedlock as a bond of moral obligation.

Nevertheless, there are long periods in the history of this living tradition when no appreciable growth can be discerned. One such period followed the age of the Reformers and the Caroline divines which had seen the emergence of a conception of sexual relationship distinctively Anglican in certain of its features; but now, after some two centuries of virtual dormancy, a notable reawakening of interest has begun—though in circumstances quite unlike those which heralded or accompanied earlier times of creativity and progress in this field. In the past, western

Christian sexual thought developed slowly and somewhat
erratically in response to internal pressures arising from various
causes such as the demands of anti-heretical apologetic, or the
needs of the ecclesiastical courts. During the last hundred years,
however, the external pressures have been greatest, although in
recent decades they have reacted upon the Church to produce a
mounting internal pressure, both theological and pastoral. But
the challenge from without has been so swift and strong that it
has precluded the leisurely debate, the gradual process of reflection, adaptation, and assimilation which formerly marked the
successive stages by which the tradition evolved; yet it has
nevertheless already provoked a radical re-examination of the
principal elements in Christian sexual thought—and this, in its
turn, has led to certain tentative reformulations based upon more
accurate scientific knowledge or deeper theological and philosophical insight.

Let us consider very briefly some of the factors which now
compel the theologian to approach the Christian sexual tradition
in a critical or a sceptical spirit. In the first place, he must needs
take account of the discoveries of medical science which have
transformed our understanding of the human body, and of
developments in the fields of biology and genetics which have a
special bearing upon sexual studies. He will recall that the
Fathers and the Schoolmen were fully acquainted with, and did
not hesitate to make use of the best science of their day, crude or
erroneous though it may often now appear; yet at the same time
he will not forget that his situation is very different from theirs.
Unlike them, he no longer shares with other scholars and thinkers
a fund of knowledge common to every educated man; this is an
age of the specialist, and much that is relevant to his proper concern with sexual relationship will lie within the province of
experts in other branches of learning and research. Consequently
the theologian must be content to accept the limitations which
oblige him to draw upon the contribution which such experts can
make to his own particular studies; it is his duty, however, to see
that he is sufficiently and correctly informed about their proved

conclusions and warrantable speculations—and it is his right as a fellow-student to expect their co-operation, as it is theirs to count upon his reciprocation.

Naturally many findings of the medical scientist and the biologist confirm, and even illuminate traditional Christian sexual teaching and ideas; equally, there are others which call in question well-established and hitherto unchallenged or unexamined assumptions. The bearing of modern scientific thought upon the Church's theology of sex is too large a topic for cursory treatment, but two specific instances relating to matters of physiological and biological detail will serve to illustrate the point under discussion. They have been chosen because they refer particularly to two recurrent features in the tradition—androcentricity, and the attribution to coitus of an inherent evil or sinful quality.

A remarkable influence has been exerted upon our sexual attitudes by what can only be described as an exaggerated and superstitious reverence for semen which derives from the scientific theories of antiquity. According to the Greek philosophers and physicians, who had no knowledge of ovulation in woman, nor of the process of conception, the human embryo was concocted from a mixture of semen and menstrual blood. The woman's real contribution, however, was simply that of providing a suitable place where this mixture could coagulate into the fœtus.[1] Her rôle was little more than that of a well-equipped incubator in which the seed was deposited by coitus; there is no difference, says Galen, between sowing the womb and sowing the earth.[2] In his view, semen is comparable to the seed of plants —indeed, the very word implies this; the ejaculate possesses all its 'faculties' from the beginning and has, in effect, the attributes of the fertilized human ovum.[3] Aristotle explains that it is a bodily distillation containing the quintessence of useful nutriment, refined into its highest form;[4] and from it the human being is

---

[1] Cf. Job x. 10.
[2] *De fac. nat.* i. 6.
[3] Ibid, ii. 3.
[4] *De gen. animal.* i. 18.

made. Potentially it has a sentient soul, but the menstrual fluid with which it congeals (the feminine element) only contains potentially the parts of the body and a nutritive soul.[1] Precisely the same view was held by the Fathers,[2] and is epitomized in the statement by Clement of Alexandria that semen is *met' oligon anthrōpon*—something almost, or about to become, Man.[3]

This notion of semen as a substance 'almost human' overshadowed the sexual thought, not only of antiquity[4] but of the whole western world until the sixteenth century brought at last the discovery of ovulation in woman, and a more accurate understanding of the process of conception; and it has left its mark upon our sexual attitudes and our ideas of venereal behaviour and morality. The belief that the essential matter out of which human beings are formed is produced exclusively by the male, and that the female is merely a suitable breeding machine, undoubtedly furnished yet another and very powerful argument in favour of the subordination of woman. Furthermore, the feelings of awe naturally associated with a secretion to which such remarkable properties were attributed explains why even its involuntary emission during sleep was treated as a 'pollution' requiring precautionary measures of a penitential character. Horror at its 'misuse' or 'waste' at least partly explains the recently prevalent view of male masturbation, and the fact that homosexual acts by men (and sodomy in particular) have been so severely reprobated and punished[5] while, quite illogically, similar practices by women

---

[1] Ibid. ii. 3.

[2] Cf. Pacian, *de bapt.* vii; *Recog. Clem.* viii. 26, 28, 32; Athenagoras, *de resurrect.* xvii; John Chrysostom, *in epist. I ad Cor.* xvii, 2; xli. 2; *in epist. I ad Thess.* vii. 2; *in epist. ad Hebr.* xxiii. 2; Methodius, *conviv.* viii. 6; Augustine, *de bono conj.* xx; *de civ. Dei,* xiv. 23; *de nupt. et concup.* ii. 29; *de anima,* iv. 6 [5]; *de Trin.* xii. 6; xv. 27; Gregory I, *moral.* ix. 52; xxiii. 15.

[3] *Pæd.* ii. 10.

[4] See also Philo, *de op. mund.* xxii. 67. An Egyptian text of the sixth dynasty (c. 2400 B.C.) reflects the idea that semen is, as it were, Man in fluid form, when it describes his creation as the result of an act of masturbation; see J. B. Pritchard (ed.), *Ancient Near Eastern Texts relating to the Old Testament* (Princeton, 1950), p. 6.

[5] See my *Homosexuality and the Western Christian Tradition,* p. 164, for further discussion of this question.

have usually been ignored or dismissed as mere feminine lewdness; and it has also been in some measure responsible for religious opposition to contraception.[1] Although the ancient theories of the nature of semen and the process of human conception have been rendered obsolete by medical science, the wrong attitudes engendered by these theories are likely to prove more obdurate to reform, being rooted in emotional prejudices or taboos[2] which are not easily dissipated by factual enlightenment alone.

Inaccurate knowledge of the structure and functions of the body was also responsible for the idea that coitus is sinful or evil. Augustine and Aquinas estimated the morality of human behaviour by certain *a priori* criteria according to which the good act must at least be rational, under the control of the will, and in general calculated not to hinder the pursuit of the contemplative ideal which represented the *summum bonum* of Man's life. When measured by these standards, coitus appeared to be miserably and inherently defective; it could not be accomplished without "bestial movements", and was accompanied by an inordinate and mounting excess of venereal emotion which fettered the reason and culminated in the uncontrollable 'apoplexy' of the orgasm.[3] That the generation of children (a good thing *per se*) should require the performance of an act so brutish and irrational could only be explained as a penalty consequent upon the Fall; hence it was

---

[1] Another example of the deduction of moral conclusions from incorrect facts may be found in *Summa Theol.* III Suppl. lxiv. 3 and 4, where Aquinas (or his editor) condemns coitus during menstruation on the ground that offspring conceived at that time are usually born deformed, lame, blind, or leprous—whereas, of course, conception cannot result from such coitus.

[2] A further instance of such taboos is the survival in certain Christian circles of various prohibitions connected with menstruation. Thus some women will abstain from reception of the Holy Communion during, and for a period before and after menstruation, invoking (as in one such case which came to my knowledge) an alleged 'Church tradition', although no such abstinence is taught by any Christian Church—indeed, its necessity was denied by Gregory I.

[3] Clement of Alexandria, *pæd.* ii. 10, attributes to Democritus the saying that coitus is a "lesser apoplexy" (*apoplēxin smikrē*), but Aulus Gellius, *Noct. Attic.* XIX. ii. 8, ascribes a similar opinion to Hippocrates who, he says, terms *coitus venerius* a "minor epilepsy" (*mikron epilēpsian*)—the allusion being obviously to the orgasm.

supposed that in Paradise the congress of the sexes would not have been attended by the turpitude and emotional disturbance which now made it seem inconsistent both with the good life as conceived by the ancients, and with the 'religious' life as mediæval Christianity chose to define it.

Had the Fathers and the Schoolmen understood the physiology and the psychology of venereal intercourse, and the neural mechanisms by which the orgasm is caused, they could never have concluded that coitus is an evil or sinful act. Unfortunately, however, they did not know that the proper performance of coitus demands the very sensual excitation and emotional abandonment which they deplored as inordinate, and that the orgasm, far from overwhelming the reason by which it should be controlled, is simply a reflex discharge of motor impulses which the will can do no more than initiate. In other words, they were unaware that the phenomena which they attributed to the effect of the Fall were actually ordained by God as part of the normal operation of the human body; and that coitus in Paradise, as they conceived it, was not only unnatural but also impossible. Thus advances in scientific knowledge have rendered untenable a view of physical sexuality which has obsessed the mind of the Church for more than fifteen centuries, and has profoundly and adversely influenced the sexual attitudes of the West.

For the theologian, however, the discoveries made in physiology and biology are perhaps less important than the remarkable developments which have taken place in the fields of psychology and sociology. In the former, the work of two outstanding specialists may be taken as typical in its significance. Notwithstanding the criticisms which have been directed at his system and the modifications which it has undergone at the hands of his followers, Freud's pioneer investigations have a permanent value for the theological study of sexual relationship, both intrinsically and because of the further researches which they have inspired. The establishment of a connexion between neurosis and sexual repression, the disclosure of a 'sexual' determinant underlying human attitudes and conduct, and the elucidation of the sexual and relational factors which govern the child's emotional development, have all proved to be of the greatest consequence for an understanding of man and woman in themselves and in their relationships. No less illuminating in a different way are the analytical studies of Jung in which he attempts to probe the depths of the individual and the collective unconscious. His theory of the existence of complementary sexual images in the individual unconscious—the feminine or *anima* in man, and the masculine or *animus* in woman, has made a profoundly original and suggestive contribution to the metaphysical interpretation of sex, while the relation of these images to the male and female archetypes of the collective unconscious throws light upon the problem of sexual stereotypes in society.

During the last four decades a useful though somewhat unequal literature, dealing with the undefined area lying between psychology, sociology, and case history, has resulted from research into the marital and other sexual relationships of men and women in contemporary western society.[1] This has recently been supplemented by the detailed studies undertaken by the late Dr Kinsey and his associates,[2] who broke new ground by enlisting the techniques of statistical investigation in order to discover the patterns of venereal behaviour typical of modern Americans; and a similar but more broadly based enquiry has also been conducted into the life of the English woman.[3] Many of these general surveys are illustrated by individual case-histories, though sometimes the personal stories themselves, together with comment

---

[1] Among the better known of such surveys are: K. B. Davis, *Factors in the Sex Life of Twenty-Two Hundred Women*, New York, 1929; R. L. Dickinson and L. Beam, *A Thousand Marriages*, London, 1932; G. V. T. Hamilton, *A Research in Marriage*, New York, 1929; E. Slater and M. Woodside, *Patterns of Marriage*, London, 1951; C. S. Ford and S. A. Beach, *Patterns of Sexual Behaviour*, London, 1952—the last includes much anthropological evidence, and compares human and animal behaviour.

[2] A. C. Kinsey and others, *Sexual Behaviour in the Human Male*, Philadelphia and London, 1948; *Sexual Behaviour in the Human Female*, Philadelphia and London, 1953.

[3] E. Chesser, *The Sexual, Marital, and Family Relationships of the English Woman*, London, 1956.

and analysis, comprise the main interest—as in Dr Henry's exhaustive account of some eighty men and women addicted in various degrees to homosexual practices.[1]

These specialists' researches have made available a great volume of information concerning the conduct and attitudes of people in an area of life where formerly all was assumption and guess-work, and they make an important contribution to the raw material upon which the theologian, the moralist, and the pastor must work when dealing with sexual relationships. Nor can the first, at any rate, neglect the results of the painstaking investigations made by anthropologists into the sexual ideas and customs and the matrimonial institutions, both of less developed contemporary societies and of the earlier societies from which our own has evolved—particularly in view of the vestiges of taboo which, as we have already observed, still survive in our culture. To give only one of many possible examples of the value of anthropology, we may instance the special interest which attaches to Dr Margaret Mead's studies of certain primitive tribes in New Guinea,[2] whose organization demonstrates the effect of sexual conventions and stereotypes in determining the social rôles played by men and women—a matter of central relevance to certain problems of western culture today.

Perhaps the greatest difficulty with which the theologian has to contend is the lack of comprehensive critical studies in which the facts concerning sexual relationship are not only assembled, but correlated and presented systematically. True, he has one such compilation at hand—but more than half a century has elapsed since Havelock Ellis began to collect and collate the medical, historical, psychological, and anthropological data relating to the different aspects of human sexuality and sexual experience, and to publish his researches in successive volumes of the monumental *Studies in the Psychology of Sex*; and the rapid accumulation of

---

[1] G. W. Henry, *Sex Variants*, London, 1950.

[2] See *Sex and Temperament in Three Primitive Societies*, New York, 1935; London, 1935; a summary account will be found in G. H. Seward, *Sex and the Social Order* (London, 1954), pp. 97 ff.

material since that time, as well as the broadening of the whole field of investigation, makes it improbable that any comparable synoptic treatment of the subject could now be attempted. This, however, does not exclude the possibility of correlation on a more restricted scale, and one neglected but urgent task is to explore the relevance of theology to the varied studies which are now included under the general title of 'sexology'. Meanwhile, despite its inaccuracies and limitations, Ellis's *magnum opus* stands as a reminder of the extent to which our sexual knowledge has been enlarged since the Christian tradition settled into its present form —and the extent, therefore, to which that tradition now requires re-examination.

No less important than the scientific and secular developments in regard to sexual matters are those which have taken place in philosophy and theology. In connexion with the former it will be sufficient to recall the appearance in Germany in 1923 of a small book which has been called a 'Copernican turning-point' in the history of human thought. This was the work entitled *I and Thou* in which Dr Martin Buber expounded his philosophy of personal relation, and offered an interpretation of human confrontation which has, among many other things, profoundly illuminated our understanding of the metaphysical aspects of sexual love and marriage. His teaching has already compelled us to examine and challenge more than one assumption of the Christian sexual tradition. We have to ask, for instance, whether it is possible any longer to rest content with the conventional theological treatment of matrimony as a sacrament, and an ecclesiastical institution primarily, if not exclusively intended for the procreation of children; or whether it ought not rather to be considered as in essence a distinctive personal union to which certain blessings (including offspring) are generally annexed, and which social or religious need or custom invests with appropriate institutional forms.

Whatever reformulation of the Christian doctrine of marriage may eventually result from the impact of Buber's thought, it cannot be gainsaid that he has driven the theologian to examine the intrinsic relational structure and meaning of the matrimonial *henosis*, with the important consequence that for the first time in the history of the Church serious theological consideration is being given to the nature and significance of the specific love which draws man and woman together and unites them as one-flesh. Valuable preparatory contributions to this new field of study had already been made by the Russian Orthodox philosophers Bulgakov and Solovyov,[1] and more recently their work and that of Buber has been supplemented by the original and suggestive 'theology of romantic love' developed by Charles Williams from themes in Dante's *Vita Nuova, Convivio,* and *Commedia.* Moreover, the theological 'discovery' of sexual love has prompted further enquiry into the nature of Man and his capacity for this particular kind of relationship, with the result that the metaphysical implications of sexual differentiation have assumed a cardinal importance for the theologian; sex in human beings can no longer be explained simply as a reproductive contrivance, for it is seen to have a personal value which is entirely independent of its generative purposes. This, too, is likely to necessitate reconsideration of certain features of traditional teaching.

Account must also be taken of the fact that biblical criticism has established a more reliable text of the Scriptures than any formerly available to scholars, and has elucidated the structure and authorship of most of the sacred writings in the Canon, thus making possible a more accurate exegesis. Furthermore, the lexical method of interpretation has revealed or illuminated afresh the thought-forms and abstract concepts of the Bible, and has disclosed beneath its diversity of material a remarkable consistency and unity of purpose which has given new meaning to its authority in the Church as the inspired Word of God. Researches in ancient history, in Rabbinics, and in comparative religion have also contributed to a better understanding of Scripture.

---

[1] For Solovyov, see *The Meaning of Love* (transl. Jane Marshall), London, 1946, and abridged in *A Solovyov Anthology* (London, 1950), III, § 3.

Consequently we now approach and handle the Bible, certainly with no less reverence, but at the same time with a better
technical equipment than that possessed by the Fathers, the
Scholastics, and the divines of the sixteenth and seventeenth
centuries—though we remain none the less indebted to them for
their own insights into the meaning of the Scriptures. The fruits
of this enhanced competence, and of textual knowledge not
available in the past, are to be seen in the advances in scholarship
which have taken place in almost every department of theology
during the present century. It is significant that their impact has
hitherto been least evident in Christian thought upon sexual
relationship, but the studies which have left their mark in so many
other fields can hardly fail eventually to affect this one also;
indeed, their influence is even now plainly discernible, and is
likely to increase considerably with the growth of theological
interest in sexual questions.

Already certain important changes of opinion have resulted
from biblical studies. For example, the conclusion of most
reputable scholars that, on text-critical grounds, the 'excepting
clause' in Matt. xix. 9 can no longer be accepted as an authentic
saying of Jesus, has markedly affected attitudes to divorce within
the Church. It has caused many Christians to reject the venerable
and widely-held belief that the Lord had authorized, or at least
had not forbidden, the remarriage of an 'innocent' husband during
the lifetime of a wife whom he had put away for adultery. This
has not led to a solution of the problem of divorce and remarriage,
but it has meant the shifting of the debate to other ground.

Biblical criticism has also served to focus attention upon several
questions which urgently demand reconsideration—and among
them, the sexual thought of St Paul, whose teaching in this respect
has generally in the past been treated selectively and interpreted
on an *a priori* basis, with the result that it has been misrepresented
both by Christians and, more recently, by rationalists. Thus his
conception of coitus and its place in married life, as set forth in
1 Cor. vi. 12–vii. 6, has rarely, if ever, been fully, faithfully, and
sympathetically expounded, while on the other hand his theory

of the relative status of the sexes has been received quite un-
critically, and with a deference which has hitherto virtually
precluded any examination of the subject within the Church.
Again, the Apostle's regulation in 1 Cor. vii. 15 concerning the
cohabitation of converts with their pagan partners has been
accepted without further scrutiny, on the dubious authority of
Ambrosiaster, as authority for a 'Pauline privilege' in favour of
the Christian spouse which is textually unwarranted, and implies
an unacceptable distinction between Christian and non-Christian
marriage.

One notable idea of St Paul, that of marriage as a symbol of
Christ and the Church, has figured considerably in Christian
sexual thought, yet its full implications have still to be explored,
and may well be illuminated by researches in the field of comparative religion. The use of nuptial and sexual imagery in the service
of religion is certainly very ancient, although it is alien from our
habits of thought and, in its more sensual aspects, repugnant to
our moral sense. It is found in Greek city state cults and in the
Mysteries, and is intrinsic to the fertility and kingship cults of the
near-Eastern world, but there is evidence that its origins lie far
more remotely in the past, for it seems to have been a feature even
of the religion of Neolithic Man. Doubtless this association of
sexuality with religion is partly to be explained by the need to
ensure the continued fecundity of the earth and the domestic
animals, but that does not exhaust its significance. To the retro-
spective theologian it will also appear as an important, if un-
suspected element in a more profound and spiritual pattern of
ideas which embraces the prophecy of Hosea and the fifth chapter
of the epistle to the Ephesians. It suggests a clouded and imperfect
intuition that human sexuality has a certain sacred quality; there
is even, perhaps, a dim perception that coitus looks beyond itself
and beyond all crude exaltation of the generative powers to find
a deeper meaning on another plane than the sensual and physical.

No doubt any such notions were at first closely connected with
a primitive sense of superstitious awe, just as later they owed
something to the ecstatic experience of coitus and the orgasm, but

if we trace them to their psychological roots we shall find that they have their ultimate source in the subtle interpenetration of sexuality and spirit which is a distinctive feature of human personality. One of the most notable (and least recognized) achievements of the Hebrew religion was to refine and spiritualize this sexual element, and so to make it the fitting symbol and vehicle of a great theological truth. The transcendent holiness of Yahweh forbade any attempt to realize in a sensible form, or to represent in the rites of a Mystery, his unique *hieros gamos* with Israel, while the interpretation of the Sinaitic covenant as a marriage threw into relief the relational aspect of sex, thus transferring the emphasis from fertility to the personal *henosis* (the union of man and woman as one-flesh) which coitus initiates and consolidates.

It is, therefore, of special significance that in the Song of Songs the canon of Scripture may well preserve a fragment of the resurrection part of a Canaanitish fertility cult liturgy associated with the worship of Tammuz and Ishtar,[1] which has undergone extensive redaction in the course of attempts to accommodate it to the Temple cultus, yet still bears the stamp of its origin while speaking convincingly to the Christian of sexual love as a veritable "flame of fire from Yah".[2] The comparative study of religion has already thrown light upon the sexual thought of the Bible, but it has assuredly much more to contribute before the pattern of ideas underlying the association between religion and sexuality is fully illuminated. Meanwhile it is already possible to say that the Scriptures affirm the insight behind the crude sensualism of the fertility cults and the Mysteries which, transformed, purified. and elevated by the Hebrew religion, attains its final and most profound expression in the teaching of St Paul—namely, that human sexuality, and particularly the act of coitus, has something of a sacred quality. To this truth the Church has always

---

[1] See W. H. Schoff (ed.), *The Song of Songs: a Symposium* (Philadelphia, 1924), and especially the essays, "The Song of Songs and the Fertility Cult" (T. J. Meek) and "The Offering Lists in the Song of Songs" (W. H. Schoff); also Claude Chavasse, *The Bride of Christ* (London, 1939), pp. 37–42.

[2] Song of Songs, viii. 6.

unconsciously witnessed, despite its assertions to the contrary, by the doctrine that through coitus alone husband and wife become one-flesh and their union assumes the symbolism of Christ and the Church.

No survey of recent influential developments in philosophy and theology would be complete without reference to the work of thinkers such as Brunner, Reinhold Niebuhr, and Barth. Confronted on the one hand with the rival anthropologies of Nietzsche, Marx, and the psychologists (to mention but a few), and on the other with the assumptions about humanity implied by industrialism and by modern totalitarian theories of the state, they have sought to develop a Christian doctrine of Man which meets the challenge of secular conceptions, offers a cogent interpretation of his contemporary predicament, and does justice to the results of biblical criticism and the discoveries of natural science. The study of sexual relationship and its problems has benefited considerably, though often incidentally, from their discussion of the questions which are posed by Man's transcendent yet creaturely condition, by his destiny as a free being who is nevertheless under obligation to live in responsible obedience to God, and by his paradoxical situation in belonging simultaneously to the realms of nature and of spirit.

Even this brief and necessarily superficial account of advances in knowledge in so many diverse fields of study and research which bear upon the relationships of men and women indicates the extent to which the western Christian sexual tradition now requires critical examination. More than the mere factual accuracy of its ideas and the soundness of its doctrine is in question; there is also the problem of communicating a true Christian conception of sex and marriage to a society which during the last hundred years has experienced a succession of rapid and confusing changes which are by no means yet at an end, and which have created a situation vastly different from that to which the traditional teaching of the Church in these matters was adapted and addressed. Both the theologian and the pastor face a condition of affairs quite unlike that which was envizaged only three centuries ago by George Herbert and Jeremy Taylor, or that in which, even more recently, John Keble, W. F. Hook, and R. W. R. Dolling ministered. Human problems may not change fundamentally in themselves, but the factors which cause them and the circumstances in which they occur can alter very greatly—and this is well illustrated by the social and cultural revolutions which have taken place in little more than three or four generations.

Having referred already to the influence of Buber's philosophy of relation, it may be appropriate to mention first, among the great changes of modern times which have affected our thought upon sexual matters, the emancipation of western woman. This, though further advanced in some lands than in others and often recognized more in practice than in theory, has made possible that degree of personal intercourse and social co-operation between the sexes without which the meaning and responsibilities of relationship could only be partially and imperfectly realized. Little progress could be achieved while androcentric theories relegated the female sex to a position of subordination which involved political, legal, and social disabilities, as well as exclusion from many professional and other spheres in which women have since proved their competence. Not only, however, has the removal or the mitigation of sexual disqualification enabled women to play an invaluable part in public life and in the service of the community, but a new understanding of the complementarity of male and female, and a growing experience of the creative possibilities of partnership between men and women, has led also to the emergence of new and more satisfactory patterns of marriage and family life. Moreover, not least among the benefits accruing from her emancipation is the fact that woman herself now has the opportunity to contribute to the critical examination of the Christian tradition, and to pronounce her own opinion upon certain questions which have hitherto been handled exclusively from a masculine standpoint.

The emancipation of women is only one of the more important of a multitude of structural and functional modifications which have taken place in western society during the last hundred years—many of them, indeed, during the last four or five decades. The culmination of a long process of industrialization and consequent urbanization, resulting in a partial decay of rural life; alterations in the patterns of political government, and the emergence and sometimes the ascendancy of novel idiologies; the development of voluntary and state welfare services, and various forms of family assistance; the ever increasing range and rapidity of transport facilities; and, more than anything else, the extensive and manifold effects of two world wars—all these, in countless ways, have inevitably affected the circumstances in which men and women enter into, and work out their relationships, and therefore, to a certain degree, the character of the relationships themselves.

Furthermore, the attitude of society towards sexual and matrimonial questions has itself undergone significant changes—many of them due to scientific discovery, or to improvements in the general condition of living. Radio, the cinema, and now television have brought to bear upon the more susceptible and uncritical sections of the public new and often insidious influences which largely determine the popular view of sexual matters. An advance in literacy, though hardly in education and a capacity for thoughtful discrimination, has exposed innumerable readers to the salacious journalism of cheap newspapers and shoddy periodicals, while the commercial exploitation of 'sex' for advertisement and other purposes is all the more serious because its cheapening of values and its suggestive and stimulating effects are rarely perceived. Sentimental, pseudo-romantic notions of love have helped to encourage 'divorce-mindedness', and rejection of, or indifference to the principle of the permanence of marriage; and rationalist propaganda, often supported by specious 'scientific' arguments, has urged the need for revision of the standards of venereal behaviour hitherto upheld by the Church and generally accepted by society as desirable—even though they were not always scrupulously observed.

In the light of such a situation the traditional Christian conception of sex and sexual relationship also demands reconsideration with reference to its evangelistic and apologetic value. We have already found that the factual accuracy of its underlying presuppositions can no longer be assumed in every case, and that in certain respects it is clearly inconsistent with the modern understanding of human personality and sexuality. Now a survey of the contemporary scene prompts further questions. Is this traditional conception entirely adequate to the needs of our time, and to the tasks which confront us in the sexual realm; and is the manner in which it is commonly presented intelligible and attractive? Does it, for example, enable the Church to offer a cogent, persuasive, and theologically sound view of sex, love, and marriage to the hostile or critical humanist; to those who are perplexed by conflicting opinions as to what is right or wrong; and to Christians themselves who, catching a new and enlarged vision of God's will for man and woman, find it difficult to reconcile their own more positive insights and convictions with the negative attitudes still dominant in many Church circles? Does it suffice for a realistic and constructive handling of problems such as artificial insemination, contraception and population control, inversion and homosexual practices, and divorce and remarriage on the scale which legislation has now made possible? —to mention but a few. Merely to state such questions is to reveal the extent of the challenge to the Church; to attempt to answer them is to realize immediately both the strength and the inadequacy of the Christian sexual tradition as past ages have framed it and transmitted it to us.

The Church has not shown itself indifferent to these matters, though its approach has generally been cautious and conservative. Perusal of the reports and resolutions of successive Lambeth Conferences affords a good indication of the Anglican reaction to contemporary problems, and of the impact of some of the scientific and theological factors which have already been reviewed. Thus the influence of biblical criticism is to be seen in a change of attitude on the subject of divorce and remarriage. In

1888,[1] and again in 1908[2] and 1920,[3] respect for tradition and
uncertainty as to the precise dominical authority of the Matthæan
'exception' is reflected in a definite, though qualified and
diminishing reluctance to condemn outright the remarriage of an
'innocent' party in the case of divorce for adultery or fornication.
In 1930,[4] however, and even more in 1948,[5] a hardening of
episcopal opinion can be discerned—though the report on the
Church's Discipline in Marriage, presented to the Conference
held in the latter year, recognizes that there are still those who
would maintain that Matt. xix. 9 is an authentic saying of Jesus,
and seems to acquiesce in a conflict of views on the subject as
inevitable and insoluble, while recording agreement on disciplinary procedure. At the same time, both Conferences express a

---

[1] Resolution 4: the Church "cannot recognize divorce in any other than the
excepted case, or give any sanction to the marriage of any person who has been
divorced contrary to this law, during the life of the other party"; furthermore,
"recognizing the fact that there has always been a difference of opinion in the
Church on the question whether our Lord meant to forbid marriage to the
innocent party in a divorce for adultery, the Conference recommends that the
clergy should not be instructed to refuse the sacraments or other privileges of the
Church to those who, under civil sanction, are thus married", *The Six Lambeth
Conferences* (London, 1929), pp. (i) 119–120; cf. also Report 3, pp. (i) 132–133.

[2] Resolution 39 affirms Resolution 4 of 1888; Resolution 40, passed by a
majority of 3 (87 votes to 84) declares that "when an innocent person has, by
means of a court of law, divorced a spouse for adultery, it is undesirable that such
a contract should receive the blessing of the Church", ibid, pp. (i) 326–327; cf.
Report 8 (I), pp. (i) 396–397.

[3] Resolution 67 affirms Christ's principle of the permanence of marriage, but
concedes that a national or regional Church within the Anglican Communion
may "deal with cases which fall within the exception mentioned in the record of
our Lord's words in St Matthew's Gospel, under provisions which such Church
may lay down", ibid, p. (ii) 44; cf. Report No. VI, pp. (ii) 110–111.

[4] Resolution 11, while passing no judgement upon regional or national Church
practice within the Anglican Communion, "recommends that the marriage of
one, whose former partner is still living, should not be celebrated according to
the rites of the Church", *The Lambeth Conference, 1930* (London, 1930), p. 42.
The subject is not mentioned in Report II, and there is no reference to the
Matthæan 'exception'.

[5] Resolution 94: ". . . the marriage of one whose former partner is still living
may not be celebrated according to the rites of the Church, unless it has been
established that there exists no marriage bond recognized by the Church", *The
Lambeth Conference, 1948* (London, 1948), pt. i, p. 49.

new pastoral concern for the spiritual welfare of those whose marriages have foundered, and a new understanding of the causes of breakdown.[1]

On the other hand, the proceedings of the Lambeth Conference disclose a progressively more liberal attitude towards contraception. That of 1908 referred in its encyclical letter with "repugnance" to "an evil which jeopardizes" the purity of home life;[2] it appealed for an unconditional condemnation of all artificial methods of family limitation,[3] and expressed approval of medical opposition to such practices.[4] In 1920 grave concern was still being voiced at the spread of "theories and practices hostile to the family", but the Conference declined to lay down rules to meet the needs of every abnormal case, and contented itself with adding to its general denunciation an assertion that the primary purpose of marriage is the continuance of the race.[5] In 1930, however, by a majority vote of 193 to 67, the bishops took what was at that time an ecclesiastically courageous step, and declared that there might be occasions when "a clearly-felt moral obligation to limit or avoid parenthood", and "a morally sound reason for avoiding complete abstinence", would justify the use of contraceptive measures in the light of Christian principles.[6]

The Conference of 1930 was notable also for its recognition that "the conditions of modern life call for a fresh statement from the Christian Church on the subject of sex", and for its affirmation that "the functions of sex as a God-given factor in human life are essentially noble and creative".[7] No task confronting the Church, said its encyclical letter, was more noble or more urgent than that of rescuing this sacred gift from degradation, and lifting it "into a pure and clean atmosphere".[8] The bishops insisted that coitus has "a value of its own" in marriage, as a means whereby

---

[1] Report VA, ibid, pt. ii, pp. 98–99 and 104–105.
[2] *The Six Lambeth Conferences*, p. (i) 310; and see Report 8 (III), pp. (i) 399–402.
[3] Resolution 41, ibid, p. (i) 327.
[4] Resolution 43, ibid.
[5] Resolution 68, ibid, p. (ii) 44; cf. Report VI, p. (ii) 112.
[6] Resolution 15, *The Lambeth Conference, 1930*, p. 43; cf. Report II, pp. 89–92.
[7] Resolution 9, ibid, p. 41, and Report II, pp. 85–87. [8] Ibid, p. 22.

"married love is enhanced and its character strengthened"—though they continued to hold that the primary purpose of the union is procreation.[1] Express reference was made to the influence of ideas such as "the sacredness of personality" and "the more equal partnership of men and women", which had acquired a new significance in modern times,[2] and the report of the Conference committee dealing with Marriage and Sex stressed the "need for a Christian philosophy of sex" in which sexual relationship should be recognized as one aspect of the "life" which our Lord declared he had come to bring.[3]

Yet it is evident from its context that this plea envizaged a revolution in venereal behaviour and in sexual attitudes, rather than the institution of any radical theological or philosophical enquiry into the Christian tradition itself. Ever since the passionate exhortation of 1888,[4] so unmistakably inspired by the spirit which had animated the 'purity' movement of the closing decades of the nineteenth century and had found expression in the ideals of the White Cross League,[5] the interest of the Lambeth Conferences in sexual matters was directed more to moral and practical issues than to the encouragement of basic research or the critical examination of Church teaching. They were content, for instance, to accept and to affirm without question the mediæval theory that consent effects a marriage;[6] indeed, in 1948 the report on the Church's Discipline in Marriage stated that the union so constituted is a contract "not terminable by either party: it establishes a permanent relationship"[7]—and this, despite the fact that the canon law never treated the purely consensual bond as absolutely indissoluble, but only that which had been cemented

---

[1] Resolution 13, ibid, p. 43.

[2] Resolution 10, ibid, p. 42.

[3] Ibid, pp. 86–87.

[4] See *The Six Lambeth Conferences*, pp. (i) 130-132.

[5] On the origin and history of this organization, see my article, 'The White Cross League', in *Moral Welfare*, April, 1952.

[6] See 1920, report VI: consent is the essence of marriage, *The Six Lambeth Conferences*, p. (ii) 110; also 1948, see next footnote.

[7] Report V (A), *The Lambeth Conference, 1948*, ii, p. 98.

by consummation. It is obvious that there are many such questions which urgently demand study by the Church—and perhaps the most important of all is that to which the following chapter is devoted: the theological meaning of sex itself.[1]

---

[1] Although the question of sex is integral to the doctrine of Man (for one basic fact about Man is that humanity exists in two sexually differentiated forms), it is significant that the 1948 Lambeth Conference Committee reporting on the doctrine of Man seemed quite unaware of the relevance of sex—though it dealt with 'Youth and the Family'. Dr Kirk observes that "singularly little thought has been given to the New Testament doctrine of sex", but he shows the influence of the *zeitgeist* when he continues: "Inevitably, it starts from the mating of man and woman; there can be no other starting-point"; see *Marriage and Divorce* (London, 1948), p. 101. Actually a doctrine of sex must start, not from the mating of the sexes, but from their *being*; it begins with an attempt to answer the question, What *are* man and woman?—which is another way of asking, What is Man?

ADDITIONAL NOTE

This chapter was written before the meeting of the Lambeth Conference of 1958 (see *The Lambeth Conference, 1958*, London and Greenwich, Conn., U.S.A., 1958). The report of Committee V (op. cit., pp. 2.141 ff.), which dealt with 'The Family in Contemporary Society', is in many respects a remarkable document and shows clearly the influence of modern theological studies in sexual relation. Its first, and theologically most significant, section breaks decisively at certain points with the sexual tradition of the western Church. The nature and purposes of marriage are reformulated, and the absolute primacy of procreation is rejected; full weight is given to the personal value of coitus, and the notion that it is sinful or evil is roundly condemned; and contraception by methods "admissible to the Christian conscience" is approved as a means of family planning. There are notable passages on the relational aspect of marriage, which is described as "an essay in responsible freedom", and on the character of the Christian home and family. This report proclaims the fact that Anglican sexual thought has entered upon a new period of growth, and it will be welcomed as an encouragement to further research and study.

VII

TOWARDS A THEOLOGY OF SEX

MENTION has already been made of Barth's protest that the traditional doctrine of Christian marriage is a mere doctrine of the wedding ceremony.[1] It is certainly true that the theology of the matrimonial contract and sacrament which was elaborated in the twelfth and thirteenth centuries turned mainly upon the exchange of consent between bride and bridegroom, and that the Church has generally seemed so preoccupied with the legal and ecclesiastical aspects of wedlock as to do less than full justice to the personal and relational aspects. Consequently such institutional factors as the competence of the parties, their rights and duties, the declared objects of their union, and the effects of their mutual consent have played an unduly large part in moulding the Christian conception of marriage. None would deny that these things are important and necessarily germane to any comprehensive treatment of the subject, but they can hardly be regarded as an adequate basis upon which to build a theology of such an intimate and distinctive relationship. For that, it is essential to go behind the matrimonial institution to the persons who are its subjects—to man and woman themselves, whom God created for one another and destined for union in one-flesh; in other words, the theological study of marriage must begin with sex.

Here at the outset, however, a difficulty arises—for what is 'sex'? Words are notoriously at the mercy of time and usage. They lose their original meanings and gain new ones; they

---

[1] See above, p. 156.

survive as vulgarisms or obscenities when they have passed out of polite currency; they retain in professional or technical parlance a significance which they no longer possess in common speech; they acquire adventitious emotional associations which render them embarrassing, so that they are gradually replaced by euphemisms or circumlocutions. Eventually the primary sense may be thrust into the background or even completely superseded. All such changes seriously inhibit accurate thought and clear communication; hence every ideological development creates its own problems of language, and it may only be possible to achieve precision either by adopting a new (and perhaps artificial) terminology, or by recalling certain important words to their original significations and then persisting in their exact use. In no realm more than the sexual does this alteration and debasement of language impede the expression of ideas; indeed, few words have been more abused than 'sex' and 'sexual' themselves, for they can now hardly be employed correctly without misunderstanding. Hence the theologian who is concerned with the relationships of men and women cannot avoid consideration of semantic questions.

According to the *Oxford English Dictionary*, 'sex' in its primary sense denotes "either of the two divisions of organic beings distinguished as male and female respectively". Although this simple and basic definition takes no account of certain fundamental differences between human and sub-human sexuality, it is at least acceptable as a theological starting-point. But a much narrower conception of sex is now generally current, for in recent times (to quote the *Dictionary* again) it has come to signify more explicitly "the sum of those differences in the structure and function of the reproductive organs on the ground of which beings are distinguished as male and female, and of the other physiological differences consequent on these; the class of phenomena with which these differences are concerned". The word 'sexual' has suffered a similar change; by 1799 it already meant "pertaining to sex as concerned in generation or in the processes connected with this", and by 1878 its predominant modern sense had appeared—namely, "relative to the physical intercourse between the sexes or the gratification of sexual appetites". The latter, in turn, seems to have caused yet further restriction and distortion of the significance of 'sex', which has undergone during the last few decades so drastic a limitation, not only in colloquial and journalistic usage but also (and increasingly) in technical, that it is now employed by most people chiefly with reference to generation and, more especially, to venereal behaviour, interests, and pleasures.

Habits of speech usually betray attitudes of mind, and those which reflect the changes of sense just noted are no exception; they provide yet further evidence of the tendency, already observed repeatedly in the course of our historical survey, to place an undue emphasis upon the physical aspects of sex. Thus although 'sexual intercourse' plainly denotes nothing but reciprocal relationship and communication between man and woman, and therefore applies to any and every form of sincere encounter between them, it is nevertheless now generally accepted (and has even been written into the law of the land) as synonymous with coitus—as if there were no other modes of intercourse appropriate to, or typical of the sexes. Again, 'sex education' implies instruction in the biology and physiology of human reproduction and not, as the term would suggest, in the meaning of personal existence as male or female. Worst of all, however, 'sex' and 'sexual' have not only degenerated in signification, but have also acquired regrettable overtones and emotional content. To persons of widely differing social and cultural levels both words tend to convey at least a subtle hint of salacity, if not a crude flavour of sensuality or nastiness'; according to the disposition of the individual, they can disturb, offend, disgust, attract, or excite.

In these circumstances, what must the theologian do? If he is to abandon 'sex' to the solecistical usage of everyday life, he must find an accurate and acceptable substitute—and none appears to exist. Some have proposed 'gender', but it is for various reasons unsuitable. It would not easily pass into currency with a new and unfamiliar connotation, especially in view of the fact that its

transferred use as a synonym for 'sex' has hitherto been merely
jocular, which would inhibit its employment for serious purposes.
Moreover, its primary grammatical reference is long established,
and its tolerance of neuter forms is anomalous in the theological
context at present under discussion—added to which, there is an
incongruity about the very idea of a 'theology of gender' which is
absent from that of a 'theology of sex'. To introduce 'gender'
would prove no easier than to restore the proper use of 'sex'—
and the latter has the advantage, even when debased, of implying at least some kind or measure of personal encounter and
relationship.

Is capitulation, then, the only alternative to complete abandonment by the theologian of the term 'sex'? That would seem to be
the conclusion reached by certain writers,[1] but it is one which
cannot be entertained without grave misgiving. To lend theological approval to the degenerate usages of contemporary
journalism and colloquial speech would place intolerable limitations upon the Christian thinker. It would compel him to treat
'sex' almost exclusively as a generative or venereal phenomenon,
with the eventual result that either its personal and metaphysical
aspects would be ignored, or confusion would be caused by the
need to introduce novel terms to denote what 'sex' properly and
adequately signifies.

Thus there remains but one feasible way of securing accuracy
in this field of study—namely, that the scholar at least should
endeavour as far as possible to restrict the unqualified use of 'sex'
and 'sexual' by relating them strictly to the being of Man, and
not to his behaviour or biological functions. For the one, a more
extensive employment of 'venereal' is to be advocated, while the

---

[1] See, e.g., the excellent study by W. G. Cole, *Sex in Christianity and Psychoanalysis* (London, 1956), from which, out of numerous instances, I select the
following at random: "Luther was concerned also over the 'infinite perils' of
those who had been deserted by runaway husbands or wives, compelled by the
Church to remain unmarried, *living without sex* for a prolonged period", p. 115
(my italics). The author means, of course, "living without coitus"; to live
"without sex" is impossible—sex is not something to be acquired or lost, done or
omitted, but an ineluctable condition of human existence.

other can sufficiently be described and defined in terms of 'generation'. Doubtless there are also derogatory emotional associations attached to 'venereal', due mainly to its being connected both in the popular and in the medical mind with a disease; but its true sense is far from obsolete, and it serves better than any other word to denote all that pertains to the physical and coital impulses and desires of men and women, and to their carnal intercourse.

Rehabilitation of 'sex', 'sexual', and 'venereal' is not likely to be easy or rapid, and may well be resented and resisted. But there would seem to be no conceivable alternative, at any rate for the theologian and the philosopher, if precision of thought and statement are to be ensured. It is valueless to contend that popular usage is now generally intelligible; certain agreed terms and expressions may suffice for the loose and often studiously vague communications of every day, but the meanings which they carry are evidently inadequate for theological purposes, and their use must inevitably encourage careless thought in a field where accuracy is vital, and assist the maintenance and propagation of the wrong attitudes which have proved so harmful in the past.

This necessary digression into semantics should have been sufficient to vindicate a precise use by the theologian of 'sex' and its cognates, and of 'venereal', as something more than a pedantic or quixotic archaism. It will also have suggested very broadly and roughly the possible scope and content of a theology of sex. Since sexual differentiation is one of the principal and most significant human characteristics, it will be obvious that sex is the proper concern of those studies which have to do with what is generally termed the doctrine of Man. It is appropriate, therefore, that we should turn first to the creation myths in which Scripture describes the origin of humanity, in order to see whether these inspired narratives hold any clue to the meaning of Man's existence as male and female.

Neither biblical account of the creation expressly attributes sex to the sub-human orders, though the emergence of plant life yielding seed and bearing fruit certainly implies structural specialization for the purpose of propagation,[1] as does also the benediction, "Be fruitful and multiply", which is spoken upon fish and fowl,[2] and may be assumed in the case of beasts and creeping things.[3] On the other hand, it is specifically stated of Man that God made him male and female; but it is significant that although he, too, participates in the divine blessing,[4] human sexuality is not associated explicitly with generation. Rather, it is linked directly in the myths with that essential quality of human nature which contributes to Man's uniqueness and sets him in a place of his own, apart from all other creatures—namely, his personality and consequent capacity for entering into responsible relationship with God and his fellows.

In the earlier (J) creation story the first human pair cleave to one another, not merely to procreate their kind, but to establish a relationship of such intimacy and significance that they are said to become one-flesh.[5] In the later (P) source the personal and relational element is still further emphasized. Twice the statement: "male and female created he them", is brought closely into apposition with the mysterious and pregnant declaration: "God created Man in his own image, in the image of God created he him";[6] and in one place it is amplified by the important addition: "he . . . called their name Adam"[7]—that is, Man (*'ādhām*). Although the idea of Man as a being made in the divine image only becomes fully meaningful in the light of Christian doctrine, it implies even in this Old Testament context that human sexuality is something more than adaptation for generation—that it has, in fact, a metaphysical import.

The precise nature of God's image in Man has long been a topic of discussion among theologians,[8] and various interpretations

[1] Gen. i. 11–12.
[2] Gen. i. 22.
[3] It is clearly indicated in God's words to Noah after the flood, Gen. viii. 17.
[4] Gen. i. 28.
[5] Gen. ii. 23–24.
[6] Gen. i. 27; v. 1.
[7] Gen. v. 2.
[8] See D. Cairns, *The Image of God in Man* (London, 1953).

have been advanced; but upon one point at least there has always been substantial agreement—namely, that the image (however defined) is to be conceived as a property or faculty of the individual. Some have found it in human spirit, freedom, or rationality; others in the dominion over the lower creation committed to Man by God; and others again in an original righteousness lost at the Fall, but restored to the believer by the operation of grace. Even Augustine, who discovered a triple form of the image in Man, confined his speculations to the individual and located the three-fold structure of the *imago Dei* first in self-love (*amans, amatum, amor*),[1] then in self-knowledge (*mens, notitia sui, amor sui*),[2] and finally in memory (*memoria, intelligentia, voluntas*).[3] Recently, however, another conception of the image has been formulated, which seeks to explain it dynamically in terms of human confrontation as exemplified by the two primary relationships of Man with God and with his neighbour—and this bears directly upon the theological meaning of sex in humanity.

According to the later of the two creation narratives (that in the 'priestly' or P source of the Pentateuch), God thus announces his purpose to create Man: "Let us make Man in our image (*tselem*), after our likeness (*dᵉmūth*)".[4] Two points are to be noticed about these Hebrew words. First, they do not represent different ideas, as Irenæus and others after him supposed; either they are synonymous terms in a parallelism, or *dᵉmūth* is intended to define *tselem* more exactly. Secondly, both words imply a reference to the original or prototype, rather than to the copy made from it; hence any attempt to explain the meaning of the divine image in Man must begin with God and his nature and not, as in traditional expositions, with the individual human being.

How, then, did P conceive the divine prototype after whom Man was fashioned? To such a question no answer can be given; we do not, and cannot know what idea the priestly author entertained of God. The plural forms "us" and "our" may point back

---

[1] *De Trin.* vii. 10 [14].
[2] Ibid, ix. 5 [8].
[3] Ibid, x. 11 [17].   [4] Gen. i. 26.

to an original polytheistic element in the myth; they may simply be plurals of majesty; but it is most unlikely that they disclose any intuition of the Godhead as a social entity. Certainly they cannot, as Tertullian thought,[1] be interpreted as an indication that the writer held something equivalent to the Christian doctrine of the Trinity; yet they suggest none the less that he envisaged God as associating others with himself in some mysterious way as partners in the act of creation, and that he regarded Man as constituted in some sense after the pattern of a plurality of supernatural beings.

But conjecture about P's notion of the Deity is ultimately irrelevant to the present discussion. We who read his words have received a fuller knowledge of God, whose Holy Spirit interprets the inspired text to us in the light of that revelation. The God of Genesis is our God; yet we know him now, not as undifferentiated Being, but as a divine unity of three 'Persons' in harmonious confrontation. Consequently the words spoken at the beginning of the sixth day of creation assume a new and more profound meaning; they express the Creator's resolve to crown his works by making a creature in whom, subject to the limitations of finitude, his own nature should be mirrored. For the Christian, the *imago Dei* must have a Trinitarian reference—though it will be in terms of an *analogia relationis*, not of an *analogia entis*. Man in the image of God is essentially a 'being-in-relation', and human existence is essentially 'existence-in-community'.

The precise content of this relational image has been the subject of much theological discussion, during which some apparently fundamental disagreements have been registered. There is admittedly no dispute concerning the Godward aspect of the image, for Man's relation with his Creator is unanimously recognized as an obvious and essential element in the *imago Dei*—though it does not concern us here. Controversy has developed, however, in regard to the nature of the Manward aspect of the image—that is, the relation between Man and his neighbour, and two conflicting

---

[1] *Adv. Prax.* xii.

conceptions have been advanced, one by Barth and the other by Brunner.

Barth maintains (and his idea is of great significance for this discussion) that the relational image of God in its Manward aspect is specifically and exclusively sexual, and consists in the general relationship of man and woman.[1] Brunner, on the other hand, finds the image in every responsible I-Thou relation,[2] and criticizes Barth's view on the ground that sexual polarity is not itself "the distinctive element in Man which differentiates him from all other creatures", but is only "one strand in this element"[3]—though he would allow that the male-female principle in humanity constitutes, as it were, "a secondary *imago*, a reflection of the divine purpose, and at the same time the natural basis of true community".[4] Dr Cairns substantially endorses this opinion; he grants that "the whole nexus of personal relations between one sex and the other is an example of personal relations *par excellence*",[5] but contends nevertheless that the determinative factor in the responsible relationship between man and woman is personal rather than sexual—though he admits that the two are "singularly fused",[6] and makes no attempt to distinguish between them.

Clearly, the validity of Brunner's conception of the image cannot be gainsaid; the relational *imago Dei* in its Manward aspect may properly be defined in the broadest terms as consisting in the confrontation of 'I' and 'Thou'—not only because Man has an innate capacity for relation, but also because humanity is fundamentally relational in its structure. Brunner insists that Man is not an isolated, individual entity, but "a 'two-fold' being"; he has

---

[1] K. Barth, op. cit., III/1, pp. 206 ff.; 529 ff.

[2] E. Brunner (transl. O. Wyon), *Man in Revolt* (London, 1939), pp. 91 ff.; *Dogmatics* II: *The Christian Doctrine of Creation and Redemption* (London, 1952), pp. 64, 75 ff. D. Cairns, op. cit., pp. 146–205, gives a summary and a critical estimate of the teaching of both theologians, touching upon many aspects of the subject of the *imago Dei* which are necessarily excluded from the present discussion.

[3] *Dogmatics* II, p. 63.

[4] Ibid, p. 65.

[5] Op. cit., p. 176.

[6] Ibid, p. 175.

been made, "not simply as two human beings, but as two beings who necessarily belong to one another, who have been created for this purpose, and whose whole nature is ordered in this direction, that is, as two beings who cannot *be*, apart from each other".[1] In other words, since God is love, his image in Man must be exhibited in terms of love—however else it may also be expressed; and this requires both an ability to love and an 'Other' towards whom love can be shown. Human destiny, therefore, can rightly be described as "fellowship in love".

Yet this idea of the image, though profound and comprehensive, fails to do full justice to the relational complexity of Man's structure or to the inner meaning of his sexual polarity—rather surprisingly, in view of Brunner's perception that human sexuality, unlike other distinctions such as race, colour, ability, and temperament, "goes down to the very roots of our personal existence, and penetrates into the deepest 'metaphysical' grounds of our personality and our destiny".[2] As these words imply, sex in Man is more than a mere faculty or attribute—much more, certainly, than a generative or venereal phenomenon. In the race, it is a divisive factor separating humanity into two radically different yet mutually complementary elements—male and female; in the individual, it is an informing and governing principle which permeates his being to its depths, and conditions every facet of his personality and his life. These two aspects of sex determine the character of the man-woman relationship in both its general and its particular forms, and at the same time distinguish it from non-sexual relation.

Both the sexual and the non-sexual relations, of course, are equally modes of true human confrontation, and of meaningful and responsible personal encounter, yet they are also structurally and qualitatively distinct. First, in every sexual relation of integrity man and woman enter together into a new dimension of experience, entirely different from that of non-sexual meeting, in which they discover a fresh understanding of humanity and another way of being human. Each genuine sexual encounter

---

[1] *Dogmatics* II, p. 64.   [2] *Man in Revolt*, p. 345

brings to them its own measure of mutual completion and fulfilment, such as cannot be attained through non-sexual relation; there is satisfaction of their deepest longings for personal communion, and mediation of a special self-knowledge—that is, of the metaphysical significance of sexuality, which is one of the profoundest and most baffling enigmas of human existence.

Secondly, each actual relation between man and woman has a potential creativity quite different from any belonging to non-sexual relation. In every form of human encounter a certain tension is engendered and must be discharged, either constructively or destructively, but the tension caused by sexual polarity, with its principle of complementary differentiation, is unique both in quality and effect. While it may certainly lead to a particularly disruptive intensity of antagonism and hatred, it can also be released creatively in a great variety of ways through many kinds of relationship—now in the procreation of children, now in the evocation of latent personal characteristics or powers, now in the special achievement of a distinctive common life as one-flesh in marriage, now in fruitful co-operation for the advancement of the common good.

These considerations leave no room for doubt that Man is a 'two-fold' being, not simply in respect of the neighbour relation, but also and pre-eminently in respect of the sexual relation; and that the latter is of such a kind and quality as to constitute in a special and peculiar sense the Manward relational aspect of the *imago Dei*—though this is not to deny that the image may also to a certain extent be discerned in non-sexual forms of human confrontation. The objection advanced by Brunner against such a concept of the image of God—namely, that sexual polarity is not peculiar to Man, implies a misconception of the nature of human sexuality. Man cannot truly be said to possess sex after the manner of other creatures, for in him (as Brunner himself observes[1]) 'animal' sexuality is caught up into personality and permeated by spiritual and psychical elements which completely overshadow and transform its crude biological character—whence

---

[1] *Man in Revolt*, p. 347.

it is possible to say that he "does not know the animal sex instinct". Strictly speaking, therefore, human sexual polarity cannot be compared with that of the lower orders of life, for theirs is simply a polarity of male and female, while ours is one of man and woman—that is, of beings in whom sex is a metaphysical as well as a biological distinction.

Man, then, is in the image of God in its Manward aspect primarily by virtue of his essential structure as a bi-personal male-female unity in which (relationally, of course, not numerically) the coinherence of Father, Son, and Holy Spirit is reflected in terms of finite existence. This is the meaning of the passages in the P source of Genesis which describe his creation, when they are interpreted in accordance with a trinitarian conception of the divine nature. When God created Man as male and female, he did not make two independent, self-subsistent beings—two 'individuals', ontologically separate and bound together by no closer tie than that of a common humanity and the need to co-operate in social life and in the propagation of the species. On the contrary, he created one dual 'being', an *'ādhām*, consisting of two empirically distinct yet correlative personal components, one male (*zākhār*) and the other female (*n^eqēbhāh*). Each, though completely and autonomously human, postulates and is naturally orientated towards the other, so that together they are impelled to realize their mutual belongingness as the constituent elements of Man in the many forms of relationship through which sexual fulfilment can be achieved—and chiefly that of union as one-flesh in marriage.

In this conception of the *imago Dei* there is actually no real novelty, for even in rabbinical thought the image of God is associated with the idea of Man as a sexual duality—though the latter notion is developed exclusively with reference to marriage, and is never applied to sexual relation in general. Thus among the Midrash sayings on the text: "It is not good that the man should be alone",[1] there is one by R. Hiyya ben Gamda concerning the unmarried man,[2] to the effect that "he is not a whole man,

---

[1] Gen. ii. 18.　　　　　[2] Quoted in G. F. Moore, op. cit., ii, p. 119.

for it is said, And he blessed *them*, and he called *their* name 'Man'".[1] Again, commenting upon the latter words, R. Eleazar ben Pedat declared that "any man who has no wife is no proper man",[2] while other rabbis held that he who remains single diminishes the likeness of God.[3] R. Simeon, as recorded in the *Zohar*, states explicitly that "God does not place his abode in any place where male and female are not found together, nor are blessings found save in such a place, as it is written, 'and he blessed them and called their name Man on the day that they were created': note that it says *them* and *their* name, and not *him* and *his* name. The male is not even called man till he is united with the female."[4] Other sayings,[5] however, indicate that these ideas were not necessarily connected with a simultaneous creation of the sexes, though R. Samuel bar Nahman in the third century and R. Jeremiah ben Eleazar in the fourth interpreted Gen. i. 27 to mean that the *'ādhām* was at first androgynous[6]—a notion more congenial to Greek[7] than to Hebrew modes of thought.

A conception of the making of Man very different from that given by the priestly writer in the first chapter of Genesis is presented by the earlier (J) creation myth in the second chapter, the purpose of which is obviously to explain, among other things, the origin and nature of sex. Here there is no reference either to the image of God, or to the simultaneous appearance of male and female. With naïve and anthropomorphic imagery, the narrative tells how Yahweh formed from the dust of the ground an *'ādhām*, whom he set in the garden of Eden to cultivate it. Then, seeing that it was not good for this *'ādhām* to be alone, he created the beasts and the fowls; but although the *'ādhām* demonstrated the authority implicit in his humanity by giving them names, he could find among them no partner morally and intellectually compatible with himself. Yahweh accordingly proceeded to

---

[1] Gen. v. 2.   [2] *Yeb.* 63a.   [3] *Gen. Rabbah*, xvii. 2; cf. *Yeb.* 62b.

[4] *Ber.* 55b, see *The Zohar*, transl. H. Sperling and M. Simon (London, 1931), i. p. 177.

[5] E.g., *Keth.* 8a; *Ber.* 61a (God's original intention was to create two beings, but in the end he only created one).

[6] *Gen. Rabbah*, viii. 1.   [7] Cf. Plato, *Symposium* 189D–190A.

fashion such a partner by casting the 'ādhām into a deep sleep, extracting one of his ribs, and building it into a woman whom the 'ādhām welcomed as bone of his bone and flesh of his flesh, and called 'ishshāh because she was taken out of 'īsh—that is, 'man', the male human being.[1]

So far as the present discussion is concerned, the central problem in this narrative is the precise significance of the terms 'ādhām and 'īsh. Broadly speaking, the former is a generic term for Man (Mankind), while the latter denotes the individual man (the human male). But there is no doubt that in the mind of the Yahwist both words were virtually equivalent in meaning; the woman receives the name of 'ishshāh because she was taken out of the side of 'īsh, although in fact she was made from a rib of the 'ādhām. This assimilation between 'Man' and 'man' was inevitable; it was the natural consequence of the androcentric situation out of which the myth emerged, and which it was partly designed to explain. The Yahwist treats 'īsh as synonymous with 'ādhām because in his view, as in that of antiquity generally, the male was the true 'Man', embodying in his person the plenitude of humanity, while the female was conceived as a subordinate (and sometimes defective) being who derived both her existence and her meaning from him—she was made after him, out of his substance, and for his special benefit.

This view of the ontological relation subsisting between man and woman is reflected even in the language of the J myth, where the terms used to distinguish the sexes carry an unmistakably discriminative overtone; 'īsh comes from a root meaning 'strong', and 'ishshāh from one meaning 'soft' or 'delicate'. In the P narrative, however, male and female are differentiated by abstract words which signify nothing more than sexual contrast and complementation; though their origin is obscure, zākhār and n°qēbhāh appear to be derived from roots denoting respectively 'the sharp one' (that is, the one with a penis) and 'the perforated one' (that is, the one with a vagina). Similar verbal changes are made in the Septuagint, where anēr and gunē in the J source

---

[1] Gen. ii. 7 ff.

become *arsen*'and *thēlu* in P—these being neuter forms of the comparatively colourless words *arsēn* and *thēlus*. Thus the language used by the priestly editor to describe the creation of man and woman is consistent with the idea that Man is relationally in the image of God in respect of his sexual structure, while that of the Yahwist reveals an androcentric tendency which is in keeping with the presuppositions of his time, and with his ætiological purpose.

Until anthropological research and the evolutionary theory supplied a more accurate explanation of Man's origin, the story in the second chapter of Genesis was accepted without question as an exact and authoritative account of the historical beginning of the human race in a single man named Adam[1] from whom both the first woman and the rest of mankind derived.[2] The fact that such a view is no longer scientifically tenable cannot, however, lessen the mythological significance of the narrative, nor is its value diminished because it appears to contradict the first chapter in depicting a successive, and not a simultaneous creation of the sexes. The two sources certainly present very different conceptions of the same divine act, yet they have an essential consistency which is immediately revealed when the earlier one is interpreted in terms of Man's sexual duality as a relational *imago Dei*.

According to the Yahwist, God first created an *'ādhām*. By this, the myth signifies that he formed, as it were, a figure representative of Mankind—a typical entity possessing the quality of

---

[1] In the Pentateuch, *'ādhām* (without the article) is used as a proper name only in Gen. iv. 25 (J) and v. 1, 3–5 (P)—cf. with the latter passage v. 2, where *'ādhām* still retains its generic sense: it is evident there that the author is concerned to mark the transition in usage from the generic term to the proper name. The LXX introduces some confusion by an arbitrary use of the proper name in places not warranted by the Hebrew, and is followed by the Vulgate and the English versions. *'ādhām* is rendered by *anthrōpos* (Vulg. *homo*) in Gen. i. 27–28, ii. 5, 7–8, 15, 18; but in ii. 16 (Yahweh addresses the *'ādhām*) and the following verses there is an abrupt change to *Adam*—generally, though not always, without the definite article. In ii. 24 *anthrōpos* (Vulg. *homo*) occurs again (for *'īsh*, translated in ii. 23 by *anēr*); and in ii. 25, *Adam*.

[2] Cf., among many instances, Augustine, *de civ. Dei*, xii. 21 *ad fin*.

humanity,[1] yet in no definable or even comprehensible sense an individual human being, and certainly not an historical 'man'—the Adam of Jewish and Christian tradition. This protoplast was so constituted that it contained within itself a relational principle which God proceeded to realize by resolving the *'ādhām* into its correlative component elements, and investing them with concrete personal existence as a sexual polarity of man and woman. Thus we may say that the Yahwist conceives the creation of sex as a process involving two stages—first, the making of an *'ādhām*, and then its separation into *'īsh* and *'ishshāh*, whereas the priestly editor thinks rather of a single act by which *'ādhām* is brought into being through the simultaneous formation of *zākhār* and *n⁰qēbhāh*. Both authors, however, express the same basic truth in different ways: the creature Man, whom God called into humanity from some earlier 'pithecanthropoid' condition, is fundamentally a sexual 'being-in-relation'—and as such, P adds, he reflects the Creator's nature.

Before leaving the Genesis creation stories, one point calls for brief comment. The interpretation of the Yahwistic myth just suggested may seem to represent it as a Hebrew version or counterpart of the universal myth of the androgyne. It is important, therefore, to appreciate that the two have nothing essential in common, despite certain apparent but deceptive similarities. The androgynous conception of sex excludes any idea of genuine meeting and self-communication between man and woman, and tends to find expression only in narcissism or self-regarding love.[2] It also denies the reality of sexual antithesis and complementation, and has no goal but an ultimate fusion of male and female in the undifferentiated unity from which it supposes that they originated. The biblical myth of the *'ādhām*, on the contrary, recognizes sex as the personalization of an ontological distinction in Man, and sees the destiny of the sexes fulfilled in every kind of responsible and creative relationship between them, and specially

---

[1] Thus the *'ādhām* exercises the dominion over the lower creation bestowed upon Man, when it names the animals.

[2] In *Dogmatics* II, pp. 64–65, Brunner comments upon this aspect of androgyny.

in that of union as one-flesh. It stands for the integrity and freedom of man and woman as individual human beings, even while it holds them together in an inescapable belongingness.

We may now define more precisely the scope and content of a theology of sex. Its main concern will be to study both the nature and the personal and social consequences of Man's sexual duality as an image of God; and to this end it will reject any such narrow conception of human sexuality as that it is merely a form of specialization for the purpose of reproduction. Rather, it will seek to exhibit the generative function as one among many aspects of a complex creative dynamic which can be released through a limitless variety of relationships, to the benefit both of individuals and of society. Such a theology will thus treat chiefly of what man and woman *are*, not of what they *do*—though by applying the principles and insights so established, it will attempt to elucidate the many practical problems which constantly arise in connexion with the ecclesiastical, social, legal, matrimonial, and venereal relationships of the sexes.

The business of a theology of sex may partly be described in another way by saying that it will to a large extent be concerned with the two primary obligations created by Man's constitution as a 'dual being'; these are, the preservation of sexual integrity, and the acceptance of sexual partnership—or as Barth expresses it, the double duty to live 'as man *or* woman' and 'as man *and* woman'.[1] The first of these obligations means the affirmation of sex as a gift from God which Man may neither reject nor seek to transcend in a quest for some 'higher' condition of virtual asexuality. From the standpoint of contemporary thought in general, it may seem nonsense to speak of denying or transcending sex—for what can Man do but accept his sex? In terms of biological, physical sexuality there is, admittedly, no alternative; male and female must acquiesce in their respective natures as they received them.[2] But with sex as a metaphysical phenomenon this

---

[1] Op. cit., III/4, pp. 165 ff.; 181 ff.

[2] So-called 'changes of sex' in human beings, though much publicized when they occur, are very rare phenomena (comparatively speaking), and cannot be

is not so, for it is possible to adopt towards one's own masculinity or femininity an attitude which amounts, in effect, to nothing less than a denial of all that sex signifies—a refusal to assent to one of the basic facts of personal existence.

Thus there is always a danger that rebellion against false or unworthy conceptions of sex may lead to rejection of sex itself. The movement for the emancipation of women, for example, found expression not only in a proper assertion of feminine rights and a salutary attack upon androcentricity, but also (at least on the part of certain protagonists) in what amounted to a positive refusal of womanhood. Nor is the latter an attitude typical only of the militant feminism of the past; Mlle Simone de Beauvoir can still assert that "one is not born, but rather becomes, a woman".[1] By this, she means that sex in Man is essentially an extrinsic condition—an effect of environment; as a girl grows up, social pressures of various kinds gradually mould her into a 'feminine creature' who has no independent meaning or autonomous being of her own, but draws her significance (such as it is) from the male—the true 'Existent' over against whom she stands for ever as the 'Other'. From this secondary, derivative rôle there can be but one way of escape; in order to become a real and self-subsistent person, woman must renounce or rise superior to her sex, with the subservience and 'otherness' which it is thought to imply, and must re-establish herself as a human being. Mlle de Beauvoir clearly fails to appreciate that to be human one must be either male or female; in her anxiety to repudiate false notions of sexuality, she falls into the error of repudiating sex itself—thus denying an intrinsic element in the humanity which she desires to restore to woman.

If the emancipation movement was characterized by a 'flight from [falsely-conceived] femininity', we now seem to be witnessing what may be described as a 'flight from [falsely-conceived]

---

accepted as in any sense a refutation of the proposition here stated. In any case, we know very little about the nature, causes, and consequences of such 'changes,' especially from the personal and metaphysical standpoint.

[1] S. de Beauvoir, *The Second Sex* (transl. H. M. Parshley, London, 1953), p. 273.

masculinity'.[1] Just as nineteenth-century woman eventually found it impossible to sustain the artificial, 'angelic' sexual rôle demanded by 'Victorian' convention and sentimental idealism, so modern man is beginning to demonstrate in a variety of ways his inability to live up to the exaggerated conception of maleness which has been fostered by war, and by a highly competitive economy conducive to the encouragement of aggressiveness and 'toughness'.[2] In each case, however, reaction against false notions of sex has taken the form, not of corrective effort directed to the inculcation of sounder ideas, but of a tendency to rebel against sex itself, and to represent it as devoid of all real significance.

Other kinds of sex denial are more subtle, and are often more deeply rooted and persistent. Every culture develops its own conceptions of what is 'masculine' or 'feminine' and these, gradually becoming formalized, affect social structure and attitudes. Such conceptions are expressed in the qualities and attributes which are held to be typical of, or desirable in men and women; in the status of the sexes *vis-à-vis* one another and the community; in the functions, rights, obligations, and privileges allocated to each; and in the approved patterns of sexual behaviour. Such social sexual stereotypes are generally quite arbitrary, and are never universal or unvarying—though some are relatively widespread and enduring; but they always indicate the sexual ideas of a culture, and reflect or produce both true and false notions of sex.

History and anthropology offer many illustrations of the social stereotyping of sexual rôles and character, but there are few clearer or better-known instances of the phenomenon than that provided by Dr Margaret Mead's studies of three contrasted New Guinea tribes.[3] In two of these tribes, sexual distinction has virtually no social significance. The Mundugumor way of life

---

[1] There is a discussion of the contemporary 'flight from masculinity' in A. Kardiner, *Sex and Morality* (London, 1955), pp. 160 ff.

[2] It is significant that as the art and literature of the time tended to sustain the nineteenth-century feminine ideal, so the cinema, the popular novel, and the strip-cartoon have played their part in the modern cult of the 'he-man' and the 'super-man'.

[3] See p. 246, n. 2, and the works there cited.

encourages in both sexes an unhappy, falsely-'masculine'[1] aggressiveness of the worst kind, while the concern of the Arapesh for
the welfare of the next generation unites male and female in a
gentle, affectionate, co-operative partnership which expresses
what would commonly be regarded in the West as a 'feminine'[1]
social ideal. Among the Tchambuli, on the other hand, sexual
distinctions are maintained in the tribal community; but owing
to the peculiar social rôles assigned to the sexes, the resultant
relational and cultural pattern is quite unlike that of the West—
although the women are theoretically subordinate they are
actually dominant, while the men are passive and accept a
dependent status. These examples alone show what different
meanings the terms 'masculine' and 'feminine' can have; they
also remind us that our own sexual concepts are to no small
degree stereotypic, and cannot be regarded as necessarily final or
determinative.

In the Christian West no less than in primitive New Guinea
powerful influences operate (as they have always done) to ensure
that the sexes conform to cultural standards, and to the ruling
conceptions of the respective social rôles appropriate to men and
women. This moulding process begins almost in the cradle, and
at a very early stage the child is made aware that the community
has certain sexual expectations, some of which may conflict with
personal inclination. Trivial though they may be, comments of
disapproval such as "little boys do not play with dolls", or "little
girls do not play with trains", introduce the child to basic stereotypes which grow more familiar and comprehensive with the
passage of years until they serve to delimit two artificial and
mutually exclusive realms—the 'man's world' and the 'woman's
world'. During adolescence and throughout adult life many
insidious pressures continually enforce upon the individual a
communal notion of what is 'manly' or 'womanly'—and with
this the majority unconsciously complies. Thus the attitudes and
values inculcated in one generation are automatically transmitted

---

[1] Here, 'masculine' and 'feminine' are, of course, used in the conventional
sense determined by western stereotypes of sexuality.

to the next—unless intervening factors prove strong enough to change or modify the prevailing patterns of sexual relation.

One of several such factors in modern times has been the emancipation of woman—and this, combined with the many social changes of the last half-century, has affected considerably the sexual ideas and relational structures of the West. In particular, it has weakened to a marked degree the androcentricity which stands out as one of the dominant sexual stereotypes of the western Christian tradition, and is still sufficiently entrenched to prevent or retard necessary reforms and developments. Nothing has been more productive of false sexual concepts and standards than the notion of male headship and privilege, and its subsidiary or dependent assumptions concerning the respective functions and capacities of man and woman. But it is necessary to be vigilant, lest new ideas of sexual relation themselves give rise to unsound values and bad stereotypes: hence the importance of watching with special care the effect of certain myths, relational patterns, and ideals which are inculcated by various media of mass communication.

The cultural stereotyping of sexual rôles and characteristics, and the consequent danger that false standards and notions may be established as socially normal or even desirable, leads directly to the question of the ontological meaning of sex. Has Man no self-understanding to guide him—no natural sense by means of which to distinguish true from false conceptions of manhood and womanhood? Here, the Yahwistic creation myth is illuminating. When God purposed to create sex, he first cast the *'ādhām* into a deep sleep, and then accomplished his will by resolving the primordial 'human being' into its complementary elements—male and female, *'īsh* and *'ishshāh*. The *'ādhām* did not know what had been done during those moments of unconsciousness, and the divine secret has never been revealed. Man is aware of the fact of sex, but he has no intuitive comprehension of its significance; the knowledge of being a man or a woman does not, of itself, convey any understanding of the meaning of manhood or womanhood. Thus sex remains a profound and baffling enigma of personal existence, the mystery of which can never be dispelled by excogitation—and certainly not by studying what is now both popularly and scientifically called 'sex', or by venturing upon casual venereal experiments. This, perhaps, is one of the most unpalatable of all truths to an age which thinks that it knows 'all about sex'.

Where, then, is the place of understanding? Again, the myth is suggestive. It tells how God brought *'ish* and *'ishshāh* together—thus signifying how the sexes meet, first in an encounter wherein each perceives in the other both self-likeness and self-difference, and then in a more intimate and permanent relationship of mutual self-committal wherein they are united as one-flesh. Here, on two distinct levels of personal confrontation, man and woman become aware of the meaning of sex; each discovers that this is made known, not through reflection upon the nature of the individual self, but through an experience of meeting in what Buber calls the 'world of Thou'—that is, the realm of responsible personal relation.

This can be expressed in another way. Strictly speaking, one who is solitary, or among others of the same sex, is not conscious of sexuality in the metaphysical sense; for to be aware of being male or female—of possessing certain sexual attributes such as the primary and secondary characteristics, conveys no inward intimation of the personal significance of manhood or womanhood. But let such a person enter into a genuine relationship with one of the complementary sex; he or she is immediately conscious of a new dimension of experience, of confrontation by another who is also human, yet human with a radical difference—and in that experience, something of the meaning of sex is perceived. True sexual knowledge, in other words, is always existential and dependent upon a capacity for sincere and responsible relational ventures; it can never be derived at second-hand from social stereotypes or conventional ideas of what is manly or womanly.

Furthermore, sexual knowledge is not knowledge of the kind that can be expressed or communicated in any way; otherwise the metaphysical significance of sex could be defined precisely enough to prevent confusion between true and false ideas or relational patterns—so tending to reduce the danger of the false developing unchecked. Rather, it is an interior awareness of the meaning of manhood or womanhood which is experienced only in the immediacy of sexual encounter, and disappears with the termination of meeting. Reflection upon past encounters may bring consciousness of having once known, and anticipation of knowing again, but the content of the knowledge itself can neither be recalled nor predicted. Nor can such knowledge ever be other than fragmentary, particular, and impossible to generalize or formulate; the full meaning of sex always remains God's secret, and all human insight here is at best but clouded and imperfect. In so far as Man attains any degree of understanding, it is due to the quality of his sexual relationships—and right relationship, therefore, is ultimately the only source of sound sexual values and a true conception of sex.

The importance of right relationship leads to consideration of the second of the two obligations already mentioned—that of sexual partnership. This obligation is laid unconditionally upon all men and women, and does not pertain simply to marriage. The common life of one-flesh is obviously the central, exemplary form of sexual partnership—but it is not the only one; the necessities and opportunities of communal existence involve the sexes in an infinite variety of associations fraught with personal or social consequences, and God demands of them a willing acceptance of their relational responsibilities. Man's constitution as a 'dual being' means that male and female were created with reference to one another, and are indissolubly bound together by a natural tie of mutual dependence. Each needs the other's help, not merely for procreative and domestic purposes, but in all the manifold concerns and enterprises of human life—especially the social and political, where the common good demands harmonious co-operation between the sexes.

In the past, genuine partnership (and therefore cross-fertilization of mind and spirit) between man and woman has been greatly hindered by androcentric theories of sexual status and function which are inimical to human well-being and progress. It is contrary to the best interests of a community that either sex should accumulate for itself such power as men have hitherto enjoyed; this cannot but inhibit the creative insights and energy which flow from sexual polarity, and may well partly explain the recurrent crises by which mankind has always been menaced. Woman has been excluded from any effective constitutional share in the conduct of public affairs, and social and educational disabilities have deprived her of means to refute the arguments by which man has buttressed his position of privilege. Even 'emancipated' woman has found herself at a disadvantage, for she has been compelled to compete against man on his terms, in a 'man's world' where conditions have conduced neither to full and willing partnership, nor to the exercise of her natural feminine genius and gifts. In the face of such obstacles her achievements have already been notable, but her direct influence in the higher counsels of Church and State is still relatively slight, and it is certain that the limited concession of 'equality' with man in certain spheres has neither solved all her problems nor satisfied her deepest personal needs.

Fifty years ago, in connexion with emancipation, reference used to be made to the 'woman's question'. Neither then nor later was it recognized that there is also a 'man's question' which has never been fully considered, and which many are not disposed to acknowledge or to take seriously. None the less, the two 'questions' are interdependent, and cannot be isolated one from the other. It is futile to discuss woman's social rôle, and to assume at the same time that man's has been predetermined and must not be disputed. There can be no satisfactory solution to the cultural problem of sexual relation until man himself sees that his own social rôle is not self-evidently that which tradition has assigned to him. The fact that God created Man as a sexual duality means that male and female, as isolated individuals, have been given no fixed and clearly-defined social status or function. They have simply been called to a life of partnership in all things—and as partners, therefore, they must seek together in love and humility to understand and fulfil their common destiny as Man. For each sex this is bound to prove a hard demand at first. While headship has its powers and privileges, subordination is not without its compensations and its opportunities for exploitation. If man and woman are to live creatively in the state of belongingness for which they were made, they will need honesty and courage to renounce old prerogatives and pretences, to welcome and assume new responsibilities, and to adventure forth side by side in confidence and mutual trust—ready to learn through experiment in relation what God, in his wisdom, has ordained that they can learn in no other way.

The obligation of partnership thus laid upon the sexes can be evaded or rejected in other ways than those which have already been discussed, and one of these ways requires special consideration because of its bearing upon Christian history and institutions. One dominant feature in western Church tradition, as we have seen, has been the conviction that virginity is the ideal, 'angelic' state of life, and that venereal activity (even within marriage) cannot take place without distraction from spiritual things—or, according to the more extreme view, without pollution or even sin (though the latter may be excused by an intention to procreate). Hence monastics and the clergy were bound to a rule of perpetual continence which was increasingly interpreted (especially in the case of monks and nuns) as requiring more or less strict segregation of the sexes; and this inevitably engendered suspicions and fears, and seriously inhibited creative encounter and co-operation between man and woman. Against all one-sex institutions and orders, therefore, as against all vows of celibacy (compulsory, and even voluntary), there is set an insistent question-mark; save as urgent, emergency expedients framed to meet a temporary crisis,[1] they are only justified if they do not hinder free and healthy partnership between the sexes.

Here it is important to guard against misunderstanding. Nothing that has just been said is directed against celibacy as such, but only against false conceptions and applications of the idea of

[1] See K. Barth, op. cit., III/4, pp. 184–185.

celibacy, particularly within the Church. Too often the obligation of partnership is misinterpreted as an obligation to marry, with the result that all Christian liberty in the sexual realm is denied. Under the old dispensation, admittedly, marriage was regarded as a duty because generation was held to be imperative; if the Jew must propagate the holy seed of Abraham, the Gentile no less must beget future citizens to serve the state and to maintain the cultus—hence (among other things) the importance attached to certain aspects of fertility religion, the peculiar scandal of adultery, and the enduring reproach which rested upon the single and the barren. But *post Christum natum*—after the coming of *the* Seed for whom all previous generations of the Chosen People were preparatory, procreation ceased to be a necessity, and carnal birth "of blood . . . of the flesh . . . of the will of Man"[1] yielded in significance to spiritual rebirth "of water and of the Spirit".[2] For the first time man, and woman also, enjoyed a right of choice; they might serve God either as married or as single, according to the calling which each had received.[3]

The error of the Church was to make an artificial distinction between the two vocations—to present celibacy as the nobler and more meritorious way, although neither in fact is holier or higher or more pleasing to God than the other, and each after its own fashion offers the fullest opportunities for the practice of the religious life and the pursuit of sanctity. But whether the Christian is called to celibacy or to marriage, he may not forget that in a sense more profound, perhaps, than that intended by the Apostle, "neither is the woman without the man, nor the man without the woman, in the Lord".[4] Upon married and single alike God lays the same ineluctable obligation to live in belongingness, one sex with the other—and from this there can be no dispensation. A man or a woman is free to adopt the celibate life, but not to refuse or evade the duty of partnership; and the celibate is likewise free

---

[1] Jn. i. 13.
[2] Jn. iii. 5.
[3] Cf. 1 Cor. vii. 7.
[4] 1 Cor. xi. 11.

to follow any particular rule or discipline, provided that it does not, by express direction or customary interpretation, inhibit or preclude free personal intercourse and creative encounter with the complementary sex. There is nothing inherently contrary to relational principle in the idea of the 'regular' community life—indeed, as the Ferrar experiment at Little Gidding showed, it has many unexplored possibilities and could be adapted to a large variety of needs and circumstances; but conventional conceptions of monasticism are still too often infected with the dualism of the Christian sexual tradition, and need reconsideration in the light of the mutual responsibility of man and woman. Nor are celibacy and monasticism alone in question; there are numerous Church societies, guilds, and associations which are constituted on a single-sex basis, and are hardly calculated to uphold the obligation of partnership.

Ecclesiastical institutions are not the only ones open to criticism; there are many single-sex clubs, schools, and colleges (not to mention more august bodies) which call for realistic scrutiny. Their existence is often bound up with certain patterns of social life, and with stereotypic notions of sex, and a wealth of andro-centric sentiment and argument would be rallied to their defence;[1] but against them, too, stands the question-mark. Segregation is particularly difficult to justify as an educational principle; not only may it encourage false sexual ideas and values, but it also prevents boys and girls from learning through school experience a lesson which is vital for adult life—namely, that each sex must recognize, accept, and act responsibly towards the other. The natural basic social unit, the family, is itself a co-educational community, and sets the pattern for more artificial groupings. A co-educational school system, therefore, will be found to afford the best oppor-tunity to inculcate those relational concepts and standards which are the essential matter of true sex instruction, and to provide the

---

[1] It is always instructive to study the arguments advanced by men against the intrusion of competent women into institutions such as stock or woollen exchanges, which have always been exclusively male preserves. The latest instance has been the opposition to that part of the House of Lords reform plan, which admits women to the Upper Chamber as life peeresses.

proper background against which to impart the factual knowledge about reproduction which commonly passes for 'sex' education. This is not to deny that the single-sex class may have pedagogic utility, at least for the teaching of certain subjects at certain stages in the child's development—but only in the general context of that free association between the sexes, in play as well as in work, which is most conducive to normal progress towards emotional maturity.

Obviously it is impossible here to deal fully with all that is implied by the obligations of sexual integrity and partnership, but enough will have been said about the theological principles of sex and sexual relation to indicate the extent of their bearing upon social, political, and ecclesiastical questions, and to suggest the benefits which could accrue from their practical application. In conclusion, several subsidiary points call for brief discussion.

First: in pleading for recognition of the importance of a theology of sex, some consideration must be given to St Paul's assertion that in Christ "there can be no male (*arsen*) and female (*thēlu*)".[1] This has generally been interpreted to imply that for those who have become sons of God, and have entered upon the new life of faith, even the natural distinction between man and woman is meaningless. Lightfoot's version,[2] "there is no room for male and female" (later adopted by Moffatt), emphatically expresses this view, which recalls the sexual antipathy of patristic thought.[3] If this correctly represents the sense of the saying, sex for the Christian is reduced to insignificance, and the theological principles outlined in the preceding pages are rendered nugatory.

The text in question, however, can be construed differently and more satisfactorily, and its true meaning emerges when it is read in conjunction with the similar passage in the Epistle to the

---

[1] Gal. iii. 28.

[2] Cf. J. B. Lightfoot, *St Paul's Epistle to the Galatians* (London and Cambridge, 1896), p. 148.

[3] The cryptic saying attributed to Jesus by the encratite *Gospel according to the Egyptians* (see above, p. 39) bears a curious superficial resemblance to the Apostle's words, but there is no evidence of direct influence.

Colossians.[1] In both places, St Paul is at pains to stress the unity which all believers attain in Christ, regardless of natural condition or secular status; in Galatians he illustrates his theme by reference to the basic divisions of race, class, and sex, while in Colossians he cites in particular the distinctions germane to the problems of the local Church—hence the absence of any allusion to male and female. But it is significant that in each case more is involved than mere distinction. Jew and Greek, bond and free, circumcision and uncircumcision, typify not only the diversity but also the divisive antagonisms of contemporary life; the Apostle is concerned, not with human division as such, but with the kind of division which is caused or intensified by mutual hostility and exploitation. When Christ makes all to become "one Man", he does not abolish distinctions themselves (for they ought to be a source of enrichment to both individuals and the community), but only the sinful disposition which uses them as a pretext for estrangement and hate. Unity, for the Christian, is something far removed from a featureless uniformity.

This is the context in which St Paul's reference to male and female must be set. Between the sexes there is also an antagonism —but of a different kind, deeper and more subtle than the enmities which bring races, creeds, and classes into collision. It emanates from the immemorial androcentricity which has corrupted the social and personal relationships of man and woman, so that instead of being creative and integrative, they have become negative and even destructive. In Christ this, too, is done away—but not, of course, sex itself, for sex is a metaphysical as well as a physical and cultural distinction, and cannot be abolished without destroying Man's intrinsic nature. Rather should it be said that in Christ man and woman are delivered from the power of false ideas of sexuality which inhibit true relation, and are enabled to become what God created them to be —to realize a genuine manliness and womanliness.

In this connexion the Colossians passage is specially significant. The Apostle exhorts his readers to remember that as a result of

---

[1] Col. iii. 11.

their conversion they have "put off the old Man (*anthrōpon*) with his doings, and have put on the new Man, which is being renewed unto knowledge after the image (*eikona*) of him that created him"[1]—and that in the life of regeneration which they have now entered mundane distinctions no longer count, for "Christ is all, and in all". Here the reference is clearly to the original creation of Man as it is described in the first chapter of Genesis, and in one respect the analogy drawn by St Paul bears directly upon our discussion.

The Manward relational aspect of the *imago Dei*, as we have seen, consists specially in Man's constitution as a sexual duality. Renewal of the new Man "after the image" of his Creator, therefore, involves more than renovation of the individual believer's character by the interior spiritual action of divine grace; it includes also the restoration of God's image in Man—that is to say, of harmonious creative relation between man and woman. Moreover, this process of renewal is "unto knowledge". Primarily, in the context, this refers to the genuine *gnōsis* which can only be attained through Christ, as opposed to the false *gnōsis* of those who were leading the Colossians astray; but this does not exclude also a more general sense, suggesting progressive acquisition of insight into the purpose of God as expressed in the creation of Man—and therefore into the true nature and meaning of sex as the structural basis of Man's existence as a 'being-in-relation'. In Christ, then, we may certainly say that "there can be no male and female" as that distinction is conceived by androcentric theories, for in him both such theories themselves, and the antagonisms and false values which they engender, are done away. But this does not mean that sexual distinction, as such, becomes of no account; on the contrary, it is in Christ that sex assumes its real significance, for in him alone can man and woman find the disciplined freedom which enables them to learn through their relational experiences something of the deeper meaning of their masculinity or femininity.

---

[1] Col. iii. 10.

When discussing the theological aspect of sex it was stated that the difference between man and woman is radical—that their relation is one of polarity no less than of mutual complementation. How can this be reconciled, on the one hand with the fact that there seems to be a certain measure of biological equivalence between the sexes,[1] and on the other with the view now commonly held, that each sex contains within itself both masculine and feminine components?

The former point is best considered in connexion with the evolutionary purpose of sex. In the most primitive, unicellular animalcules reproduction occurs asexually by means of binary fission—a method of propagation which merely results in an endless reduplication of more or less identical organisms. Such, apparently, was the primordial condition of things—but a momentous change took place with the emergence of sexual specialization; infinite possibilities of variety arising from the combination of inherited characteristics were implied by the fact that reproduction, in all but the simplest creatures, now required the co-operation of two dissimilar and, to an increasing degree, complementary individuals, Sex thus became first an instrument essential for the progressive development of ever higher and more complex forms of life, and eventually the most pronounced and significant of the differences within the several species. The culmination of the whole evolutionary process in Man brought into play a new factor—personality; and this served further to sharpen and deepen in the human kind the division already caused by sexual distinction, so creating between man and woman a profound metaphysical antithesis which stands in a clear contrast to any biochemical equivalence at another level of their being.

---

[1] Thus C. L. Evans, *Principles of Human Physiology* (London, 11th ed., 1952), instances the fact that the sex hormone in Man is not completely sex-specific (p. 1141), and that œstrogenic (female hormone) and androgenic (male hormone) substances are found to be present in the urine of both men and women (pp. 1125, 1138, and 1141). Furthermore, the suprarenal cortical hormones are nearly related chemically, and in large doses can produce both androgenic and œstrogenic effects (pp. 1141–1142). It also seems that the pituitary substance which stimulates the growth of the gonads is probably the same in both male and female (p. 1141).

Here, then, there is no inconsistency between the view of human sex presented by theology on the one hand, and by science on the other; each is concerned with a different aspect of Man's nature, which it seeks to elucidate in terms of its own insight and discipline. The theory of personal bisexuality, however, involves considerations of another and more complex kind bearing upon the relation between sex and those qualities which together constitute the distinctive character of the individual personality. Humanity, as we have seen, exists either as manhood or as womanhood—aberrations such as hermaphroditism are irrelevant to the metaphysical question now under discussion. Personal characteristics likewise exist, not abstractly, but only as they are exhibited concretely (and therefore differentially) in male or female; that is to say, they are distinguished qualitatively by sex. Consequently it cannot be said that any human attribute pertains exclusively or even specially to man alone or to woman alone, for each (according to his or her sex) possesses fully the nature of Man, and all that belongs thereto. On the other hand, it follows equally that masculine and feminine variants of what may be termed 'basic' human characteristics (such as gentleness, aggressiveness, tenderness, and so forth) cannot be conjoined in the same individual. Metaphysically speaking, man is always purely masculine and woman is always purely feminine—a statement which would be truistic, were it not that the contrary opinion is so commonly assumed and maintained.

It is not difficult to understand how the notion of an individual psychical bisexuality arose. As its stereotypes of manliness and womanliness develop, every culture tends to identify some personal qualities with one sex and some with the other, and to label such qualities 'masculine' or 'feminine' accordingly. But the traits so classified are never intrinsically sex-specific, though each, of course, will have its manly and its womanly form; all, in the appropriate sexual mode, are present as elements in the personality of male and female alike. Every individual, therefore, will normally reveal characteristics which are deemed by convention not to be congruous with, or becoming to his or her sex—a fact which invites from those who accept a sexual analysis of personal qualities the plausible but erroneous explanation that in each man there is something 'feminine', and in each woman something 'masculine'. In other words, the theory of individual bisexuality is simply a by-product of false conceptions of the sexual factor in personality, and rests upon nothing more substantial than *a priori* supposition. Although it has been widely popularized, and appears to be regarded as axiomatic by many psychologists,[1] it lacks both empirical authority and metaphysical justification, and cannot be admitted by the theologian.

It is sometimes suggested that rejection of the theory of individual bisexuality throws doubt upon the reality of the Incarnation, and of the redemptive work of Christ. How, it is asked, can God in Christ be said to have taken humanity in its fullness if, in fact, he only assumed masculinity? The contention is that this theory safeguards the central truth of the Christian faith because it guarantees that God united to himself elements both of manhood and of womanhood, thus becoming completely and not partially Man. Actually, however, such a view destroys rather than secures the reality of the Incarnation and the Redemption, for it asserts that God took upon him something other than our true nature. Personality is never bisexual. Since there are only two ways to be human—that is, as man or as woman, so there were only two possible forms for a genuine Incarnation to take. It was, therefore, part of the 'scandal of particularity' that God must assume Man's nature as man[2]—just as he had also to assume it as a Galilean Jew of the first century; but as man, Christ redeemed Man, and not merely men.

---

[1] It has not, however, received unanimous support from psychologists, and in particular has been rejected by Dr Sandor Rado, for an account of whose teaching see W. G. Cole, op. cit., pp. 263 ff.; and see also A. Kardiner, op. cit., pp. 164 ff., for an adverse criticism of this theory in relation to homosexuality. It is possible that the theory of individual bisexuality may partly be due to misunderstanding of Jung's categories of *animus* and *anima*; these, of course, relate not to qualities or aspects of personality, but to archetypal images residing in the unconscious.

[2] With the obvious reasons why he did not take womanhood, we are not here concerned.

Finally, there remains the critical question of the status of woman.[1] From the dual constitution of Man, as we have seen, two ineluctable obligations arise: to preserve one's sexual integrity, and to accept the principle of sexual partnership. To these, Barth would add a third: to acknowledge and maintain the order established by God in the sexual realm, according to which the woman is ontologically subordinate to the man as her 'head'.[2] He is conscious of the fact that this conception of her status is now not universally upheld, and is therefore at some pains to explain that it does not imply male tyranny or female subservience. Man has no advantage over woman, and woman concedes no superiority to man, but she realizes her humanity most fully by acquiescing in his leadership and initiative, and her secondary status has its own honour and greatness. Her submission is always the expression of free decision, while his pre-eminence is possible only because it is grounded in deep humility. Upon this subordinative relational structure, however, human order depends—and for that order man, being the stronger, must assume responsibility; woman, on the other hand, will demonstrate her maturity by co-operating with man, and by accepting her appointed place within the order in obedience to the divine will. Between the sexes there is no spiritual inequality; nevertheless the headship of man and the subordination of woman are facts which cannot be ignored or explained away, and an ordinance of God which society disregards at its peril.

Despite Barth's careful (indeed, almost anxious) qualifications and reservations, it is evident that there is basically but little difference between his theory of sexual status, and the familiar

---

[1] In discussing this question, the reader will notice that I reach a conclusion which is directly opposite to the one stated in the Appendix on 'The New Testament Doctrine of Subordination' in *The Mystery of Love and Marriage*, pp. 129 ff. In that Appendix I attempted (not without misgiving) to justify the traditional theological view that woman is subordinate to man. Further study has shown that the misgiving was not without cause, and that the attempt was misconceived. It is evident that such a notion of sexual order is untenable, and the pages which follow are, therefore, in the nature of a retraction.

[2] Op. cit., III/4, pp. 188–202.

androcentric assumptions of Christian tradition. These assumptions rest mainly upon the teaching of St Paul, whose definition of the relation between the sexes has always been regarded by the Church as possessing special authority. It is unnecessary, however, to consider the circumstances and details of this teaching, for we are only concerned here with the principle to which the Apostle appeals when he directs that women must be veiled as a mark of their subordination when they pray or prophesy, that they must keep silence in church, and that they must not teach or in any other way usurp dominion over men.[1]

The principle itself is stated quite categorically in the first epistle to the Corinthians: "the head (*kephalē*) of the woman is the man"; he is "the image (*eikōn*) and glory (*doxa*) of God", but she is only "the glory of the man",[2] and must "be in subjection" (*hupotassomai*) as the law demands.[3] In the epistles to the Ephesians and the Colossians, and also in the first epistle of Peter, it is applied specifically to marriage: "the husband is the head (*kephalē*) of the wife, as Christ also is the head (*kephalē*) of the Church".[4] Wives, therefore, must "be in subjection" (*hupotassomai*) to their husbands,[5] and must "fear" (*phobeō*) them[6]—requirements which are balanced, it is true, but in no way mitigated by the commands to husbands that they, for their part, must love their wives as Christ loved the Church, avoiding bitterness against them, and honouring them as weaker vessels who are none the less "joint-heirs of the grace of life".[7]

---

[1] 1 Cor. xi. 3 ff.; xiv. 34–35; 1 Tim. ii. 12. It is irrelevant here that the second and third passages may not be authentically Pauline; or that there are (on certain interpretations) apparent contradictions between 1 Cor. xi, which implies that women are permitted to speak in assemblies for worship provided the proprieties governing female behaviour are observed, and the other two passages, which appear to prohibit women from speaking or teaching in any circumstances. For a discussion (from the conservative standpoint) of the textual and exegetical problems involved, see F. Zerbst, op. cit., pp. 31–58; and see also the standard commentaries, *ad. loc.*

[2] 1 Cor. xi. 3, 7.   [3] 1 Cor. xiv. 34.   [4] Eph. v. 23.
[5] Eph. v. 22, 24; Col. iii. 18; 1 Pet. iii. 1 (cf. 5).
[6] Eph. v. 33; cf. 1 Pet. iii. 6.
[7] Eph. v. 25, 28, 33; Col. iii. 19; 1 Pet. iii. 7.

What is the significance of the term *kephalē*, as it is used in these passages to describe man's superordinate status? There is good reason to think that in St Paul's thought it has virtually the same meaning as *archē*—that is, 'origin' or 'first cause'.[1] In classical Greek, admittedly, the two words have nothing in common, but in the Septuagint they are brought into close association as alternative and interchangeable renderings of the Hebrew word *rōsh*, which means 'head', while *archē* is also used to translate the feminine form of *rōsh—rēshīth*, the dominant sense of which is 'first' or 'beginning'. We may fairly assume that this Old Testament assimilation of *kephalē* and *archē* was familiar to the Apostle, and that it largely determined the language in which he sought to define his conception of the structure of sexual relation. When, therefore, he describes the man as 'head' of the woman, there can be little doubt that he uses *kephalē* in the sense of *archē*, thus attributing to the male sex an ontological priority from which the man's apparent social and marital pre-eminence over the woman is derived.

The source of this idea is obvious—indeed, it is clearly revealed by St Paul's assertion that "the man is not of the woman, but the woman of the man: neither was the man created for the woman, but the woman for the man".[2] His view of sexual relation is governed by the conviction that God not only created the sexes in the order and manner described in the second chapter of Genesis, but also signified thereby and established for all time the status proper to each. Moreover, it is evident that St Paul sees a reflection of this divinely ordained pattern in the structure of society, in the axioms of jurisprudence, and in the "custom" (*sunētheia*) of "the churches of God".[3] When he declares that "the head of the woman is the man", he undoubtedly expresses what he believed to be a theological principle; but it is important to remember that he also states an undisputed assumption of contemporary law and social life. Likewise, when he says that "the

---

[1] For a fuller discussion of the connexion in St Paul's thought between *kephalē* and *archē*, see S. Bedale, 'The Meaning of *kephalē* in the Pauline Epistles', in *The Journal of Theological Studies* (NS), v. pt. 2, October 1954, pp. 211–215.

[2] 1 Cor. xi. 8–9.   [3] 1 Cor. xi. 16.

husband is the head of the wife", and when he bids wives "be in subjection" to their husbands, he not only invokes the same theological principle, but also recognizes as a matter of fact that the wife is theoretically and practically *hupandros*[1] or subordinate to her husband, being under his authority as that was variously defined by law and religion, and upheld by convention and usage.

In short, the subjection of woman was part of a social pattern which was universally accepted and inculcated in the ancient world, and not something peculiar to primitive Church teaching and discipline. From one point of view, indeed, the New Testament regulations concerning feminine status and activity simply reflect the conservatism of early Christianity in its social attitudes; they are obviously adaptations of precepts from the 'codes of subordination' which were then current in both Jewish and Hellenistic circles, and were widely employed as methods of education in the duties and obligations of civic and domestic relationship.[2] St Paul, however, is not content to regard this social pattern as a mere secular phenomenon; he sees behind it the primordial law of God investing it with divine authority and immutability. Hence his condemnation of what, according to this standard, was disorderly in the public worship at Corinth; male and female, he allows, are spiritually equal in Christ—yet even baptism cannot alter their personal standing *vis-à-vis* one another, as decreed by the Creator.

From what has been said, it will be clear that St Paul's idea of a divine law behind the principle of male headship is no more than a literalistic inference from the account of Man's creation given in the second chapter of Genesis. In the final analysis, therefore, his conception of the general status of each sex relative to the

---

[1] Cf. Rom. vii. 2, where *hupandros gunē* is the term used to designate a married woman. It is true that at this time Roman women were acquiring virtual independence by means of the subterfuge of *trinoctii absentia* (see above, p. 3), but the principle still stood.

[2] See further on the codes governing social relationships, as they are reflected in the New Testament, E. G. Selwyn, *The First Epistle of St Peter* (London, 1946), pp. 419 ff.

other stands or falls upon a plain question of fact. Is it true, we have to ask, that God derived woman from man—that he made her subordinate, and destined her to remain so for ever? To this, only one reply is possible: no positive evidence of any kind can be adduced in favour of such an idea, while on the other hand there are compelling reasons (both theological and scientific) for rejecting it as untenable.

The Scriptures themselves record no direct and positive word of God assigning to women in general a rôle of subjection,[1] nor does the author of the myth specifically draw any subordinative conclusion of his own from his description of the making of *'ishshāh*—and the belief that he intended nevertheless to imply what he did not express depends entirely upon *a priori* considerations. More significant, however, is the fact that in treating the Yahwist's story as decisive, St Paul ignores the brief but pregnant account of Man's origin which is set forth in the preceding chapter, though the latter is at once more profoundly suggestive from the theological point of view, and more consistent with the indications of anthropogeny. The priestly writer depicts creation as the immediate effect of God's spoken word. The divine utterance, "Let us make *'ādhām*", therefore, is no mere proposal to create, but the initiation of a creative act itself—the act whereby Man was brought into existence as a 'being-in-relation' and a sexual duality. We may state this in another way by saying that the Creator's fiat called into humanity, not an individual or isolated individuals, but a community or communities within which male and female were constituted in a new and special relation of personal equality and complementary interdependence as an image of his own Being. But however we may attempt to interpret the mystery of Man's creation, there is neither theological nor scientific warrant for perpetuating the crude notion that woman was made from man's bodily substance, and that he is virtually her *raison d'être*. Consequently no justification exists for describing man as woman's *kephalē* or head in the sense of *archē*

---

[1] The significance of Gen. iii. 16 is discussed below.

or origin, and the principle of feminine subordination, as expounded and applied by St Paul, thus proves to be without foundation.

It may be urged, however, that the Apostle correctly discerned the principle underlying sexual relation, although he adduced the wrong argument in its support. Those who maintain this opinion would contend that even if man is not in fact woman's *archē*, he is none the less truly her *kephalē*. We have, then, to ask whether God, at the creation, established between the sexes an order of headship and subjection which is immutable because it is inherent in the very constitution of humanity—so that without it Man would not really be Man. For this view, too, there is clearly no express scriptural authority—apart, of course, from what is stated or implied in the Pauline and Petrine writings, which cannot (for the reasons already discussed) be accepted as decisive; and above all, it has no place in the teaching of Jesus. Nevertheless, certain arguments are commonly advanced in its favour, and at these we must glance briefly.

It is sometimes claimed that if Man's sexual duality is indeed an *analogia relationis* of the divine Being, then the hierarchical order within the Trinity must necessarily have its counterpart in a corresponding order between man and woman. But this contention begs important theological questions. The Church has never officially endorsed the opinion, first advanced during the patristic age,[1] that the Father is the *principium* in the Godhead, and it is salutary to recall in this connexion Dr Leonard Hodgson's caution against "attempts to find the unity [in the Trinity] by treating one of the [three] elements as ultimate and reducing the others to terms of it".[2] But even if a subordinationist conception of the Godhead were conceded, the quasi-sexual parallelism between the two masculine terms, 'Father' and 'man', would certainly not warrant the conclusion that the latter's ontological relation to woman is in any way comparable to what is predicated of the relation between the first and the other two Persons of the

---

[1] See, e.g., Hilary, *de Trin.* iv. 16; Basil, *c. Eunom.* iii.

[2] *The Doctrine of the Trinity* (London, 1943), p. 88.

Trinity. Moreover, since man is not woman's *archē*, it is difficult to appreciate in what sense he could be said to have the status of *principium* in the sexual relation. On the other hand, if subordinationism is rejected, the *analogia relationis* would require also the rejection of the principle of hierarchical order in the sexual realm; nor could that principle be maintained by alleging (as some have done) the subjection of the incarnate Son to the Father—an argument which merely substitutes for the Trinitarian analogy one drawn from Christology for which no scriptural or other authority can be furnished. We are bound to conclude, therefore, that Man's constitution as a sexual *imago Dei* neither implies nor justifies any idea of male headship.

But the theological defence of man's superordination has more often been based upon arguments which are essentially empirical. It has been asserted that God endowed him more generously than woman with qualities such as physical strength, reasoning power, judgement, and practical ability, thus signifying that his proper office is to plan and decide for the common good, and to exercise responsible leadership in human affairs. Her inferior genius, on the other hand, indicates that she is destined only for a secondary rôle, being qualified for none but domestic and subsidiary employments—though there are compensating privileges, and especially maternity, to alleviate the disadvantages of subordination. This view, obviously, is simply a modified and refined version of the traditional androcentric attitude to sexual relation. Woman is no longer dismissed in Aristotelian terms as *hōsper arren pepērōmenon*[1]—a defective or misbegotten male, nor is she even stigmatized in the language of Christian divines as weak, foolish, inconstant, imbecile, vain, and incapable. But it is still assumed none the less that, compared with man, she is innately and irremediably deficient in certain essential respects; and this conjectural deficiency is alleged as the theological explanation and justification for her subjection.

Recent social developments, however, have deprived this argument of its plausibility, for the defects which were supposed

---

[1] *De gen. animal.* ii. 3.

to be intrinsic to the feminine character can now be traced in large measure to inadequate education, persistent inculcation of stereotypic ideas of the 'womanly', and lack of opportunity to learn the lessons which experience alone can teach. Emancipation has rapidly and effectively given the lie to many of the androcentric assumptions which were current in the immediate no less than the more remote past. Although women have only been able for a few decades to play a large-scale part in political and professional life, commerce, and industry, they have already shown themselves as a sex to be far from deficient in qualities hitherto regarded as peculiarly masculine, and therefore indicative of superiority. In the discharge of routine duties their efficiency is as great as that of men—if not often greater, while it is abundantly clear that the latter have no monopoly of the capacity for direction and leadership—though here few enough of either sex display real pre-eminence. In short, the empirical argument in favour of male headship has been substantially refuted on empirical grounds—and it is important to appreciate that the refutation has its negative as well as its positive aspects. While woman has actively and successfully vindicated herself against man's imputations of incompetence and personal inferiority, it can hardly be said that he, on his part, has convincingly demonstrated in the conduct of human affairs those qualities of headship to which he has laid claim as a divine endowment; indeed, both past and present history offer a telling indictment of his hollow pretence to superordinate status—and a salutary warning to her, lest the change in her situation should tempt her to a similar arrogance.

Rejection of the Pauline principle that the man is head of the woman does not, of course, imply that there is no order in the sexual realm. Indeed, the Apostle himself rightly discerned such an order, and attributed it to the will of God; but he also made the understandable mistake of identifying this order with contemporary patterns of relation and assumptions about sexual status. Consequently he defined it in hierarchical terms which presupposed the subjection of woman, and thus invested with an appearance of divine sanction the androcentric social and legal theories of antiquity. How, then, should we think of sexual order? Perhaps the theological reconsideration of sex in the first part of this chapter may suggest a more satisfactory conception than the rigid categories of Christian tradition.

Sexual order may be described as the general form of relation subsisting ontologically between male and female as personal constituents of the dual being, Man. Like sex itself, this order is essentially a divine secret or mystery—something known immediately to God alone; he has not expressly declared it by revelation, man and woman have no abstract and intuitive comprehension of it, and it cannot be deduced from biological or psychical data about the sexes, or from their established social rôles and functions. As with manhood and womanhood, its meaning can only be discovered existentially—that is, through sincere and responsible relationship; and even so, the knowledge thus gained is of such a kind that it cannot be formulated or communicated, any more than can the special self-knowledge acquired through sexual encounter. Consequently sexual order is not amenable to precise, categorical definition; all that can be said is that despite infinite possibilities of variety due to personal factors, it always remains intrinsically an order of mutual complementation wherein neither sex is subordinate or superordinate to the other.

From sexual status in general we must now turn in conclusion to the form of the relation between man and woman in marriage. It is unnecessary to dwell upon the familiar sentence pronounced against woman after the Fall: "in sorrow shalt thou bring forth children; and thy desire shall be to thy husband, and he shall rule over thee".[1] The fact that her subjection is represented as a punishment for sin shows that it does not belong to the pattern of matrimony as originally constituted. The author's purpose in recording the divine condemnation is obviously ætiological; he explains that because of her transgression, woman can now only enjoy the satisfaction of her sexual needs at a double cost—that of

---

[1] Gen. iii. 16.

enduring the pains and inconveniences of frequent child-bearing, and the indignity of a subordinate if not servile condition.

The traditional notion of woman's status in marriage rests principally upon an inference from St Paul's teaching in his epistle to the Ephesians. The statement: "the husband is the head of the wife, as Christ also is the head of the Church",[1] has not infrequently been taken to imply that the subordination of the wife belongs to the essence, at least of Christian wedlock, by virtue of the latter's sacramental character or symbolism. The passage in which these words occur, however, though certainly somewhat complex in its argument, cannot be made to support the view that because Christ's union with the Church is described analogically in terms of matrimonial relationship, it follows that every husband is ontologically the head of his wife, as Christ is head of the Church.

There are two possible interpretations of St Paul's reference to headship in Ephesians, dependent upon the construction of the term *kephalē*. This may, as in other instances, be synonymous with *archē* ('origin'), or it may simply denote 'overlordship'— which is probably its meaning in the significant declaration earlier in the epistle, that God had set Christ to be "head (*kephalē*) over all things to the Church, which is his body".[2] With the first alternative we have already dealt fully when considering the general form of sexual order.[3] If St Paul intended to convey the idea that the man (as husband) is related to the woman (as wife) in the same way that Christ is related to the Church, because in each case the former is 'head' of the latter in the sense of 'origin' or 'cause', then the comparison must be rejected as without foundation—valid though it would have seemed to the Apostle; for while Christ can properly be described as the *fons et principium* of the Church, the analogy (as we have seen) breaks down completely at the human level. Woman certainly did not derive her being from man, nor does she derive her significance from him.

---

[1] Eph. v. 23.   [2] Eph. i. 22–23.   [3] See above, pp. 294ff.

It is doubtful, however, whether St Paul uses *kephalē* in this passage otherwise than in its normal sense, and his argument is best interpreted accordingly. Between the form of marriage in the ancient world and the union of Christ with the Church he perceives an obvious but significant correspondence, for in each case the relation is one of headship and subordination. Therefore he enjoins Christian husbands and wives to imitate the example of the supernatural union—the husband by loving his wife as Christ loved the Church, and the wife by obeying her husband willingly and joyfully as the Church obeys Christ; but he neither asserts nor implies that the husband's headship is in any way derived from or dependent upon that of Christ. Nor does the nuptial analogy itself, the representation in wedlock of the spiritual marriage between the heavenly Bridegroom and his Bride, rest upon the parallel between divine and human superordination— though it is to the latter that the Apostle appeals, and from it that he draws his teaching. The analogy is essentially relational— between the *henosis* of Christ and the Church, and the *henosis* of man and woman as one-flesh; and in it the ancient religious symbolism of sexual union, already elevated and transformed by the Prophets, attains its fulfilment. Consequently rejection of the wife's subordination does not invalidate the analogy, but simply requires a revision of the terms in which its ethical and personal implications are expressed. Thus, because marriage is a relation of mutual and not unilateral love, the exemplary love of Christ for the Church stands as a pattern to be imitated by the wife no less than the husband; indeed, the full moral and theological significance of their *henosis* only emerges when the notion of male headship is discarded in favour of a higher conception of sexual order.

INDEX

ABBOT, George, 218
Abduction, 70, 73, 106, 142
Abelard, Peter, 122, 139
Abortion, 24, 69, 70, 72, 100
Abraham, 15, 61
Achelis, H., 33
Acts of Andrew, 36, 39, 40
    of John, 36, 39, 40
    of Judas Thomas, 36, 39, 40
    of Paul and Thekla, 36, 39, 40
    of Peter, 36, 40
    of Peter and Andrew, 40
    of Philip, 40
Adam, 53, 54, 58, 135, 171, 189
Adamnan, 107
Adeodatus, 50
'ādhām, 265, 271–5, 280, 297
Adultery, 8, 69, 70, 159, 160, 161, 175, 176, 205
Affinity, 129, 130, 144–8; spiritual, 146–8, 163
Alan of Lille, 140, 158
Albert the Great, 134, 136, 140, 155
Alexander of Hales, 139
Algar of Liege, 122
Allport, J., 193, 194, 201, 206
Ambrose, 20, 22, 23, 24, 25, 28, 32, 33, 46, 47, 51, 62, 63, 76, 77, 83, 84, 97, 119, 120, 142, 143
'Ambrosiaster', 32, 85, 96, 97, 115, 236, 250
Ammon, 41
Amphilochius of Iconium, 70, 87
Andrews, Lancelot, 189, 198, 208, 220, 221
Androcentricity, 62, 64, 68, 100, 157, 163, 181, 200, 201, 234, 242, 253, 273, 274, 277, 288
Androgyny, 275
anēr, 273, 274
Angus, S., 9
Anselm of Laon, 121, 122
Anselm of Lucca, 110, 153
Apelles, 37
Apocrypha, New Testament, 36, 39–41
Apostolic Canons, The, 84

Apostolic Constitutions, The, 20, 25, 29, 31, 32, 38, 45, 47, 66, 67, 68, 69, 70, 99
Aquinas, Thomas, 112, 113, 115, 134–9, 153, 155, 157, 159–62, 171, 208–10, 243
Arcadius, 116, 142
archē, 295, 297–9, 302
Aristotle, 135, 157, 241, 299
Arnobius, 44, 45
arrhæ, 79, 80, 117
arsen, 274, 287
Artemia, 42
Asceticism, 4–6, 10–12, 20, 25, 36–42, 98, 233
Asterius of Amasea, 84, 88, 89, 94
Athanasius, 20, 24, 46, 63, 72
Athenagoras, 44, 45, 82, 242
Augustine of Canterbury, 47, 59
Augustine of Hippo, 20, 22–5, 28, 32, 33, 37, 38, 41–5, 47, 49–60, 64, 77, 83, 84, 86, 89–95, 97, 99, 100, 114, 119–21, 133, 135, 138, 139, 142, 144, 147, 161, 162, 165, 171, 220, 233, 237, 242, 243, 266, 274, 287
Augustus, 81
Aulus Gellius, 80, 243
Ayliffe, J., 191, 205, 212

BAILEY, D. S., viii, 10, 147, 156, 158, 159, 191, 197, 210, 213, 242, 258, 293
Bainton, R., 9
Bandinelli, Roland (*see also* Popes; Alexander III), 105, 128, 145
Barbatianus, 28
Barth, K., 156, 252, 260, 268, 284, 293
Basil of Cæsarea, 21, 23, 24, 32, 35, 66, 67, 70, 83, 84, 87, 144, 298
Basilides, 38
Basilidians, 38
Beach, S. A., 245
Beam, L., 245
Beauvoir, Simone de, 277
Beacon, Thomas, 184, 191, 194, 196, 198, 200–4, 217
Bedale, S., 295

Bede, 106, 107
Benedict Levita, 145
Benediction, nuptial, 75–7, 79, 141, 183, 189
Berkeley, Gilbert, 218
Bernard of Pavia, 145, 146
Bestiality, 70, 72, 159, 160, 161
Betrothal, 75, 76, 77, 78, 79, 80, 123, 125, 126, 128, 129, 132, 206
Bevan, E., 2
Beveridge, William, 190
Bicknell, E. J., 189
Bigamy, 70, 174, 175
Bisexuality, 290–2
Bona Matrimonii, 22, 43, 91, 135, 137, 155, 197, 199
Bonaventura, 112, 140, 141, 154, 155
Boniface, Count, 32
Boniface of Maintz, 104
Book of John the Evangelist, The, 39
Bramhall, John, 194
Brunner, Emil, 252, 268–70, 275
Buber, Martin, 247, 248, 253
Bucer, Martin, 198
Bulgakov, S., 248
Bullinger, Henry, 215
Bunny, Edmund, 221
Burchard of Worms, 109, 110

CADALUS, 149
Cainites, 38
Cairns, D., 265, 268
Calfhill, James, 188,
Calvin, John, 169–78, 180, 182
Canons of Hippolytus, 46
Canute, 107, 117
Cardwell, E., 183, 185, 191, 192, 197, 198, 205, 206, 211, 212, 214, 215, 216, 217
Carpocratians, 38
Carrington, P., 12
Castration, self-, 72
Catharism, 158
Celibacy, clerical, 29, 38, 71, 102, 133, 148–52, 153, 163, 167, 168, 169, 180, 190–3, 233, 239, 284
Chadwyck, Healey, C. E. H., 212, 215, 218
Charibert, 108
Charles the Great, 109
Charles, R. H., 12
Chavasse, C., 9, 251
Chemnitz, Martin, 175, 176
Chesser, E., 11, 245
Children, 1, 3, 14, 15, 24, 25, 99, 100, 181, 203, 204
Clandestinity, 131–2, 142, 188, 204–5
Clarke, W. K. L., 21, 65

Clement of Alexandria, 25, 26, 37, 38, 39, 44, 45, 62, 63, 64, 76, 82, 119, 196, 242, 243
Clement of Rome, 99
Coitus, 2, 9, 10, 11, 41, 42, 44–9, 52, 133–8, 145, 171, 172, 186, 205–8, 249–52, 257, 258; abstinence from, required or commended, 41, 42, 73, 133, 134; antipathy to, 44, 45, 46, 48, 98, 232, 233; contaminated with evil, 102, 134–6, 164, 165, 243, 244; disparagement of, 37, 40, 44 ff., 164–7, 206; part of, in the formation of marriage, 118–30, 132, 133; during lactation, 45; after the menopause, 45; during menstruation, 45, 208, 209; in Paradise, 53, 54, 58, 134, 244; pleasure of, 45, 48, 54, 56, 59, 133, 134, 136, 172; during pregnancy, 45, 209; prohibited, 47, 48, 134; purpose of, 44, 45; *retro*, 159; Schoolmen, attitude of, 133, 137; sinful, 136, 171
Cole, W. G., vi, 263, 292
Colet, John, 165, 166, 235
Collins v. Jesset (1703), 205
Comber, Thomas, 198, 199, 201, 204, 207, 221
Commodian, 63
Compilations, The, 126
Concubinage, 50, 69
Concupiscence, venereal, 23, 53–6, 58, 59, 133, 136, 140
Confarreatio, 3
Conjugium initiatum and *conjugium ratum*, 125
Connolly, R. H., 45, 46
Consanguinity, 141–4, 206
Consent, 75–8, 80, 117, 118, 120–33, 137–9, 141, 155, 156, 163, 186, 205, 221, 222, 230, 239, 258, 260
Constantine, 76, 81, 108
Constitutions and Canons Ecclesiastical (1604), 185, 205, 212, 214, 218, 222–5, 227, 228, 231
Consummation, 118, 120–5, 127, 129, 130, 139, 179, 259
Contraception, 257
Contract, matrimonial, 154, 239, 258–60
Cosin, John, 88, 198, 218, 219, 224, 225
Councils:
　Agde (*C. Agathense*), 506—31, 71, 72, 73
　Aix-la-Chapelle or Aachen (*C. Aquisgranense*), 789—103; I, 816—68

Councils:

Angers (*C. Andegavense*), 453—31, 71, 72, 73, 84

Ankara (*C. Ancyrense*), 314—24, 29, 35, 71, 72, 73

Arles (*C. Arelatense*) II, 442-52—31, 32, 35, 71, 72
  5th cent. [sometimes dated 314]— 72, 73, 82, 84
  IV, 524—31

Auxerre (*C. Autissiodorense*), 578— 31, 71, 72, 73, 144

Barcelona (*C. Barcinonense*), 599—72

Bourges (*C. Bituricense*), 1031—104, 145, 149

Braga (*C. Bracarense*), II, 563—35, 72, 99
  III, 572—71

Carthage (*C. Carthaginense*), 390—30
  VI, 401—30
  348—35
  XI, 407—84

Chalcedon (*C. Chalcedonense*) 451— 67, 72, 73

Chalon-sur-Saône (*C. Cabilonense*), II, 813—110

Clermont in Auvergne (*C. Arvernense*), 535—71, 72, 144

Compiègne (*C. Compendense*), 756— 109, 145

Constantinople (*C. in Trullo*), 692— 24, 29, 31, 67, 147

Elvira (*C. Illiberitanum*), 305-6—24, 30, 35, 71, 72, 73, 82, 144

Ensham (*C. Aenhamense*), 1009—107

Epaon (*C. Epaunense*), 517—31, 67, 72, 144

Florence, 1439—140

Friuli (*C. Forojuliense*), 791—103

Gangra (*C. Gangrense*), ?343—29, 38, 73, 99

Gerona (*C. Gerundense*), 517—72

Hertford (*C. Herudfordense*), 673— 106

Hippo (*C. Hipponense*), 393—35, 71, 72

Huesca (*C. Oscense*), 598—71

Irish, under St. Patrick (*C. Hibernicum*), II, c. 456—72, 107; [I, actually 8th cent.—107]

Kiersy, 858—116

Laodicea (*C. Laodicenum*), mid-4th cent.—32, 68, 72, 73, 77

Lateran (*C. Lateranense*), I, 1123—150
  II, 1139—150
  III, 1215—150

Lerida (*C. Ilerdense*), 524—24, 35, 72, 73

Councils:

Lyons (*C. Lugdunense*), 583—71, 72

Mâcon (*C. Matisconense*), I, 581—71, 72
  II, 585—31, 72, 73

Maintz (*C. Moguntinum*), 847—145, 147
  1049—149

Meaux (*C. Meldense*), 845—116

Nantes (*C. Nannetense*), 8th cent.— 103

Neocæsarea (*C. Neocæsarense*), ante 325—29, 32, 71, 72, 84

Nicæa (*C. Nicænum*), 325—35, 38, 67, 72

Nîmes (*C. Nemausense*), 394—67

Orange (*C. Arausicanum*), 441—31, 67, 71

Orleans (*C. Aurelianense*), I, 511—31, 72, 73, 144
  II, 533—31, 67
  III, 538—71, 72, 73, 144
  IV, 541—31, 71, 72
  V, 549—71, 72

Paris (*C. Parisiense*), III, 557—72
  V, 613—32

Paris (*C. Parisiense*), VI, 829—103, 109, 110

Pavia (*C. Ticinense*), 1022—149

Prague (*C. Pragense*), 1346—147, 148; 1355—148

Rheims (*C. Remense*), 1049—103

Rome (*C. Romanum*), 386—30, 71; 402—30, 71, 72; 465—31, 71; 721—145; 826—104; 853—104; 1051—149; 1059—149; 1074—149

Rouen (*C. Rotomagense*), 1072—103, 145

Saragossa (*C. Cæsar-Augustanum*), 691—33

Seville (*C. Hispalense*), I, 590—35, 72

Soissons (*C. Suessionense*), 744—103, 109

Toledo (*C. Toletanum*), I, 400—30, 31, 71, 72
  447—37, 99
  II, 527-31—35, 71, 72
  III, 589—71, 72
  IV, 633—35
  VIII, 653—30
  IX, 659—30
  XII, 681—103
  XIII, 683—33
  XVI, 731—30

Tours (*C. Turonense*), 461—30, 31, 71, 72; 567—71, 72, 144; 1060— 103

Councils:
Trent (*C. Tridentinum*), 1545-64—179
Tribur (*C. Triburense*), 895—111
Turin (*C. Taurinense*), 401—30
Valence (*C. Valentinum*), 374—31
Vannes (*C. Veneticum*), 465—72, 73, 84, 85
Vernon-sur-Seine or Verberies (*C. Vermeriense*), 756—108-10, 145
Worms (*C. Vormatiense*), 829—103; 868—145
Courson, Robert de, 134
Cox, Richard, 215
Cranmer, Thomas, 185, 190, 191, 213, 214, 215
Creativity, sexual, 270, 282, 283
Cross, G., 152
Cudworth, Ralph, senr., 207
Cudworth, Ralph, junr., 200
Cummean, 107
Cynics, 4
Cyprian, 33, 35, 61, 66, 77, 98
Cyril of Alexandria, 63
Cyril of Jerusalem, 20, 66, 68, 99

DAMIANI, Peter, 122, 148, 165
Danby, H., 74
Dante, 248
Davenant, John, 193, 194, 201, 202, 204, 206, 210
Davies, K. B., 245
Deaconesses, 65-9
Demetrias, 41
Demiurge, the, 37, 42
Desertion, 70, 72, 106, 176, 224
desponsatio, 77-80, 125
Dibdin, L., 212, 215, 218
Dickinson, R. L., 245
Didache, The, 20, 69
Didascalia, The, 45, 46, 66, 68, 99
Digamy, 20, 21, 30-2, 38, 70, 72, 91, 153
Diocletian, 76
Diogenes, 4
Dion Chrysostom, 8
Dionysius of Alexandria, 45, 47
Divorce and remarriage, 2, 5, 73, 82-97, 99, 103-10, 175-7, 206, 211-29, 249, 255, 256, 257
Divorce *a mensa et thoro*, 82, 83, 91, 92, 212, 217, 218, 219, 225
Dolling, R. W. R., 253
Donne, John, 198, 220
Double standards, ethical, 14, 19, 26, 42, 153, 180; of venereal morality, 2, 3, 5, 91, 100, 237
Dualism, Hellenistic, 100

Duchesne, L., 75, 78
Dudden, F. H., 62
Duns Scotus, John, 112, 140, 143, 154
Dunstan, 107
Durand of St Pourcain, 141

EBERHARD OF BETHUNE, 158
Ebionism, 10, 36
Eckert of Schönau, 158
Edward VI, King, 191, 215, 216
Egbert, Abp., 106
Eleazar ben Pedat, Rab., 74, 272
Elizabeth I, Queen, 185, 192, 201, 215, 217
Ellis, Havelock, 246, 247
Encratism, 36, 38, 42
Epictetus, 9
Epiphanius, 32, 37, 38, 67, 68, 84, 87
Essenes, 5, 36
Eusebius of Cæsarea, 23, 35, 37, 72
Eustace Deschamps, 158
Eustathius of Sebaste, 38
Evans, G. L., 290
Eve, 53, 54, 58, 64, 135, 171, 189, 235
Exposure of infants, 24, 99

FAMILY, 2, 4, 5, 14, 23, 24, 25, 40, 99, 180, 181, 203, 204, 236, 237
Farnell, L. R., 9
Fellatio, 159
Feltoe, C. L., 75
Fertility religions, 250, 251
Finian, 107
Fitzgerald, A., 26
flammeum, 75
Fœticide, 70
Ford, C. S., 245
Fornication, 69, 70, 72, 87, 159, 160, 161, 205, 209
Foxe, John, 214-6
Frazer, J. G., 9
Frere, W. H., 184
Freud, S., 244
Fulke, William, 188, 194

GALEN, 241
Gandulph, 127
Gee, Edward, 190
Gennadius, 27
Germanus of Paris, 108
Gibson, Edward, 182, 183, 184, 185, 191, 192, 193, 205, 212, 214, 218
Gnosticism, 36, 37, 38, 42
Goodman, Christopher, 201
Gorgonia, 64
Gospel of Bartholomew, The, 32, 39
Gospel according to the Egyptians, The, 39, 287

Gospel according to the Hebrews, The, 66
Grace, matrimonial, 140, 141
Gratian, 105, 110, 111, 113, 125, 126,
 127, 128, 129, 145, 146
Gregory of Florence, 158
Gregory of Nazianzus, 20, 21, 26, 32,
 34, 64, 77, 100
Gregory of Nyssa, 21, 23, 35, 44, 45, 65
Gregory of Tours, 108
gunē, 273

HADDAN, A. W., 106, 107, 111
Haddon, James, 213
Halcombe, T. R., 26
Halitgar of Cambray, 110
Hall, Joseph, 190, 193, 194, 204, 206,
 224, 225
Hamilton, G. V. T., 245
Hammond, Henry, 206, 223, 224, 228,
 229
Hastings, J., 33
Haw, R., 185, 205, 212, 214, 216, 217,
 219
Headship, male, 292–303
Helvidius, 27, 101
Henry VIII, King, 182–5, 194, 204
Henry, G. W., 246
Herbert, George, 193, 253
Hermann of Cologne, 183
Hermas, 20, 32, 33, 36, 65, 82, 83
Hieracas of Leontopolis, 38
hieros gamos, 9, 251
Hilary of Poitiers, 46, 298
Hildebrand (see also Popes: Gregory
 VII), 110, 149, 150
Hillel, 8, 74
Hincmar of Rheims, 110, 111, 120, 145
Hippocrates, 243
Hippolytus, 31, 37, 38, 46, 65, 69, 100
Hiyya ben Gamda, Rab., 271
Hodgson, L., 298
Holt, Chief Justice, 205
Home, 1, 2, 15, 23, 24, 25, 26, 180,
 181, 196, 197, 203, 204, 236, 237
Homilies, The, 187
Homosexual practices, 4, 69, 70, 72,
 106, 158, 159, 160, 161, 242
Honorius, Emperor, 35, 81, 108, 116,
 142
Honorius of Autun, 122
Hook, W. F., 253
Hooke, S. H., 9
Hooker, Richard, 194, 201
Hooper, John, 198, 214, 216
Hopf, C., 198
Hosea, 250
Howard, Catherine, 185
Howson, John, 221

Hugh of Pisa, 133
Hugh of St Victor, 111, 113, 123,
 125–7, 129, 131, 139
Hugh of Strasbourg, 140
Hutchinson, Roger, 194

IGNATIUS OF ANTIOCH, 65, 66, 74, 99
Image of God in Man, 265–9, 271, 275,
 289, 294
Impediments to marriage, 70, 72, 74,
 142–8, 163, 177–9, 184–6, 229
Incest, 70, 109, 159, 160, 161, 206
Infanticide, 24, 69, 72, 99
Institution of a Christian Man, The, 184,
 186, 189, 191, 197, 206, 211
Irenæus of Lyons, 37, 38
Isaac, 61
'ish, 273–5, 280, 281
'ishshāh, 273, 275, 280, 281, 297
Ishtar, 251
Isidore of Seville, 80, 120
Isomachus, 62
Ivo of Chartres, 110, 112, 114, 121, 122

JACKSON, Thomas, 202
Jacob, 61
James, E. O., vi, 3, 100
James, M. R., 32, 39, 66
Jeremiah ben Eleazer, Rab., 272
Jerome, 19–21, 23–5, 27, 28, 32–4, 37,
 42, 44–7, 49, 50, 63, 64, 67, 68, 77,
 83, 84, 96, 98–100, 119, 122, 137,
 158, 165, 171, 172, 208
John Cassian, 25, 41, 42, 93
John Chrysostom, 19, 20, 22–4, 31, 32,
 34, 35, 44–7, 60–3, 65, 77, 84, 95,
 96, 99, 119, 120, 242
John of Damascus, 20, 23
Johnson, John, 107
Joseph and Mary, marriage of, 119,
 124, 138, 139, 153
Jovinian, 27, 28, 101
Joyce, G. H., vi, 77, 78, 79, 95, 96,
 105, 110, 112, 121, 126, 131, 140,
 143, 174, 176, 205
Judicium Clementis, 106
Julius Cassianus, 37
Jung, C. G., 245, 292
Justin Martyr, 24, 44, 65, 72, 82
Justinian, Emperor, 31, 33, 35, 67, 76,
 106, 118, 142, 176

KARDINER, A., 278, 292
Keble, J., 253
kephalē, 294, 295, 297, 298, 302, 303
Keturah, 61
Kidd, B. J., 168
Kiddle, M., 12

Kinsey, A. C., 245
Kirk, K. E., 6, 10, 15, 20, 24, 27, 52, 259
Kittel, G., 33
Knowledge, sexual, 280–2, 289

LACEY, T. A., vi, 97, 163, 219
Lactantius, 24, 63, 84, 94 ·
Lambeth Conferences, vii, 255–9
Langdon-Davies, J., 156
Laski, John, 214
Latimer, Hugh, 194
Laud, William, 218
Law, William, 193
Lea, H. C., 150, 152, 153
Legislation, ecclesiastical, relating to sexual behavior, 69–74
Leontius of Antioch, 72
Lewis, C. S., 59, 156
Lietzmann, H., 20
Lightfoot, J. B., 66, 287
Liguori, Alphonso di, 210
Lindsay, T. M., 174
Lloyd, C., 184, 186, 191, 197, 206, 208, 211
Lombard, Peter, 112, 122, 125–8, 130, 131, 134, 137, 139, 145, 155
Lot, 60
Lothair II, 110
Louis the Pious, 109
Love, romantic, 18, 156; sexual and marital, 170, 196, 197, 247, 248
Lucretius, 159
Lupton, J. H., 165
Luther, John, 169
Luther, Martin, 168–71, 173–8, 180–2, 233, 235, 237, 263

MACARIUS OF ALEXANDRIA, 26–7
Macclesfield, Earl of, 219
Mace, D. R., 1
Macmillan, A. T., 3
Macrina, 65
McClure, M. L., 75
Maitland, F. W., 117, 127, 138
Maitland, S. R., 201
Man, creation of, 265–9, 271–5, 295–7; his nature, 252; a sexual duality, 268, 270, 271, 275, 276, 289, 297
Manicheans, 52, 56
Manicheism, 50
Mansi, J., 110
manus, 3, 4
Marcion, 21, 37, 83
Marriage, 1, 2, 3, 5, 36, 100; asceticism in, 11; blessings of (*bona matrimonii*), 43, 197, 199—*and see* Bona

matr.; compared with baptism, 90; and celibacy, 20–4, 239; clerical, 180, 190–3; defence of, 99, 237; depreciation of, 36 ff., 98, 99, 235, 236; formation of, 6, 75–80, 115–31, 236, 239; heretical views of, 36 ff.; impediments to —*see* Impediments; indissolubility of, 110–15, 125, 129, 222, 225, 227, 236—*and see* Divorce and re-marriage; institutional conception of, 154, 236; mixed, 72, 95, 96, 97; non-Christian, 19, 97, 100, 111–15, 164, 188; purpose of, 3, 197–200; attitude of Reformers, 170–4, 180; in Roman law, 80, 81, 116, 117, 118; St Paul on, 9, 11, 12, 14; symbolism of, 60, 92–4, 99, 102, 121, 125–7, 131, 132, 139, 140, 186, 199, 250, 302; in Teutonic law, 117; the common life in, 196, 197; a lesser good, 42, 43, 235, 236
Marriage bond, its nature, 88–96, 225
Marriage ceremonies, 74–80
Marriage Service, 183, 184, 197, 199, 212
Marriage sacrament—*see* Sacramentum.
Martin of Tours, 44
Martyr, Peter, 213–5
Marx, K., 252
Mary, 64; perpetual virginity of, 138, 139
Mary, Queen, 193, 201
Mary, Queen of Scots, 201
Masturbation, 159–61, 242
Matrimonial causes, Church's jurisdiction in, 116, 117, 154, 174, 175, 179, 182, 183
Mattheolus of Boulogne, 158
Mayor, J. B., 138
Mead, Margaret, 246, 278
Meek, T. J., 251
Melanchthon, Philip, 176
Menstruation, 45, 47, 243; coitus during, 45, 159, 208, 209, 243
Merkens, A. G., 65
Methodius, 20, 22, 45, 98, 99, 242
Metsch, J. L., 174
Michælangelo, 181
Milan, 149
Minucius Felix, 20, 24, 25
Mishnah, 74
Moffatt, J., 101, 287
Moneta of Cremona, 158
Montanists, 38
Moore, G. F., 1, 8, 271
Mortimer, R. C., 97, 105, 109, 163, 219

mundium, 106, 108, 117
Musonius Rufus, 8

*Necessary Doctrine and Erudition for any
    Christian Man, A,* 184, 187, 189,
    191, 197, 206, 211
Nectarius, 65
Neo-Platonism, 50
Neo-Pythagoreanism, 5
*n*ᵉ*qēbhāh,* 271, 273
Niceta of Remesiana, 76
Nicholas de Tudeschis, 114
Nicolaitans, 38
Niebuhr, Reinhold, 252
Nietzsche, 252
Nocturnal emissions, 47, 160, 242
Northampton, Marquess of, 217
Northumberland, Duke of, 215
Novatians, 38
Novatus, 61
Nullity, 74, 177, 206, 229
nuptiæ, 75, 77, 78, 80

Œpke, A., 33
Olivi, Peter John, 140
Olympias, 65
Onan, 208
One-sex institutions, 284, 285; schools,
    286
Onesiphorus, 40
Optatus, 77
Origen, 60, 72, 82, 83, 93
Orphism, 5
Ovid, 172

Pacian, 61, 242
paiderastia, 4
paidophthoria, 4
Paley, William, 232
Palladius, 65
Panormitanus, 114
Paphnutius, 29
Parker, Matthew, 185, 192, 211, 214,
    218
Parshley, H. M., 277
patria potestas, 3
Paul of Samosata, 35
Pauline privilege, 96, 97, 111–15, 176,
    177, 229, 230, 236, 250
Paulinus of Nola, 25
Pelagians, 52
Pelagius of Laodicea, 41
Petavius, 87–8
Peter the Chanter, 134, 139
Philo, 5, 242
Plato, 22, 272
Plautus, 80
Pliny, 66

Plutarch, 8
Pollock, F., 117
Polycarp, 65
Polygamy, 70, 179, 226
Polygyny, 60, 174
Ponet, John, 201
Pontitian, 51
Popes:
    Alexander III, 128–31, 145, 146
    Alexander VI, 181
    Boniface VIII, 112, 130
    Calixtus II, 150
    Callistus, I, 99, 100
    Celestine III, 130
    Damasus, 144
    Gelasius I, 31
    Gregory I, 23, 30, 45, 47, 48, 59, 63,
        71, 103, 133, 134, 145, 148, 150,
        233, 242, 243
    Gregory II, 103–5, 109
    Gregory VII (*see also* Hildebrand),
        30, 110, 149–51
    Gregory IX, 126, 129, 130, 146
    Honorius III, 130
    Innocent I, 30, 31, 33, 71, 84
    Innocent II, 126, 150
    Innocent III, 112, 128–30, 133, 143,
        146, 150
    Julius I, 146
    Leo I, 30, 31, 33, 71, 120, 121
    Lucius III, 140
    Nicholas I, 75, 78, 80, 110, 120
    Nicholas II, 149
    Pascal II, 146
    Paul IV, 181
    Siricius, 28, 30, 71, 76, 77
    Stephen III, 103
    Urban III, 130
    Zacharias, 103, 145
porneia, 82, 84
Pre-contracts, 185
Prideaux, John, 221
Priscillianists, 37
Pritchard, J. B., 242
Proctor, F., 184
Procurers, 69
Prodicians, 38
Prostitution, 3, 4, 72, 161–64, 182,
    206, 210
Pseudo-Clement, 35, 36, 39, 44, 45, 48,
    99
Pseudo-Clementine writings, 242
Pseudo-Cyprian, 41
Pullen, Robert, 111, 133

Rabanus Maurus, 110
Rado, Sandor, 292
Rape, 70, 73

Reformatio Legum Ecclesiasticarum, 183, 185, 197, 206, 212–16, 220, 225
Reformation, The, 167 ff.
Regino of Prüm, 109, 134
Reissenbusch, Wolfgang, 168, 170, 171
Relation, philosophy of, 247; sexual, 268–70
repudium, 81, 103
Reynolds, Edward, 219
Rich, Lady Penelope, 218
Richard of Middleton, 112
Ring, in marriage, 75–80
Robinson, J. A., 67
Rogers, Thomas, 188
Ross, Lord, 218, 223, 224
Roth, Stephen, 173
Rougement, Denis de, 156
Rufinus, 28
Rusticus, 42
Rye *v.* Fuliambe, 217

Sacramentum, Matrimonial, 89, 92–4, 114, 115, 118, 123–6, 131, 132, 139–41, 154, 178, 179, 186–90, 199, 231, 236, 239, 260
Sadducees, 91
Sahidic Heptateuch, 46, 47, 65, 66, 70
Saint, W. P. le, 21
St Paul, 9–14, 19, 33, 34, 46, 49, 51, 57, 82, 93, 94, 96, 114, 119, 165, 171, 175, 178, 195, 207, 233, 249, 250, 251, 288, 289, 294–8, 300, 302
Samson, J., 226
Samuel bar Nahman, Rab., 272
Sanchez, T., 157
Sanderson, Robert, 205, 206, 221
Sandys, Edwin, 198, 204
Sarah, 15, 61
Sarmatio, 28
Saturninus, 37
Saxony, John Frederick, Duke of, 174
Schaff, D. S., 152
Schaff, P., 167, 168, 169, 179, 181
Schoff, W. H., 251
Selwyn, E. G., 296
Semen, 241–3
Separation (*a mensa et thoro*), 70, 73; *see also* Divorce and remarriage
Severians, 37
Severus of Antioch, 23, 31
Seward, G. H., 246
Sex, 257, 260–303; its meaning, 260–4, 280, 281, 282; misuse of the term, 261–3; its nature in Man, 269–71, 276, 277; denial of, 277, 278; creativity of, 282, 283
Sexual relation, the form of, 301–3
Shammai, 8, 74

Simeon, Rab., 272
Simon, M., 272
Simonians, 38
Simplician, 51
Slater, E., 245
Socrates, the ecclesiastical historian, 29, 38, 41, 72
Sodomy, heterosexual, 159; homosexual, 161, 242
Solovyov, V., 248
sōphrosunē, 4
Sozomen, 29, 41, 65, 67
Sperling, H., 272
sponsa, 77, 78, 80, 125
sponsalia, 75, 78–80
Sponsorship, 146–48
sponsus, 77, 78, 80, 125
Statuta Ecclesiæ Antiqua, 31, 32, 35, 66, 67, 68, 72, 73
Statutes of the Apostles, 46
Stawell, Sir John, 218
Stereotypes, sexual, 245, 246, 278–80
Stillingfleet, Edward, 221
Stoicism, 5
Strabo, Walafrid, 147
Strype, John, 190, 191, 215, 217
Stubbs, W., 106, 107, 111, 117
subarrhatio, 75, 76
Sulpitius Severus, 44
Swinburn, H., 205
Syneisaktism, 24, 33–35, 72, 137
Synesius of Cyrene, 26

Tametsi, decree, 179, 205
Tammuz, 251
Tancred, 141, 142, 145
Tappert, T. G., 168
Tatian, 37
Taverner, Richard, 198
Taylor, Jeremy, 195–8, 201–4, 206–10, 225–7, 230, 253
Tertullian, 20, 21, 24, 31, 32, 35, 37, 38, 45, 46, 49, 50, 63, 64, 65, 68, 75, 76, 77, 78, 82, 83, 91, 99, 158, 267
Testament of the Lord, The, 47, 65, 66, 68, 70
Teutberga, 110
thēlu, 274, 287
Theodore of Canterbury, archbishop, 105–7, 110, 111, 145, 159
Theodore of Mopsuestia, 33
Theodoret, 37, 41, 68, 72, 84, 88, 89, 94
Theodosius II, emperor, 35, 76, 81, 108, 116, 176
Theonas, 41
Therapeutæ, 5
Thornborough, John, 218

Thorndike, Herbert, 193, 194, 218, 220–2, 225, 228
Thorpe, B., 134
Timothy, 36
Tollinton, R. B., 26
Tractarianism, 234
Tradition, Christian sexual: its character and growth, 232–40; impact of modern thought upon, 240, 241, 244–54; criticism of, 240–3, 247–50, 252, 255
Traheron, Bartholomew, 201
Trigamy, 70, 72
Trinity, symbolism of, in Man, 266, 267, 299
trinoctii absentia, 3
Tulloch, J., 200
Turner, C. H., 40
Twelve Tables, The, 3
Tyndale, William, 172, 184, 188, 190, 194, 198, 200, 204, 216

ULPIAN, 79, 80, 123
Ussher, James, 207

VACARIUS, 127
Valentinian III, emperor, 81
Venereal, meaning of, 263, 264
Venereal acts, morality of, 158–61, 205–10
Victorinus, 51
Vigilantius, 27, 101
vinculum, 90–2, 94–6, 114, 115, 223, 224, 231, 239
vinculum juris, 127
Virginity, 5, 12, 14, 20, 21, 22, 23, 27, 28, 42, 98, 102, 153, 163, 169, 172, 179, 180, 193, 194, 195, 196, 233, 234, 284, 285
Virgins, order of, 65, 66
Vows of continence, 164, 167–9, 178, 179

WATKINS, O. D., vi, 81, 83, 95, 96, 104, 105, 106, 107, 113, 141
Weller, Jerome, 182
Whitaker, William, 188
White Cross League, 258
Whitgift, John, 200, 217, 221
Wickmann, John, 176
Widows, order of, 65, 66, 69
Wilkins, D., 184
Wilkins, John, 219
William I, King, 117
William of Auvergne, 141
William of Auxerre, 140
William of Champeaux, 122, 126
Williams, Charles, 18, 156, 236, 248
Williams, N. P., 2, 55
Willibrord, 106
Wilson, H. A., 75
Wolferinus, Simon, 176
Woman, her status, 2, 3, 6, 15, 16, 17, 61, 62, 100, 157, 253, 293-303; attitudes to, 2, 3, 17, 62-5, 73, 157, 173, 200-3, 234, 235; subordination of, 62, 157, 173, 234, 242, 250, 273, 277, 283, 284, 293-303; ministry of, 65-68, 173, 294; responsible' for the Fall, 64, 235; emancipation of, 253, 277, 280; social rôle of, 283
Woodside, M., 245
Woolf, B. L., 20, 168, 175-9
Wordsworth, J., 30
Wotton, Thomas, 203
Wyon, O., 268

XENOPHON, 62
Xystus, 136, 137

ZĀKHĀR, 271, 273
Zerbst, F., 65, 68, 173, 294
Zwingli, U., 168